Anyplace But Here

Anyplace But Here

ARNA BONTEMPS *and* JACK CONROY

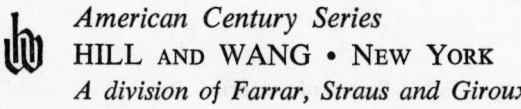

American Century Series
HILL AND WANG • NEW YORK
A division of Farrar, Straus and Giroux

Originally published as *They Seek a City*

Standard Book Number (clothbound edition): 8090–2715–1
Standard Book Number (paperback edition): 8090–0085–7
Library of Congress catalog card number: 66–15898

Manufactured in the United States of America

8 9 10 11 12 13 14

Preface

WHEN JACK CONROY and I first began to compare notes on Negro migrations within the United States, our desks were about twenty feet apart. We were both employed as editorial supervisors on the Illinois Writers Project of the WPA. Not far away, at a similar desk, was a serious young supervisor who never wasted much time but whom I thought I saw making eyes at a slender young typist in the secretarial pool. He was Nelson Algren. Across the big room, in an area assigned to the radio unit, one occasionally saw the energetic and personable young figures of Studs Terkel and Lou Gilbert, both clearly marked for bigger future roles in television and the movies, respectively.

Katherine Dunham, Richard Wright, Frank Yerby, Stuart Engstrand, and George V. Martin had worked at these same desks just weeks or months earlier, and some of them returned occasionally to see how things were going. Meanwhile, their successors continued to fill the files with gleanings from old Illinois newspapers and other library sources. After Conroy and I got steamed up about Negro migrations, we began to pay even closer attention. We discovered, for example, that Katherine Dunham, who had been working for a doctoral degree in anthropology at the University of Chicago, had directed a bit of research toward a study of Negro cults in Chicago, and that this had led her writers to collect information about the groups that later became widely known as Black Muslims. We came across an inspired day's work by a writer who had done nothing but list the names of storefront churches on one street in the southside ghetto. And what names they were!

The Project ended suddenly, but not before it and others like it had made publishing history with the excellent series of state guides and other books and pamphlets of regional or local interest, often of substantial value to later researchers. Peripheral benefits, sometimes too intangible to be measured by linage or pagination, were often noted, and the opportunity for development afforded the likes of Wright and Yerby and Algren was matched by the revitalization of old timers like the poet Fenton Johnson who had been hit even harder by the depression. While Johnson's *WPA Poems* did not get published as a collection, they obviously did him a lot of good.

When the Project came to an end, a publisher who had heard about our interest in the migration story encouraged us to develop it. We went to work, and *They Seek a City* was published in 1945.

One thing about the impulse we had tried to trace was apparent from the first. Another became apparent later. We soon realized that we were dealing with currents that were still running vigorously and that we could not tell when or where they would crest. To that extent our book was premature. But the disasters ahead in Watts and Chicago and Harlem which were later to focus intense light on this fantastic population shift, with all its dislocations, could not have been foreseen. Nor could they have been understood prior to the events of the fifties and sixties, disclosing the depth and intensity of the Negro American's drive toward freedom. Needless to say, twenty years of change and unforeseen developments have made it necessary to recast most of the original chapters of the book and to add a number of new ones.

ARNA BONTEMPS

Contents

Preface v
Prologue: Mudtown 1
I Du Sable: Man of the Midlands 12
II To the Western Passes 21
III Toward the North Star 32
IV John Brown's Friend 43
V "Leave a Summer Land Behind" 53
VI Across the River from Slavery 72
VII They Met at the Fair 88
VIII Darktown Strutters 111
IX The Invisible Migration 122
X Strangers 135
XI The Exodus Train 158
XII Trouble in Canaan 175
XIII "Beloved and Scattered Millions" 191
XIV Registered with Allah 216
XV Calling the Children Home 247
XVI Trail of the Whitetops 257
XVII Karamu 278
XVIII Moon of the Migrant Tides 287
XIX With Brotherly Love 307

XX Freedom's Frontier 315
XXI Chicago: Queen of the Inland Sea 321
Epilogue 343
A Selected List of References and Sources 349
Index 361

Anyplace But Here

PROLOGUE

Mudtown

THE FIRST BLACK MEN in the American midlands—not counting a few who were brought in chains to work the salt mines—were fugitives and wanderers. They came thrashing the wilderness grass like frightened animals, and at night they cast their aching, exhausted bodies on the ground and slept. In the morning they rose up, filled their lungs with the free air of God's country, and swore it was different from the air of bondage. The difference, they reasoned soberly, was exactly the difference between night and day. One doesn't have the same mind in the dark at night as he has in daylight. Things don't seem the same under the stars. The wisdom of the evening, like as not, will turn out to be the foolishness of the morning. And the things a man values in slavery may not appeal to him in freedom. The air made the difference. That's why folks always talked about going North and breathing the free air.

Many such folks came to Illinois. There they paused to get their bearings, and some stayed put, but others moved on. In Chicago, a city once described by the Shawneetown *Gazette* as a perfect "sinkhole of abolition" and the rival of Boston and Cincinnati in that respect, they boarded lake vessels and embarked on the last leg of the journey to Canada. A certain few, beguiled by stories of the West Coast, thumbed their noses at the frozen North and headed for California.

Of course those were the days of the bloodhound, the slave catcher, and the kidnaper. A spirited boy called "Young Tom" had to wriggle a rope from his wrists and lash a pack of dogs till they whimpered before making good his escape. Brutal, shaggy-maned agents of the slave system invaded the North in pursuit of runaways and did more by their harsh, inhuman methods to crystallize sentiment against the South than did the passionate literature of the day. Racketeers, posing as agents, snatched up free men of color along with an occasional white who could not offer immediate "proof" of his whiteness and hustled all off to slavery together. But the stream of fugitives continued to pour out of the Slave States.

After Emancipation the stream became a flood. Old "Pap" Singleton, calling himself the "Black Moses" of his people, led a host of "exodusters" into a land sanctified by the memory of John Brown of Osawatomie. The flood backed into Kansas City and St. Louis, rose like a tide in Ohio, Michigan, and the Indian Territory. It reached New York and Boston on the East Coast, San Francisco and Seattle on the West. But this was not a stream of fugitives and runaways. This was a migration of freedmen—newborn children setting out to make a new life in a new world.

The pre-Civil War migration of fugitives had followed the rivers, the steamboat lines, and the wagon paths from South to North. With the railroads came lateral East-to-West migration. The couriers of this new movement were black firemen, dining-car waiters, Pullman porters. Young boys left home to run on the road and never returned. "If I don't come back," some of them said, "I'll write you a letter." Many kept their promises, scribbling terse, illiterate notes inviting friends and relatives to come along and live like people. They observed in their quaint dispatches that *things* were better in Denver or Rochester than in Memphis or Birmingham. They did not mean working conditions when they said *things.* When they meant working conditions, they said working conditions. When they said *things,* they referred to the free air. Other boys, the bitter, disillusioned, poetic ones, packed their guitars with their change of shirts and announced to the world that they would go so far away from the South it would cost five dollars to send a post card home. Nobody need expect to hear from *them!*

Old people too tired to move, young ones who enjoyed a favor or two in the South, and others who were just plain scared to leave stayed at home, watched their friends slip away, and tried to understand the thing they saw before their eyes. The impulse to go, as it appeared to them, seemed to work like a fever. It had progressive symptoms. The first might be anger, disappointment, hope, or just a tendency to dream, but the second was always discontent and restlessness. Then eyes that swept the horizon. Finally, flight.

They noted, too, that white folks got mean when times were hard, that they usually jumped on the Negro when their own affairs were in a bad way. Sometimes the Negro jumped first. In the old days during slavery or later on share farms where freedom of action was denied, the one who planned a getaway would shout, "Bird in the air!" When all faces turned heavenward to search the sky for a pair of wings, the Negro would dash for freedom. Before those most deeply concerned realized what was happening, he would be on his way. So hard times pushed the colored man away from the South, and good times pulled him to the North. There was nothing to make one want to stay.

The biggest movements, however, occurred about once every twenty years. The Fugitive Slave Law of 1850 brought to a peak the travel on the Underground Railroad. Freedom touched off the push of 1870. Another big one followed the Chicago World's Fair in 1893. A huge one paralleled World War I, and still another began with World War II. No one has measured or charted these migrations of Negroes from the South too accurately. The movements haven't generally been recognized as migrations till they are well under way or perhaps tapering off. Yet the results of the movements have been neither vague nor mysterious.

A few years after the big World War I migration reached its peak, a Negro Baptist congregation bought a massive stone building on Chicago's South Side. It had a Hebrew inscription graven across its façade, for it had been a Jewish synagogue before the district "went colored." Around the converted house of worship were the run-down remainders of better days—baroque mansions built by the white gentry who long since had moved on. Their proudly embellished iron fences had rusted and fallen to the ground. Loose sections were furtively or boldly carried away by ragged Negro boys eager to coax a few pennies from the junkman. No grass or flowers grew on the lawns worn slick by trapped black feet. The spacious rooms, some with ornate chandeliers still depending from the high ceilings, had been cut into tiny cubicles crammed to bursting with dark-skinned citizens constantly forced to push outward against the four walls of their cages—to struggle like drowning men against the rules and animosities that tried to "restrict" them to the parts of the city that had become dismal with overcrowding and the odor of death, stagnation, and decay.

In the years that followed World War II, a frenzy for civic improvement seized Chicago. One of its main manifestations was tearing down "substandard" or slum dwellings and replacing them with high-rise apartment buildings too expensive for the poverty-stricken residents who had previously lived in the area. So the Negroes moved out of the former synagogue, and it, like the surrounding low-rent apartments, crumbled from the assaults of the wrecker's big swinging iron ball. The other Negro ghettos were already full or bursting. If the displaced persons attempted to "invade" lily-white neighborhoods, they were met with hostility and even violence. A tight ring of "white" suburbs girdled the Black Metropolis like a strangling noose. The few subdivision, small-down-payment-and-easy-monthly-terms developers who solicited Negro buyers for their jerry-built, cheaper-by-the-dozen "little boxes" (as the popular song called them), built on tracts that in days past were open fields, signified their willingness by illustrating their advertisements with pictures of smiling Negro couples and their happy, romping children. The endorsement of Jesse Owens, Negro track star turned businessman, was the go-ahead signal used by one enterprising realtor.

During World War II, Negro migrants seeking the high wages of the airplane factories and shipyards occupied the "Little Tokyos" of Los Angeles and San Francisco, replacing Japanese Americans who had been uprooted by the government and "located" farther inland. How handsomely some unscrupulous real-estate speculators profited from the plight of the departing and the need of the arriving is another story. Many of the Japanese Americans eventually returned, adding to the congestion. They and the Negroes often shared the same ghettos. But the Negro migrants kept coming. In 1962, it was estimated that two thousand Negro newcomers were entering California each month. Most of these came from Texas, Louisiana, Oklahoma, and Arkansas. The 1960 census numbered more than a million Negro residents in the state, a sizable percentage of whom had come during or after World War II.

Another result was seen in little Negro towns such as Robbins and Lovejoy in Illinois, in neighborhoods such as Mudtown in dozens of cities. Perhaps the original Mudtown is in Topeka. One cannot be sure; it is a disputed honor. Besides, Mudtown is as uniform as Middletown. It is as real, as American. Mudtown is that embarrassing section of the Northern city in which the new people from the South erected those absurd little shacks to house themselves till they could move on—or perhaps do better. The Furlough Track in Los Angeles was one of the Mudtowns. Perhaps its history is typical.

First there was a farmhouse in a clump of lacy pepper trees. It was an old house of a style not now common in the Far West. A walnut grove surrounded the grounds, and a mile-long palm drive led to the big road. Then came the steel rails, the railroad lines on the east, those of the electric interurban trains on the west side of the property. The land between lost its charm as the home place of people whose taste in rural situations required clean, smokeless air as well as exotic trees. Mexican section workers settled in a eucalyptus grove along the tracks, in a cluster of whitewashed hovels built by the railroad company. Later the whole stretch of land was sold and subdivided. About a dozen substantial cottages were built, some of them almost attractive. Then—all unexpectedly—came the migrants, and Furlough became another Mudtown.

Since it was not easy for carriages or carts to enter the community, thanks to embankments and fences along the railroad right of way, wagon paths became obscure in this deep-rutted Mudtown, and grass grew a foot high in its principal streets. Cows and goats were tethered on that part of Holmes Avenue that reached into the neighborhood. A half-grown cinnamon bear was chained to a stake on a side lot. Flocks of pigeons circled over the rooftops and settled on the towering birdhouses that had been erected for them on twenty- and thirty-foot poles. Honeysuckle covered slat fences, tumble-down verandas, and outhouses, and filled the air with an unexpected sweetness.

"So this is where the colored folks live," a tired little man once remarked on reaching the neighborhood at night, following a long and exhausting journey from Louisiana. Then he added sorrowfully, "I mighta known."

From where he stood he could see Furlough's one street lamp, a flickering orchid light about two blocks away. He began to complain bitterly that there is nothing for the Negro anywhere. But presently an enormous orange moon came up, a moon that made the tiny Mudtown community seem small by comparison, and the old fellow found himself gaping with wonder. "Look!" he cried. "That moon—did you ever see anything like it?" A moment later a freight train thundered on the Alameda tracks. The kerosene lamps trembled. Mudtown quivered and shook like a toy village. The newcomer decided to reserve judgment. The very slightness and unreality of this trash-and-paper district changed his outlook.

The next day he walked around. Trash, indeed! Some of the houses had actually been built of scraps of tar paper tacked over frames constructed of scarred planks and broken strips. New people had crowded in on the older and better situated ones in disconcerting ways. One old couple, a shriveled, birdlike pair with dirt-encrusted fingernails and tattered flannel feathers, were evidently sleeping in a tree, in what had apparently been a playhouse built among the branches for the children of the inhabitants of the original farmhouse. Entering and leaving their nest by a ladder, the scrawny old doves managed somehow to give the impression that they could easily have flown to their roost had they elected to do so.

The little old man who arrived at night got his fill of Mudtown in a day or two. He had dreamed too long of a complete break with the South. He left a jar of real cane syrup and a bag of giant pecans with the family that had put him up and packed his wicker bags again and headed across the tracks. He never learned that Mudtown was more than trash and paper and scrawny birds with flannel feathers.

Those who remained longer made some surprising discoveries. They learned, for example, that Red Eagle, the broad-shouldered Negro who lived alone, talked little, and dressed like an Indian, was actually named Red Eagle. His parentage was obscure, but there was little doubt that he had grown up and lived most of his life among Indians in Oklahoma. Recently he had worked as a cowboy, and his shack was filled with the exciting paraphernalia of his occupation. One or two friendly youngsters who managed to break through his shy and diffident shell had been shown the wonderful objects. The kids had learned that Red Eagle knew all about ornaments made of silver, all about ropes and knots, but nothing much about the ways of his fellow Negroes and nothing at all about their songs and laughter.

He knew, if most people did not, what Philip Durham and Everett L. Jones have since written about the Negro cowboys in their book *The Negro Cowboys* (1965):

> Now they are forgotten, but once they rode all the trails, driving millions of cattle before them. Some died in stampedes, some froze to death, some drowned. Some were too slow with guns, some too fast. But most of them lived through the long drives to Abilene, to Dodge City, to Ogallala. And many of them drove on to the farthest reaches of the Northern range, to the Dakotas, Wyoming and Montana.
>
> They numbered thousands, among them many of the best riders, ropers and wranglers. They hunted wild horses and wolves, and a few of them hunted men. Some were villains, some were heroes. Some were called offensive names, and some others were given almost equally offensive compliments. But even when one of them was praised as "the whitest man I've ever known," he was not white.

The two tall brothers who lived in a small house in a thicket also became familiar to those who spent more time in this little Mudtown of the Far West. For some unexplained reason these brothers would have no neighborhood children in their yard or climbing their trees. Frequently in the afternoon, when they returned from their work, they would arm themselves with leafy switches, beat through the bushes and the branches, scare up a half dozen or more brats and drive them off the lot with shouts and threats and waving arms. The children, frightened out of their wits, referred to the towering brothers as "the giants." Yet a few of them continued to explore that forbidden yard when they thought no one was home only to come leaping from it eventually like cottontails.

But the stomping, shouting "giants" were less fearful than was another character who came to Mudtown a few years later. The woman called Tump—whose real name is not important—first made a reputation in Mudtown by walking in the middle of the road instead of following the footpath. She worked as a car cleaner in the railroad yards beyond the tracks, but nobody ever asked her any questions. Tump wasn't friendly. She tried to pick fights with people who gave her howdy. She carried a knife, and the word was that she would as soon fight men as women. Her only pleasant contacts with her neighbors were in crap games with the rough crowd of men, and these were likely to be qualified pleasures for the men involved. Tump's speech was unnecessarily profane. It was too ripe and infested for even the rounders and the scamps. Most of them tried to avoid playing with her on the grounds that there was a limit to such profanity—even with them. They may also have had a reason which they did not state: Tump's quarrelsomeness, her readiness to turn the fun into a brawl.

Yet there are those who remember this community fondly. Some talk about the picnics held in a lantern-hung summerhouse and under the pepper trees that surrounded it. They recall ribbons and bright silks in the Fourth of July sunshine, and bands playing under the trees at night. They mention unforgettable services in one or the other of the two little Mudtown churches, particularly the Sunday night when the quartet of boys from Tuskegee gave a program which started folks to humming spirituals they thought had been left down home. They still talk about the Mexican storekeeper and his pretty daughter Julia, and they remember the even prettier colored girl named Alameda who looked more Mexican than Julia.

And in this Mudtown, as in all the others, there was a sprinkling of the sheltered homes of educated Negroes trying earnestly to inspire and maintain ideals and aspirations in their children. There was, for example, a quietly dignified "Y" secretary with his soft-spoken, well-dressed brown children. And there was a retired college teacher whose son was doing well with his violin. A score of others were sending their children to high school or college. Among the offspring of this group were some girls who would soon become public school teachers in the Los Angeles system; some boys who were headed for better-than-average pulpits; a prospective dentist was among them, a lawyer, and a couple of doctors—

all in a community without a sidewalk, a community served by a single street lamp.

But these were not the gaudiest talents among Furlough's kids. One bright-eyed youngster became in later years a trumpeter in Duke Ellington's first band. Another, fighting under the ring name of Baby Joe Gans, came close to a welterweight championship of the world. Furlough folks knew him as Babe Slaughter. One grew up to play the title role in the sound-film version of *Uncle Tom's Cabin,* not to mention other movie parts. One went to U. C. L. A. and became an All-American end and track star. One became a writer of books. An equal number of young people, equally talented, deliberately turned their backs on the values that are often reckoned as success. Mudtown, with its hundred or so houses, with its migrants fresh from the South, and its across-the-tracks status, was on the verge of proving itself a wholesome and fertile community—when something happened.

Mudtown and its extension known as Watts awakened to the fact that it was a ghetto and a slum. That was the end. All who could get away fled. Those who remained—trapped—sank to indifference and then despair. A crushing weight fell on the spirit of the neighborhood when Mudtown learned that it was hemmed in, that prejudice and malice had thrown a wall around it. As long as residence there seemed temporary and accidental, everything was fine, but the ghetto consciousness, the knowledge of restraining pressure from without, the awakening of children born in the community to the fact that they were rated as aliens and outsiders in the total life of the city and the state was more than the vitality of any neighborhood—let alone Mudtown—could bear. Something had to crack.

In the case of Furlough, calamity was postponed by replacing it with a housing project, the Pueblo del Rio. For a few short years Mudtown thought it had realized its dream when it saw small Negro, Mexican, white, and Filipino children splashing in a wading pool. Where once there were two hundred and forty-six homes of all kinds, including—no doubt—even the nests in the trees, it could count nearly five hundred units, housing that number of families, thoroughly integrated. Where Tump once elected to walk in the dusty road rather than follow the footpath and where the brother "giants" switched the neighborhood brats for trespassing, classes in home arts and family living were conducted. Lawns and gardens, day nurseries and playgrounds, community meeting rooms and staff offices replaced tumble-down verandas and back-yard sheds, vine-grown lean-tos, and slat fences. Houses by Paul R. Williams, the now famous Negro architect, replaced the shotgun shacks in which Tump and her cronies played at dice.

While the conscience that conceived public housing for the denizens of Mudtown held the winds for a time, an earthquake in 1932 may have accomplished the same thing for the neighboring area of Watts, a stone's throw away. But the migrants kept coming, and the tensions continued to build. Nevertheless, this was the spot where the moon seemed so incredibly big, the earth so small and shaky to the little old wanderer from the South; where the quartet from Tuskegee thrilled the homesick folks at church; where the clean-punching Babe Slaughter learned his footwork; where James Lowe recited Shakespeare; where young Arthur Whetsol practiced on his trumpet; where Woody Strode's touchdowns for U. C. L. A. were born.

In a sense this book is the story of Mudtown's dream. It seeks to place the generic Mudtown in American life and culture. More important, however, it tries to tell the story of some of the people who came to Mudtown, as well as to some other places in the North and West and East, in such a way that the reader may realize the migratory impulse as personal experience. We think this experience has a deep meaning for all America. We believe it has had more to do with our history than is commonly known. We believe it is a thing America must reckon with as we look to the future.

Of course the story of internal migration of Negroes in the United States has perhaps as many threads as the story of the nation's westward expansion. The front is wide, and the period of the movements covers more than a hundred years. And just as every man who went West had his own personal reasons, so every Negro who left the South behind was motivated by a set of circumstances peculiar to himself. Obviously there is a limit to the number of these that can be told in a single volume. We have made a selection which seemed to us representative, and we have tried to focus on those which have clear meaning for the nation as a whole.

The migrations have followed no set route. Starting at any point in the South, they have moved in every possible direction. In most cases, however, the migrant has headed for a convenient dispersal point in the North or on the border; he has paused to take his bearings in Cincinnati or St. Louis and then moved again. Traditionally and geographically, the whole period of migration considered, the most important of these dispersal points has been Chicago.

Hence, our starting point. . . .

CHAPTER I

Du Sable: Man of the Midlands

THE INDIANS used to say, with straight-faced merriment, no doubt, that the first white man in Chicago was a Negro. Of course they were talking about Du Sable, the trader who built his log house at the mouth of the Chicago River in 1779 and lived there for more than sixteen years; and their remarks suggest that they were keen enough to understand that culture, rather than color, makes the man. Du Sable's heritage was French, despite his dark, Negroid features, and this makes his story of special interest. Here was a man who fitted not at all into the accepted pattern; he was neither a slave escaped from the bondage of the South, nor, from what we know about him, a man who was brought to these shores against his wishes.

Sometimes referred to as Au Sable, Du Saible, De Sable, Sabre, or Le Grand Sabre, the man Jean Baptiste Point Du Sable was probably born about 1750. No one can say just where. Milo M. Quaife, historian of the Great Lakes, indicates in his book *Checagou* that the lineage of a Du Sable family can be traced back to France in the early part of the seventeenth century. At that time the ancestral name was Dandonneau. Members of this family migrated to Canada, where a descendant came to be known as Dandonneau "Sieur du Sable." This, the historian offers, followed a custom of the time whereby second names were occasionally added to family names. Thus La Salle, the explorer, acquired his euphonious sobriquet by affixing it to Robert Chevalier, the name his parents gave him.

Quaife found that succeeding generations of Dandonneaus had

been known as "Dandonneau and Du Sable," and that these names had earned a certain prominence in the high-heeled circles of New France's aristocracy. Members of the family later moved to the settlement at Detroit, and there—thanks to the tendency of wives of the period to sign their own family names beside those of their mates—their peregrinations may be traced through marriage and baptismal records kept by the churches. However, if this is the true lineage of the mulatto Du Sable, still another custom of the period must be recalled: the common practice which allowed a child, if he elected to do so, to be known by his mother's, rather than his father's name.

Another chain of possibilities, when carefully linked, enables Quaife and others who like his thread to link the dark frontiersman with the Du Sable family of lofty French ancestry. The name Du Sable is found to have been conspicuously associated with Indian traders throughout the Northwest Territory. The Negro Du Sable was a trader. He lived and operated in the Northwest. His name in all its forms was strikingly similar. His color? That, too, can be explained by a time-honored custom: the uninhibited cohabiting of Frenchmen with Negro and Indian women. In an existing document Point Du Sable refers to himself as a "free Negro."

But there is perhaps just as much basis for the tradition that Du Sable was a Haitian who migrated to New Orleans and then pushed up the Mississippi to Checagou in the hope of founding a colony of *hommes de couleur libres* in the lake region. His education and tastes, which may have been acquired in France, can as well be explained by the custom of the free mulatto groups of New Orleans and Cap François to send their children to Paris for study as by Dandonneau and Du Sable ancestry. In either case, the man of whom we speak was definitely on the spot where Chicago now stands before July 4, 1779. And, curiously enough, he steps into history under a cloud of deep suspicion.

In 1779 the British were in control of the vast territory surrounding the lakes. Having recently seized it from the French, they were now eager to make it secure. At the same time, however, the American colonists were on their hands in a rather troublesome way. The result was that the question of the loyalty of the inhabitants was a very real one to Colonel Arent de Peyster, British commandant at Michilimackinac, whose business it was to uphold the authority of his government in the region. Naturally, the colonel had given special attention to his most prominent colored subject. In his official report of July 4, 1779, he observed: "Baptist Point de Saible, a handsome Negro, well educated and settled at Eschikagou, but was much in the interest of the French."

The partiality of Du Sable toward the French is easily understandable. So much so, from the point of view of the British officer, that De Peyster wasted no time trying to build a case against the brown man. So much so, from the point of view of the shrewd frontiersman, that Du Sable did not wait to see what the colonel's next move would be. Colonel de Peyster promptly ordered the Negro detained under suspicion of "treasonable intercourse with the enemy." Somewhat more promptly Du Sable disappeared.

The colored man was well on his way to Detroit when the military overhauled him. The report of Lieutenant Thomas Bennet, De Peyster's arresting officer, throws a revealing light on the personality and reputation of the man he was sent to capture. "I had the Negro, Baptist Point de Saible, brought prisoner from the River Du Chemin," Bennet stated. "Corporal Tascon, who commanded the party, very prudently prevented the Indians [these being British allies, of course] from burning his home or doing him any injury." Evidently nobody rushed the prisoner or tried to rough him up, for the report added carefully: "He secured his packs, et cetera, which he had taken with him to Mackinac." Bennet concluded his remarks with these forthright words: "The Negro, since his imprisonment, has in every way behaved in a manner becoming to a man of his station, and has many friends who give him a good character."

The charges of the British against Du Sable were soon dropped, and he was released. But that is only the beginning of his conquest of his captors. Patrick Sinclair, the British governor of the territory, who thought he knew a first-rate man when he saw one, was so impressed by Du Sable that he immediately retained the former captive's services for his own enterprises. In what capacity Sinclair employed the prominent Negro during his first year is not clear, but the work may have been supervisory. Du Sable appears to have had contacts with the governor's far-flung interests, for during the following summer a delegation came to Sinclair from the "Pinery," an establishment founded by the governor on the St. Clair River south of Port Huron, asking a change in their setup and requesting that Du Sable be put in charge. The governor honored the delegation's proposal and sent Du Sable to take over the management of the Pinery, replacing a Detroit Frenchman whose conduct of the business had provoked complaints. There is no indication that the colored man's handling of the operations at the Pinery was in any wise unsatisfactory.

Du Sable's sojourn in this section continued until 1784. Meanwhile, his accounts with Detroit merchants, some of which have been preserved, show that he never regarded his stay as more than a sojourn. He retained his Chicago address, and he continued to carry on business and to keep alive his contacts west of the lake. He even extended his landholdings. In the same year Sinclair assigned him to manage the Pinery Du Sable set about to develop a plot of eight hundred acres at Peoria, and three years later he legally established his ownership of the property.

In the sixteen years that followed his return to his Chicago trading post, Du Sable clearly established himself as a man of affairs by frontier standards. A typical transaction at his place is recorded by Hugh Howard, agent for a Detroit merchant. Howard and his Canadian boatmen stopped at Du Sable's post in the spring of 1790. They obtained forty-one pounds of flour, twenty-nine pounds of pork, and a supply of baked bread in exchange for thirteen yards of cotton cloth—of excellent quality. They also swapped their canoe for a pirogue. This routine business would seem to indicate the character and scope of the Negro trader's activities.

One of the legends which Du Sable has inspired pictures his home place as a cabin in the wilds—a cabin, no doubt, on the scale of those provided for slaves on Southern plantations. Such is the influence of the stereotype on the minds of men. Actually, the cluster of buildings which constituted his trading post included a log house forty feet by twenty-two, a bakehouse, a dairy, a smokehouse, poultry house, workshop, stable, barn, horse mill, and perhaps others. Like most successful pioneers, Du Sable worked at a number of occupations. The buildings on his place, together with the number and variety of tools listed in an inventory of 1800, show that he was not only a trader but also cooper, husbandman, miller, and several other things besides. It is senseless to try to fit him into the pattern of life and manhood imposed by the cotton country.

A feeling of comfort and well-being came over the dark trader in the early autumn of 1788. When leaves began to fall from the trees, he felt himself in a reflective mood. Memories of a full life crowded into his thought. They were tinged with sadness. Though he was still a young man in the fullness of his strength, Du Sable realized that time was passing. He had a sense of things gone. Beside him his patient Catherine stood, her hand in his, drawing nearer to him as the earth turned and the pageantry of the seasons marched through their green Eden. Catherine, the ruddy Potawatomi Indian girl who had run to meet him through blowing leaves when first he came into the forest, was no longer young, no longer light on her feet, or flushed with color. Catherine was stout and middle-aged and brown as an oak leaf. Their son had come to early manhood. Their daughter Suzanne herself was nearing the end of childhood. Soon— Already a certain Jean Baptiste Pelletier had shown an interest. Suzanne was an attractive girl. She was also the daughter of a prominent trader in the lake country.

Du Sable pressed the hand of the devoted Catherine, no doubt, as he told himself that one thing was lacking. Their life was not complete. The falling red leaves reminded him that he had neglected to marry Catherine as the Church required—the church of his youth and upbringing. Though their union had long ago been twice blessed, he couldn't help thinking that a higher state of blessedness was possible; he did not feel entirely satisfied. Besides, think of the difference to Suzanne and her children! There was a Catholic priest at Cahokia. Catherine must get into a boat with him and make the journey. He couldn't fully explain, of course, Catherine being an Indian, but this was most important. It was an inner need.

On the twenty-seventh of that October the brown couple stood before a man of the Church and recorded their marriage. If we wish to picture the Potawatomi woman by Du Sable's side, we must use our imagination. Concerning the groom, however, we are better informed. Contemporaries left us word that Du Sable was "about six feet tall," that he was "of commanding appearance," "handsome," "of very pleasant countenance." Catherine was probably proud of him on that fall day in Cahokia. Perhaps she even whispered in his ear that he had never looked so fine before.

There is some evidence that Du Sable began to see things in a new light after the marriage journey to Cahokia. Perhaps the South had begun to creep into the Northwest. Perhaps, even in his situation, he had not always escaped the sting of racial arrogance on the part of newcomers. Maybe he was offended by the kind of interest they showed in Suzanne. Possibly, on the other hand, it was none of this, but only that his Potawatomi wife assured him that her people were nearer to him than these others, that among them he could be a great man and a leader of men. Perhaps she won his pity by reciting the evils her people had suffered at the hands of the invaders. But whatever the cause, Du Sable came home from Cahokia and began gradually to orient himself toward the Indians and away from his white associates on the frontier.

Symptomatic of his change, perhaps, was the fact that he rid himself of twenty-one of the twenty-three specimens of European art which had earlier been listed among his possessions in the Day Book of James May of Detroit—among them such doubtful masterpieces as *Lady Strafford, Lady Fortesque, The King and the Rain, The Magician and Love and Desire* (or *The Struggle*). Why Du Sable divested himself of his art "treasures" is not explained by any contemporary source, and it may well have been that, being a trader first and a lover of art second, he was unable to resist the prices these works commanded on the lakefront in the 1790s. It may as easily have been, however, that he had lost his taste for the stuff. Subsequent developments are not entirely out of tune with the second possibility.

Two years after Du Sable and Catherine said their wedding vows, their daughter Suzanne was given in marriage to Jean Baptiste Pelletier. This second union was duly registered, as was also the birth of a daughter Eulalie in Chicago on October 8, 1796. Meanwhile, Jean Baptiste Point Du Sable, Jr., went his own way and settled in the vicinity of St. Charles, Missouri. The venerable Du Sable, *père,* was working quietly toward other objectives. He was building political fences—with the Indians.

The details of these fascinating activities are, unfortunately, not a matter of record. Yet a few facts remain to suggest the outline of the unwritten story. The year his granddaughter was born Du Sable appeared at Mackinac as the leader of a band of Indians in birch canoes. The British garrison greeted his arrival with a salute of cannons. Somewhat later he stood for election as chief of the surrounding Indian tribes. He was defeated. That result does not seem important at this date, for the very fact of Du Sable's candidacy for such power and authority among the Indian nations of the lake region seems remarkable enough, but Du Sable did not take it that way. He was deeply disappointed, if we may judge by his actions.

In May of 1800 he sold his Chicago interests to Jean La Lime of St. Joseph, John Kinzie and William Burnett witnessing the transaction. The bill of sale, written in French, was recorded in the Wayne County Building in Detroit. The sale brought Du Sable 6,000 livres, or something like $1,200, and he promptly shook the dust of the lakefront from his feet. He never returned.

This move on the part of the trader has puzzled some of those who have tried to reconstruct the fragmentary outline of his unusual life. Perhaps it is because they have failed to measure the depths of his disappointment. What he did not know when he left Chicago was that misfortune was waiting for him at every bend in the road.

First his horses were stolen by Indians. In December of the year in which he sold his trading post Du Sable appeared in court in St. Clair County, Illinois, and testified that he had seen the animals and their captors in the vicinity of Peoria. The case was transferred to the Indiana Supreme Court where it was scheduled for trial the following March.

Here the wanderings of the man become vague, his story spotty. We don't have the outcome of the litigation over the stolen horses, and we know no more about the disposition made of his other landholdings or about his own activities during the next five years. But the years between 1805 and 1814 were apparently spent in and around St. Charles, Missouri, where his son lived. Real-estate transactions have been found to establish this point.

A man of comfortable means, past sixty years of age, known and respected throughout the midlands, a good friend of Jacques Clamorgan, the influential Spaniard of St. Louis, Du Sable had earned a contented retirement in a small but attractive house not too far from the homes of his children and grandchildren. Somewhere along the way, perhaps during that obscure five-year period that followed his removal from Chicago, he had buried his wrinkled brown Indian wife. In St. Charles, too, leaves were falling. Fortunately, there was a Catholic church and cemetery there. To both of these Du Sable felt himself quietly, sweetly drawn.

But sixty is not a great age for a man of Du Sable's fiber. What's more, St. Charles was anything but a place in which to contemplate the earth's autumn, the body's dissolution. Frontiersmen and scouts and fur traders and Indian fighters thronged the little outpost town. The place hummed with the music of adventure. Almost daily the whitetops lumbered through its streets headed for Boone's Lick and the western passes beyond. Du Sable, whose close association, at one time or another, with Frenchmen, Englishmen, Indians, and Spaniards would seem to indicate a certain facility in languages, must have listened to a lot of stories in St. Charles—and told a few. Now and again, no doubt, he set his mind on those western hills of which so much was being said. Perhaps there was still one more kick left in the old dog. But, no—his children would have none of it. The western passes were not for men past sixty.

While he waited and dreamed and hoped, time passed, and Du Sable grew old and feeble, indeed helpless, in his St. Charles home. In June of 1813, he transferred a house, lot, and other property to his granddaughter Eulalie Baroda, now the wife of Michael Derais, in return for her promise to care for him the rest of his life and then to bury him in the Catholic cemetery. But Eulalie Baroda failed to keep her promise. Sixteen months after divesting himself of his property, Du Sable had to apply "for the benefit of the law relative to insolvents."

Soon thereafter he died. And despite the failure of his granddaughter to care for him as she had promised, he is buried in the

St. Charles Borromeo Cemetery. His grave lies among those of François Duquette; Major James Morrison, trader and salt manufacturer at Boone's Lick; Rebecca Younger, wife of Coleman Younger, the Missouri outlaw, and other pioneers of the western midlands.

Though his relatives neglected Du Sable in the twilight of his years, the city he founded eventually got around to commemorating him in some measure. There is the Du Sable High School at Forty-ninth and State streets, with a painting of "The Black" hanging in one of its corridors. A plaque on the northeast approach to the Michigan Avenue bridge across the Chicago River marks the spot where his trading post stood. An earlier plaque is in the Chicago Historical Society. And when the names of eight eminent Illinoisans were chosen to adorn the frieze of the Illinois Centennial Building at Springfield in 1965, Du Sable's was one of these.

CHAPTER II

To the Western Passes

ABOUT THE TIME Du Sable settled in St. Charles, a Virginian, a man of property and a former officer of the American Revolution, migrated to the same section of the country with more than a score of slaves. Some of these appear to have been his own offspring. And there is also reason to believe that the old fellow had the decency to free those he had sired soon after settling them in the fork of the Mississippi and Missouri rivers.

At any rate, a fourteen-year-old mulatto boy, Jim Beckwourth from the "Beckwourth Settlement," as the community was known, was apprenticed to George Casner, a blacksmith of St. Louis, in the year 1812 or thereabouts. The apprenticeship lasted five years and ended violently. Young Jim took to courting a girl of the town and staying out late at night. His boss disapproved and cautioned the boy against such behavior. But at nineteen Jim was much too wild to be reached by safe counsels. He continued to keep his own hours and, presumably, to see the lady of his choice.

One morning, after one of those late sessions, old George Casner began to spit fire as his helper entered the shop. He gave the husky youth a tongue-lashing that was intended to force a showdown. It worked. Jim's anger flared, and Casner drove home the words he had been trying for weeks to get across. Jim would mend his ways or he would be fired. There were no two ways about it. This was final. Instead of taking his medicine, however, Jim came back with a few strong words of his own and assured his principal that he would continue to do as he damn pleased. Moreover, he wouldn't take a cussing from George Casner or anybody else.

The blacksmith spat into the glowing forge, pivoted around, and hurled his blacksmith's hammer at the young Negro apprentice. Jim stepped aside. The hammer clattered against the wall. Even then, however, Jim declined to let the matter drop. He picked up the hammer and threw it back at Casner. That was the last straw. The blacksmith flung off his leather apron and rushed into the boy with both fists flying. Nothing could have pleased Jim Beckwourth more. He parried the blacksmith's blows easily, and he delivered his own counterblows without much trouble. In the end Casner gave the rugged brown boy a polite dismissal, and Jim went to his rooming house conscious of having burned his bridges. Now he was on his own. He would have to make a new life for himself.

He had been in his room only a few minutes when he discovered that he wasn't yet through with George Casner. The blacksmith followed Jim home and instructed the landlady to refuse him lodging and meals. This led to another scuffle, and again Jim more than held his own. This time Casner went out and called a one-armed constable. By the time this individual reached the boy's lodging, Jim was ready for anything. He drew a pistol and advised the officer to mind his own business if he wanted to stay healthy. The constable took the suggestion, but Jim suspected that he had only gone to summon more help, and while he was away, the blacksmith's apprentice went into hiding. Three days later he shipped on a keelboat to the mines on Fever River. Again he was discovered and detained by his former boss. This time he was sent home to his father to get straightened out. His father tried to persuade Jim to return to Casner and complete his apprenticeship, but Jim's cup was full. What's more, he said, he wanted to see some of the world. The father agreed finally, and young Jim Beckwourth rejoined the expedition of Colonel R. M. Johnson heading for the mines in the section which is now Galena, Illinois. Jim worked as a hunter, with the responsibility of providing meat for the company of more than one hundred men.

A year and a half later, having accumulated seven hundred dollars in cash, Jim left the expedition, returned to Beckwourth Settlement for a visit with his folks around St. Charles, and then made a trip down the river to New Orleans by steamboat. He didn't enjoy fabulous New Orleans, for he contracted yellow fever and was ill throughout his stay. But when he returned to St. Louis, something big was waiting.

Beckwourth, who was around St. Charles at the time Du Sable was swapping stories with scouts, Indian fighters, trappers, and hunters of the western wilderness, had pined to see the Rocky Mountains since boyhood. A variety of contacts with Indians, some friendly, some hostile, had done nothing to dim his hope. He spoke in his memoirs of a "growing wish to travel." Perhaps it is fair to read into this guarded statement a reference to stresses and pulls that have motivated all Negro migrations in the United States. Beckwourth and his collaborator, T. D. Bonner, were at some pains to purge from his story all indications that the hero was a colored man, born in slavery and heir to everything that that status implied in the early decades of the nineteenth century, but the fact remained, and others—including Francis Parkman—refused to let it be forgotten.

When he had shaken off the effects of yellow fever, Beckwourth found employment with General William Henry Ashley's Rocky Mountain Fur Company. Neither he nor the general say in just what capacity the robust young Negro was engaged, but his duties included blacksmithing, wrangling, hunting, trapping, and Indian fighting. He may also have been the general's body servant. The company was composed of twenty-nine men at the time Jim joined it, and soon thereafter the outfit was headed for the Far West by horse and pack mule.

Everything happened to Jim Beckwourth on this fur-gathering expedition—everything. "Fur companies in those days," says Jim in the dictated memoirs, "had to depend upon their rifles for a supply of food. No company could possibly carry provisions sufficient to last beyond the most remote white settlements. Our food, therefore, consisted of deer, wild turkeys, bear meat, and even, in times of scarcity, dead horses. Occasionally a little flour, sugar, and coffee might last over to the mountains; but those who held these articles asked exorbitant prices for them, and it was but few who tasted such luxuries." Trapping the beaver was a relatively simple matter compared to the hazard and adventure of providing food for the company. And Jim saw times of such critical shortage that the men commenced to look at each other with an obvious, evil intention. Fortunate for them all, at such times, was the presence of Jim Beckwourth, for Jim was a dead shot with a rifle, and he had a wonderful way of landing a buffalo or deer just at the moment when the outfit was wavering on the edge of starvation, madness, and cannibalism.

Another life essential on which the fur company counted for survival was mounts. The men required an ever-increasing number of horses as the outfit pushed farther and farther from its base and into the wilds. With the Indian tribes practically devoting their lives to horse stealing, this became another problem of great urgency and peril to General Ashley's men. At this savage business, too, Jim proved himself invaluable to the fur trader and his company.

Then there was the Indian fighting and scalp-collecting which went hand in hand with the other activities and could not be separated from the need of horses. Apparently the fur companies accepted this desperate guerrilla fighting as a part of their business. The casualties to their own forces they took as a matter of course, and they seemed to reckon as nothing the lives of the Indian foes. Jim Beckwourth was as good as the best at this end of the work. What was equally important, he was born lucky. Showers of arrows fell around him harmlessly. In time he actually began to imagine that he couldn't be killed by an Indian.

Along the way, by his own account as well as the general's, Jim Beckwourth rescued Ashley from a wounded and infuriated buffalo, saved him from drowning in Green River, pouted and fell out with his employer over an angry epithet that slipped from Ashley's lips, made up after the general had apologized, consented to continue with the party. What it was that General Ashley called Jim Beckwourth is not recorded, but it can be imagined, for Jim wanted to settle the issue with blood—and on the spot. And when General Ashley said as much as a man could to make it right, Jim still felt the sting. One gets the impression that he never really liked the general thereafter. There is a word which, spoken in wrath and in a vile tone, will awaken that kind of unforgiving hatred in a colored man, but only one. Perhaps General Ashley used it. If the part of the story on which the accounts of both men agree—the saving of the general's life by Jim, et cetera—is true,

Beckwourth's bitterness must be excused. General Ashley, on the other hand, probably didn't know that Jim would take the "epithet" so seriously. He seems to have allowed Jim a right to be angry over what was said and to have tolerated the Negro's rather drawn-out pout.

When the company returned to St. Louis, it brought enough skins to make General Ashley a rich man. The men were paid off handsomely, and all repaired to Le Barras' hotel to enjoy themselves. Here the celebration continued for a couple of days, at the general's expense, and included drives through the town in carriages hired by the general. To the mountaineers and trappers and such folk in the carriages were added a number of girls, says the memoirs, and we are left to picture them as—well, as the kind of frontier girls who liked to ride in carriages with mountaineers and trappers just back from the wilderness and out on a spree.

In his liquor Beckwourth became such a mighty man that he volunteered to remove from the boat the grizzly bear the company had brought along to be delivered—with grim humor—as a present to an officer friend of the general's in St. Louis. Evidently the spirits were adequate, for Beckwourth assures us he not only led the beast off the boat, but also brought it to the officer's house and there tethered it to an apple tree with a chain. Only when he turned to leave did the bear spring at Jim. The chain held.

Somewhat later Jim looked up Eliza, his former girl friend, and revived the old spark. Now they could be married. But no—duty came first. The general came to him with an urgent request. He desired to send a message to William L. Sublette, captain of trappers in the vicinity of the Great Salt Lake. The matter was most urgent. General Ashley was prepared to offer Jim Beckwourth a thousand dollars to deliver it.

The Rocky Mountain Fur Company had been in St. Louis only a week when the general made his proposal, but the offer sounded good. Romance could wait a few months. And think how much sweeter with that extra thousand dollars! With many sad glances and sorrowful murmurs and cries of "dear girl" and "I care not for money" and bursting floods of tears, the break was finally managed. Not, however, till Jim had promised to return speedily to part no more till death should separate them. Jim admits that the tears were not all Eliza's. "My heart sought relief from its overcharged feeling in the same way."

Almost immediately he and his one companion on the journey were on their way, each provided by the general with two excellent saddle horses and a pack mule between them. It was years before he thought of poor neglected Eliza again. But this forgetfulness cannot be charged entirely to callousness. Things happened. And they were not ordinary things. Scarcely once during the next fourteen years did Jim have time to ponder anything more remote than the business in hand.

Jim reached Sublette by the hardest route and after months of delay. While attached to Sublette's camp, he accepted another mission. This trader was interested in establishing a post among the Blackfeet. His problem was to find a man who would risk his scalp to look after it. Jim, who had already knocked off a few Blackfeet, did not hesitate to accept the assignment. He counted on his reputation as a killer of Blackfeet to help rather than hinder him. "To the Indian," he reasoned, "the greater the brave, the higher their respect for him, even though an enemy." He neglects to mention, what others have told us, that actually Jim Beckwourth, like any number of mulattoes, looked very much like an Indian. Evidently his first employers in the wilderness, the company of Colonel R. M. Johnson, had exploited this circumstance by making Jim their contact man with the Sacs on Fever River. And General Ashley's use of the colored man as a wrangler may also have been for the same purpose. Later, of course, the evidence became conclusive, for Jim, as we shall note, was pawned off on another tribe as one of their own.

Jim's main accomplishment with the Blackfeet was the acquiring of two wives—both daughters of the chief—under the most startling conditions. The first daughter was accepted by Beckwourth, following her father's suggestion, for very practical reasons: he considered such an alliance a guarantee of his personal safety among the Blackfeet as well as an excellent sales advantage. When, however, the Blackfeet brought in a few scalps of people Jim knew and threw a dance in celebration, Beckwourth became enraged—or so he says—and ordered his wife not to join in the dancing. Presently reports came to him. What dancing his wife was doing! Why didn't he come and join? In a tantrum Jim rushed out to the scene, struck the woman a fearful blow with the side of his battle-ax, and dragged her out of the circle, apparently dead. A few minutes later the Blackfeet were ready to lynch the angry Beckwourth, but the chief restrained them. Obedience, he reminded them, was a virtue which all of them required of their women. Even though his own daughter was involved, he could not blame this man for doing what any Blackfoot would have done to a disobedient woman. Instead of punishing the brave who dwelt among them, he was prepared to offer him another wife, a sister to the first and much prettier.

All this Jim took with excellent grace, and modestly accepted the younger daughter of the wise old chief. That night the slumbers of the newly mated pair were interrupted by a whimpering beside their couch. It was the first wife. She had only been stunned. Now she was back, penitently begging to be accepted. She would never be disobedient again. Jim said, "Well, all right," or something of the sort, and let her stay. When he left the Blackfeet a few days later he sent both of his ex-wives presents: some dress patterns he was able to pick up at Sublette's trading post.

Beckwourth's adventures reached a climax in his association with the Crow nation. Somewhat earlier a fellow trapper had amused himself by telling one of the braves of that tribe a little romantic fiction which seemed to fit the circumstances. Evidently the Crow had marveled at the presence of the brown Beckwourth with the company of trappers. Instead of giving him the rather complicated truth, the fellow with the ripe imagination reported something simpler and far more credible. White-Handled Knife (the name the Snakes had given Jim), he said, was actually a Crow. When the Crow brave asked how that could be, he recalled a bit of familiar Crow history. A number of years ago the Cheyennes had fought the Crows, killing a thousand or more men and capturing large numbers of women and children. The Crow nodded. He remembered the event perfectly well—as all old Crows did. Well, the trapper added, White-Handled Knife had been one of the children captured by the Cheyennes at that time. He was not only a Crow but the son of a leading brave. The Crow was deeply impressed. He and his companion hurried home and reported the news.

Nothing happened to Jim immediately, as a result of this completely convincing yarn, but a few weeks or months later he reaped the rewards. While following traps in the vicinity of Powder River he wandered into a herd of horses attended by Indians. He had walked into the territory of the Crows. Immediately word went to the chief of the nation and all his people that the kidnaped Crow had come home, and Jim was given a reception worthy of a returning hero. The first problem was to identify him. Which of the stolen sons was Jim? That was settled by an elderly woman, the wife of Big Bowl, who suggested that if he was the boy she had lost, he would have a small mole on one of his eyelids. Jim's eyelids were promptly stretched and examined. And sure enough, a small mole was found on one of them. That settled it. The family of the old woman, her husband, her other sons, and her four unmarried daughters, swept the happy, astonished Negro into their arms and made him one of them.

The daughters, Jim's new sisters, earned the right to dress their long-lost brother in proper leggings, moccasins, and other appropriate garments. The new "father" announced to the nation that the lost was found. Then he went out and brought in three fine daughters of one of the greatest braves and told Jim to take his pick. Jim selected Still Water, the oldest of the three, because her name appealed to him, and almost immediately he was plunged into the fierce wars of the Indian nation which had adopted him.

The accounts of Beckwourth's fighting and scalping as a Crow brave grow almost monotonous. They are relieved only by stories of horse stealing and little domestic touches like painting the anxious face of his newest wife (a time-honored Crow custom) on his return from battle. But Jim did not find the scope of these activities disagreeably narrow—not for a long time, anyhow. He had a lust for danger, and he fought best when the odds were the greatest. Indeed, his zest and prowess earned him such proud names as Bull's Robe and Medicine Calf and raised him, eventually, to the rank of chief of the Crow nation.

Finally the savage life commenced to pall. Where Point Du

Sable, a man of peace, owner of twenty-three paintings, had failed to reach the position of authority among the Indian tribes to which he aspired, Jim Beckwourth, the taker of scalps, the painter of women's faces, overcame all obstacles. To his credit, however, it can be said that he renounced the savage life while he was still in the good graces of the tribe. Perhaps something happened to remind him of Eliza, the girl in St. Louis whom he had promised to marry. In any case, he walked away from the land of the Crows—breaking an unfinished romance with Pine Leaf, an alluring woman warrior of the tribe—and made his way back to the city in which he had left the tearful Eliza fourteen years earlier. Eliza, he imagined, would be waiting. She wasn't. She had married a couple of weeks before he arrived.

So it was back to the Crow nation for old Jim. They rejoiced at his return, and Pine Leaf gave herself to him, having completed a vow not to marry till she had garnered a hundred scalps to repay the loss of her brother in battle. But even Pine Leaf was not enough. Jim Beckwourth could no longer be happy in the tribal life. Five weeks later he left it again.

At this point in his story Beckwourth appears to have been touched with an almost monumental restlessness—a restlessness approaching that of some of the Greek gods. His activities range from St. Louis to New Orleans to the Seminole country in Florida and back to St. Louis again. Then he turns in the other direction and covers the country from St. Louis to Mexico to California. Along the way Jim fought the Indians with United States forces, traded with outlaws, acquired a Mexican wife, guided wagon trains across the Rockies, discovered an unfamiliar pass leading to California, bought and settled on a ranch on Feather River. In 1854 he met in San Francisco a writer named T. D. Bonner. To this individual old Jim dictated the memoirs which Harper & Brothers published in 1856. But even then James P. Beckwourth wasn't finished.

After a blank space of four or five years history picks up his story, thanks mainly to Le Roy R. Hafen of the State Historical Society of Colorado and to Frank S. Byers, son of an old Denver newspaperman who knew the amazing Jim. Beckwourth was involved, or accused of being involved, in some organized horse stealing in California and requested by the Regulators of that country to leave the section—at his own convenience. Old Jim pulled up and made a roundabout journey to Denver. There he operated a store for an old associate of Sublette. Later he settled on a nearby ranch. Meanwhile, he married Elizabeth Lettbetter, the daughter of Denver's first laundress. The marriage didn't last, and presently the old boy took up with an Indian woman called Sue.

In the twilight of his Homeric life Beckwourth got word of his old cronies of the Crow nation. Perhaps memories of Pine Leaf, the woman warrior who captured his heart, returned to trouble him. But it is a fact that he took advantage of an opportunity to go back to their country. The government sent Jim with two others to try to pacify the still-fighting Crows. At Absaroka he was received handsomely by his old companions. A feast was spread in his honor. At Absaroka, however, Jim fell sick and died.

In the year in which Beckwourth's *Adventures* were published, Francis Parkman, the Boston historian, bought a copy and wrote on the flyleaf: "Much of this narrative is probably false. Beckwith (a variant spelling of the name) is a fellow of bad character—a compound of white and black blood. . . ." Nearly fifty years later, in 1902, Hiram M. Chittenden, historian of the fur trade, repeated and expanded the same judgment. Others have described Jim as a "noted old liar." In 1918, however, a competent historian, not concerned with the mixture of Beckwourth's blood, gave the story a careful inspection, comparing it wherever possible with other sources. Harrison Clifford Dale's labors, a phase of his monograph on the Ashley-Smith Explorations, were directed toward checking the authenticity of Beckwourth's report, nothing else. It is enough to say that Beckwourth's reputation for veracity has been rising ever since. Dale suggested that the old romancer could be believed—now that the record was checked—when talking about any subject but himself. Bernard De Voto, in the Americana Deserta edition of the *Life and Adventures*, advises the acceptance of the man's personal story as neither truth nor falsehood but mythology.

Others will probably want to give old Jim credit for telling as much truth about himself as the records show he told about related matters. The broad outlines of his career seem to be definitely established: it is the story of a Negro born in slavery and looking for something better in America.

CHAPTER III

Toward the North Star

THE WICKEDNESS of human slavery was never more keenly felt by the slave than at the time of the old master's death. Then it was that the black man, sick with apprehension, shuddered in his quarters and waited for the worst to happen. If the owner's financial affairs were left in bad shape, his people might be sold and scattered as a means of paying debts. If a division of his property was required by the heirs, his slaves could look forward to separation from their families and friends. If a younger master inherited the entire Negro population of the estate, the slave could still afford to shudder for his own future. Not all sons inherited the humane attributes of their fathers.

Levin Steel was one who shuddered. His old owner had died, and a younger master had taken over the plantation on the Eastern Shore of Maryland. All of the uncertainties of this changed situation came into the young Negro's mind. Naturally he was filled with fear. But in time this fear changed to another feeling. "By what right," Levin asked himself, "does a man hold another man in bondage?" If it were said that the owner bought and paid for the slave, then Levin wanted to know how it was that human property could rightly be passed from one man to another as an inheritance. Certainly something more was involved here than came into consideration when inanimate wealth was at issue. Thus Levin's first apprehensions were compounded with a kind of thought that made him miserable indeed. Soon he grew so unhappy that he made a reckless decision, and he went directly to the young master and stated it bluntly. "Massa," he said, "I'd sooner die than stay a slave."

To Levin's surprise his young owner took a reasonable view of his decision. Perhaps he was convinced that the Negro meant what he said. At any rate, it was the master who suggested a price at which he would permit the slave to purchase his freedom. And within a few years, by working overtime and by hiring himself out, Levin managed to accumulate enough money to complete the deal. He went North, changed his last name to Still, to avoid any connection with his former status, and settled in the neighborhood of Greenwich, New Jersey.

But freedom for Levin Still was by no means all sweetness. He had been compelled to leave Cidney, his wife, and the youngsters, two boys and two girls, she had borne him in slavery. He consoled himself, however, with the hope that now he would be able to work toward their freedom too.

Cidney, a most remarkable woman, had encouraged him in his plan, but this did not prevent a little righteous scheming on her own part. She was as dissatisfied with slavery as was her husband, and she was equally convinced that God was against the institution. When Levin went North—early in the nineteenth century—she also discovered that loneliness can sometimes put outlandish thoughts in a woman's head. To her it suggested running away from the Maryland plantation and joining Levin in New Jersey.

How Cidney Still finally made the hazardous journey has not been recorded, but her accomplishment can be simply stated. She arrived in Greenwich with her four small children after a flight which many men fugitives found exceedingly perilous when traveling alone. She jubilantly rejoined her husband, and together they set about to get a grip on the responsibilities of freedom. They had scarcely made a beginning when a party of slave catchers came upon the family and dragged the wife and children back to the Eastern Shore.

But the slavers underestimated Cidney Still. They took her back to Maryland, and they may have punished her in other ways, but they failed to change her mind on the question of freedom and her ability to achieve it. She began at once to plan a second attempt.

This time, of course, she would be under more strict observation. If she made a break, the capturing gang would be better prepared to follow. Everything would be harder. Cidney turned the whole matter over in her head and carefully revised her strategy. This time she would leave her boys behind. Peter and young Levin were but eight and six years old respectively, but their grandmother would keep an eye on them, and when they were grown, they would be able to win their own freedom as their mother and father had done. Her little girls, both of whom were infants, were different. Separation from them would probably be permanent. She would not leave her daughters in slavery, despite the problem of carrying two infants in her arms from eastern Maryland to Greenwich, New Jersey. In the middle of the night Cidney kissed her sleeping boys, wrapped her daughters in such rags as she could find, and again headed toward the free country.

Once more she reached New Jersey successfully. And this time she did not forget to reckon with pursuing slave catchers. She and Levin withdrew from Greenwich to the heart of the pines in Burlington County, about seven miles east of Medford. Here, in a neighborhood thinly settled by small farmers who supplemented their incomes by wood chopping, charcoal burning, marl digging, and cranberry picking, Levin Still bought a tract of about forty acres and adopted the manner of life of his poor neighbors. And here, by carefully concealing his family history, he and Cidney and the girls remained safe from capture. Levin prospered in his fields. Cidney thrived in her home and bore her husband a total of eighteen children. The youngest of these, William Still, born October 7, 1821, was destined to fill an important place in the history of the Underground Railroad.

William Still's childhood, like that of his brothers and sisters and of the neighbors' children in that part of New Jersey, was spent in fields of corn and rye, potatoes and garden vegetables. The farm stock consisted of a horse and a yoke of oxen. As William and his brothers grew older, wood chopping claimed more and more of their time, because a forty-acre farm was no adequate support for a family the size of the Stills'. Before he was sixteen, William astonished the community on one occasion by putting up a cord of market wood before noon. This was pointed out as a neighborhood record for a boy of his age.

Cordwood was carried into Medford, a rich agricultural section settled by Quakers. Here the Stills and other people of the pines disposed of their wood and farm products, their charcoal and cranberries, by exchanging them for groceries, marl, lime, and other essentials. When they were needed to help with harvests or for other work, the Still boys also hired themselves to these Quaker farmers for day work. Among these people William made many friends, as he had also done among the poorer folks back in the pines.

Despite friendly relationships in both communities, however, young William's youth was never entirely free from the stings of prejudice. At school some of the children resented the presence of dark classmates. One afternoon a crowd of them waylaid William on his way home and shoved him off a bridge into the water. Thereafter the teacher had to dismiss the colored Stills earlier than the other children, so that they could get a safe start. But, as things developed, the teacher himself proved to be the cause of the antagonism manifested by the other children; and when this was discovered by Levin Still—who had not sweated to earn freedom for the sake of seeing his offspring humiliated in this way—the father withdrew his children and voluntarily terminated their opportunities for schooling. William was seventeen when a change of teachers in the school made it possible for him to return and take up where he had left off. The new teacher took an impartial attitude, and the hostility of the students was quickly reduced. Before the term was out, the bad feeling had practically vanished. The next year William returned to his studies and ten weeks later terminated his common school education.

Meanwhile, in the home of Thomas Wilkins, an elderly bachelor, William received his introduction to the work that was to occupy most of his time and energies in adult life. Wilkins, who lived with his two aged sisters, had in his employ a giant Negro whose free status was at least questionable. A fine property, by reason of his intelligence as well as his physical powers, this firm-willed black man was constantly hounded by slave catchers. Up to this time, however, none had laid a hand on him, for he had announced his determination not to be captured alive. But one rainy night during William's youth the big fellow's former owners sought out Wilkins' house and sent a colored decoy to the door to say that he had a message for the ex-slave, one that had to be delivered in person. Reluctantly the huge black man came down from his hiding place in the attic to face the stranger. As soon as the door was opened, a gang sprang from the shrubbery, rushed into the house, and began beating the powerful Negro with clubs and fists. The odds were hopelessly against him, but the fugitive fought back manfully for a while. Then, his strength gone, he was seized by his captors and held fast as they began clamping handcuffs on his wrists. But elderly Mr. Wilkins and his aged sisters had not lost interest in this invasion of their home. As the men scuffled, one of the old ladies quietly reached for the fire shovel, ran it into the coals, and showered the ruffians with glowing embers. To say that the slave catchers were astonished is to put it mildly. In the panic that followed they left one handcuff dangling. The bruised Negro was quick to take advantage of his opportunity. He sprang into action again and, using the loose handcuff as a weapon, promptly put the whole crowd to flight.

After this rather odd victory everyone in the household agreed that the only wise course would be to remove the runaway to a safer spot. Moreover, they were of the opinion that no time should be lost. He must leave immediately. It was here that they decided to call in William Still and another colored boy and ask the two to escort the hurt and bleeding black man through the pine forest to a place they knew in the vicinity of Egg Harbor about twenty miles away. William and Gabriel Thompson, his young brother-in-law, made the wet trip through dripping trees and sloshing fields. They reached home the next morning. It had been a wretched night and a most exhausting journey, but through it William had discovered the adventure of freedom. Thereafter his quest became the freedom of all slaves.

About this time he discovered and subscribed to the *Colored American,* first antislavery newspaper in this country owned and published by colored men. It was edited by Charles B. Ray and Philip Bell of New York, and the abolitionist tone of the sheet led the local postmaster to assume some of the authority of a censor and to withhold the papers from William for several weeks at a time. He then compelled the boy to pay excess postage in order to get them. This shabby trick was about the last straw for a young man who had just reached twenty and who day by day was becoming more and more sensitive to the ugly little extensions of slavery that reached him among the pines of New Jersey. He decided to leave home and try the world.

The next spring he went to work as a farm hand at Evasham Mount. He worked here a year. Then his father died, and young William went into the wilderness to search his own heart and try to find God. By the middle of 1844, after pondering William Miller's lectures on the Second Coming of Christ, he had his answer: Christ *must* come back to the earth. There was no other hope. With this assurance he was ready to face an evil world. He set out for Philadelphia.

William Still reached Philadelphia just in time to witness bloody riots between "native American" and Catholic elements in the city, and the bitterness of the street fighting he saw stunned the young Negro. A large Catholic church, just then being erected at the corner of Fifth and Girard, a very short distance from William's stopping place, was fired by the mob and was saved from total destruction only by an extra effort on the part of firemen. Many Catholic churches were completely reduced, as was much other property. The police soon recognized their own helplessness in the volcanic situation. When the military was called out, the mob wheeled cannon into line and faced the soldiers on equal terms. Muskets and ordnance were thrown into the fight. There were charges and countercharges, with great bloodshed. Rioting settled down to pitched battle. A detachment of soldiers encamped on a common directly in front of William's quarters. The young man from the Jersey pines imagined every moment that the next cannon ball would collapse the tottering house in which he lived.

But the strife ended without damage to this particular old property and without harm to the boy who had found lodging there, and soon William was on the streets looking for work. His first job was in a brickyard. Then he tried driving a cart on shares, doing general hauling. A few weeks of this convinced him that he would never make the money he needed in this way, and he returned to his old place in the brickyard. The next winter he went into business for himself, opening an oyster cellar on Second Street, but "a plausible fellow of comely proportion, dignified manner, and excellent speech, who passed himself off as a member of the Baptist church and a pronounced friend of the colored race," borrowed William's working capital and brought the enterprise to bankruptcy. But William still had the vacant cellar on his hands, so he accepted the offer of a porter friend to engage in the secondhand clothing business, the porter (who worked in a store) to furnish the old clothes while William did the selling. This partnership lasted exactly three days. William Still had the unusual experience of going bankrupt twice in a single week in totally different business ventures. The last plunge left him penniless in a big city with winter coming on. But other work came his way, as builder's helper, as waiter, and as butler in a well-to-do home. Then in the fall of 1847 he heard that a clerk was wanted in the Pennsylvania Anti-Slavery Society, the office of which was located at 107 North Fifth Street. He applied for the position and got it.

The starting salary was small, $3.75 a week, but the work was more in line with his abilities than the things he had been doing, and the chance actually to help in the cause of abolition was an opportunity he wouldn't have turned down for anything. William Still quickly learned the details of the office. He became acquainted with all the leaders of the antislavery movement in Philadelphia. On the side he worked as janitor at the Apprentices' Library at Fifth and Arch to supplement his salary. Later, of course, the Anti-Slavery Society raised his wages and made this offtime work unnecessary. But by then William Still had another side job that was vastly more exciting and more important. He had become associated with the Underground Railroad.

Though thoroughly organized in Pennsylvania, through a vigilance committee, the Underground work was strictly confidential. Essentially the Underground Railroad was a system for assisting fugitive slaves. It had many branches in the North and some in the South, but all looked toward the North Star and led to freedom, either in the States above the Mason-Dixon line or in Canada. Half freedom was achieved by the slave who made his way across the

Ohio River or into Pennsylvania or New Jersey. In this territory, however, he might be pursued, overtaken, and returned to bondage. The probabilities varied. But in Canada the runaway was beyond the reach of the slave system. The Canadians gave the fugitives refuge, but refused the slave catchers permission to invade their land. The Underground Railroad, then, was the humane enterprise on the part of people opposed to slavery for helping runaway slaves to reach free territory.

Sometimes the work consisted of feeding and housing the poor travelers between legs of the journey. Sometimes it involved driving them in wagon or buggy to a given point. Again it meant listening for knocks at the door at night and going to the window to whisper a few directions to those who could give the password. The road was forever changing, and it had as many twists and turns as has the trail by which the fox eludes his hunters.

Soon after William Still connected himself with the Vigilance Committee of Philadelphia, a middle-aged fugitive was sent to him for an interview. By then it had become Still's duty to learn something about people of this sort, to ask questions, and to give advice. A brief conversation brought out the fact that this fugitive was Peter, one of the young sons of Still's parents whom Cidney had left behind when she stole away with her infant daughters. More than forty years had passed since that time, and Peter was handicapped by complete ignorance of his mother and father and their other children. He had been sold from the Eastern Shore plantation soon after Cidney disappeared the second time and had grown to manhood in Alabama without knowledge of his background. But William knew the story of Cidney's escape, and he told it to his brother for the first time in Philadelphia.

This strange meeting led to dramatic efforts to rescue the wife and children of Peter. The first suggestion was to raise money to buy the freedom of the family, but this could not be followed because Alabama law did not permit slaves to purchase their own freedom or the freedom of wife or children. Peter had won his through the co-operation of a Jewish friend who became his nominal master after the slave had raised enough money to make the purchase. The wife and children of Peter were finally rescued by Seth Conklin, a white man who had been so touched by the story of Peter's life that he readily volunteered to risk his own in the undertaking.

The meeting with his brother Peter led William Still to a determination to get fuller information about the fugitives who passed through Philadelphia and to keep more adequate records of the Underground Railroad work there. He was most favorably situated to do this, and his notes and papers and records accumulated rapidly. After the Civil War publishers began to bid for them. They appeared in book form in 1882—a large volume filled with quaint and fascinating experiences.

Hundreds of fugitives passed through Philadelphia in William Still's day. Some of them were disguised. Others came in boxes with strange labels on them. Many walked into the offices of the Anti-Slavery Society and told stories which later excited a whole generation of Americans and became a literary type somewhat comparable to the Western story. These tales are now known as slave narratives. Today surviving copies are the objects of many collectors. Some libraries have acquired more than one hundred and fifty titles.

William Still's work was known and appreciated by William Lloyd Garrison, Horace Greeley, Charles Sumner, and most of the other important opponents of slavery. Many of them hailed his book of *Underground Railroad Records* enthusiastically.

Perhaps the most exciting personality to emerge from this great mass of unorganized papers is that of Harriet Tubman. This strange, heroic woman appears and reappears like the haunted spirit of freedom itself. "The next arrival numbered four passengers and came under the guidance of 'Moses,'" one entry states. In parentheses "Moses" is said to be Harriet. Again a letter shows her following a group in a stage, keeping a sharp eye on her charges. Another time Thomas Garrett is writing to ask what has become of Harriet. He hasn't seen her for a long time. When he is told reassuringly that the brave "conductor" is still at work, still returning again and again to lead her people out of slavery, just as she herself had escaped from a plantation in Maryland years earlier, he is greatly cheered.

Still saw much of Harriet Tubman. She passed through Philadelphia on her first journey to freedom, and she was in and out of the offices of the Anti-Slavery Society during the period of Still's connection with it. She was evidently a woman who made a strong impression on people.

A small black woman with a prominent scar on her face and a wide gap between her front teeth where two had been knocked out, she had suffered brutal treatment in slavery because of her will to freedom. Later she had escaped from Maryland's Eastern Shore and made her way to upper New York and then to Canada. But Harriet Tubman was a woman to whom individual liberty was not enough. She hated *slavery*. Very soon she was returning to the land of bondage to encourage and assist others who groaned under the yoke. By repeated trips of this kind she became expert in the techniques of escape and began to lead men and women to freedom by the dozen, then by the score, finally by the hundred.

Her exploits became legendary in the North; in the South a high price was put on her capture. It was never collected. Meanwhile, however, the little shrunken woman bobbed up at antislavery meetings and conventions all over the North. People would whisper in awe and point her out. "That's Harriet Tubman." John Brown knew and admired her and drew inspiration from her, so much so that he always referred to her as General Tubman. A report of the Senate Investigating Committee mentions her in connection with Harpers Ferry. W. E. B. Du Bois suggests that only sickness, brought on by overwork and exposure, prevented her actual presence at that historic moment. She died in the city of Auburn, New York, in 1914. The next year a distinguished audience unveiled a bronze tablet to her memory on behalf of the city, and the mayor urged everyone to put out flags "that the memory of faithful old slave Harriet Tubman may be honored." The tablet was later mounted on the front entrance of the Cayuga County Courthouse, where it remains to the present time. In 1943 Harriet became the subject of an admirable biography by Earl Conrad—an even finer tribute.

Harriet Tubman was not the most famous slave to escape bondage via the Underground Railroad. Frederick Douglass and William Welles Brown were both vastly superior in culture and learning. These men were intellectuals, writers, and orators, and they stirred hundreds of audiences in the United States and in the British Isles. But in neither was the sheer passion for freedom any stronger. No greater tribute can be paid to William Still of Philadelphia than to say that he worked hand in glove with such a woman till their purpose had been accomplished.

CHAPTER IV

John Brown's Friend

ON A MARCH NIGHT in 1856 a band of men moved furtively through the unlighted streets of Chicago. They stopped before a darkened house. Then the leader went to the door and rapped sharply while the others waited in the shadows. Presently the door opened, and a shaft of yellow lamplight fell on the man outside. He was tall and gaunt, with piercing eyes and a flame-touched beard. The individual behind the door extended his hand.

John Brown greeted Allan Pinkerton, noted detective—later to become Abraham Lincoln's bodyguard. Pinkerton, an active abolitionist, took some of the men into his house and found places for the others. They were all John Brown's men. All, that is, except eleven escaped slaves. Pinkerton then took Brown to the home of a mutual friend with whom Brown had stayed on other occasions. That friend was John Jones, free Negro, prominent businessman and leader in the fight for equal rights.

The following day the detective raised nearly six hundred dollars at a "lawyers' meeting" to assist the group on its way to Canada. He also obtained a car on the Michigan Central Railroad from Colonel O. G. Hammond, general superintendent, "who personally saw to it that the car was stocked with provisions and water." Late that afternoon the party left for Detroit. Brown himself had taken an earlier train to make sure of meeting Frederick Douglass there. This was the last time the two old friends were to meet. John Brown went on to Harpers Ferry and his death. John Jones went on to become one of Illinois' most eminent citizens and a leader of his people.

John Jones had been born on a plantation in Greene County, North Carolina, late in the year 1816 or early in 1817. His mother was a free mulatto, his father a German named Bromfield who had settled in the eastern part of the State, not far from the Tidewater. As the child of a free woman, Jones himself was born free, but his mother, fearing that his father or his father's relatives might attempt to enslave him, apprenticed the young child to a man named Sheppard, who agreed that the boy should be taught a trade.

Sheppard moved to Tennessee and there bound the lad over to a tailor named Richard Clere, who lived near Memphis. After working with Clere for a while John was hired out by his employer to a Memphis tailor. In Memphis the young man met and fell in love with Mary Richardson, daughter of a Negro blacksmith. Dissatisfied with the lot of free Negroes in Tennessee, the Richardsons presently left the State and moved to Alton, Illinois. John Jones remained in Memphis to finish his term of service.

Soon he was beset by other troubles. Young Jones learned that the heirs of Clere, whose death was expected momentarily, were planning to claim the apprentice as their property and to sell him into slavery. There were hints that he would be sent to Texas, then an independent republic, from which escape was almost impossible.

Jones immediately secured permission from his employer, who had no part in the plot, to return to North Carolina to obtain legal evidence of his free status. Needless to say, he wasted no time en route. John Jones's ride to Carolina for his freedom papers is a thrilling tradition. He never forgot the tedious throb of galloping feet on the long and lonely errand. A few days later he returned—the evidence in his pocket.

In January of 1838 Jones filed a petition addressed to Judge V. D. Barry of the Eleventh Judicial District, then holding court in Somerville. The petition set forth that John Jones, alias John Bromfield (for he was sometimes called by his father's name, sometimes by his mother's), was born free about the middle of November 1816; that he was brought from North Carolina to Tennessee by an individual to whom he was bound as an apprentice until he should be twenty-one; that by sale or otherwise he had passed among several bonds until by purchase he came to Richard

Clere, a tailor, for the purpose of learning the trade; that Clere hired him out during the years 1836 to 1837 and thereby forfeited all right to the custody of his person. On these grounds Jones requested that he be brought into court and discharged on a writ of *habeas corpus*. Thus his status would become a matter of unquestioned record.

On January 16, 1838, after consideration of Jones's petition, the court ordered his release from the service and custody of Clere and ruled that he be allowed to go at liberty. The discharge papers which Jones obtained that day remain in the Chicago Public Library to which they were presented by him.

In all, Jones remained in Memphis about three years, working and saving his money. Then in 1841 he struck out for Alton, following Mary Richardson. He arrived with $100 in his pocket and promptly proposed to the fair octoroon whose queenly beauty became a legend in later years. She accepted him, and they were married. Almost immediately Jones and his young wife were precipitated into seething events—the formation of antislavery societies, the organization of the Liberty party, the spread of abolitionist sentiment, and activities connected with the Underground Railroad. Alton was the starting point of one branch of the road which ran northwest to Jacksonville, through La Salle and Ottawa, and then to Chicago. Evidently the militantly antislavery atmosphere of Chicago, terminus of all the most Western routes, attracted John Jones, for with his young wife and infant daughter, Lavinia, he headed northward. With freedom papers in his luggage, he had little to fear from suspicious fellow travelers during the seven-day journey by stage and canal.

The Jones family arrived in Chicago on March 11, 1845, and rented a one-room cottage at the northwest corner of Madison and Wells streets. Jones also rented a small shop standing where the Clark Street entrance of the Sherman House is now located. There he set himself up as a tailor and solicited the patronage of the townspeople. If, as has been alleged, abolitionists financed the establishment of his business, he must have recommended himself to them before coming to Chicago. The Jones's capital of $3.50 was used to furnish the home. By pawning his watch Jones raised enough money to purchase two stoves, one for the home and one for the shop. O. G. Hanson, a Negro grocer, allowed the new family credit to the amount of $2.00.

In the days that followed Jones devoted himself to work and study and unremitting activity in behalf of his race as a whole. He learned to read and write mainly by his own efforts. L. C. Paine Freer is supposed to have done all Jones's writing for him for a while after the tailor settled in Chicago. But when the kindly lawyer-businessman suggested that Jones acquire the art for himself, the tailor applied himself so seriously that he learned not only to write but also to read and to do both with distinction. Through all the succeeding years, Jones and Freer, the courtly abolitionist, continued to be friends, working together for the defeat of slavery in all its forms. Freer survived John Jones by thirteen years and is buried in Graceland Cemetery, Chicago, just a few steps from the grave of his old friend.

Jones was easily the outstanding Negro in the Midwest in 1860. His business prospered from the first, and his voice and pen became increasingly powerful in the struggle for emancipation. His home was a popular rendezvous for abolitionists, black and white. It was also a station for the Underground Railroad, and through it passed scores of fugitives on their way to Canada. With George DeBaptiste (also a free man of color and brother of Richard, the noted editor and churchman) Jones also worked to arrange safe "depots" in other Negro homes and in churches.

In 1853 the State legislature passed a law prohibiting the immigration of free blacks to Illinois. The abolitionists sprang to arms. The Negroes of the State rallied with grim determination. John Jones was in the forefront of this fight, as were L. C. Paine Freer and Dr. C. V. Dyer, the wealthy physician whose name is so closely linked to the cause of freedom in Chicago. Frederick Douglass, by then a national figure, came to lecture during October. Douglass, the amazing ex-slave orator, worked actively with Jones. In subsequent years he generally stayed at Jones's home when in Chicago. Jones, too, made speeches up and down the State, lobbied, and gave generously of his wealth, which by now was not insignificant.

In his autobiography Douglass recalls with amusement a trip he and John Jones made through Wisconsin during those antislavery years. A hotel in Janesville accepted the colored men as guests but set them apart to eat by themselves at mealtime. Wincing at the segregated arrangement, Douglass observed—loud enough for the other guests to hear—that he had noticed white and black horses eating from the same trough in the stable of the hotel. There seemed to be perfect harmony between the animals, and he was left to infer that the horses of Janesville were more civilized than its people. The guests in the dining hall took the remarks in the spirit in which they were intended, laughed, and pleasantly rearranged the seating.

Despite his active role in the struggle against slavery, John Jones conducted his business so well that he was able to purchase important property, including the location at 119 Dearborn Street —now occupied by a prominent Chicago department store—where he set up a merchant tailoring establishment. He gave notice to his customers of his new and favorable location in the following newspaper ad:

JOHN JONES. Clothes, Dresses and Repairer. Gentlemen, I take this method of informing you that I may be found at all business hours at my shop, 119 Dearborn Street, east side between Washington and Madison, ready and willing to do all work in my line that you may think proper to favor me with, in the best manner possible. I have all kinds of trimming for repairing gentlemen's clothes. Bring on your clothes, gents, and have them cleaned and repaired. . . . Remember, garments left with me are in responsible hands. I am permanently located at 119 Dearborn Street. Yours for work, J. JONES.

The year 1856 saw the birth of the Republican party at the State anti-Nebraska convention in Bloomington, where Abraham Lincoln raised his voice against further extension of slavery. Although the new party—composed of abolitionists, Free Democrats, and Democrats—was unsuccessful in national elections, many victories were recorded in Congressional districts and for State offices. In the same year a convention of the Negro citizens of Illinois met at Springfield to petition for the rights of Negroes in the State. John Jones was one of the most active participants. The following year another legal victory was scored when it was decided that the laws of other States recognizing slavery could not affect the condition of a fugitive in Illinois. The defeat of proslavery forces in Kansas further cheered the abolitionists, while the Dred Scot decision spurred them to efforts to build and strengthen the Republican party.

In 1861 the catastrophe predicted by John Brown descended on the nation. The Negroes of Illinois, while not admitted to the armed forces as combatants until two years later, aided the Northern effort in every way they could. Only a few months before Fort Sumter was fired upon Negroes meeting in Chicago had been urged to win their liberties "by the use of their strong right arms." It was an idea which had first been recommended by Alexander Hamilton during the Revolutionary War. But not until 1863 did these willing arms find use in the War between the States. They then gave a good account of themselves despite restrictions and discriminations practiced against them in uniform.

The lot of Negroes in Illinois was not noticeably improved during the first years of the war, but after the defeat of the Democratic majority in the State elections of 1864 Illinois rallied to the support of the national administration. In that year, too, John Jones published his forceful pamphlet, *The Black Laws of Illinois and a Few Reasons Why They Should Be Repealed,* printed by the Chicago *Tribune*. The booklet was an eloquent plea for full citizenship rights for the Negro. It reviewed his condition under the Black Laws and urged that they be abolished. Jones addressed one adroit argument to the lawmakers, most of whom were men of property:

> You ought to, and must, repeal those Black Laws for the sake of your own interest, to mention no higher motives. As matters stand now, you cannot prove by us that this or that man (if white) ran into a valuable wagonload of merchandise and destroyed it; therefore you are liable to lose hundreds of dollars any day if your wagons are driven by colored men, and you know they are, in great numbers.

Jones was referring to the inability of a Negro to testify in court against a white man under the existing Black Laws. He noted that he was paying taxes on $30,000, yet could not vote, and reminded the legislature that the Negro inhabitants of Illinois numbered seven thousand. He predicted that petitions requesting repeal of the Black Laws would be presented to them "this winter from all parts of your state, . . . signed by your most respected and financial citizens." During the debate on repeal in 1865 one State Senator expressed his willingness to vote for a special act enfranchising Jones himself, for whom he entertained respect and kind feelings, but not the entire race.

John Jones had bigger plans. He made speeches, wrote articles, circulated his pamphlet, and led in the organization of Negro and white groups in every part of the State. He lobbied throughout the session of the legislature while the proposed repeal was under consideration. The results of these efforts were indicated by the *Tribune* in its issue of January 16, 1865:

> Petitions continue to pour into the General Assembly from all parts of the state for the repeal of the infamous Black Laws and of other laws upon our statute books placing disabilities upon the black race in the state. The petitions are signed by a large number of leading men of the state, very many of whom, four years ago, voted against their being stricken from the statute books of Illinois. These Black Laws will be repealed—there is no doubt of it.

The final vote came late in January. The Senate counted 13 to 10 for repeal; the House 49 to 30. The Negroes and all other friends of liberty were overjoyed. Church bells rang; glasses were lifted in toasts to the success of the campaign. The fuse lighted by John Jones fired the cannon that hurled the blast which brought victory.

Of course the campaign for the liberation of the Negro did not stop with the repeal of the Black Laws. The legislature went on to endorse the federal amendments granting suffrage to the race, which in Illinois alone had put eighteen hundred and eleven soldiers in the field to preserve the Union. Illinois became the first State to ratify the 13th Amendment, one day after Congress voted to submit the resolution to the legislatures of the various States. The 14th and 15th Amendments were passed with equal speed. As the sixties closed, the basic laws of the land declared the Negro free and equal. It was the culmination of a long and bitter struggle by Negroes and their white co-workers.

In 1866 Jones went to Washington with a committee headed by Frederick Douglass to call on President Andrew Johnson in the interest of suffrage for freedmen. The committee feared that Johnson, who was said to favor colonizing the race abroad, would not endorse progressive legislation for Negro rights unless he was subjected to pressure.

Meanwhile, John Jones's fortune continued to grow. In 1871, prior to the great fire, it was estimated at close to $100,000. He was not only the most affluent Negro in the Midwest but one of the wealthiest in the country. The great fire reduced his possessions somewhat, but he remained a well-to-do man by contemporary standards.

Shortly after the fire, Jones's name was proposed for the Cook County Board of Commissioners, short term, by a nonpartisan "Fireproof" ticket. He was elected almost without opposition. He was re-elected for a three-year term in 1872, but in 1875 he was defeated along with some other commissioners as a result of alleged participation of board members in a conspiracy. When the case came to trial, however, Jones was acquitted, there being no evidence whatever against him. He was one of the first of his race in the North to win an elective office of importance, and the first in Illinois. Following his defeat in 1875, another colored county commissioner was not elected again for nearly twenty years. During his incumbency, Jones was active in the fight against separate schools for the children of the two races, an issue not settled by law until 1874.

In 1875 Chicago newspapers reported an unusual reception in the Jones home. The family was celebrating the thirtieth anniversary of their residence in the city. Very fittingly the event coincided with the signing of the Federal Civil Rights Act by President Grant. And prominent Chicagoans, white and colored, came in great numbers to honor the Negro who, for them, represented the possibilities of his race. The *Tribune* spoke of a continuous throng of friends and acquaintances who remembered the early years of the struggling tailor and who had stood by him for three decades and observed his rise.

Everybody was impressed by the Jones home on Ray Street. When evening fell on the waves of visitors, the parlors presented a beautiful picture. They were brilliantly lighted. Hanging mirrors were entwined with wreaths of evergreen. Mantels were ornamented "with camellias, roses, and orange blossoms." Over a center door adjoining two parlors was an inscription artistically wrought in wax. Another such inscription had been placed above a framed engraving of the signing of the Emancipation Proclamation in the rear parlor. Engravings of Mr. Lincoln, John Brown, President Grant, Chase, Sumner, Horace Greeley, and Joshua R. Giddings were suspended against the white walls of the front parlor. Elsewhere large oil paintings of Jones and members of his family had been appropriately placed.

A quadrille orchestra played during the evening hours. As the evening wore on, Jones drew his older friends aside to entertain them with stories of his thirty years, while his daughter "with ease and grace marshaled the young people who desired to enter into the terpsichorean pleasures." This went on for hours.

The few remaining years of the life of Illinois' most honored colored citizen were spent quietly in the house on Ray Street, where the family became widely known for its charming hospitality, the mellow wisdom of its head, and the queenly grace and hauteur of his fair wife. Since his name was not mentioned in newspaper accounts, it is improbable that Douglass attended the thirty-year anniversary party, but Jones had heard the leonine platform giant lecture on John Brown in Farwell Hall a few weeks earlier and entertained him at his home. Perhaps on this occasion the two men exchanged memories of their zealous friend. In a newspaper interview Jones stated his belief that John Brown had arms buried in the Cumberlands—arms that would someday be found. Douglass delivered another address in Chicago in February 1877. The following month Douglass assumed his duties as United States marshal for the District of Columbia. Jones devoted himself more and more to donations to charitable institutions and other philanthropies; much of his large fortune went in this manner during the late years of his life. He died May 27, 1879, after a long illness. The next day his body was carried to Graceland Cemetery, followed by "an immense concourse of friends and well-known citizens."

John Jones's funeral was given full coverage by the press. The line of march, the lists of mourners, persons walking and those in carriages, the floral pieces—all were detailed and enumerated. And once again the experiences of the man were sketched. Chicago evidently liked the story of John Jones, merchant tailor, free man of color. His success was both an object lesson and a promise.

Perhaps some of the credit belongs to the community which, in those days, did not confine the lives of men like John Jones to a ghetto. He lived and worked as a man—not a Negro—though he never lost his identification as a colored American. It was not as a Negro that he conducted his business or was elected to political office or built his home. And it was not as a Negro, but an American, that he was buried at Graceland in the section which also contains the graves of Freer, Pinkerton, and other friends of the struggle. On Pinkerton's imposing monument one learns that here is a man who "sympathized with, protected and defended the slaves, and labored earnestly for their freedom." The fact that John Jones lies near by completes the story.

CHAPTER V

"Leave a Summer Land Behind"

Whence came these dusky legions,
Braving the wintry wind?
For our snow-bound, icy regions
These fleeing, dusky legions
Leave a summer land behind.

They fly from the land that bore them,
As the Hebrews fled from Nile;
From the heavy burthens o'er them;
From the unpaid tasks before them;
From a serfdom base and vile.

—"Exode" by W. H. Stillwell in the
Chicago *Inter-Ocean,* March 12, 1881.

ON A SPRING DAY in 1880 a slight, light-colored Negro man sat restlessly in the antechamber of a committee room in which United States Senators were questioning a seemingly endless procession of witnesses. The man was getting along in years—past seventy-one —but he appeared to be more energetic than many of the younger witnesses waiting their turn.

His full, quick eyes darted expectantly to the door leading into the inner room each time an attendant opened it to call a name. He ran his fingers nervously through his wavy iron-gray hair; he stroked his scraggly chin whiskers and twisted the ends of his mustache. His feet kept up a constant shuffling, as though they were anxious to be up and away. Now and then he fished a heavy silver watch from his pocket and regarded it worriedly. He spread open a fat scrapbook he had been clasping under his arm, turned the pages slowly, scanning the newspaper clippings it contained. He could not spell out the separate words, but others had read them to him so many times he almost knew them "by heart." This was not surprising. They were all about himself.

At length the attendant opened the door and called out, "Benjamin Singleton!"

"That's me!" cried the impatient witness, almost dropping the scrapbook in his haste. Remembering the solemnity of the occasion, he slowed down as he made his way across the floor. Holding his slender form proudly erect, he entered the committee chamber with dignity.

Democratic Senator Daniel W. Voorhees, "the Tall Sycamore of the Wabash," chairman of the senatorial committee investigating the phenomenal Negro exodus from the South to the North, was getting a little tired of the whole business when Benjamin Singleton entered. Much of the previous testimony had repudiated the Democrat's contention that the Republicans had sponsored the importation of Southern Negroes into Indiana and other Northern States in order to win political control.

Voorhees had just undertaken to shake the testimony of Henry Adams of Louisiana, a Negro veteran of the Union Army. Adams resolutely stuck to his story of violence and murder directed against the freedmen and of the cheating of Negro farmers by plantation owners. Even women and children, he asserted, were not spared the wrath of hate-filled rebels who had writhed at the sight of Negroes in political office and positions of responsibility during the reign of the "carpetbaggers." Now the "carpetbaggers" had pulled out, restoring the reactionary element to undisputed control again. One Negro witness had observed succinctly, "If I votes the Republican ticket, I wakes up next morning in a graveyard."

After the triumphant Democrats returned to power in the South and re-established "white supremacy," the more spirited Southern Negroes found their lot almost unbearable. Return to Africa was out of the question for most of them, even if they had desired to go. But there was the North, where Negroes, theoretically at least, enjoyed equal rights with white people. By hundreds and eventually by thousands Negro migrants began to push northward. A great exodus got under way. Within a short time it assumed such proportions that investigation by the Senate was ordered.

Politicians, sociologists, planters, industrialists, and many others aired their opinions before the committee. Some of the testimony brought a beaming smile of approval to the face of Senator Voorhees. Andrew Currie, mayor of Shreveport, Louisiana, testified that most of the colored people of the South were contented and prosperous and that there was no reason why an industrious and law-abiding Negro should migrate. A disgruntled minority numbering less than one per cent of the total Negro population, aided by white agitators from the North, was stirring up all the trouble, he contended. There were even some black folks who voiced their entire satisfaction with conditions in the South and branded as irresponsible troublemakers and shiftless loafers their brethren who were pulling up stakes and striking out for the North. Other Negro witnesses had an unprintable name for these collaborationists.

Benjamin Singleton's contribution to the investigation brought no joy to Senator Voorhees and his Democratic confreres. The chairman hammered away at the elderly Negro, trying to establish his point that the Republicans were the propelling force behind the exodus.

"*I* am the whole cause of the migration. Nobody but me," Benjamin Singleton repeated time and again, jutting his square jaw till its sparse whiskers bristled. "I am the Moses of the colored exodus!"

Though his testimony was less vehemently bitter than some offered (Singleton was such a mild and friendly person that all of his followers and most of his acquaintances called him "Pap"), "the Moses of the colored exodus" was firm in asserting that the freedman in the South was no better off than he had been under slavery—worse, if anything. The only escape for the colored man, he said, was to make his way to a new country where he could develop his own agriculture and industry, found his own institutions and conduct his own courts, make his own laws. It must be some place where there weren't too many white folks around to hamper and persecute. "Pap" had become convinced that white and black were like oil and water, and could never mix successfully.

Soon thereafter the senatorial committee investigating the exodus wound up its affairs. It had recorded testimony covering seventeen hundred printed pages, but it had arrived at no definite conclusions. The Democratic majority—despite evidence to the contrary supplied by "Pap" Singleton, Henry Adams, and others—stuck to its original contention that the mass migration had been engineered by the Republicans as a political maneuver, and named as a secondary impetus the greed of railroad and steamship companies seeking passenger business. Republican Senator Windom submitted a minority report, vigorously dissenting. As the din of verbal battle died away, the Chicago *Evening Journal* ventured a doleful prediction:

> It is barely possible that the Democrats may learn one lesson from this investigation, and that is that the North is still a Canaan for the oppressed and outraged race, and that, unless they should be accorded better treatment by the Democratic ex-slaveholders, the cotton, corn, and rice fields of the South will in time become dreary and unfruitful wastes.

Strangers who encountered Benjamin Singleton in his later years at times were inclined to take the old man as an inveterate windbag, but there was always something so delightfully ingenuous and transparently honest about him that few found his boasting annoying. And he had some justification for bragging a little, as we shall see.

"The Moses of the colored exodus" was born a slave in Nashville, Tennessee, in 1809. He had been trained as a carpenter and cabinetmaker, but for some reason—possibly because of his restless and independent disposition—his master sold him a dozen times or more, sometimes as far away as the Gulf States. Each time he ran away, and doggedly made his way back to Tennessee. This monotonous routine tired him at last, and with weariness came the call of free soil. After three abortive attempts he reached (by way of the Underground Railroad) Windsor, Canada, in the province of Ontario, just across the river from Detroit. He might have been safe there to pursue his trade, but by this time he had become a man with a purpose. He could not sleep easy in his bed while other black men across the river and back in the Southland were denied the air of freedom in their lungs.

"Pap" recrossed the river and established himself in Detroit as a scavenger. Though he never told much about his activities in Detroit, where he remained until 1865, we may suppose that "Pap's" scavenger cart carried many a black runaway through the streets to and from his "secret boardinghouse for fugitive slaves," as he later described it. Then Lee surrendered to Grant at Appomattox. The South was beaten. "Pap" still couldn't get Tennessee off his mind, and he got to thinking about how it would be down home now that no man was master and no man slave. By George, he'd go back there and find out! His work with the Underground Railroad and the scavenger cart was finished anyhow.

Disappointment and disillusionment awaited Singleton in Tennessee. Vengeful rebels, smarting from their recent chastisement, had regained power with the Democratic party, and the Negroes—regarded by many as the cause of it all—were punished in innumerable ways. Jailed for petty offenses, they often found themselves farmed out to the same planters who had formerly owned them, and their status, if anything, was worse than under legal slavery. They were denied the educational and social facilities they had been led to expect, harried by the Ku Klux Klan, and discriminated against in general. The dream of "forty acres and a mule" faded away. Contract farming kept the Negro tenants hopelessly in debt from one year to the next, since they were obliged to procure all their supplies from a commissary maintained by the planter, who chalked up goods at exorbitant prices, such as sixty cents a pound for bacon, thirty cents a pound for sugar, and thirty-five cents a yard for calico. Fifty cents might be charged for a plug of chewing tobacco, a dollar and fifty cents to two dollars for a gallon of molasses which would fetch no more than twenty-five cents at St. Louis.

Singleton believed that the Negroes would fare better if they segregated themselves in some new territory. He formed the Tennessee Real Estate and Homestead Association for the purpose of settling ex-slaves on subsistence farms, but Tennessee land proved to be too high and the atmosphere there too charged with racial prejudice. "The whites had the lands an' the sense an' the blacks had nothin' but their freedom, an' it was jest like a dream to them," he said later.

Singleton eventually discarded Tennessee as unsuited for Negro colonization. After considerable investigation, he decided upon Kansas, State of "Old John Brown." The idea of emigration to Kansas fired the imaginations of even the most illiterate peasants of the Deep South, for the song "John Brown's Body" and the story of the fiery old abolitionist's martyrdom at Harpers Ferry were known to all.

Brilliantly colored chromos depicting the fortunate lot of freedmen who had been sagacious enough to remove to Kansas found a ready sale among Negroes throughout the South. One of the most popular of these revealed an "exoduster" and his family sitting down to a lavishly spread dinner table in a tastefully arranged room, while through the open windows were disclosed barns bulging with plenty, sleek cattle and horses, and fields heavy with ripe crops. Steamship and railroad companies, as the Democrats of the exodus committee had maintained, did profit from migration, but there is little or no evidence that they had a hand in *starting* it. Once the movement was under way, however, the enterprising transportation companies helped it along with enticing circulars about the benefits of life in the New Canaan, offering special excursion rates.

"Pap" formed various colonies in Kansas and boasted late in life that he had led 82,000 Negroes out of the South. This figure, however, is known to be greatly exaggerated. The numbers grew with "Pap's" age.

The people of Kansas, though for the most part favorably disposed toward the "exodusters," could not easily accommodate all of them, and "Pap" Singleton began to think of other refuges. He visited Indiana and Illinois, not only to spy out the land for colonization sites, but to campaign for Garfield, Republican candidate for President. Indiana had already received a number of Negro pilgrims, but little response was aroused in Illinois. "Pap" later credited himself with winning the two States for Garfield, maintaining that he had visited Democratic chieftains and threatened to lead 250,000 Negroes up from the South unless Indiana and Illinois were found in the Republican column. The alarmed Democrats, "Pap" claimed, stayed away from the polls, and the desired result was obtained.

A few rebuffs were not enough to daunt a seasoned warrior like "Pap." He had been spreading the gospel of emigration for more than a decade, spending six hundred dollars of his own money for circulars which he had managed to dispatch to every remote corner of the South. Some were carried abroad by itinerant preachers; railroad porters and steamboat hands distributed others. Unlettered though he was, "Pap" was a forceful and pungent speaker and often voiced his distrust of and contempt for "educated" Negroes and politicians. Following his fruitless visit to Illinois, he told a St. Louis *Post-Dispatch* reporter (who evidently embellished the recital somewhat):

> The colored race is ignorant and altogether too simple, and invests too much confidence in Professor Tom Cat, or some of the imported slippery chaps from Washington, Oberlin, Chicago, or scores of places whence are sent intriguing reverends, deputy doorkeepers, military darkies or teachers, to go often around the corrals and see that not an appearance of a hole exists through which the captives within can escape or even see through.

As time went on the colonization movement took on the character of a fraternal order or a religious body. Numerous local branches conducted meetings, and songs such as "The Land That Gives Birth to Freedom" added fervor to the proceedings. Copies of these songs, crudely printed by Negro craftsmen, sold for ten cents, and the proceeds were added to the colonization funds. Churches, halls, and schoolhouses echoed to:

> *We have held meetings to ourselves to see if we can't*
> *plan some way to live.*
> *Marching along, yes, we are marching along.*
> *To Kansas City we are bound.*
> *We have Mr. Singleton for our president. He will go on*
> *before us and lead us through.*
> *Marching along,* et cetera.

For Tennessee is a hard slavery state, and we find no
friends in that country.
Marching along, et cetera.
We want peaceful homes and quiet firesides; no one to
disturb us or turn us out.
Marching along, et cetera.

The settlers of Nicodemus, one of the several colonies planted by Singleton, sang:

Nicodemus was a slave of African birth,
And was bought for a bag full of gold,
He was reckoned a part of the salt of the earth,
But he died years ago, very old.

Chorus:

Good time coming, good time coming,
Long, long time on the way;
Run and tell Elijah to hurry up Pomp
To meet us under the cottonwood tree,
In the great Solomon Valley,
At the first break of day.

The reference to Nicodemus being obscure to a great many of the "exodusters," they fell into the habit of pronouncing the name "Nigger Demus."

Southerners who had wished merely to chastise the Negroes and "put them in their places" began to realize that their zeal was having an effect they had not anticipated. Not only plantation hands but skilled artisans were heading North. Both force and persuasion were employed to convince the Negro that the South was his true homeland, and even Negro leaders such as Frederick Douglass became alarmed at the prospect. Douglass maintained that the Negro had been too impatient, that he had not given democracy enough time to reassert itself in the South, and that he should stand by to assist in the progress. The Chicago *Inter-Ocean* inquired of Mr. Douglass why *he* had not remained in the South as an example for his persecuted race.

Professor Richard T. Greener, dean of the Law School of Howard University and later national secretary of the Emigration Aid Society, opposed Douglass' view. He said,

> Before the war the Negroes in the Southern cities and larger towns were the carpenters, bricklayers, stonemasons, and, in some instances, manufacturers on a small scale. Send him [the Negro] West, and open up to him the life of an agricultural laborer, a small farmer, a worker in the mines or on the great lines of railways, and you will soon find out what a steady, cheerful worker he is, and what a peaceful citizen and desirable acquisition he will become. . . . In pursuit of freedom years ago we endured the cold of Canada, the rigor of the Northwest and of New England. I see no reason to fear the effect of any climate on our race now. . . .

The Port Gibson (Mississippi) *Reveille* demanded that all those who encouraged the exodus should be "dealt with as are other incendiaries outside the law," while the Wilmington (North Carolina) *Star* reproached the Northern backers of the movement for unwarranted meddling. The Macon (Georgia) *Sun,* though deprecating faintly the flogging of a woman by Mississippi vigilantes searching for Prince Johnson, charged with "trying to induce the Negroes to emigrate to Kansas," added: "If the Negro Johnson is guilty, as charged, of trying to influence Negroes to abandon their crops, he should be drummed out of the country."

Those friends of the exodus who placed reliance upon more direct measures were not passive. General Thomas W. Conway, an active advocate of migration, announced in St. Louis that if steamboat companies, influenced by Southern interests, continued to refuse transportation to Negroes desiring to leave the South, he and his associates planned to charter a boat and to proceed downstream, using firearms if necessary, to deliver out of the land of bondage those waiting at river ports. Several hundred Negroes were reported to have armed themselves near Caroline and Leoti landings, Mississippi, and proclaimed their determination to confiscate the first passing steamboat and to compel it to carry them as far as possible toward Kansas.

More articulate Negroes throughout the nation seriously and collectively considered the migration and its effects. Henry Adams, the Union Army veteran who testified before the Senate investigating committee, was instrumental in calling the New Orleans Colored Convention in April 1879. Adams, like "Pap" Singleton, was illiterate, but a man of energy, courage, and ability. Returning to Louisiana in 1869 with an honorable discharge from the Union Army, he was deeply agitated by the treatment being accorded his "liberated" people. He traveled on foot from city to city, plantation to plantation, to organize a committee whose members, at one time totaling five hundred, journeyed to every locality in the South to survey conditions. The New Orleans convention met to deliberate over these findings, and adopted a resolution recommending "organized and systematic emigration."

The National Colored Convention assembled in Nashville the next month, and resolved: ". . . That it is the sense of this conference that migration of colored people to those States and Territories where they can enjoy all the rights which are guaranteed by the laws and Constitution of the United States, and enforced by the executive departments of such States and Territories, should be encouraged, and we ask of the Congress of the United States an appropriation of $500,000 to aid in the removal of our people from the South."

Though a large section of the Southern press and many public officials professed to see in the exodus a temporary and not extremely significant phenomenon, planters and civic leaders organized a convention of both white and Negro citizens which met in Vicksburg, Mississippi, May 6, 1879, to discuss means of regulating the migration. The more militant delegates of both races were outtalked and outvoted by a controlling element of Southerners intent upon keeping on hand a stable and docile reservoir of labor. Little more than speechmaking and a few timid resolutions purporting to reaffirm certain rights of the colored citizenry resulted from the conclave.

"Pap" Singleton's good news about "Sunny Kansas" spread farther and had more effect than even he had reckoned. Emigrants not only from Tennessee and Kentucky but from the uttermost recesses of the South swarmed to the State, many of them pausing en route in Cairo, East St. Louis, or other points in Illinois. Though both Negroes and whites tried to keep them moving on to their original destination and formed organizations for that purpose, not a few tarried or made their way to Chicago. The plight of destitute "exodusters" on the bleak Kansas plains soon excited national concern.

At the beginning, only colonists of some substance, able to maintain themselves until they could make a crop, had been invited. Kansas seemed even more attractive to the have-nots, and there was no holding them back. Once they made it to Kansas, they reasoned, their troubles would be over. Though he had not taken the possibility of such a development into account, "Pap" was inclined to defend the right of the disinherited to seek a better land.

"What are homestead laws for?" he demanded. "It's not the rich white folks that take up homestead claims in new territory; if they're rich enough, they're satisfied to stay where they are. Why shouldn't the black folks have the same right to make a fresh start, even if they are poor?"

This abstract "right" was of scant comfort to the shivering pilgrims from Madison Parish, Louisiana, who disembarked from a Mississippi River steamboat onto the cold granite cobblestones of the St. Louis levee on a snowy day in early February 1879. They wore light summer clothes, and most of them were barefoot. They gazed at the snow with wonder and terror. Few of the adults and none of the children had ever seen snow before.

The colonization companies did their best to cope with the situation. They erected clapboard barracks, pleaded for donations of clothing and food. The hospitality of the State of "Old John Brown" was strained to the breaking point. The City Council of Atchison passed an ordinance prohibiting the "importation of paupers." The authorities at Leavenworth halted a steamboat full of "exodusters" in midstream and forbade it to approach the riverbank. At Topeka irate citizens descended upon the rude barracks being constructed to house the destitute migrants and, after razing the buildings, threw the lumber used in them into the river.

Other white jayhawkers were more kindly disposed. They organized the Kansas Freedmen's Relief Association and began a systematic campaign of assistance. The Emigration Aid Society undertook the task of raising funds on a national scale.

"Would it not be wise," the Chicago *Inter-Ocean* suggested (April 11, 1879), "for the churches of Chicago to move into the benevolent work of aiding the colored people who are fleeing from Southern oppression to homes upon our Western prairies?"

The churches responded. The Chicago branch of the Emigration Aid Society arranged meetings and collected funds. An ex-slave, described as the prototype of Harriet Beecher Stowe's Uncle Tom, lectured at the Emmanuel M. E. Church for the benefit of a Kansas "exoduster" colony. The Chicago *Inter-Ocean* solicited contributions and listed among other donations $19.17 from the churches of Peotone, Illinois, a small hamlet. John Deere, Moline manufacturer of agricultural implements, sent $100 and expressed his fear that the exodus might be "carried too far" and thus "result to the disadvantage of all concerned." Colonel Robert Ingersoll offered $1,000 to the fund. Railroad and express companies agreed to transport relief supplies free of charge.

The despairing cry of the "exoduster" reached across the sea. Sympathizers in London sent 50,000 pounds of goods, $8,000 in cash. The London *Times* commented:

> What is most to be desired is the quiet but firm interposition of the central government to insure the Negro protection and equal justice. The time seems to have come when this task must be undertaken more boldly; and it is to be hoped no political exigencies will interfere with so plain a duty.

P. D. Armour, a Chicago packer, went out to see for himself, and on his return told of a visit to Wyandotte, Kansas:

> Here is where the refugees are crowded to the number of nearly 2,000. . . . They cannot exist there, for the town is poor. The churches, private houses, and halls were full, and many of them had to lie out on the docks over Sunday without shelter. . . . I talked with a great many of them and was surprised at their intelligence. I asked them where they thought they were going. They said only North to escape persecution. . . . They had no idea that they were going to a land of plenty or idleness, but simply to a land of freedom.

So impressed was Armour that within a short time he had collected twelve hundred dollars from Chicago business firms and put the money at the disposal of the Kansas sufferers.

There were also voices urging the Negroes to go back to the South with its more temperate climate. Surely, after the rigors of Kansas in the wintertime, Dixie seemed like a welcome haven of refuge. Though they had not found the bright El Dorado they had envisioned, or anything approximating it, few of the "exodusters" elected to make the return trip.

Elizabeth L. Comstock, a Quaker missionary, busied herself with errands of mercy among the Kansas clients of the Freedmen's Relief Association. There she met and became friends with Sojourner Truth. The indomitable old crusader, angel of mercy to black soldiers of the Union Army, was now nearing the end of her row (she died in 1883), but her eye was still bright, her step firm, as her strong black hands worked at preparing food and tending the sick. Miss Comstock talked to many "exodusters" and began to understand why they preferred death on the cold Kansas prairies to retreat to the balmy Southland. She wrote to a friend in Chicago:

> The latest horrible case of mutilation and amputation that we have heard on good authority is this: A respectable colored man came here last spring, worked hard, earned enough to buy a lot, build a cottage, and save $100, and then returned to bring his wife and family. The brutal Regulators seized him, cut off both his hands, and threw him into his wife's lap, saying, "Now go to Kansas to work."

Despite demands for federal assistance and the actual introduction of several bills in Congress, relief remained on a voluntary basis, though most of it, it is true, marshaled by the Emigration Aid Society and distributed by the Kansas Freedmen's Relief Association. Horatio N. Rust of Chicago was particularly active in soliciting and forwarding money, food, and clothing. To him John Brown, Jr., wrote (April 20, 1879) from Put-in-Bay Island, Ohio:

> . . . It seems to me of importance that these people be aided to reach lands, and be helped until they can help themselves on lands that are opened to homestead entry, or that can be obtained cheaply. . . .
>
> The Northwest can furnish lands of the richest soil in quantity sufficient to meet any probable demand for many years to come—can re-

ceive the entire Negro population of the South, if these should leave, and yet have room for the poor whites of the South, and the emigrating poverty-stricken people of Old World; and all these would find their homes too widely separated if each family were located on every quarter section of the really desirable land found there.

If we would gladly see the higher qualities of the American citizen of African descent brought out in this country or in any other, we must, in my humble opinion, help him to get a foothold where lands are good and cheap, in a latitude where the climate, instead of inviting to habits of indolence and lack of thought, will, on the other hand, be an ever-present stimulus, urging him and his children on to better conditions and a higher life.

Though assistance poured in from everywhere, the situation of the "exodusters" remained critical for some time to come. On January 15, 1880, the Chicago *Inter-Ocean* inquired:

Will the government and the people of the land let them [the "exodusters"] starve to death in the sight of plenty, even while the press is teeming with denunciations of England's inhumanity toward the Irish poor? If they were white men, nobody doubts that aid would soon reach them. New Orleans had five deaths from yellow fever, and the demands were so pressing that $10,000 was at once placed at the disposal of her authorities by telegraph from Washington. We poured money and luxuries into stricken Memphis, and even the government found the constitutional right to appropriate $800,000 for a board of health, with tents and government rations. It is true there was some difference. A man dying with yellow fever might infect his neighbor, but a "frozen nigger" is only out of the way.

All the excitement over the Kansas "exodusters" put "Pap" Singleton in a difficult position, but he was not willing to acknowledge that his thesis that Negroes ought to be segregated into communities of their own was wrong. He could see, however, that continued mass migration of poverty-stricken Southern Negroes to Kansas not only would wreak disaster on them (at the same time destroying their confidence in the Moses who had led them out of the land of Egypt), but also would alarm and antagonize the authorities of other regions in which he might want to locate colonies.

"Pap" was willing and even eager, therefore, to consent to the publication of pleas, bearing his name, in both Southern and Kansas newspapers urging prospective homeseekers to stay away from Kansas, since it had more newcomers than it could possibly accommodate. Though he felt constrained to advise Negroes to halt the stampede to Kansas, "Pap" still joined issue with opponents of migration such as Frederick Douglass and P. B. S. Pinchback, Negro lieutenant governor of Louisiana in the Reconstruction period. Migration in itself was good and necessary, "Pap" argued. It would be necessary to find another and more hospitable clime than Kansas. Canada? He gave it up after a little investigation. Too cold—and the Canadians might grow as weary of a mass movement as the Kansans had. Liberia or Ethiopia? Maybe that was it. "Pap" became interested in the campaign of Bishop Turner to resettle American Negroes in these fertile sections of the African homeland. "Pap" made an effort to divert migrants to Colorado and Nebraska, but few heeded his recommendations in that respect.

An inquisitive traveler passing through Kansas in the autumn of 1964 recalled the stories of "Pap" Singleton and the pilgrims he had led from a "summer land" into what he and they hoped would be a Promised Land. The only surviving colony among those planted by "Pap" was Nicodemus on the High Plains. The traveler found that the township of Nicodemus had shrunk from a population of perhaps 800 at one time to about 131 when a count had been taken the previous spring. Most of the descendants of the black pioneers who had toughed it out in sod dugouts among the buffalo grass, prairie dogs, and rattlesnakes had moved farther westward toward more enticing vistas—mostly to Colorado or California. The colonists had won a victory over the inhospitable land, coaxed the bleak prairie into productivity, and established a community that thrived for a time.

Some of the heirs of the "exodusters," like Arthur W. White, had prospered materially even beyond the grandiose dreams of "Pap." He was farming one thousand acres of wheat land, and had a large herd of cattle. Nevertheless, the Negroes felt they were living in an enclave surrounded by white territory. Mrs. White said they had white friends with whom they occasionally exchanged visits, but that it had been a long time since they had enjoyed any "real relationship" with their white neighbors in general. The wall between was still strong. "Things were better in the old days," a seventy-nine-year-old veteran of the colony mourned. He remembered that in the early years there were few white people, and they, faced by a common enemy in the wind and weather and the stubborn soil, were inclined to fraternize with their companions in misery—the "exodusters." When the whites became more numerous, and particularly when unregenerated Southerners arrived with their prejudices, there was a change in the atmosphere. Most of the white townspeople in 1964 endorsed the spirit of the Civil Rights law, but they did little or nothing to oppose the *de facto* segregation enforced by the attitudes of a few hard-core segregationists. Until Kansas passed an antidiscrimination law in 1961, the restaurants in Hill City refused to serve Negroes and the motion-picture theater segregated them. "It often made me mad that I couldn't buy a Negro farmer a cup of coffee when he came to town to talk business," a farm official in Hill City confessed. Hill City was named for an Indiana land speculator, W. D. Hill. He had come to Kansas to help the "exodusters" find land on which they could settle, and, presumably, find freedom from the restrictions they hoped they had left behind.

The Chicago *Evening Journal* in a report (February 7, 1881) on the status of the immigrants to Indiana, discussed a year earlier by the Senate exodus committee, indicated a cheery sequel to migration as a contrast to the dolorous picture in Kansas:

> The thousands of Negroes who went to Indiana a year ago from North Carolina and Virginia have been absorbed, and are distributed all over the state. The resident Negroes supplied them with clothing, furnished them temporarily with food, and found homes for them in the farming districts. Their labor was needed, and they are doing well. They are paying their own way, except in the matter of public taxes, and they are pretty well contented, though the cold weather is a trial to them. They thrive on the "hog and hominy" that is the staple diet of the rural districts, and add to it many luxuries in the form of nuts, rabbits, coons, and squirrels. They are social in their habits, and fond alike of dancing, religious meetings, and political discussions. Their children go to school, and the next generation will have larger wants, and also a larger capacity for supplying them.

Not a few of the migrants who achieved a measure of financial success in Kansas had taken an active part in politics in the South during "carpetbagger" days, and some of them had been elected to office. Now, they complained, they could vote but were never nominated for elective positions. "Pap" in 1881 organized the "United Links," a fraternal society "to consolidate the race as a band of brethren." Each meeting appropriately opened with the singing of "John Brown's Body." Singleton appears to have been active in politics at various times, and the "Links" wielded some influence in that direction, though in a not very clearly defined manner. A far, fair country where the black man could enjoy unmolested the fruits of his labor was still the bright, impalpable dream possessing "the Moses of the colored exodus," who grew more and more proud of his title as the years sped by.

"Pap" had his consolations, though he had spent all his savings on his various colonization projects. His need became so great at one period that he was compelled to ask the newspapers to run a statement that he would welcome donations of food or clothing to be left at a certain warehouse. The newspaper added its own endorsement of Singleton's personal integrity. In 1882 the Negroes of Topeka staged a big picnic and birthday party for "Pap" in one of the city parks, charging five cents' admission. "Pap" was delighted and gratified by this recognition and sent invitations to national, State, and city dignitaries, from the President down. None of these attended, though some sent polite notes of regret which "Pap" gave to the newspapers for publication. He directed that the names of prominent people invited be put down on the program as speakers, even though most of them had already declined. Nobody missed them, anyhow. The affair was a grand success, beginning at sunrise with a salute of one hundred guns and ending at sunset with a similar volley. The festivities netted "Pap" a nest egg of fifty dollars. A barbecue held on his next birthday ended with a profit of $274.25.

While Cleveland was campaigning for the Presidency in 1884, a rumor spread throughout the South that the Democratic candidate proposed to re-enslave the Negroes if he won the election. It was supposed by many that even Northern Negroes would not be immune. Perhaps this prospect served to spur "Pap," his eyesight failing him rapidly and his voice so ravaged that he could scarcely speak above a whisper, into a renewed search for a New Canaan for the black man. Somebody had published a letter in a St. Louis newspaper suggesting that the island of Cyprus, just ceded by the Turkish infidels to the British, might welcome Negro colonists. "Pap" started to St. Louis to consult with the writer of the letter and then to raise funds to go to Cyprus on a tour of investigation, but he knew he couldn't make it by himself. He enlisted the aid of a glib young Negro preacher upon whom some of the old man's most ardent well-wishers looked askance. The duo ran out of funds in St. Louis, however, and the pilgrimage had to be abandoned.

The next year found "Pap" heading the United Transatlantic Society to encourage and facilitate emigration to Africa. Though it referred quite a number of applicants to other societies dedicated to the same purpose, the organization never sent an expedition of its own. Smooth-tongued preachers and fast-talking promoters attached themselves to the United Transatlantic Society, as they had to Singleton's other enterprises, but no suspicion of fraud or chicanery ever attached itself to the old man himself. During its several years of operation the society accomplished little more than to pass resolutions favoring "Negro national existence."

Like many another hedged-in man, "Pap" discovered a scapegoat upon which to vent his frustration. In his later years he inveighed against "the scum of foreign powers" pouring into the country from oppression-ridden lands across the sea. These, "Pap" said, ". . . emigrate to America and put their feet on our necks." They could live and save money, he complained, where a Negro would starve. He provided a concrete example: "Steam laundries and Chinamen have forced three thousand Negro women and children of Kansas once fully engaged in washing and ironing into idleness, and hundreds of them into prostitution."

"Pap" was eighty-three when he died in Topeka in 1892. He was very feeble and very tired, but he liked to talk about the great exodus and his part in it right to the end. The newspapers had been neglecting the old man a little, but his death set them to reminiscing about the vanished era when "Pap" supplied good copy every day of the week. "Pap" would have liked the obituary notices about him. He would have pasted them proudly in his big scrapbook with its yellowed clippings, all of them about "the Moses of the colored exodus."

CHAPTER VI

Across the River from Slavery

In 1834 James Gillespie Birney, a Southern lawyer, a devout Presbyterian, and former owner of slaves, decided to quit beating around the bush. He submitted his resignation as vice-president of the Kentucky Colonization Society, outlining his reasons in a letter first published in the *Western Luminary* of Lexington. Slavery, Birney reasoned, would be increased by the colonization plan. What's more, he could no longer reconcile the issues involved with the religion he professed or with basic morality. So, like Edward Cole of Albemarle, Virginia, and many other men of conscience from the Slave States, he joined the forces of freedom and determined to give the foes of human liberty the pommeling they deserved.

The next year he helped to organize the Kentucky Anti-Slavery Society. He also attended a meeting of the American Anti-Slavery Society in Cincinnati. His impression of the latter was that the membership was ineffective. Birney's own approach was set forth in May of the same year in a speech before the New York meeting of the society. He advocated a united effort by all forces opposed to slavery, and he proposed to sound this note in New England too. Before he could get there, however, the struggle got under way in Kentucky, and Birney had to rush home.

Birney had already completed plans to publish an antislavery weekly in Kentucky, the first issue having been scheduled for August 1, 1835, but his opponents heard about it and they rallied to strike first. They invaded his quarters, rifled his mail repeatedly, and got set to mob him as he returned from New York. In that final objective they were frustrated, but they did succeed in making it impossible for the new weekly to appear on August 1, and eventually they forced Birney and his publication out of the State. In January of 1836 the first number of the *Philanthropist* was issued from New Richmond, near Cincinnati on the Ohio side.

The move to the area around Cincinnati, unfortunately, failed to shake his tormentors from the trail of James G. Birney. Within a few months another mob was after him. On July 30 it swept down on the shop in which the *Philanthropist* was published, destroyed all the copies it could find, threw the type into the street, and broke up the printing press. By that time the pack was howling. It reached the home of the printer, but somehow this individual managed to save himself from evidence of complicity—in the eyes of the mob. It swept past the homes of Birney and his friends, giving them an anxious moment or two. A more logical next step, the leadership then suggested, might be Church Alley, the Negro section, Cincinnati's original Mudtown. To this neighborhood the wild crowd hastened.

In Church Alley, however, they received a strange reception. Two guns opened fire through the cracks in the walls and the broken windowpanes. The mob fell back to catch its breath and reshuffle its strategy. A few hours passed. Then a second assault was made. But Church Alley moved faster. The returning mob found that the Negroes had slipped quietly out of their little Mudtown community. Though they must have been perplexed by this unprovoked attack, they were probably glad enough to get away from the squalor in which they had been trapped. Finding no Negroes to attack, the mob entered the houses, emptied them of their contents, and destroyed all the stuff in the streets.

The following year James G. Birney gave up the *Philanthropist* and moved to New York. By this move he changed his base of operations, but he later proved that he had only begun to fight slavery. He didn't stop till he died in 1857, and even then he left three sons who did the Union plenty of good in the years that followed.

How much he bequeathed to the colored people of Cincinnati by way of incentive cannot be measured, of course, but it is interesting to note that more than one contemporary observer declared that the progress made by this group of free Negroes between 1835 and 1840 compared favorably with any group advance in the world over a similar period of time. A summary of this progress was included in Barber's "Report on the Condition of the Colored People in Ohio, 1840"; it was also mentioned in newspapers of the same year, but perhaps a better indication of what it was like may be gathered from examples cited by Carter G. Woodson in a study of the community published seventy-six years later in the first volume of the *Journal of Negro History*.

Woodson discovered that these 2,255 individuals accumulated, despite almost fierce opposition, $209,000 worth of property during these years, not counting personal effects and three churches valued at $19,000. Some of the property included in the estimate consisted of land purchased in Ohio and Indiana. A group of colored men of the city, he found, organized in 1839 "The Iron Chest Company," a real-estate firm which built three brick buildings and rented them to whites. A Negro who had paid $5,000 for himself and family had also been able to buy a house for them valued at about a thousand dollars. Another freedman, having been a slave till he was twenty-four, acquired two lots valued at $10,000, not to mention three hundred and twenty acres of land in Mercer County. Still another, worth $3,000 in 1836, raised it to nearly $15,000 in 1840, including seven houses in Cincinnati and four hundred acres of land in Indiana. A woman who had been a slave till she was thirty-four was able to lend $2,000 to a white lawyer of the city, getting a good mortgage as security. And another who had been on the auction block in 1832 spent $2,600 for her freedom and the freedom of her family and saved enough more to buy two brick houses worth $6,000 and five hundred and sixty acres of land in Mercer County, valued at something like $2,500.

Obviously such prosperity did not develop in a vacuum. At least two explanations were immediately apparent, and the prettier of the two was the steamboat on the river. Transportation by steam was increasing rapidly on the Ohio River, and Cincinnati was one of its most important landings. This meant the employment of strong-armed Negroes on the docks and personable and intelligent ones in the cabins of the vessels. The work to which they were most frequently assigned on board was service to the traveling public, but a few of the more capable ones became stewards. It may be assumed that tips were good. The favored stewards had the opportunity to earn additional income by care and enterprise in placing of orders for supplies. A number of these ex-stewards were found to have invested their savings in successful business ventures in Cincinnati.

The other explanation of the progress of Cincinnati Negroes between 1835 and 1840 was less colorful perhaps, but equally wholesome. It was the rise of the Negro mechanic. Earlier a hard struggle had been waged on this front, for white mechanical workers were frightened by bad dreams at the first appearance of free colored men working at the skilled trades. But thanks to the *Philanthropist* and other voices that had no stake in the division of trained hands along color lines, this campaign had been won by 1835. By then colored mechanics were getting all the work they could do. Blacks and whites not only worked side by side in these trades, they fraternized together. They patronized the same barbershops, went to the same places of amusement. In fact, many white artisans sought employment with Negro master workmen. This fact was noted at least three times by the *Philanthropist* in 1840 and 1841. The Negro contractors, it was reported, had earned the reputation of being more uniformly reliable as paymasters.

Naturally the thoughts of these 2,255 energetic, aspiring Negroes soon turned to their children. Having escaped slavery themselves, they were anxious that their offspring should widen the gap between their freedom and slavery. Education seemed to be the first step. In 1840 these free colored people of Cincinnati sent sixty-five of their children to the schools conducted by Reverend Denham and Mr. Goodwin, paying $3.00 per quarter for each pupil, and forty-seven to Miss Merrill's school, at the same tuition rate. Meanwhile, another fifty-four youngsters were attending the school of Miss Seymour, supported by the Ladies' Anti-Slavery Society. Cincinnati Negroes were clearly bent on educating their children. What's more, they were paying for it—in large measure—themselves.

Four years later they were ready for a high school. James H. Perkins, a prominent white citizen, stated in the press that the students of one of the schools attended by colored children had shown by examination that they were as good as any others in the city. Impressed by this readiness and capacity to learn, no doubt, Hiram S. Gilmore, a British clergyman and a gentleman of wealth, bought a lot at the east end of Harrison Street and erected on it a building of five large rooms and a chapel. In the yard he provided apparatus for physical training. With this building and equipment he opened the Gilmore High School in 1844.

As an institution for educating young Negroes it was a most advanced step, and there are indications that no expenses were spared to make it a success. Excellent teachers were employed, and the curriculum included Latin, Greek, music, and drawing, along with the more usual offerings of an English course. The Reverend Gilmore acted as principal, though he did no teaching. Associated with him for a long time was his brother-in-law, Joseph Moore, who taught the more advanced classes. Dr. A. L. Childs was in charge of the department of elocution and Professor W. F. Colburn directed the music studies. These two appear to have done outstanding work. During the vacations they made regular tours through Ohio, New York, and Canada, presenting their more talented students in concerts and exhibitions. On these tours they were accompanied by Reverend Gilmore himself, possibly for money-raising purposes, for the profits of the trips—which appear to have made them worth repeating—were used to provide books and clothing for worthwhile students who happened to be without resources of their own.

Despite successful vacation tours by the music and elocution students, despite an enrollment of several hundred tuition-paying students, the Gilmore High School was not self-supporting. Reverend Gilmore's idea of a secondary education for the children of free people of color was always a few notches above anything the normal income of the school could provide. In addition to his own contribution of grounds, buildings, and perhaps his own services, the institution needed—and got—financial support from the liberal element of white people of the community. It also received some unblushing support from below Mason and Dixon's line.

Students were drawn to the Gilmore School from as far south as New Orleans. It was never a secret that most of these were the mulatto children of rich Southern planters. So important an element was this group in the school's program that a white slaveholder, a graduate of Amherst, was employed on the teaching staff. Other institutions later established for the education of Negroes—some of them still in operation—were in the beginning intended mainly for this group of mulattoes toward whom their slaveholding sires retained traces of natural affection. There is a rich lore in Negro colleges about the ways of old rebels and their children. Some of their correspondence with the schools survives, and some of the oldest teachers remember the days when these individuals were frequently seen in the principals' offices beaming on their golden offspring. The Gilmore High School may have been the first institution in the North to serve the purposes of this group.

In later years the students of Reverend Gilmore's school repaid their debt. One of them, Pinckney Benton Stewart Pinchback, son of Major William Pinchback, white planter of Holmes County, Mississippi, became lieutenant governor of Louisiana. He was also elected United States Senator from Louisiana, but he was refused admission. Pinchback and his elder brother were sent to Gilmore High School in 1846. They remained till 1848, returning home just before Major Pinchback's death. The old man's passing produced the usual confusion in families like his. A dozen years earlier the major had taken his beautiful slave girl to Philadelphia and set her free. All told, before and after that date, she had borne him ten children. They, too, were technically free. But when the father died, the administrator of the estate sent the mother and her children bucketing to Cincinnati, as he said, to prevent white heirs of the estate from attempting to enslave them. There was, of course, nothing to prevent these more distant relatives from ruthlessly stripping the family of all its rightful inheritance, and this they promptly did. Napoleon, the oldest son, was shattered by the experience and lost his mind in Cincinnati. Pinckney, who had been his companion at the Gilmore High School, went to work as a cabin boy on a canalboat on the Miami Canal, running from Cincinnati to Toledo. None of the other children of the Pinchback family lived very long, and Pinckney's tragic boyhood blossomed into bitter manhood.

Pinchback followed the steamboats on the Red, Missouri, and Mississippi rivers till the outbreak of war between the States. By

1861 he had risen to the position of steward, the highest attainable to a man of color. War then interrupted the business, and Pinchback, abandoning the *Alonzo Childs* at Yazoo City, made his way to New Orleans, despite a Confederate blockade. The following year he got into a fight with his brother-in-law, John Keppard, and wounded him. Civil authorities, habitually indifferent to crimes committed by Negroes on other Negroes, released him on bail. He was awaiting trial when the military picked him up, speedily tried and convicted him of assault with attempt to murder, and sentenced him to two years in the workhouse. Three months later, however, he was released to enlist in the First Louisiana Volunteers. Almost his first assignment in the Army was to assist in enlisting the Second Louisiana regiment. During this recruiting drive Major General Benjamin F. Butler, commanding the department of the Gulf, issued his historical order No. 62, calling upon free men of color of Louisiana to take up arms in defense of the Union. Pinchback asked to be transferred to this new work. The request was granted, and he was assigned to open a recruiting office at the corner of Bienville and Villeré streets in New Orleans. Within a week he had a company ready for muster. Pinchback became captain of the outfit when, thirty days later, they officially became part of the Second Louisiana regiment. Presently the question of equal rights for colored soldiers arose, and Pinchback and other Negro officers found themselves up against a wall of prejudice. A year later, despairing of the fight, Pinchback and the other colored officers resigned. Pinchback made another try, following a personal interview with General N. P. Banks. Given authorization to recruit a company of colored cavalry, Pinchback went out and promptly brought in his men, but the general refused to commission the originator of the command as captain, and Pinchback gave up the game—so far as the Union Army in Louisiana was concerned. In 1865 he and H. C. Carter went to Washington to seek authority from the President to raise a regiment of colored men in Ohio and Indiana, but the surrender of the Confederacy intervened.

For two years following the war Pinchback was an angry man going from city to city in the South and denouncing the unjust treatment to which Negroes were being subjected by lawless elements in the defeated States. Then, when Congress enacted the Reconstruction Acts, he returned to New Orleans and organized the Fourth Ward Republican Club. This was the start of a political career which was to lead him into a long series of appointive and elective offices, culminating with lieutenant governorship and election to the United States Senate. His seat in the Senate was hotly contested, then denied. But while the issue hung in the balance, the Washington correspondent of the New York *Commercial Advertiser* sent his paper an interesting dispatch. In it he spoke of the "pastoral phraseology" of the "blue-grass Democrats" who had determined "to give that nigger some sleepless nights before he gets his seat." He had noticed Pinchback gliding "around the chamber like a bronze Mephistopheles, smiling sardonically." The essence of the contest, as the *Advertiser*'s correspondent saw it, was that "the mad obstinacy and devilish cruelties of the White League in the South recently have made Pinchback's support a party measure." He added, "Aside from the political view of the question, Pinchback's presence in the United States Senate is not open to the smallest objection, except the old Bourbon war whoops of color. He is about thirty-seven years of age, not darker than an Arab, less so than the Kanaka. Like Lord Tomnoddy, 'his hair is straight but his whiskers curl.' His features are regular, just perceptibly African, his eyes intensely black and brilliant, with a keen, restless glance. His most repellent point is a sardonic smile which, hovering continuously over his lips, gives him an evil look, undeniably handsome as the man is. It seems as though the scorn which must rage within him at sight of the dirty, ignorant men from the South who affect to look down upon him on account of his color, finds play imperceptibly about his lips." After contrasting Pinchback's attractive manners with those of the "Texas and Louisiana Yahoos who shout 'nigger, nigger, nigger' in default of common sense or logic," the correspondent concluded with the observation that "Mr. Pinchback is the best-dressed Southern man we have had in Congress from the South since the days when gentlemen were Democrats."

The sardonic Pinchback retained Republican confidence despite the refusal of the Senate to seat him, and three years later he was still knocking at its door. But twilight had come to the hopes of the

Reconstruction, and Pinchback remained outside. He had good reason to grow more and more cynical. Few men anywhere have been more completely, from birth to death, fortune's fool.

Another student of the Gilmore High School, James Monroe Trotter, was appointed recorder of deeds in the District of Columbia by President Grover Cleveland. Like Pinchback, Trotter was born in Mississippi. After attending Gilmore High he went to school in Hamilton, Ohio, and gave special attention to the study of music and art. He had moved on to Massachusetts when the Civil War broke out; and when Frederick Douglass started recruiting colored men for the Fifty-fourth Massachusetts, Trotter enlisted. He rose to the rank of lieutenant before it ended. In Boston he was made superintendent of the registered-letter department, but after eighteen years of service in this office he objected to local political maneuvers, resigned, turned on the Republicans who had appointed him, and voted for Cleveland. The appointment to the Washington post followed. Trotter is also remembered as the author of one of the most highly valued early books on Negro music, *Music and Some Highly Musical People*.

John Mercer Langston, great-uncle of the Negro poet Langston Hughes, was another distinguished alumnus of Reverend Gilmore's school. In looks John M. Langston, part Indian and part Negro and part Anglo-Saxon, was simply Langston Hughes with a beard. But he also had distinctions of his own. He was born in Louisa County, Virginia, in 1829. When his slaveholding father died, he was given his freedom as a result of provisions in the owner-parent's will. He went to Gilmore High and prepared for Oberlin College. He failed to gain entrance to law schools of the country, declining a suggestion that he pawn himself off as an Indian from South America or some such place, and had to spend several anxious years trying to enter the profession he had elected. Finally Philemon Bliss of Elyria, Ohio, took the young man into his office for study. Langston took his obstacles in stride in Ohio, worked for abolition—as did his brother Charles—and rose in his profession. After the Civil War he was invited by General O. O. Howard to act as general inspector of the schools of the freed people of the country. In the same year he was admitted to practice before the Supreme Court of the United States, on the motion of James A.

Garfield. But he continued to act as inspector of the Freedmen's schools, traveling throughout the South, till he was offered the deanship of the new Law Department of Howard University. Later Langston was appointed minister resident and consul general to Haiti by President Hayes. He held this post for nearly eight years. When he returned to the United States, he was elected by the board of education of Virginia to the presidency of the Virginia Normal and Collegiate Institute, now Virginia State College.

But these were not the only pupils of the Gilmore High School who turned out to be first-rate. Peter H. Clark became the principal of a secondary school in Cincinnati. Joseph H. Perkins was called "the great orator of the Ohio Valley." Phillip Tolliver became a presiding elder of the African Methodist Episcopal Church. John I. Gaines earned the fine descriptive phrase, "Nestor of public-school advocates." And Thomas C. Ball became known, locally at least, as an artist.

Meanwhile Cincinnati's Mudtown produced an assortment of vivid talent unaided by formal schooling. A good example was the artist Robert S. Duncanson who, at about twenty-two, painted "The Trial of Shakespeare," a canvas which remains in Cincinnati to this day. The painting came to light about a year before the Reverend Gilmore opened his school, and all existing evidence seems to indicate that Duncanson was entirely self-taught. Little beyond this fact can be said definitely about his early life, but the date of his birth is given as 1821. A letter in the *Liberator* for August 21, 1846, describing a bedraggled young artist of quaint and haphazard living habits, may or may not have referred to Duncanson, but as a revelation of the artist's personality it has been questioned. Duncanson was undoubtedly a young man of fierce pride with a lust for complete freedom. He demonstrated both in later life. If he gave the impression of being more run down at the heels and out at the elbows than is common even among hopeful, aspiring artists, possibly this can be credited to the compounding of hardships which came of being a free Negro as well as a blithe creative spirit on the American frontier in 1843. Duncanson appears to have mingled freely with white artists of Cincinnati, but that was not enough. A place to sleep, food, and a few clothes were essential, and the business of providing them was likely to involve harsh contacts with people who had no feelings whatever about art but some very strong ones about color. Whatever Duncanson's experiences in Cincinnati had been, he left the city soon after his struggles to become an artist had come to the attention of antislavery groups. All subsequent references to his Cincinnati years speak of the hardships by which they were remembered.

But the whole story is not reflected in the sensitive young man's unhappiness in Cincinnati and his decision to go away. Before leaving Duncanson produced a "painted poem" suggested by Tennyson's "The Lotus-Eaters," an item good enough to make a strong impression on the British when it was shown in London a few years later and, indeed, to win the wandering artist an invitation to visit the poet laureate at his home on the Isle of Wight. Two rather fulsome descriptions of "The Lotus-Eaters," both emanating from London, have survived, though the painting itself has not.

Young Duncanson was commissioned by Nicholas Longworth of Cincinnati to paint a series of mural landscapes for the Longworth Mansion, now the Charles P. Taft Museum. These appear to have been done while the artist was still in his early twenties, while the Gilmore High School was flourishing, and the community of free men of color continued to enjoy the reputation of being one of the most progressive sections of the city. The Longworth murals have been preserved. When considered in the light of their time, the general status of art in the West and in the nation as a whole, the specific pressures exerted by a society that was less than half convinced that a colored man had a soul—considered in this light, the murals are clear evidence of Duncanson's talent. They also testify to the fact that his gifts were not entirely unrecognized or unappreciated in the city in which he grew to manhood.

Duncanson was in Canada for a few years after leaving Cincinnati. Antislavery groups—which always took pleasure in discovering and encouraging Negro talent—sent him abroad and gave him an opportunity to study and develop. He returned to the United States after the Civil War, broken in health, wandered into the West again and, presumably, ended his life in a Detroit hospital for the insane.

Two contemporaries of Duncanson's in Cincinnati were far more conspicuous in the life of the community than was the artist. Neither, however, has been quite so well-favored by posterity. The first was Henry Boyd, a Kentucky freedman who invented and patented a corded bed which became popular throughout the Southwest. Boyd set up a manufacturing business in which he employed as many as twenty-five men on a strictly interracial basis. Evidently his beds were good. He became one of the well-to-do men of the city. But trouble followed—trouble from colored people who saw in his labor practices something which they took to be encouragement to miscegenation, trouble from whites who were just plain jealous of his success. The whites burned him out, and the colored turned up their noses. Boyd's children and grandchildren married whites and vanished across the caste line.

Duncanson's other prosperous contemporary among the free colored people of Cincinnati was Robert Gordon, formerly the slave of a wealthy yachtsman of Virginia. Assigned by his master to manage a coalyard in Richmond, Gordon is said to have handled the business so well that the grateful owner allowed the Negro to sell the slack for his own profit. Gordon made the most of his opportunity, acquiring customers among small manufacturers and blacksmiths, and before long he was able to purchase his freedom. In 1846 he arrived in Cincinnati, a heavily built, light-brown man with a full beard. For a man who had just stepped out of slavery his dignity was impressive. But even more remarkable for a freedman was the fact that he came to town with money—real money by frontier standards.

Naturally the coal business attracted him, and Gordon brought to it shrewdness as well as energy. He acquired a large yard in the bottoms and was soon doing so much business he had to hire bookkeepers. He bought coal by the barge from Pittsburgh dealers, unloaded it at his own docks on the river, and hauled it in his own wagons. When white competitors tried to break him by a price war, he sent mulattoes who could pass for white to the rival companies and bought up all the coal in town at the cutthroat prices. Instead of being broken by the price war, Gordon exhausted his competitors. A few months later the Ohio River froze and remained locked for months. During this time Gordon had the coal market cornered. He made a killing and remained in business till 1865, when he retired—a man of wealth. His descendants transferred their interests to Chicago, and one of them, Dr. Gordon Jackson, married Mae Walker, daughter of A'Lelia Walker, daughter of Madame C. J. Walker, who made a million dollars on a hair-straightening preparation and built a mansion on the Hudson.

Another facet of Negro life in Cincinnati in the time of Duncanson, Boyd, and Gordon in the years that followed the closing of the Gilmore High School came to focus in Bucktown, the district east of Broadway between Sixth and Seventh and ranging through the bottoms to Culvert Street. Bucktown was a city jungle. Lafcadio Hearn visited it in the seventies in company with two police officers who happened to be seeking a female thief. What he saw caused his senses to tingle, for he was a man with an eye for exotic color.

To his surprise, Hearn discovered that by no means all of Bucktown's inhabitants were black, though Negro rousters from the river boats were a solid element in the population. Bucktown's people were as likely to be white as black and somewhat more likely to be one of the shades between. But "white, tawny, brown, or black," Hearn suggests, all were "Ishmaels bound together by fate, by habit, by instinct, and by the iron law and never-cooling hate of an outraged society." Even so, the writer became almost lyrical in describing these disinherited folk and their way of life for the *Commercial Gazette:*

> As the violation of nature's laws begets deformity and hideousness, and as the inhabitants of Bucktown are popularly supposed to be great violators of nature's laws, they are vulgarly supposed to be all homely if not positively ugly or monstrously deformed. "A Bucktown hag" and "an ugly old Bucktown wench" are expressions commonly used. This idea is, however, for the most part fallacious. The really hideous and deformed portion of the Bucktown population is confined to a few crippled or worn-out, honest ragpickers, and perhaps two or more ancient harlots, superannuated in their degrading profession, and compelled at last to resort to the dumps for a living. The majority of the darker colored women are muscular, well-built people, who would have sold at high prices in a Southern slave market before the war; the

lighter tinted are, in some instances, remarkably well favored; and among the white girls one occasionally meets with an attractive face, bearing traces of what must have been uncommon beauty. Gigantic negresses, stronger than men, whose immense stature and phenomenal muscularity bear strong witness to the old slave custom of human stock breeding; neatly built mulatto girls, with the supple, pantherish strength peculiar to half breeds; slender octoroons, willowy and graceful of figure, with a good claim to the qualification pretty, will all be found among the crowd of cotton-turbaned and ebon-visaged throng who talk alike and think alike and all live alike.

A Negro known as Webster was called the "Mayor of Bucktown," and another called Jim Allen became a legendary figure as the hard-fighting cop assigned to that dangerous beat. Indeed, tough Jim Allen and his partner, another colored cop named Miller, are credited by some old-timers with cleaning up Bucktown by sending most of its more savage denizens to hospitals or workhouses.

So Bucktown was already becoming a romantic memory when a small, dark colored boy, completely unremarkable in appearance, took a job as janitor in the Cincinnati Conservatory of Music. His name was Gussie L. Davis, and he had previously worked on railroad trains as a Pullman porter. On one of his runs he had been associated with a poetic conductor named Frank Archer, a native of Hector, New York, and each of them had been stabbed to the heart when they discovered one day a coffin in the baggage car and learned that it contained a dead woman, the mother of a little family which was traveling tearfully in another part of the train. Archer was moved to verse, and he set down the facts of the ballad in a composition called "Mother," which was printed in an upstate New York newspaper. Gussie L. Davis went back to Cincinnati and pondered the elements of the tragedy as he swept the halls of the Conservatory of Music. Later he wrote his own lyrical version of the story and set it to music. The result was "The Baggage Coach Ahead," a landmark in popular song writing in America; and the unsophisticated Gussie, the Cincinnati Pullman porter and janitor, won the distinction of drawing more American tears than perhaps any other man of his time.

Gussie L. Davis became one of the most prolific song writers of his period. He used the ballad form then so highly favored by tenor singers in minstrel shows, but neither his music nor his lyrics had any special connections with the South or with Negro life. His first published composition was issued by a local concern. It carried a picture of a rather surprised-looking young Negro described on the cover as Cincinnati's only colored composer. Legend has it that the elated Gussie would stand outside the shopwindow for whole days at a time in order to say to folks who stopped to look at the display of sheet music, "That's me. I done it."

Davis gravitated to New York City, became a mainstay of the rising publishing firm of Edward B. Marks, and gave his generation many of its most popular hit songs, including "Down in Poverty Row," "The Fatal Wedding," "In a Lighthouse by the Sea," "We Sat Beneath the Maple on the Hill," "Send Back the Picture and the Wedding Ring," as well as "The Baggage Coach Ahead."

Perhaps no musician in Cincinnati could do more with a Gussie L. Davis tune than dapper young Wendell Phillips Dabney who, in his studio at Wurlitzer's, gave lessons on the guitar, banjo, mandolin, and *bandurria.* A classmate of Will Marion Cook's at Oberlin College, Dabney had come to Ohio from Richmond, Virginia, and started the new life as a member of a college string combination which sometimes played in the Oberlin theater. He was a self-taught musician, but his pupils in Cincinnati—as in Richmond—frequently came from the wealthiest families, and his two string orchestras—one white, one colored—were in demand for receptions honoring guests as famous as Prince Hohenlohe and William Jennings Bryan.

But Dabney had a greater love than music. His heart sang constantly, but it sang of people—people of all classes and kinds. Before long he closed his studio to enter politics, become a city paymaster, and edit and publish a highly individual weekly newspaper called the *Union.* More important, perhaps, he began to collect the anecdotes that were to make him, in time, one of the most pleasant raconteurs his race has produced in America.

When asked for reminiscences of Gussie L. Davis, this jovial, racy editor, to whom all memories were golden, began to recall his last meeting with Paul Laurence Dunbar, an evening with James Weldon Johnson, an encounter in a rooming house in New

York City. All he could remember about the young composer he had met in Cincinnati in 1894 was that Gussie left the impression of having been well dressed. Was he tall or short, gay or thoughtful, easygoing or ambitious? Dabney could remember nothing but Gussie's songs.

CHAPTER VII

They Met at the Fair

FOUR HUNDRED YEARS after a Genoese adventurer and promoter heard his weary sailors joyfully cry out, "Land ho!"—and none too soon for the safety and comfort of the audacious Cristoforo Colombo—a wonderland commemorating this event arose along the shore of Lake Michigan in the city of Chicago. The gaudy palaces and stately halls were not quite so impermanent as a Hollywood movie set, and from a slight distance, at least, the building of "staff"—a composite of cement, glycerin, and dextrin resembling marble in appearance though not in durability—seemed very impressive indeed.

The World's Columbian Exposition, which officially opened in May 1893, was designed to celebrate four centuries of American progress in all fields of endeavor and the arts, and people poured in not only from the adjacent hinterlands but from far regions and distant cities to goggle at the new inventions on display and to participate in the gaiety possible at such an exhibition even in those days. To the respectable and genteel females of that era the sinuous wrigglings of "Little Egypt" were just as scandalous as the bubble and fan manipulations of Sally Rand were to their more sophisticated granddaughters forty years later in the Streets of Paris concession at the Century of Progress on the lake shore a little north of the site of the White City of 1893. And no doubt the males of the nineties were just as attentive.

At any rate, almost everybody heard about the big doings in Chicago, and wanted to get there. This, of course, included Negroes in adjoining states and in the South. The Negroes of Chicago wanted to feel that they had a hand in the affair too. A club of Negro women calling themselves the Woman's Columbia Auxiliary Association drew up resolutions requesting that "the Negro be given some consideration in the World's Fair exhibits." A copy of these resolutions was sent to Judge Albion W. Tourgée, author of *A Fool's Errand* and a prominent friend of the colored people. Judge Tourgée promised to use whatever influence he might be able to exert toward assuring Negro representation.

August 25 was eventually set as a tentative date on which the progress of the Negro race in America would be observed. The Colored Men's Protective Association, when asked for an endorsement, replied that such an action would smack of segregation and the organization could not approve it. Nevertheless, August 25 was decided upon. A committee on arrangements reported that 10,000 Negro visitors were expected from Tennessee, Kentucky, and Ohio alone. A letter signed by a number of colored citizens appeared in the newspapers to urge that the day not be regarded as a "watermelon festival" or cakewalk jubilee, but a "refined and dignified" assembly of "cultured Afro-Americans."

The signers had ample reason to worry about the manner in which the newspapers, at least, would regard Negro Day, which became generally known as Colored American Day as the event approached. Two years before I. Garland Penn had published a book on the Negro press in the United States in which the attitude of the white newspapers toward Negroes had been given considerable attention.

About the same time (ten years after ratification of the Thirteenth Amendment) the Chicago *Evening Journal* noted:

> In calculating the features of the "war of the races" in the South, it would be well to remember that white men, and not the Negroes, have charge of the telegraph wires and dispatches. Some of the *white* dispatches are black with lies, and though highly *colored,* do not favor the blacks.

Evidence of white control of the printed word was not confined to the South. Newspapers adhering to the Democratic party almost invariably treated the Negro with undisguised hostility, while even the Republican press ordinarily regarded all his activities as likely subjects for heavy-handed humor. Especially favored were items tending to fortify legends relating to the Negro's appetite for watermelon and chicken, his reliance upon the razor as a weapon, the thickness of his skull (accounting for miraculous escapes from injury), his fondness for gaudy colors and fantastic attire, his inordinate fear of ghosts, and his extraordinary speed in retreat from danger.

While attention was centered upon those unfortunate enough to become involved with the police, the most eminent colored people were not immune to ridicule and abuse. As early as April 9, 1862, the Chicago *Times* published under the caption "The Irrepressible Nigger vs. History" a complaint from a reader who had attended a lecture by Wendell Phillips, and, as he put it, "heard his elaborate eulogy upon that distinguished 'darky' of San Domingo, Toussaint L'Ouverture." "As Mr. Phillips has made the irrepressible nigger his special study for many years," the correspondent contended, "he ought to be well informed in every particular that concerns this interesting race." He then disputed two minor historical points brought up by the celebrated orator, and concluded: ". . . These may suffice to show how much confidence may be placed in a man who evidently reads history only to exalt and glorify the African race."

Later in the year the *Times* commented at length upon the thieving, indolent habits and general unreliability of the many "contrabands" in the city. One of these, the paper said, had been hired by a man who "had no great faith in her capabilities," and assigned her to the simple task of sweeping out the bedrooms. The *Times* went on:

> . . . She did it with a vengeance. A bottle of pure tokay, kept convenient for sudden attacks of night sickness, first attracted her attention, and its contents were quickly abstracted to the amount of about a pint. She then started downstairs, with a vase in one hand and a gold watch in the other; but, slipping, reached the bottom sooner than intended, smashing her cargo into smithereens, and cutting herself severely.

By October of 1862 the *Times* had become even more concerned over the influx of dark contrabands and vouchsafed its conviction that "these sons of Ham would most of them be improved only in the good old country style of treating that part of the pig which bears the name of their common ancestor—to cure: first pickle, then hang." As a horrible example, the newspaper re-created a scene in police court when

> . . . two Negroes, black as the ace of spades, were arraigned, in company with two white women, on a charge of disorderly conduct. They were living together in one house, indulging in the most intimate relations, and with unblushing impudence claimed to be lawfully married. . . . All the neighborhood has suffered from these vile Negroes and trebly vile women—worse by far than the lowest *nymph du pave,* who nightly prostitutes herself to white men. To what depth of degradation must a female sink before she can submit to such a fate; and how utterly perverted must be all the desires and instincts of an original pure and noble nature. Such are, indeed, "angels fallen into the lowest corners of the deepest hell."

Politically sympathetic newspapers, such as the Chicago *Inter-Ocean,* could not resist punning at the expense of Negroes. This item appeared November 18, 1874:

> Abraham White, who is BLACK, ungallantly assaulted Lizzie Black, who is WHITE, and was fined $25 by Justice Boyden yesterday morning, which had the effect of rendering Abraham White, black, blue, and Lizzie Black, white, happy.

The Chicago *Evening Journal,* on May 20 of the same year, quipped:

> A Danbury little darkie refused to go to church 'kase he didn't want to look like a huckleberry in a pan of milk.

And a short time later:

> A Louisville Negro fell asleep on the top of a high building and rolled off. He didn't complain of the fall—and never will.

This 1879 fashion note appeared in the *Inter-Ocean*:

> "Bandana" dresses do not "take" very well with cultivated and refined women, but colored lady help go into raptures over them.

The danger of such handling of Colored American Day by the press was effectively avoided, however, and the event drew together in Chicago a group of Negroes destined, as spokesmen and interpreters of their race, to influence not only the attitudes of their own people but, in varying degrees, those of the world. One of these was Paul Laurence Dunbar, a young poet, who had just published the traditional "slender sheaf" of first poems and had landed a much-needed job as assistant to the aged abolitionist orator, Frederick Douglass, who was in charge of the Haitian Pavilion at the fair. Another was Ida B. Wells, already established as a militant champion of Negro rights. There was also Robert S. Abbott, then principally known as the tenor of a Hampton quartet which frequently toured the country. Wendell Phillips Dabney, to whom admirers had already awarded the title of "World's champion guitar player," was also at the fair, visiting with his friend and classmate, Will Marion Cook, the composer, who was very busy with the entertainment features of Colored American Day.

Douglass, Dabney maintains, did not wholly approve the Negro Day idea, but Cook had persuaded him to deliver the principal address. Douglass, perhaps, felt the stigma of segregation sensed earlier by the Colored Men's Protective Association. Others had argued that other racial groups had had their special days, so why shouldn't the Negro? At any rate, the day came, and the aged Douglass appeared tired and dispirited as he stepped upon the platform. He began to read falteringly from a manuscript typed for him by a relative, Charles Mitchell, later to become a United States official in Liberia.

A group of white men in the gallery began to jeer at Douglass, and at first easily drowned out his voice. Then the old warrior shook back his white mane, his nostrils distended, and he threw the prepared manuscript to the floor. The sonorous organ-toned voice that had held so many audiences spellbound in the past rolled forth in almost undiminished volume as he discoursed scathingly on the treatment accorded "free" Negroes in a free land. He condemned the cowardly evasion which prompted some people to solve the Negro question by ignoring it; this he called "hiding the black baby under the bed." The scoffers were won over by his surging, passionate eloquence. "The vast audience went wild," says Dabney, recalling the remarkable scene, "and its applause rocked the building, echoed and re-echoed even over the lake."

The rest of the program was received with enthusiasm. Joseph Douglass, the favorite nephew of Frederick, played the violin. The elder Douglass loved music, and was no mean hand himself with the violin. The shy young poet from Dayton, Paul Laurence Dunbar, recited some of his poems; Harry T. Burleigh's baritone solo brought him encore after encore. The whole thing, naturally, was a triumph for the entrepreneur, Will Marion Cook.

Wendell P. Dabney had been associated with Cook at Oberlin College and had played guitar in an orchestra formed by Cook, violinist, and Cook's brother John, a pianist. In 1907 he established the *Union* as "a strictly old-time newspaper conspicuous for independence and originality," its masthead carrying the legend, "Poor but proud—little but loud." It survived in Cincinnati for nearly half a century thereafter, every issue enlivened by the editor's pungent comment and his picturesque recollections of earlier days. Dabney died June 4, 1952.

The unobtrusive young poet who shared the platform with Frederick Douglass on the evening of Colored American Day at the World's Fair carried throughout his short, harried life the memory of the old lion's magnificent response to the challenge to battle. Paul Laurence Dunbar's father, Joshua, had been a fighter too. Before the Civil War he took the Underground Railroad to freedom in Canada. There he learned the plasterer's trade and also how to read. Eagerly he devoured the newspapers and books carrying tidings of the struggle being carried on by both white and black lovers of liberty. When the War of Emancipation broke out, Joshua, though comfortably situated, had to get into the fight. He enlisted in the Fifty-fifth Massachusetts Infantry, which covered itself with tragic glory in the course of the war. It is quite possible that he knew Frederick Douglass, for the latter made several speaking tours to enlist recruits for this regiment. With peace, the elder Dunbar did not return to Canada, but settled down and married a young widow in Dayton, Ohio, where Paul was born on June 27, 1872.

"This child will be great someday and do you honor," Joshua

told his wife. But he did not live to see his prophecy fulfilled, though there were strong indications of it when he died, leaving Paul fatherless at twelve.

Never a hardy specimen physically, Paul's interest during his schooldays centered in reading and writing. He felt little of the sting of racial prejudice, for his teachers encouraged him and he was popular with his classmates. He wrote the graduation song for his high school class, of which he was the only Negro member.

Even when his poverty forced him to take a job as elevator boy in an office building, Paul, absorbed in his poetry, did not find life too unpleasant. People in the building talked to him about his writing, and bought copies of his first book of verse, *Oak and Ivy*. The business manager of the United Brethren Publishing House, which printed the book but did not market it, "stood good" for the one hundred and twenty-five dollars asked as a guarantee.

Paul's summer at the World's Fair as Frederick Douglass' assistant in the Haiti building did not make him rich. Douglass had no funds with which to pay his modest salary of five dollars per week and had to dig it out of his own pocket, none too heavy with wealth. There were compensations, however. Paul met Richard B. Harrison, then a dramatic reader, and "De Lawd" helped the budding poet to sell copies of his *Oak and Ivy*. Then there was the association with Frederick Douglass which later helped to put iron into the soul of the frail youth when he encountered some of the things Douglass had fought all his life.

On several previous occasions the young poet had felt some of the evangelical fire of the old crusader. One such occasion was in Toledo in the spring of 1893, when a Dr. Chapman, recently returned from a tour of the South, arose in a meeting of the West End Club to comment on his trip. Dr. Chapman, not knowing that Paul, having been invited to read some of his poems, was also present, pointed to him as an exception to the general run of Negroes. His travels, Dr. Chapman said, had convinced him that, while an occasional Dunbar might stick up his head and attain distinction, the mass of Negroes, because of their inherent inferiority, were doomed to a subordinate position. Dunbar, trembling with emotion, arose to deliver with a passion he was seldom able to command in his later years as a trained elocutionist a poem he had not intended to include in his repertoire. It was his "Ode to Ethiopia," an effective answer to the abashed critic of the Negro race.

Dr. H. A. Tobey, superintendent of the Ohio State Hospital for the Insane in Toledo, helped Dunbar in one of his darkest hours of poverty by buying several copies of *Oak and Ivy* for distribution among his friends. He admired the poet's verse, but did not meet him for some time after he had first read it. "Thank God he's black!" Tobey exclaimed when he first saw Paul. Asked for an explanation, Dr. Tobey said that genius in a Negro inevitably would be attributed to the white blood in his veins. Paul gave no visible evidence of having any. Here again the sensitive young poet was fortunate in his association with a white man, for Dr. Tobey not only became a warm friend and patron (with none of the humiliation usually associated with "patronage"), but he brought Paul into intimate communion with several other notables of Toledo—"Golden-Rule" Jones, the spellbinding reform mayor; Brand Whitlock, also a mayor and, in later years, an author and diplomat as well. When Paul died Dr. Tobey said:

"I never loved a man so much. 'Golden-Rule' Jones, Brand Whitlock, and myself—we three were great cronies, because we were cranks, I suppose, but we took Paul in and made him one of us."

Financial success eventually came to Dunbar. His prose and verse commanded high prices from the leading periodicals of the day. No "elocutionist" could get along without a volume of his very recitable verse. But his lungs were failing fast, and he could not escape the tormenting race question, pleasant though most of his own relations with white people were. His lecture tours brought him into contact with white people not so considerate as the friends who admired and respected him and strove in every way to hide the ugly face of racial intolerance from him. But they couldn't shield him everywhere and at all times. Once Paul walked into the lobby of the Kenmore Hotel in Albany, New York (not Birmingham, Alabama), and stopped at the desk to register. The clerk asked him what he meant by this behavior.

"There's a room reserved here for me. I'm Paul Laurence Dunbar," Paul replied. And there was, for Mrs. Merrill, a local patron of the arts, *had* reserved not merely a room but a suite for the poet.

"Oh no, there ain't! Not for *you!*" the clerk said insolently.

Paul stood his ground, and the clerk at length scanned the list of reservations. Sure enough, there was a Paul Laurence Dunbar. Incredible! The perplexed clerk called the manager, who exploded with indignation.

"Call the police and tell them to come down here and get a crazy nigger!" he directed the clerk. But he was uneasy about Paul's invocation of the name of Mrs. Merrill, prominent in the city. When Mrs. Merrill herself appeared to insist that the distinguished poet be given every consideration, mine host yielded, though with no good grace. Dunbar, of course, emerged from the experience with no sense of triumph.

Ella Wheeler Wilcox, "Poetess of Passion," had heard the up-and-coming young colored poet recite when he was first beginning to make his mark. "The Warrior's Prayer" moved her to tears, and as Dunbar finished his recital of it she impulsively embraced him and cried: "Go on, Paul! Go on!"

There were others even more eminent, such as W. D. Howells. Colonel Robert Ingersoll, the silver-tongued agnostic orator, especially admired "Ere Sleep Comes Down To Soothe the Weary Eyes" and said it was "as profound as 'Thanatopsis' and as musical as 'Hiawatha.' "

A lecture engagement in London came later. Also a stint as an assistant in the reading room of the Library of Congress, this position secured for him by Colonel Ingersoll. He stuck it out fifteen months, feeling like a bird in a cage. Then more trouble from the hemorrhages which were to become worse until he died, two years younger than Byron at his death—only thirty-four. In the fall of 1899 Paul went to Denver. At first he was inspired and invigorated by ". . . great, rolling, illimitable plains and bleak mountains standing like hoary sentinels guarding the land." But soon he referred to Denver as "the city where so many hopes are blighted . . . and through which humanity struggles with hot, strenuous life."

In his pain and despair Dunbar turned to a comforter that has addled the life of more than one man of genius—the bottle. Under the influence of liquor, he felt a transient fire that might burn until he could finish a recital with something of his old polish and verve. As is almost always the case, the bottle became the master and not the servant.

This became painfully apparent at a recital in October 1900, arranged for Dunbar in Evanston, Illinois, by Professor P. M. Pearson of Northwestern University. A large audience of university people and citizens of the town assembled. The beginning time came and Dunbar did not appear. The chairman looked at his watch and fidgeted. So did the audience. Half an hour late, the poet walked onto the stage, rather unsteadily. Few knew he was drunk, however, until he had mumbled the first lines of a poem, stumbled, repeated, stood, and looked vacantly, trying to remember. Some of the spectators laughed, others rose and stalked out in righteous indignation. It may be that, as Paul stood there in impotent befuddlement, his sad mind returned to Colored American Day at the World's Fair and to the recollection of how Frederick Douglass had handled a jeering audience. Dunbar gave few recitals after that.

Frederick Douglass was not far from the grave when he lashed back so magnificently at his tormentors that evening as the bashful young poet sat on the platform with him. He died two years later. Paul wrote a sonnet about him, and saluted him as "no soft-tongued apologist." When Dunbar was reaching his own twilight—so short a time past the brief blaze of noon—he thought more and more of the stout old battler. Benjamin Brawley has said that Dunbar called despairingly for "the blast-defying power" of the leonine wraith to "give comfort through the lonely dark." But Douglass could not or would not answer from the shades. Perhaps his approval was not as fervent as that of Brand Whitlock, Colonel Robert Ingersoll, W. D. Howells, and Ella Wheeler Wilcox.

Ida B. Wells, another of the World's Fair group of Negroes who spoke or were to speak through the printed word, had commented frequently and with point on the prevailing attitude of the white press toward her race. Already she had attained a reputation as a journalist and a crusader against lynching. While attending the exposition, she collaborated with Frederick Douglass, I. Garland

Penn, and Ferdinand L. Barnett on writing a booklet recording the achievements of American Negroes and refuting the false impressions created by most of the newspapers.

Ida B. Wells was born in Holly Springs, Mississippi, four years after the close of the Civil War. When she was fourteen and a student at Rust College, a Freedmen's Aid Society School in the village, both her parents were stricken with yellow fever, and she found herself burdened with the support of four younger children. She not only discharged this obligation, but managed to continue classes at Rust. Later she spent a summer at Fisk University, where she contributed to the school publication. After teaching a rural school for a time, she won an appointment near Memphis, and shortly afterward one in the city. She began to write steadily for the *Living War*, a local Negro paper.

After six years in the classroom, during which her work appeared in many Negro publications under the pseudonym "Iola," Ida B. Wells forsook teaching to become half owner and editor of the Memphis *Free Speech.*

Free Speech became an increasingly effective voice against racial injustice; it circulated extensively throughout the Mississippi delta and was peddled by railroad newsboys. Indications were that a prosperous life for the paper lay ahead. In May 1892 three young Negro businessmen of Memphis were lynched, and *Free Speech* charged that disgruntled white competitors had instigated the deed. So telling were the paper's denunciations that one dark night a crowd of hoodlums descended upon the plant, demolished the press and office, and chased the editor from town.

Undaunted, she arrived in New York and resumed her condemnation of lynching, writing for the New York *Age*, which had published her work before she fled from Memphis. Publisher T. Thomas Fortune described her as "one of the few of our women who handle a goose quill with diamond points, as easily as any man in newspaper work. If 'Iola' were a man," Fortune continued, "she would be a humming independent in politics. She has plenty of nerve, and is as sharp as a steel trap." Shortly after her arrival in New York, "Iola" established a lasting friendship with the elderly Frederick Douglass. She published also the *Red Book,* said to be the first authentic record of lynching in America, and became associated with Monroe Trotter, Harvard graduate and sometime editor and publisher of the Boston *Guardian.*

The Woman's Loyal Union presented Ida B. Wells with a gold pen, symbolizing her journalistic achievements, and a purse of $700 to finance a lecture tour in Great Britain. Late in 1892 she sailed for London in response to an invitation from the Anti-Caste Society of Great Britain. Her lectures evoked a tremendous response, and the press and churches of the British Isles resounded with outcries against lynching. "Iola" left England in 1893 to attend the World's Columbian Exposition.

One of the journalists who collaborated with Ida B. Wells on the World's Fair booklet was Ferdinand L. Barnett, a graduate in law from Northwestern University. Barnett had founded in 1878 Illinois' first Negro newspaper, the *Conservator*. Later in the year he relinquished the editorship to Reverend Richard DeBaptiste, founder of Mt. Olivet Baptist Church, who announced that the aim of the paper would be to "discuss in a fair and liberal spirit those questions that agitate and cause an honest opinion among citizens whose aims are alike patriotic."

Ida B. Wells continued her work as a journalist during her visit to Chicago in 1893. Commissioned by the Chicago *Inter-Ocean* to investigate a recent lynching, she published a report tending to prove the innocence of the Negro victim. She organized the Ida B. Wells Club, first Negro organization of its kind in the city, and headed it until her death. Its example led to the formation of many other colored women's clubs, and, finally, their amalgamation in the Federation of Colored Women's Clubs. In subsequent years Miss Wells organized young people's and women's clubs not only in Chicago but in Louisville, a number of Eastern cities, and elsewhere. The Chicago organization bearing her name was instrumental in establishing the first Negro orchestra in the city, opened the first kindergarten for children of the district, and became a charter member of the Cook County Women's Clubs, thus dealing a blow to the color line.

When she returned to England in 1894, Ida B. Wells found that sixteen branches of the Society for the Recognition of the Brotherhood of Man had been organized in Great Britain as a result of her previous visit, and a monthly magazine, *Fraternity,* was being issued in London. Her former successes on the lecture platform were eclipsed, and once again her activities created intense interest in the United States. Not all of this interest was friendly.

So greatly were certain opposition elements in the United States concerned over Miss Wells's revelations, according to the New York *Tribune,* that they dispatched agents to England to counteract her influence. Their efforts, however, ended in ignominious failure. T. Thomas Fortune sent notices to all branches of the Afro-American League throughout the United States to hold mass meetings to endorse Miss Wells's campaign. She maintained an average schedule of ten addresses a week. A British clergyman said that "nothing since the days of *Uncle Tom's Cabin* has taken such a hold in England as the anti-lynching crusade."

Ida B. Wells returned to the United States in July 1894, to command huge audiences in New York City. Only twenty-five years of age, she was recognized as the most implacable and most effective enemy of mob rule. She told a New York gathering:

> Our work has only begun; our race—hereditary bondsmen—must strike the blow if they would be free. I have been endeavoring to tell the whole truth. I have been banished from my home for this alone. An English lady who had seen for herself the condition of our people in the South, and seeing the hopelessness of our ever arousing public opinion in the North, asked me a few days after a colored man was burned alive at Paris, Texas, February 1895, to come to England to arouse a moral sentiment in England against these revolting cruelties practiced by barbarous whites. The British people took with incredulity my statements that colored men were roasted or lynched in broad daylight, very frequently with the sanction of officers of the law; and looked askance at statements that half-grown boys shot bullets into hanging bodies and after cutting off toes and fingers of the dead or dying carried them about as trophies. They could easily have believed such atrocities of cannibals or heathens, but not of the American people, and in the land of the brave and the home of the free.
>
> But when I showed them photographs of such scenes, the newspaper reports and the reports of searching investigations on the subject, they accepted the evidence of their senses against their wills. As soon as they were positively convinced resolutions were passed asking the American people to put away from them such shame and degradation.

Antilynching leagues formed in many American cities raised funds to keep Miss Wells in the field. After a tour of the Middle West, she found larger audiences than before awaiting her in New York. At one of her lectures in Rochester, an irate Texan arose to ask the speaker why Negroes did not leave the South if they didn't like the treatment they received there. Susan B. Anthony, the renowned suffragette leader, mixed in the fray and "heatedly reproached the Texan" as she ably supported Miss Wells. At Kansas City, Missouri, an acrimonious debate was precipitated in a meeting of the Protestant Ministers' Alliance when a resolution endorsing Ida B. Wells and her antilynching campaign was introduced. Reverend S. M. Neel, described as "a Southerner," opposed the resolution with such vehemence that it eventually was tabled.

Miss Wells continued to write for the Negro press, including the *Conservator,* in which Ferdinand L. Barnett retained an interest. She knew that a strong, independent Negro press was highly desirable. In a letter to the Chicago *Inter-Ocean* she said:

> . . . Is not the North by its seeming acquiescence as responsible morally as the South is criminally for the awful lynching record of the past thirteen years? When I was first driven from Memphis, Tennessee, and sought a hearing in the North to tell what the Negro knew, from actual experience, of the lynching mania, and refute the foul slander that all the Northern papers were publishing, without question, about Negro assaults against white women, not a newspaper to which I made application would print the Negro side of this question. . . .

In the meantime, the interest of Ferdinand L. Barnett in the young crusader whom he had met at the World's Columbian Exposition had intensified to such a degree that he asked her to marry him, his first wife having died seven years before. Miss Wells accepted, and their wedding at Bethel Church in Chicago on June 27, 1895, was an important social event, the bridegroom being a prominent member of the Chicago bar and the bride well known for her lectures, her social work, and her contributions to the Chicago *Inter-Ocean,* the *Conservator,* and other publications.

Henceforth the Barnetts figured in almost every Midwestern battle against racial injustice. They have been described as "representative of the more militant body of Negro opinion long before the body acquired a leader in Dr. W. E. B. Du Bois."

The Political Equality League in 1903 asked Mrs. Barnett to address its members on "The Colored Woman, Her Past, Present, and Future." The speaker, as was her custom, presented a realistic picture of her race's plight, pointing out that "there was little employment for the Negro, and the average Negro scarcely exceeded the domestic scale." Her white hearers responded with expressions of sympathy. They fluttered about the speaker.

"My heart goes out to the colored race," said one. "Let us remember that when we say a thing against one Negro we say it against all."

"Our treatment of colored people is our national disgrace," another put in.

To these effusive well-wishers, Mrs. Barnett replied quietly: "We ask only that the door of opportunity be opened to us."

Approaching age did not diminish perceptibly Ida B. Wells Barnett's zest for the advocacy of social-reform measures. She attacked vice conditions, the housing situation, and new evidences of discrimination from the lecture platform and in newspaper articles, notably in the Chicago *Defender*. In 1913 she was appointed adult probation officer, the first of her race in Chicago. She contemplated and even announced her candidacy for the State Senate. But her seemingly inexhaustible energy spent itself at last, and she died on March 25, 1931, at the age of sixty-two, after an illness of only two days. The writer of an obituary article in the *Defender* remembered her as ". . . elegant, striking, and always well groomed, . . . regal though somewhat intolerant and impulsive."

When the Federal government planned a low-rent housing project for Chicago's South Side, South Parkway Gardens was the tentative name selected. The Ida B. Wells Club, the Federated Women's Clubs, and other organizations advocated so vigorously the naming of the development after the crusader whose pen and voice had been silenced by death a few years before, the housing authorities acquiesced. Dedication ceremonies were held October 27, 1940.

Standing in close proximity to Chicago's most dilapidated slums, the spick-and-span Ida B. Wells housing project was a tiny island

—an oasis with its brave young trees and green lawns and trim flower beds. It was only a small beginning—a drop in the bucket. But the woman for whom it was named knew what it meant to build against opposition and discouragement from small beginnings. During the ensuing quarter century most of the neighboring slum dwellings were razed, and the Ida B. Wells project was surrounded by high-rise apartments too expensive for most of the people who used to live on that terrain.

But that's another story.

Another out-of-town visitor who observed Colored American Day at the World's Fair was Robert Sengstacke Abbott, almost twenty-three. As tenor of the Hampton Quartet, he had frequently toured the country. The young man listened to Frederick Douglass' speech and heard Ida B. Wells tell of the destruction of her Memphis newspaper by a mob. Abbott also was interested in journalism, and had been learning the printer's trade at Hampton Institute, Virginia.

Abbott enjoyed his World's Fair visit, and in 1897 returned to Chicago with the intention of staying. He was a fully qualified printer, but found that printing firms were reluctant to hire a Negro. He picked up odd jobs at his trade and undertook the study of law in night classes at Kent College of Law, where his closest friend and counselor was Harry Dean, subsequently a sea captain and adventurer. Dean has recounted his somewhat astounding experiences in a book, *The Pedro Gorino,* written in collaboration with Sterling North.

John R. Marshall (later Colonel Marshall of the Eighth Illinois Infantry), a Hampton graduate, was a Chicago brickmason, and to him Abbott brought a letter of recommendation from General Samuel C. Armstrong, founder of Hampton and at that time its principal. Marshall's circle of acquaintances was large and included many persons of prominence and authority. The young printer-lawyer benefited from his association with the popular brickmason.

Edward H. Morris, possibly Chicago's most successful Negro attorney of the period, told Abbott bluntly that he was "a little too dark to make any impressions on the court in Chicago," and advised a debut in a smaller town. The beginner displayed his hopeful shingle in nearby Gary, Indiana, but it was almost totally ignored by the citizens of that steelmaking community.

Giving up his attempt to practice law, Abbott fell back upon his intermittent printing jobs. But he had another idea. The evening of May 6, 1905, found him peddling on the street and from door to door copies of a four-page paper, the Chicago *Defender,* bearing an arrogant subtitle, "The World's Greatest Weekly." The publisher was also editor, business manager, and entire staff. The editorial desk doubled as a kitchen table in the apartment of Mrs. Henrietta P. Lee on South State Street. Mrs. Lee also proffered the use of her telephone, and the Western Newspaper Union, a printing company specializing in small country weeklies, was persuaded to extend as much as twenty-five dollars credit. Abbott seldom was able to pay the full amount of the bill at once, but was forced to take out a portion of the edition, sell it, and then return with proceeds to bail out the remaining copies held in escrow by the printer. Abbott's friend Marshall had introduced him to a foreman in the Chicago *Tribune* engraving plant who arranged a month's credit for engravings. A night-club proprietor championed the venture, often depositing ten dollars in his cash register subject to the demand of the hard-pressed publisher and editor. When Abbott expressed worry over the obligation thus incurred, the slate was wiped clean by insertion of an advertisement.

Though Abbott continued for some time as sole regular staff member, he enlisted a number of volunteers. Julius N. Avendorph, sports promoter and social figure, wrote about both fields of interest. Tony Langston, a bartender at the Keystone Club, took advantage of his position to gather news about frequenters of the establishment and other tidbits accessible to members of his profession. Alfred Anderson, manager of old Provident Hospital, helped out with editorials, and Dr. A. Wilberforce Williams edited a health column. Recognizing the role of the barbershop as social center and forum, Abbott called on as many as he could reach to leave papers for sale and to collect items of news, comment, and criticism deposited by customers.

James A. Scott, subsequently appointed assistant State attorney, had suggested *Defender* as a suitable name for Abbot's new paper, since Negroes of Illinois and the nation were in critical need of a vigorous defender of their rights. A great many of the preceding and contemporary Negro papers had attached themselves to one or the other of the dominant political parties (usually the Republican), and too often had subordinated the battle for justice and equality to political expediency. Abbott resolved to remain rigorously independent and to fight incessantly for Negro rights. His resolute adherence to this policy at length brought him more readers than any other "race" publisher.

One of Abbott's earliest competitors, the *Broad Ax,* moved to Chicago from Salt Lake City in 1899. Julius C. Taylor, its editor and publisher, decorated each issue with numerous likenesses of politicians, who, it has been said, often enough lent the paper financial aid to escape the uncomplimentary comments of Taylor, who excelled in personal accusations and preacher-baiting. His motto was: "Hew to the line, let the chips fall where they may." The editor was inclined to condemn ministers of the gospel who mixed politics with religion, and on one occasion said:

> The Negro race is the only race in the world to have their churches turned into political halls for faking preachers and the small-headed base white Republican politicians who contend that they can buy any "darky" preacher and a whole church full of niggers for ten dollars.

As a matter of policy, the *Broad Ax* favored the Democratic party, but expressed its willingness to print contributions from "Republicans, infidels, or anyone else . . . so long as their language is proper and the responsibility fixed." Aside from its pungent editorial style, the paper was notable as the first in Chicago to attack the tradition demanding of Negroes full and unquestioning loyalty to the Republican party. The *Broad Ax* ended its hectic career in 1927.

When the *Defender* outgrew the facilities of the Western Newspaper Union, Abbott made a printing arrangement with the Chicago *Daily Drover's Journal.* A composing-room foreman who had worked for the Hearst press persuaded him that his make-up should be more sensational and eye-arresting. Abbott agreed, and before long was being called "the William Randolph Hearst of Negro journalism." It was rumored widely that the paper actually belonged to Hearst. The *Defender* cartoonist had designed a masthead so similar to that of the Chicago *Evening American* that hurried newsstand purchasers often mistook one paper for the other to the disadvantage of the dealer, since the *Defender* sold for five cents and the *Evening American* for two. The Hearst paper filed suit for infringement of copyright, but Abbott forestalled the action by changing the masthead.

The *Defender* achieved national prominence with its vigorous advocacy of the Negro exodus from the South beginning with World War I. Circulation leaped, and Abbott added pages and various improvements. He cultivated a homey, direct style of expression, never "talking down" to his readers, and demanded that his writers follow this policy. The paper became the "bible" and inspiration of black Southerners yearning toward the New Canaan, and the "defender" indeed of those already in the North.

Beneath the slogan, "American Race Prejudice Must Be Destroyed," every edition of the *Defender* emphasized these points:

> The opening up of all trades and trade unions to blacks as well as whites. Representation in the President's cabinet. Engineers, firemen, and conductors of all American railroads and government-controlled industries.
>
> Representation in all departments of the police forces over the entire United States.
>
> Government schools open to all American citizens.
>
> Motormen and conductors on surface, elevated, and motor bus lines throughout America.

During the race riots of 1919 the *Daily Drover's Journal,* fearing mob violence, refused to print the *Defender,* and Abbott was forced to bargain with the Gary *Tribune,* whose small presses required two days to turn out an edition of 150,000. Impressed with the desirability of owning his own plant, Abbott moved a year later into his own building on Indiana Avenue, where printing equipment valued at more than $500,000 now turns out the paper.

Before Abbott died in 1940, after an illness lasting eight years, he had the satisfaction of seeing his "World's Greatest Weekly" attain a circulation larger than that of any other Negro paper. During the great migration a record of 500,000 is said to have been reached, and a consistently high figure has been maintained.

After its founder's death the *Defender* came under the control of Abbott's nephew, John H. Sengstacke, who had been groomed for the job. Abbott had died childless. Sengstacke amply justified his uncle's faith in his capabilities. He put the *Defender* on a sound financial basis and widened the area of its influence. Then he developed a chain of newspapers which included, in addition to the Chicago edition, the Gary *Defender,* the National *Defender,* the *Tri-State Defender,* the Michigan *Chronicle,* the Louisville *Defender,* and the New York *Age Defender.* In 1956 the daily *Defender* was launched in Chicago appearing Monday, Tuesday, Wednesday, and Thursday, with a feature-filled and larger weekend edition issued on Friday.

The militancy fostered by Robert S. Abbott was not perceptibly diminished under the regime of Sengstacke. For some time after the United States entered World War II, readers were exhorted to "Remember Pearl Harbor and Sikeston too." The latter reference was to a particularly brutal lynching in Missouri. The *Defender* steadily broadened its outlook and vigorously attacked all forms of racial intolerance, including anti-Semitism. Its avowed policy, of course, always had dictated such a policy, but for a long time the emphasis was almost exclusively upon anti-Negro manifestations.

An example of the *Defender's* catholicity is provided by a glance at the roster of columnists who have from time to time appeared in it. These include: W. E. B. Du Bois, then regarded as the elder statesman among Negro leaders; Langston Hughes, Negro poet and playwright; S. I. Hayakawa, Japanese American who wrote *Language in Action* and other books; Earl Conrad, white New Yorker; Jack Conroy, white Missourian; Walter White, veteran foe of lynching whose investigations often were facilitated by the fact that he easily could be mistaken for a white man; Harry Golden, white Southerner of Jewish descent; and baseball star Jackie Robinson, a Republican before he bolted to support Johnson's candidacy in the 1964 Presidential election. In 1954 and 1960 the *Defender* was the only daily newspaper in Chicago to endorse the Democratic national ticket.

During World War II, the *Defender* was sometimes criticized for comparing Hitler's racial theories with those of rampant anti-Negro fanatics in the South. Some justification for this comparison might be found in a curious book published by the American Book and Bible House in St. Louis in 1900, seven years after the lights had gone out in the World's Fair White City and workmen began dismantling the "staff" palaces beside Lake Michigan.

The Negro a Beast, or, *In the Image of God,* by "Professor" Charles Carroll, who, according to the publishers, ". . . spent fifteen years of his life and $20,000 in its compilation," descends to the nadir of racial hatred. The burden of its argument is that the Negro is not a man at all, but a superior type of ape ". . . created with articulate speech, and hands, that he may be of service to his master—the white man."

The weird hodgepodge of quotations from the Bible and the works of scientists such as Darwin and Haeckel, if we omit the religious motif, has a strangely contemporary ring. And no wonder! Some of the Haeckel references, at least, are precisely those used in the "scientific" anthropological journals and books issued under the Nazis. An example:

> The front teeth of the White, set perpendicularly in the jaw, find their strongest contrast in the front teeth of the Negro, which set slanting in the jaw. This is another character of the ape which the Negro presents. Haeckel describes as Prognathi those whose jaws, like those of the animal snout, strongly project, and whose front teeth, therefore, slope in front; and men with straight teeth Orthognathi, whose jaws project but little and whose front teeth stand perpendicularly.

Those of mixed white and Negro parentage are even worse than the pure Negro, or "beast," "Professor" Carroll maintained. Here is his recommendation for a disposition of the problem of "corrupted flesh":

> . . . The immediate offspring of man and the Negro—the mulatto —was doomed by Divine edict to instant death in the very moment of conception. Hence, neither the mulatto nor his immediate offspring can acquire the right to live. This being true, it follows that these monstrosities have no rights social, financial, political, or religious that man dare respect—not even the right to live.

The Negro a Beast is embellished with crude woodcuts pointed by melodramatic captions. An example:

The Beast and the Virgin, or the Sin of the Century. Can you find a white preacher who would unite in holy wedlock a burly Negro to a white lady? Ah! parents, you would rather seen your daughter burned, and her ashes scattered to the winds of heaven.

Certainly the comparison between *The Negro a Beast* and Nazi anthropological lore is not too remote, and, as we have seen, the same sources have been used.

The Nazis were not the only ones promulgating such theories during the World War II period. Representative McKenzie of Louisiana, placing an account of the opening of a Washington CIO canteen for Negro and white servicemen, attended by Mrs. Eleanor Roosevelt, in the *Congressional Record* inquired sarcastically:

"How can anyone be a party to encouraging white girls into the arms of Negro soldiers at a canteen dance while singing 'Let Me Call You Sweetheart'?"

To this query Mrs. Roosevelt replied: "Soldiers who come there have been in unions composed of both white and Negro members, and naturally if whites and Negroes work together, their union, when it sponsors a canteen, cannot cut out one group of its members. As usually happens, the people choose their own friends."

During the 1964 Presidential campaign millions of "hate" books in which the supposed inferiority of the Negro was stressed were distributed, usually gratis, to the electorate. In the Southern States carried by Goldwater, strongest citadels of white supremacy, the one circulating more than all the rest was J. Evett Haley's *A Texan Looks at Lyndon.* The indignant author, described as "cowman and historian," assigned practically every crime on the calendar to the Democratic candidate. One of the gravest of these, the author alleged, was "his complete acceptance of social integration by setting an example at the White House." Haley then quoted with horror and dismay a story attributed to the Chicago *Defender* for March 12, 1964. It stated that the President at a White House dance had tagged the wife of Michigan "negro" Congressman Charles D. Diggs. Afterward, it was revealed, she excitedly "showed her dimples" and "cooed" that she had "danced with the President . . .

an excellent dancer . . . twice." "At an earlier reception," Haley complained, "the colored wife of California Congressman August F. Hawkins was 'just as delighted with the Texas charmer.' " LBJ, it seemed, had cut in while Mrs. Hawkins was dancing with a young military officer, saying as he did so: "Now, let's give an expert a chance."

Veiled or open support of Nazilike racial ideas was a part of the strategy of Goldwater campaigners on both sides of the Mason-Dixon line. In the Chicago area, "the right to choose your neighbors" was frequently used. Even after Goldwater had been thumpingly repudiated, propaganda sheets calculated to poison the race relations atmosphere continued to issue from mimeograph machines and printing presses. Some of these bore the imprimatur of nonexistent organizations to which the names of respectable citizens were unauthorizedly attached. A typical one was the questionnaire distributed to Wheaton citizens who had signed "statement of conscience" advertisements in Wheaton area newspapers supporting "the right of all persons of any race, creed or national origin to rent or own housing anywhere in Wheaton."

The questionnaire, which fraudulently bore the name of Donald S. Frey, an Evanston lawyer and prominent Episcopal layman, included these queries:

> If you had your choice, would you prefer to live next to:
> ______A Negro dope addict?
> ______A white Communist?
> Do you think that more attractive grandchildren would result if:
> ______Your son married a Negro girl?
> ______Your daughter married a Negro boy?
> Would you feel prejudice against a Negro who raped your:
> ______Wife?
> ______Daughter?
> ______Both?

According to the questionnaire, answers to these inquiries would "be most helpful in planning our next moves to integrate your immediate area." It was mailed under the forged letterhead of the United Citizens' Committee for Freedom of Residence, a legitimate State-wide organization. The hate peddlers had also forged the signature of Richard C. Dunham, a credit-union executive and a director of the United Citizens' Committee.

CHAPTER VIII

Darktown Strutters

A GOOD-LOOKING brown-skinned boy was walking the streets of Birmingham one night in the early years of Grover Cleveland's second Administration. He was out of work and broke. A panic had closed the steel mills and mines around Jefferson County, Alabama, and the pipeworks at which he had been employed had laid off nearly all its hands. Down and out and wondering about his next meal, the sensitive, bright-eyed youth stopped in front of a saloon to listen to the singing of a barroom quartet. Suddenly an idea struck him, and he went inside and offered to teach the singers some songs he had learned in his hometown quartet over in Florence. The boys took him up on it.

Within a few weeks the group, augmented by its clever and enterprising young leader, was breaking down such numbers as

Old Aunt Kate, she died so late
She couldn't get in at the Heaven gate.
The angels met her with a great big club
Knocked her right back in the washing tub.

Hear dat trumpet sound?
Stand up and don't fall down.
Slip and slide around
Till your shoes don't have no tacks.

Join dat 'lection band.
Better join it while you can.
If you don't join dat 'lection band,
(Whatcha gonna do wid 'em den, brother?)
Gwine chop 'em in the head with a golden ax.

A few months later the quartet was headed for Chicago and the Columbian Exposition. Its members were riding the rods of freight trains, sleeping in boxcars, hopping from one town to the next, and stopping along the way to sing for meals and small change. Due to a postponement of the exposition—news of which had failed to reach them—the boys arrived in Chicago a whole year too early. Naturally they couldn't wait around that long. Someone suggested they try their fortunes in St. Louis, then a focal point of Northern migrations and the geographic hub of the Negro sporting wheel. Perhaps the boys could make a go of it there. The quartet headed in that direction.

Unfortunately, St. Louis was already overrun with stranded musicians. Quartets like the one young William Christopher Handy had recruited in the Birmingham saloon were a dime a dozen in the pool halls, barbershops, and hangouts around Targee Street. Neither the "Golden Ax" number nor pieces such as "The Dance of the Nixies" and "When the Summer Breeze Was Blowing" got much attention from the folks in St. Louis. The Lauzetta Quartet, as it proudly called itself, broke up, and Handy took a job helping the swipes at the St. Louis race track rub down the horses. The work was not very profitable in one sense, but it did give the erstwhile quartet leader a chance to sleep in the hay in a stall. And it kept him around St. Louis long enough to store away some of the impressions upon which he was later to base his popular classic, "St. Louis Blues."

There was hardship and want in the St. Louis of 1893. There was also crime and depravity. The Cleveland panic had done its work among Negroes; they were leaving the South in endless streams, and St. Louis was drawing more than its share of the migrants. The overcrowding which resulted produced intolerable conditions. Sitting space in pool halls became a real luxury. Thousands of vagrants slept on the cobblestones of the levee. Police brutality reached a point seldom equaled.

Officers of the law carried night sticks a yard long and learned to hurl them at the feet of fleeing migrants in such a way as to trip them up when they tried to run. The cops kept watchful eyes on such places as Victor's poolroom too. Anyone they caught nodding in a chair was likely to be arrested for vagrancy. The burden of proof was on the patron. Unless his eyes were open or his feet moving, he might be found guilty. One migrant with a glass eye managed to thwart the officers by pulling his hat over his good eye as he dozed, leaving the glass one exposed. Others managed to steal a few winks by learning to work their feet as they slept. Many of the newcomers were less resourceful, however, and out of their brushes with the law grew such popular songs as "Brady, He's Dead and Gone" and "Looking for the Bully."

St. Louis made a grim reputation for itself in those days, but Negroes were glad to accept its harsh dealings in exchange for the indignities of life in the Deep South. Some of them liked to say, as they have said with reference to Harlem, to Chicago's South Side, and to other communities of the North, "I'd rather be a lamppost on Targee Street than be the mayor of Dixie."

Of course there was another side to the city's reputation too. W. C. Handy has recalled that during his sojourn there in 1893 he saw the prettiest woman he has ever seen in his life. Other testimony of the same sort is not hard to find. Undoubtedly the elegance of St. Louis' dusky fancy girls was something startling. Their beauty and their fragrance, their rustle of silk and their jeweled garters, their diamonds like hen eggs, and their cooing voices, brought forth an exotic little world that is still remembered, by those who knew it, like a spicy dream.

Their men, called "macks," were an equally gaudy breed. The following description of them, taken from original sources, occurs in the novel *God Sends Sunday:*

> They wore gay embroidered shirts, and on their fingers, below the knuckle-length sleeves, flashed diamonds and polished nails. Their finery seemed even to exceed that of the fancy women who supported them. Gold money made into jewelry was customary, also high-roller hats, with nude women or boxers or racing horses worked in small eyelets in the crown.

They also wore box-back coats and shoes with tiny mirrors set in the toes.

A way of life equally exotic flowed from these characters. Gambling was highly favored by both men and women. The domestic relationships between the macks and their partners were reflected in the male individual's right to beat the woman upon occasion. In this prerogative only did he enjoy unqualified priority; hence "lumping," as it was called, became a symbol of his position, and he would fight another man to the death for attempting to usurp it. The hallmark of an authentic lovers' quarrel in that society was the throwing of a kerosene lamp at the beloved. A fight that failed to end in action at least this violent and spectacular was just a spat, not a clash.

Music was a necessity in the world around Targee Street. In every house there was a guitar. In many of the saloons and fancy establishments there were pianos. On these guitars and pianos of the Negro sporting world ragtime music was created. Somewhat later jazz, blues, and swing evolved from the same roots. The savage beauty of the rouged brown girls on Targee Street was behind it all.

In those days a young Negro named Scott Joplin left his home in Texarkana, Texas, and took to the road. Scott was out to make a career in music. Where he went and what he did during most of his travels can only be guessed, but his biographers have found a good many clues. In the history of American westward expansion there is the story of the Mormons who planted sunflower seeds as they journeyed so that followers could trace the way they had taken across the prairies. Scott Joplin published songs. With no intention such as motivated the planters of sunflowers, the migratory singer, pianist, and composer from Texarkana left quite as vivid a record of his wanderings. In a short biography of this "overlooked genius" which appeared in the *Record Changer,* a magazine published in the interest of phonograph record collectors and buyers, Roy Carew and Don E. Fowler showed that they could reconstruct a more or less complete story of Joplin's life from evidence revealed on his published sheet music.

Born in 1869 and raised in or near Texarkana, Joplin appears to have received early musical training at home. One account states that his father played the violin but opposed his son's childhood tendency to spend all his time at the piano on the grounds that music was a poor staff on which to lean for temporal support. Maybe his own experience had embittered him. In any case, the story is that he tried to prevail on Scott to learn a trade. He might have saved his breath. By the time the boy was twenty-one, perhaps earlier, he was on the road, earning a living at music and seeing a lot of the country at the same time.

The evidence of this is the song "Please Say You Will," published by M. L. Mantell of Syracuse, New York, in 1895 and bearing the inscription, "Song and Chorus by Scott Joplin, of the Texas Medley Quartet." One is left to surmise that the Texas Medley Quartet was singing before the public with reasonable success at that time. And the fact that another Joplin composition, "A Picture of Her Face," was published by another Syracuse publisher, Leiter Brothers, the same year would seem to establish the assumption that the quartet had sung in that city and that Joplin had taken advantage of the opportunity to place two of his songs with local publishers. Still another inference to be drawn is that the Texas Medley Quartet featured some of the compositions of Scott Joplin in their programs.

By 1896 Joplin's wanderings had carried him South again. In October of that year John R. Fuller of Temple, Texas, published a number by Joplin called the "Great Crush Collision, March." And in the following month of the same year another Temple publisher, Robert Smith, issued two other works by Joplin, "Harmony Club Waltz" and "Combination March." This evidence would seem to place Joplin in the town of Temple in 1896, perhaps in the latter part of the year.

From Temple the arrow of speculation points to Sedalia, Missouri. The Missouri, Kansas, and Texas Railway, which runs through Temple, Texas, also runs into Sedalia, one of the railroad centers of west central Missouri. Perhaps the "Great Crush Collision, March" commemorated an accident on that line. Certainly it is in Sedalia that the thread of Joplin's story is next picked up. Here the most significant period of this composer's history began.

Where Scott Joplin lost the Texas Medley Quartet and how he traveled thereafter can only be guessed, so far as the written record goes, but the fact that the year 1897 found him playing a piano in a joy spot in Sedalia is at least suggestive. By then the twenty-eight-year-old musician had evidently become one of the great tribe of wandering piano players whose genius and originality brought on the revolution in American popular music. And Scott Joplin clearly exerted a greater influence in this direction than any one of his contemporaries.

It is said that the owner of the establishment where Joplin played in Sedalia was a man of musical interests and some discrimination. Attracted by the number and variety of original stylings in Joplin's playing, this individual, according to one story, suggested that the pianist enroll at Smith's School of Music for formal training. Joplin is supposed to have accepted this advice. The legend adds that within a very short time the young stomp pianist and barroom musician was off on a creative spree, working into his compositions some of the ideas that marked his own playing.

But Carew and Fowler, Joplin's biographers, are by no means convinced that the music school was an important factor in the composer's development. Less open to question, however, is the fact that Joplin went to Kansas City in 1897 or 1898 and sold his "Original Rags" to Carl Hoffman for publication. How long Joplin had been *playing* ragtime is not known. Neither can it be said with certainty that one individual or another was responsible for *first* giving the keyboard the extra lick that made all the difference. It can be said, nevertheless, that when ragtime began to be written and published, Scott Joplin was on hand with his compositions. Moreover, his were far and away the best of the rags, the most durable and the most influential. His "Original Rags" was stomping good ragtime, fit to stand with the best, and the date of its publication speaks for itself. It was played wherever the new music was appreciated, and its influence reached to New Orleans and Memphis where jazz was, even then, incubating.

Back in Sedalia again in 1899, Scott Joplin contacted John Stark and Son, a music publishing firm which was getting ready to move its business to St. Louis. To them he showed the manuscripts of "Maple Leaf Rag," "Sunflower Slow Drag," and perhaps other rags. This proved to be the big moment in Joplin's career as well as in the history of the Starks's publishing firm and, perhaps, in the development of American ragtime music. Years later the publishers recalled:

> When he [Joplin] first came into our office, with his manuscripts of "Maple Leaf Rag" and "Sunflower Slow Drag" he had tried other pub-

lishers, but had failed to sell them. We quickly discerned their quality, bought them and made a five-year contract with Joplin to write only for our firm. . . . When we published the "Maple Leaf" it took us one year to sell 400 copies, simply because people examined it hastily, and didn't find it.

The "Maple Leaf Rag" and another Joplin number called "Swipsey Cake Walk" were both published by the Starks in Sedalia. Soon thereafter the publishers moved to St. Louis, where, thanks mainly to Scott Joplin, they earned the designation of "The Classic Rag House." Joplin followed the Starks to St. Louis and gave them such compositions as "Peacherine," "Easy Winners," "Breeze from Alabama," "The Strenuous Life," "Entertainer," "The Ragtime Dance Song," "The Chrysanthemum," and "The Cascades," all solid Joplin numbers.

By 1901 Joplin was being hailed as "King of the Ragtime Writers." "Maple Leaf Rag" was already on the way to becoming the classic of the genre. Joplin was widely imitated. Percy Wenrich, for example, called one of his compositions "The Smiler—Joplin Rag." The boy from Texarkana had practically given his name to the musical form itself. People talked about Joplin rags without always referring to one of Scott Joplin's compositions.

Scott Joplin is not easy to play. Chris Smith, another Negro song writer, summed up the problem when he said that very few people played the "Maple Leaf Rag," though a great many played at it. Indeed, the publishers themselves were compelled to take note of this difficulty. They issued the following statement:

We knew a pianist who had in her repertoire "Maple Leaf," "Sunflower Slow Drag," "The Entertainer," and "Elite Syncopations." She had played them as she thought, over and over for her own pleasure and others, until at last she had laid them aside as *passé*. But it chanced that she incidentally dropped into a store one day, where Joplin was playing "The Sunflower Slow Drag." She was instantly struck with its unique and soulful story, and—what do you think? She asked someone what it was. She had played over it and around it for twelve months and had never touched it.

In 1904 Scott Joplin followed the Starks to New York and continued to give them a stream of outstanding ragtime compositions.

But he remained in New York when the firm with which he had been so closely identified returned to St. Louis again, and it was in New York that he died in 1917.

Meanwhile, however, Scott Joplin learned something about the agony of creative genius. He was never at peace with himself. He dreamed of grand operas in ragtime. Perhaps he was never quite sure that the music which had flourished in the St. Louis saloons and the houses on Targee Street was respectable. True, he had lived to see it widely accepted by the nation as a whole, but could he be sure? If Scott Joplin failed to wonder about this, he was unlike some of his contemporaries in St. Louis. They helped to create ragtime, but they have never been sure that it wasn't naughty.

If anything could have reassured these composers, it would have been a ragtime opera. To such a project Scott Joplin turned his creative powers in the last years of his life. His first ambitious effort in this direction was recorded by the Library of Congress in 1903. It was entitled *A Guest of Honor,* but no copy was ever received by the Library, and the work was never issued by the publishers. Weak story and lyrics have been given as the reason. But Joplin was not convinced. In 1911 he published at his own expense *Treemonisha,* a second operatic composition on which he had spent his creative resources. Its failure to get a production was a cutting disappointment. Whether or not the experience had anything to do with the composer's final confusion has been the subject of speculation. In any case, Scott Joplin wandered into a complete fog before his death.

Twenty-five years later a white man named S. Bronson Campbell, himself a ragtime pianist, set about to raise a memorial to the near-forgotten "King of the Ragtime Writers." As a young man, playing over some popular numbers in the Armstrong Byrd music store in Oklahoma City, Campbell had been handed his first Joplin score by Otis Saunders, friend of the composer. Later he met Joplin personally and learned how the music should be played. The ragtime rhythm never deserted him. To him it became the music of memory.

What Joplin never realized, perhaps, was that he, more than anyone else, had provided mood music for the great migrations of Negroes from the South at the turn of the century. First the musicians themselves migrated, generally following the sporting wheel. They wrote letters home or returned and brought reports. Wherever large numbers of the newcomers settled, shacks and tenements and store fronts commenced swaying and rocking to Joplin rags. In Chicago this impulse produced the Pekin Theatre, self-styled "temple of music."

In 1905 Robert Motts, café, saloon, and gambling-house proprietor, suddenly found his activities opposed by the local clergy; the political outlook, too, was unfavorable to him. Motts decided to make a change. He, as much as anyone else, had learned to make capital of the increasing numbers of Southern Negroes in Chicago. He was familiar with their deep need of music, and he knew their willingness to pay for that form of entertainment. To his experiences with his own people, moreover, Motts was able to add impressions gained from travel in Europe, where he had admired the Continental music halls in which patrons, seated about the stage, were entertained by short plays, musical selections, and variety acts as they ate and drank. His "temple of music" on Chicago's South Side was a darktown adaptation of this European style of entertainment.

The essential difference, of course, was the kind of musical fare the Pekin Theatre featured. Cakewalks were offered, and ragtime was interspersed between waltzes, sentimental ballads, and coon songs of the nineties. And more often than otherwise ragtime took the cake. Chicagoans of all classes and colors began to discover the Pekin. Its popularity increased so rapidly that Motts was forced to expand, and in April of 1906 the "temple of music" became the "New Pekin Theatre," a regular theater with conventional stage and seating arrangement. Entertainment was provided by a stock company of composers and musicians, actors and singers, writers and directors, but the accent was still on music, and the musical play was the Pekin's specialty.

Almost immediately a stream of talented young Negroes began arriving from St. Louis and other directions. Joe Jordan became an active member of the company, composing its theme song, "The Pekin Rag," which became a national hit under the title of "Sweety Dear." Will Marion Cook, who had been around town off and on since the day in 1893 when he promoted the Negro celebration, came to the Pekin with a reputation already established, but this did not keep him from writing for the group nor from marrying Abbie Mitchell, beautiful and talented young soprano of the company. Shelton Brooks was the Pekin company's man of all work. He produced, acted, directed the orchestra, and composed. In the latter capacity he became top notch, giving American popular music a string of all-time hits in numbers like "Some o' These Days," "Darktown Strutters' Ball," "Balling the Jack," "Walking the Dog," and "You Ain't Talking to Me." Tim Brymn was a rival of Joe Jordan's for the honor of being the busiest composer in the Pekin company. H. Lawrence Freeman, whose main interest ran to heavy operatic works, nevertheless wrote some music for the group, as did also Bernie Adler, Mill Dixon, and others. Oliver Perry was the first musical director of the "New Pekin Theatre."

Star stage performers of the Pekin included Charles Gilpin, later to originate the title role in Eugene O'Neill's *Emperor Jones;* a promising young tap dancer named Bill Robinson, and a pair of versatile comedians named Flournoy Miller and Aubrey Lyles. This latter team appeared in all kinds of Pekin productions, but in none were they more appealing than in *Mayor of Dixie*. A number of years later Broadway liked them in this piece, too, when *Shuffle Along* was based on the old Pekin hit.

Of course Chicago Negroes heard more ragtime than that which was played at the Pekin. The itinerant barroom musicians who made "the revolution in 4-4 time" began to consider it a good town on the circuit as the migration moved past St. Louis. Tom Turpin who, like his brother Charles, was a familiar figure on Targee Street and who in the eighteen nineties had published "The Harlem Rag" and "The Bowery Buck," came up and played in Chicago saloons. Scott Joplin, Tony Jackson, Louis Chauvin, and Ferdinand ("Jelly Roll") Morton all included Chicago on their rounds in the ragtime period. Most of them were still active in 1914 (though the Pekin was no longer running) when Freddie Keppard, cornettist of Emanuel Perez's Creole Band from New Orleans, just arrived at the Grand Theatre at Thirty-first and State, gave the trumpet blast that announced to the North the arrival of the jazz age.

But that is the music of another migration. Meanwhile, however, the St. Louis of Targee Street, fancy girls, macks, plush parlors, high-roller Stetsons, and diamonds like hen eggs was not played out. Its two greatest songs had already been inspired, but at least one had not been written and neither had yet become a part of the cultural heritage of America. Very soon, though, all this was to follow. A lovers' quarrel on Targee Street, with violent overtones, produced the folk ballad "Frankie and Johnny." And a spasm of poignant recollection and remorse drew from W. C. Handy the "St. Louis Blues"—a song which many people in other countries believe to be the American national anthem.

CHAPTER IX

The Invisible Migration

IN HIS BOOK *The Port of New Orleans* Harold Sinclair makes a casual, almost offhand observation which might easily have been pursued further. "The number of free Negroes in New Orleans," he says, "decreased by half in the decade before the Civil War. Where did they go? There is no exact answer . . . except that nobody knows."

One could complain that the historian gave up too soon. Sinclair does indicate that it will do us no good to seek the answer in the more obvious explanations such as high death rates, epidemics, mass migrations, and the like. Nothing of that sort applies. If there were many deaths by epidemics and other causes, they are canceled out by a high birth rate. If there was a large exodus, it has not been recorded. What, indeed, became of the 10,000 free people of color who disappeared from the New Orleans census prior to the War between the States?

Perhaps a fair answer might begin with the personal history of one of them, a girl who left the city in the spring of 1856. Her name at christening was Philomene Croi Theodore, but like most youngsters reared in the Creole tradition she soon acquired from her parents a pet name to take the place of the cumbersome Philomene. Perhaps it was Berthe. Later she frequently added to or revised the names by which, at one time or another, it pleased her to sign herself. But the one which stuck longest was Adah, and it was by this name that she was known when the English poet Algernon Charles Swinburne called her "the world's delight."

During most of her life, in America and abroad, Adah was accepted as white. Obviously, she was at least a quadroon. Until she left New Orleans, however, she was just one of many light-skinned colored girls on Love Street (now Rampart) between Elysians Fields and Marigny. In the city as a whole her family was one of hundreds, perhaps thousands of the kind that was the romance (and later the embarrassment) of old New Orleans. For the free group, the *hommes de couleur libres,* was essentially a mixed-blood group. Therefore it was called colored, rather than Negro or black, and the French, with a nice eye for such distinctions, invented terms such as *sacatro* (Negro and *griffe*), *griffe* (Negro and mulatto), *marabon* (mulatto and *griffe*), *mulatto* (Negro and white), *os rouge* (Negro and Indian), *tierceron* (mulatto and quadroon), quadroon (white and mulatto), octoroon (white and quadroon) to describe the various shades.

The kind of life to which a girl like Adah could look forward in New Orleans in the first half of the nineteenth century was perhaps symbolized by the Quadroon Ball. Here, at affairs so astonishingly brilliant they almost took the breath of European visitors such as the Duke of Saxe-Weimar and Harriet Martineau, young upper-class Creoles met and made matches with fair colored girls who had been carefully reared and often well educated for just such careers in a city where connections of this kind were the rule, though marriage between the two groups was prohibited by law. But the Quadroon Balls ended in the 1840s, when Adah was still a child, and the way of life which they reflected—often wistfully romantic—began to deteriorate. It had already fallen into disrepute with newcomers to the city—the more puritanical Anglo-Saxon element of the population. In time it was represented by these, quite inexcusably, as something base and ugly, not far removed from common prostitution. Gross, back-country bumpkins with mud on their feet pushed themselves into the luxurious ballroom in later years, spitting tobacco and shouting, "So this here's the place where they used to sell the gals!" Adah saw and heard enough of this kind of behavior to know that the custom which prompted it was already doomed. But it wouldn't have suited *her,* anyhow. There was something special about Adah.

Quadroon girls of New Orleans were so uniformly beautiful they had been described as *les Sirènes* by several generations of romantic Creoles. Adah, too, was emphatically lovely, but pictures of her contemporaries do not permit us to infer that she was in a class by herself. Adah's distinction grew out of forces that worked behind that beautiful outer baggage. A wide horizon, unwillingness to accept the status to which local convention had assigned her, an ability to see life in broad panels, and a sense of adventure marked her from the rest.

It now seems, despite the apparent contradiction of her actions, that a fierce pride in what she was helped to motivate her career. What most of her biographers have seen, of course, was just the opposite, for Adah threw an abundance of dust in their eyes. Toward the end of her career she did her best to give a clue to the mystery she had created, but it was 1938—ninety years after her birth—before anyone began to take her hints, and even then some of the most obvious implications of her deeds were overlooked. Perhaps she had succeeded *too* well; her triumph over her early environment had been so overwhelming it seemed unreal.

The world—beyond Rampart Street in New Orleans—became aware of Adah in June 1861, when the city of Albany, New York, was placarded with pictures of a nude young girl bound to the back of a galloping steed. Adah Isaacs Menken, it was announced, was about to open in the title role of *Mazeppa* at the Albany Theater. Following this performance the sobriquet "The Naked Lady" was given to Adah by persons in the astonished audience, and one first-nighter went so far as to suggest that what he observed had to be seen to be believed. As the horse on which she rode disappeared into the wings, there was at first silence and then a burst of frenzy and shouting as the audience rose to its feet. "Parts of the body of this actress were exposed that God never intended to be seen by any eye other than her mother's," one reported. A year later the same picture covered the billboards of New York City, but this time the accompanying announcement was that Mrs. John C. Heenan would play the part. Three years later the whole thing was repeated in London, with Adah Isaacs Menken billed to appear in the same play at Astley's Theatre, and the following year the scene was Paris and the theater the Gaîeté. In each of these cities, with the possible exception of Paris, the theater-going public was shocked—and thrilled—at the prospect of seeing a nude woman on a stage. Particularly one with curves as appealing as Adah's, with such a sweet childlike face, with eyes as languishing as hers appeared to be.

When her performance was attacked on moral grounds, Adah calmly defended her position. There was nothing indecent about the display of the human body, she insisted. Indeed, the attitudes and poses assumed by her in the play were no more objectionable than those to be found in classical works of sculpture. And her admirers—mostly men—were much taken with the logic of her explanation. They held that she was a pure-minded, talented young woman being abused by an evil-minded world. Of course the difference between the two points of view was not composed in her day, but common ground between the factions was found on the question of Adah's beauty. On this all agreed. To a lesser extent, perhaps, there was agreement as to her talent, though there are many who still wonder whether or not it was acting talent, in the conventional sense. No matter. Swinburne thought she was the world's delight. And Charles Dickens and Charles Reade and Rossetti and Alexandre Dumas were all evidently convinced that she was *some*thing extraordinary, whether that or not. She was terrific box office.

But behind Adah's theatrical career was the real drama. Much of this became common knowledge, too, for the loves and marriages of this fascinating woman were almost as widely publicized as her performances in *Mazeppa*. She acquired four husbands in her short life, and at least an equal number of distinguished lovers. The husbands included a young Jewish music teacher—who gave her the name by which she was known on the stage—a famous prize fighter, an American humorist who wrote under the pseudonym of Orpheus C. Kerr, and a Wall Street broker. Her impact on the great men who knew her, but not as husbands, may be summarized in an entry made by the author of *The Cloister and the Hearth* in his diary and a line of poetry by Swinburne. Speaking of Adah, Charles Reade noted: "A clever woman with beautiful eyes; bad actress; made hit playing *Mazeppa* in tights; goodish heart." And in a copy of *Infelicia,* Menken's book of her own poems, the smitten Swinburne wrote: "Lo, this was she who was the world's delight." She was also the inspiration of his poem, "Delores," described by him as a revery upon "the transmigration of a single soul always clad in the same type of fleshly beauty." At hearing the news of her death, the poet remarked, "She was most lovable as a friend as well as a mistress." He had, in the view of some others, "let himself be lamentably entangled with the fair but frail American."

The elderly Alexandre Dumas, père, when chided by his talented son for his rather unbecoming May-and-December romance with Adah, replied less solemnly than Swinburne might have done, but with equal zest. "In my old age," the indomitable old romancer said, "I have found a Marguerite and am playing Armand Duval." He referred, of course, to the lovers in his son's drama *La Dame aux camélias*.

But through it all there ran a thread of mystery. Who was this woman with the beautiful eyes, the clever mind, and the enchanting body? What was her exotic secret? Where was she grown? She herself told half a dozen conflicting stories about her parentage. Some who saw her thought she looked slightly Jewish. Others imagined they saw evidences of a Spanish or gypsy strain. Adah told one she had spent her childhood in Cuba and made her bow on the stage there. She told others that this military man or that physician in New Orleans had been her father. She even dreamed up a yarn about how she had been kidnaped by Indians and lived among them for a couple of years. Not one of her accounts of her parents or background could ever be verified. On the contrary, every one of them has been completely dashed. In 1938, however, John S. Kendall, writing in the Louisiana *Historical Quarterly*, suggested—very tentatively—that if we just assume that Adah was a colored girl of New Orleans, many of the parts of her story which have hitherto been perplexing are inclined to fall into place. They do. Even more completely than he himself claimed.

Kendall is content to let the New Orleans Board of Health records, the archives of the French cathedral, and the facts set down on the marriage application in Galveston speak for themselves. And that is quite sufficient to dispose completely of most of the accounts of Adah's background to be found in encyclopedias and biographical dictionaries. On the psychological and emotional levels, however, more could have been added.

What must have happened, in actual fact, is that Adah's odyssey began when her young Jewish music teacher fell in love with her. But one or the other of them, perhaps both, were determined that New Orleans would not be permitted to make something low and shoddy of their passion. Accordingly, they resolved to be legally married. Which meant they had to leave the State. Texas was the answer. So to Galveston, that remote outpost, they went, and there they were married.

Adah was converted to the Jewish faith—to which she adhered throughout the rest of her life—and began contributing poems to the Cincinnati *Israelite*. With her young husband, who appears to have been the one true love of her life, she traveled in the South for a time and made her debut as an actress. This may have occurred at the J. S. Charles Theatre in Shreveport, Louisiana, in March 1857. Five months later she played Lady Freelove in *A Wife's First Lesson* in New Orleans when Charles took over the Varieties Theatre of that city. She was billed as "Mrs. A. J. Menken," and apparently none of her home-town friends did or said anything to embarrass her during the performance of this or other plays in which Charles presented her. The local criitcs liked the productions. But Adah failed to complete the season with the company, leaving it under circumstances which—assuming that she was "passing"—were at least provocative of speculation.

Riots broke out in New Orleans in connection with municipal elections early in the following June. Charles was obliged to close the Varieties for four days as a result of the disorders. When he resumed the plays, Adah was missing from his stock company, her place having been taken by the more established Charlotte Crampton. This replacement seems logical enough at first glance, for Crampton was a name at that time, and Menken was just a beginner. On the other hand, however, the fact that Adah's leaving coincided with the riots cannot be overlooked, and one must remember that both critics and public had been completely favorable to the productions while Adah was in them. Then why did she withdraw? And why did she never return to the New Orleans stage after she had reached stardom in *Mazeppa?* Had a jealous neighbor, say, discovered that Mrs. A. J. Menken was just plain Berthe Theodore, the girl who had run away from Rampart Street with a young Jew? Perhaps it is unnecessary to speculate. Perhaps it is enough to observe that everything connected with her appearances in these plays was falsified by Adah in later years. Adah told a reporter, after her rise to fame, that she had made her debut as "Frazie," but this was actually the role in which Crampton had opened *after* Menken had left the company. Was Adah trying to usurp the other woman's glory or was she simply seeking to build a case—putting herself in the productions after the riots to make sure nobody asked why she left the group when she did? At the same time Adah recalled for the press scenes of adulation paid her in New Orleans by Judah P. Benjamin and other prominent Jews of the city. It was all a dream. Nothing of the sort ever happened. But it is a fact that Louisiana quadroons have frequently found it convenient to imply that their lineage was Jewish. And Adah who, with no more basis in fact, sometimes hinted at a girlhood debut in Havana, apparently felt that there was something about her looks, her coloring, her features, or her expression, that required an explanation.

But now Adah was an actress. She played many roles in many theaters around the country, including New York. Somewhere along the way she lost the young husband whom she loved. He divorced her the year following the New Orleans season in the J. S. Charles company, giving "incompatibility and desertion" as grounds. A year later she was billed in New York as "Mrs. John C. Heenan," presumably the wife of the prize fighter known as the Benicia Boy. She used his name, more or less casually, for two years, and she bore the gaudy ringman a child which did not live. Adah seemed to think the fighter's name would contribute to the success of the New York run of *Mazeppa*. She soon found she didn't need it or him, so she settled on the name of her first husband and kept it the rest of her life.

Adah did *Mazeppa* from New York to San Francisco. On this tour she was accompanied by Robert Newell, the humorous writer who signed his stuff "Orpheus C. Kerr," whom she had married shortly before her decree from Heenan was granted. From San Francisco she returned to New York by boat. Somewhere on this long voyage she dropped the humorist. She may have grown tired of his gags, for Adah's taste in literature did not run to low humor, and she made this abundantly clear by her choice of friends abroad, beginning in 1864.

In London, where her *Mazeppa* was as sensational as it had been in American cities, Adah was taken up by the literary crowd. She was associated, in one way or another, with Thackeray, Robert Reece, John Oxenford, Dante and William Rossetti, as well as Dickens, Swinburne, and Reade. How near she was to this one or that has not been determined in every case. While moving among them Adah began collecting her own poems, but the pathetic little volume she called *Infelicia* did not get published till after her death. Perhaps this was because she was still too busy living.

Menken returned to New York to play *Mazeppa* in 1866. She remained long enough to contract another marriage. This one, her fourth, was to James Paul Barclay, the Wall Street broker. This unhappy man appears to have been totally bewitched by the dazzling woman. He gave her a brownstone-front house on Seventh Avenue, between Thirty-eighth and Thirty-ninth, spent perhaps $150,000 on her in three months, then—convinced, no doubt, that he could never possess the bright creature—walked out on her, went to Philadelphia, and was soon found dead there. This romance was too cyclonic for even the tempestuous Adah. She took poison, and it almost did its work.

Still ill from the dose, she was carried on board the ship that was to take her to Europe again. Other roles awaited her in the theaters of the Continent, but something much more significant was also in store. For a long time—it could have been since childhood—Adah had been attracted by the romances of Alexandre Dumas. It is a matter of record that on several occasions in London she stated publicly that if ever she got to Paris she would become "the mistress of that extraordinary man." On this trip she got a chance to make good.

Adah was presented in *Pirates de la Savanne,* another vehicle for her enchanting curves. The show did well, so well, in fact, that all the dandies and literati of Paris came to the daily levee she held in her suite at the Hôtel de Suez on the Boulevard de Strasbourg. Adah met many great names, but Alexandre Dumas did not come. But the sixty-five-year-old author did attend a performance of *Pirates* one night and Adah caught a glimpse of the unwieldy old Negro standing in the wings. He wore a stiff white piqué vest and a high collar. As he watched the show his eyes twinkled and Adah must have seen in him the wonderfully engaging old satyr that he was. Anyhow, at the close of the third act Adah—still clad in her flesh-colored tights—ran to him, threw her arms around his neck, and kissed him.

That night the usual crowd came to the Hôtel de Suez to attend Adah's levee, but the hostess did not show up. She had gone to a supper given in her honor by Paris' "king of romance." Afterward Dumas set her up in an apartment of his own. Then he took her to Bougival, a summer resort on the Seine. The two were there when Dumas' son, embarrassed by the gossip the old man's ardor was provoking, wrote his father in protest. At first Papa Dumas laughed with the laughers, but the ridicule got under his skin when a curious little triolet by Paul Verlaine appeared, beginning with the lines

L'Oncle Tom avec Miss Ada,
C'est un spectacle dont on rêve.

And the appearance of post-card pictures showing Adah sitting on his knee or leaning affectionately on his shoulder was more than he could take. He promptly broke off the affair and sued the photographer.

It is not hard to imagine Dumas' feelings, but what about Adah's? Are we to believe, as the old-line biographers implied, that this woman of the Old South, this New Orleans belle, was personally drawn to the famous old quadroon simply because she liked his books? New Orleans had the most subtle consciousness of color. Are women grown in such an atmosphere just waiting till they get to Paris to throw their arms around men like Dumas? Adah's Louisiana biographer has nothing to say on this point. But even though the psychological aspects of the question failed to arouse his curiosity, he might have noted that there were several colored men from New Orleans in Dumas' circle of acquaintances in Paris at the time. One was Victor Séjour, the popular playwright. Two others were P. Dalcour and Camille Thierry, poets. Might not this circumstance have indicated that Adah now felt there was no longer any need for her to "pass" as white? Might not her statements about "that extraordinary man" be taken as a welling up of pride, however belatedly, in what she was, in the group of mixed-blood people to which she belonged? In New Orleans these people of color were taught to think very well of their own kind. There was a sort of clan feeling among them.

Adah died on August 10, 1868. She was buried as a Jew, and on her stone were engraved words she herself had selected from Swinburne's poem "Ilicet." "Thou knowest!"

Whether or not opinion is unanimous on the question of Adah Isaacs Menken's "passing," at least it can be said that the pattern of her life is certainly a classic imitation of a colored Creole passing for white in the United States and England in the middle of the nineteenth century. Walter White, author of *Flight,* one of the most authoritative novels on the subject, may or may not have been unconscious of the close parallel between his heroine's reaction to the Negro concert singer whose achievement drew her back to the group with which she had earlier been identified and Adah's throwing herself into the arms of Alexandre Dumas.

As to the 10,000 free people of color who disappeared from the New Orleans census in the middle of the last century, one is left to assume that Adah Isaacs Menken's story is their story repeated in a gaudier context—with the exception that most of them never met a Dumas. And, of course, those who raised families of children were doubly restrained from ever indulging a wistful emotion toward the folks they had left behind. Even so, their secret did not always remain concealed.

A recent experience of a well-known white writer is suggestive. This prominent editor had been told that one of the cathedral records of births, deaths, and marriages of old New Orleans Catholics had been altered. Gossip had it that a certain priest had allowed visitors to view the record alone—with no one else in the room. The reason, of course, was to give the individual an opportunity to remove any embarrassing h.c.l. or f.m.c. from beside the names of his early ancestors. These initials indicated *homme de couleur libres* or free man of color, and that was bad for one who had been brought up to think he was "white" by local definition. The editor wanted to see for himself what had happened to the record. He, too, was allowed to inspect the book alone. The report he brought out was that the pages resembled nothing so much as old-fashioned player-piano rolls. They were fairly covered with scratched-out holes. The evidence had definitely been tampered with, though the suspicion remained.

Pre-Civil War censuses are explicit on the racial identity of the free colored group, and the figures indicate that in Louisiana four out of five of these were either mulattoes or lighter mixtures. That half of this number should have been fair enough to "pass" is completely credible. The invisible exodus continued for at least a generation after emancipation, manifesting itself now and then in the most unexpected places, and the quaint folk dogma that a drop of Negro blood makes one a Negro in America produced a series of tangled domestic problems throughout the country.

In 1907 Mrs. John Warner, a socially prominent Chicago woman and widow of a millionaire, proved to the satisfaction of a court that she was not of "tainted origin." And those who sought to deny her and her two daughters their fortune by swearing that she had "concealed the presence of Negro blood in her veins" from her late husband were completely frustrated.

The same year Dr. J. Frank McKinley appeared in a Chicago court, where he had been charged by his former wife, Mrs. Maude Cuney Hare, of "posing as a Spanish-American," to claim his seven-year-old daughter Vera. Apparently each parent of the child was light, but the mother had elected to live as a colored woman. The ex-husband had married a white woman, a Miss Caroline I. Ennis, owner of the Huntington Hotel, and made the decision to be a Caucasian. The books were opened, as it were, when the custody of little Vera came to an issue.

Meanwhile, a mild hysteria was created on the campus of the University of Chicago when it was discovered that Cecilia Johnson, described at the time as "a society leader, a swell dresser, a lavish spender, and an honor student," was not only a colored girl but a close relative of "Mushmouth" Johnson, a well-known Negro "gambling king," who was underwriting her career on the Midway. And a few years later an aging colored woman, the mother of four children, laid claim to the estate of William H. Lee, junior partner of the prominent Midwestern publishing firm of Laird & Lee, and apparently established the fact that the deceased publisher had been "passing" for thirty years.

There are even stories of successful "passing" by slaves. A number of instances occurred in which a slave girl, white enough to get by, dressed as a man and posed as the young master of a personal "slave," actually her Negro husband, and reached freedom in Canada in that way.

But not all the light-skinned Negroes of the South took advantage of this rather easy avenue of escape. There is an ever-lengthening list of capable men and women whose identification with the Negro group in America has been essentially voluntary. Such a man was Daniel Hale Williams who in 1893 gained fame as the first surgeon ever to report a successful operation on the heart. Another was Charles W. Chesnutt, the Cleveland author whose stories appeared so frequently in the *Atlantic Monthly* and other magazines around the turn of the century. And still another was the wife of Blanche K. Bruce, the Negro Senator. Of her an astonished Midwestern reporter wrote for his newspaper:

> . . . She made an exceedingly favorable impression upon her callers, and nowhere were people more gracefully or handsomely received. She wore a black velvet robe of worth and handsome diamonds. Mrs. Bruce has unusual personal beauty. . . . A stranger would suppose she was of Spanish blood.

He could scarcely believe his eyes.

Walter F. White, the distinguished predecessor of Roy Wilkins as executive secretary of the National Association for the Advancement of Colored People, sometimes used his "whiteness" to advantage in investigating and reporting lynchings, riots, and other anti-Negro disorders. An even more conspicuous example of the Negro indistinguishable as colored, though so classified by American definition, has been Congressman Adam Clayton Powell, Jr.

That the multiplying of such cases, and the results, would eventually come before the courts was perhaps inevitable in an era of civil rights concern. When the Supreme Court struck down a Florida statute which made it a crime for Negroes and whites to cohabit, on the simple grounds of race, Mr. Justice White observed that ". . . we deal here with a racial classification embodied in a criminal statute. In this context, where the power of a state weighs most heavily on the individual or group, we must be especially sensitive to the policies of the Equal Protection Clause, which . . . were intended to . . . subject all persons to 'like punishment, pains, penalties, taxes, licenses and exactions of every kind,' and no other." To this Justice Stewart and Douglas concurred by stating: "It is simply not possible for a state law to be valid under our Constitution which makes the criminality of an act depend upon the race of the actor."

The evolution of a new legal attitude toward such matters had apparently begun.

CHAPTER X

Strangers

FOUR WHITE MEN walked across a stretch of frozen marshland beside a railroad spur bisecting a field near an industrial suburb of Chicago. They did not speak as they strode along, their feet crunching the brittle spears of ice-encased grass. Now and then they dodged a clump of cattail, but they bore steadily toward the goal they were eying as they advanced. Five coaches, a baggage car, and a red caboose stood on the siding. As the men approached, four Negro men climbed down from one of the baggage cars and made their way across the field to meet the white men. Both groups halted, and black and white men eyed one another for a moment. Then one of the white men spoke.

"We're from the Chicago Federation of Labor. We want to talk to you."

"What about?" asked one of the Negroes, stepping forward from his group.

"About working at the Latrobe plant. Do you know the company is using you to fight us? That's the reason they haven't unloaded you at the plant. We don't aim to have you go in there, and if we have to we'll get rough."

"We don't want no trouble," replied the Negro spokesman, "but we got to eat same as anyone else. There's three hundred and twelve of us in them cars—men, women, and children. We ain't had nothing to eat for two days, and we just got enough water for today. We ain't got warm clothes—just what we had when we left Birmingham. All we done was come up here to make an honest living. And that's what the man told us down in Birmingham—that's what he told us we could do up here."

"It *ain't* honest," pursued the emissary of the labor unions. "You're taking the bread and butter right out of your white brother's mouth, and his women and children too. You want us to be the same as you colored men was before Lincoln freed you? Why, my old daddy fought the rebs to make your people free! I figure that gives me a right to talk to you if nothing else does."

The Negroes bowed their heads in thought. They were tremendously impressed. This kind of talk was strange, but it had great power to stir them. The union member had struck deeper than he probably knew.

"What can we do?" asked the Negro spokesman. "We don't aim to do nobody no dirt. And we ain't got much use for that company, either. They leave us out here on the prairie to starve."

"Go back where you came from—that's what you can do. Go back and let them know that the black man refused to stick a knife in the back of his white brother."

With this, the white delegation turned and walked back across the marshland. The Negroes stood watching for some time, then they returned slowly to the railroad cars. Black, anxious faces, pressed against the frost-crusted coach windows, were awaiting them. The thin, petulant wail of a baby broke through.

The next day the delegation from the Chicago Federation of Labor returned to find the cars empty. The Negro strangers, strikebreakers from Birmingham, Alabama—though penniless, hungry, homeless, and ragged in a strange land—had braved the 1901 winter in response to a plea from their white brothers. Later the general manager of the Latrobe Steel and Coupler Company announced that it had decided against using the Negro strikebreakers, and, to avoid violence, had sent them back South. But the committee from the Chicago Federation of Labor knew better.

The role of the Negro as a strikebreaker was not a new one, and it may be said that the unions were largely responsible for this condition. The Alabama Negroes brought up from Alabama in 1901 to break the strike of white workers at the Chicago plant of the Latrobe Steel and Coupler Company were typical. They knew little or nothing of labor unions, and the exclusion policy of the white unions prevented them from finding out. Ordinarily their education was attempted by means of violence and bloodshed rather than the persuasion so effectively employed by the delegation from the Chicago Federation of Labor.

The National Labor Union, meeting in Baltimore in 1866, seated several Negro delegates, but any positive position on the Negro in labor was avoided at this and successive conventions until the organization lapsed into ineffectuality in 1870. Many Negroes were aware of the advantages of labor unions, however, and continued to make efforts to form some sort of affiliation with white trade unionists.

Independent organization tempted the Negroes, too, when they became discouraged at the evasive or openly hostile policies of the unions dominated by whites. On December 6, 1869, the National Labor Convention of Colored Men met in Union League Hall, Washington, D. C. Assembled were one hundred and fifty-six delegates from all sections of the country. Isaac Myers, a ship's caulker, emerged as a leader, as did Lewis H. Douglass, a printer and a son of Frederick Douglass, who also took a prominent part in the proceedings.

From this conclave developed the Colored National Labor Union. Even its mild aims were regarded with hostile suspicion by some Negroes. One reader wrote in to the *National Era*, the union's magazine, to inquire whether the outfit was a disguise for communism, a colored affiliate of the Red Internationale intent upon plunging the country into anarchy and mob rule. There was a brief period of vigorous enrollment of Negro mechanics and factory hands in trade unions, and then the organization veered more and more toward politics. Frederick Douglass helped along this deviation from the National Labor Union's original principles, and maintained that it ought to align itself closely with the Republican party. On May 17, 1874, the *New National Era*, edited by Douglass, published an editorial on "The Folly, Tyranny, and Wickedness of Labor Unions," advancing the theory, very popular in certain quarters today, that labor unions, if given too much rein, would ruin the country. Labor unions were then at about their lowest ebb, both in membership and public esteem.

The Knights of Labor came along with a very forthright policy on the admission of Negroes. The Knights were not hypocritically advocating the inclusion of colored members in their ranks without any intention of supplementing theory with action, but they encountered numerous difficulties. Unluckily for the racial equality plank, the 1886 General Assembly convened in Richmond, Virginia. Frank J. Ferrell, a Negro delegate from New York, was selected by General Master Workman Terence V. Powderly to introduce him at the evening session. There were considerable stirrings and murmurings among Southern delegates at this, but these were nothing compared to the storm that broke loose when Ferrell reserved for himself a choice seat in one of the Richmond theaters. Upon the colored New Yorker's appearance in his box, most of the astounded and outraged patrons of the theater ". . . left the building, vowing vengeance upon the intruder who had so recklessly defied one of the rules of Richmond life."

The next day it was rumored that Ferrell intended to repeat his indiscretion, and an armed mob congregated near the theater prepared to die in their tracks rather than see the temple of the drama defiled a second time. Ferrell, at the advice of Powderly and other officials of the Knights of Labor, prudently remained in his hotel room. But the mob had had a taste of excitement, and did not intend to be thwarted so easily. Wrathful citizens descended upon the hotel which housed the K. of L. leaders and threatened them with manhandling if they did not require their colored delegates to watch their manners more closely. The newspapers took up the hue and cry, hinting that a coat of tar and feathers might look well on Powderly and that an ideal method of transportation for him would be a ride out of town on a fence rail.

Powderly did not change his mind on the racial question, but he felt it necessary to explain his attitude in the Richmond *Dispatch*. He later complained that the paper omitted those portions of his communication which they considered too damaging to their own position in the matter. The general master workman began his appeal to reason by reminding his readers of an address he had made two years previously, and recalled part of it:

The Negro is free; he is here and he is here to stay. He is a citizen and must learn to manage his own affairs. His labor and that of the white man will be thrown upon the market side by side, and no human eye can detect a difference between the article manufactured by the white mechanic and that manufactured by the black mechanic. Both claim an equal share of the protection afforded to American labor, and both mechanics must sink their differences or fall a prey to the slave labor now being imported into this country.

As if frightened at his own temerity, Powderly went on to give assurance that neither he nor Ferrell had been aware that the latter's conduct had violated any of Richmond's customs, for which both had the utmost respect. Colored delegates, Powderly went on, would not thrust themselves in where they were not wanted.

Intolerant aggressors are seldom appeased by such weasel words, as the world found out more than half a century later. The abuse of Powderly and the Knights of Labor continued unabated for quite a while, a great amount of it arriving by mail. A postal card to Powderly conveyed what the writer must have considered an unbearable insult:

As you are so much in sympathy with the Negro, will you please call over and fill our coachman's place until he gets well? Enquire on Church Hill.

Miss M———

The issue of "slave labor"—particularly Chinese—was a live one in that period. Labor leaders were incessantly charging that European and Oriental workers were being spirited illegally into the country daily by greedy industrialists seeking cheap and tractable wage hands. Sensational accounts of the smuggling of this animated merchandise filled the labor as well as the general press. In this instance, the incensed upholders of racial supremacy in Richmond ignored Powderly's attempt to divert them from their quarry—the black man.

How far the Knights of Labor drifted away from their expressed avowal of racial equality is indicated by an open letter from a Negro citizen of Chicago printed in the *Inter-Ocean* almost eight years later, in March 1894. The correspondent, taking umbrage at a solution to the problem of Negro labor reportedly proffered by James R. Sovereign, who had succeeded Powderly as master workman of the K. of L., addressed Sovereign:

I take exception to your proposition to deport the Negro back to Africa (as being the best way to solve the Negro question) as being contrary to all international law. There was a day when you preached the universal brotherhood of man. . . . Now, I will suggest an easy solution of the whole trouble—that is, for Mr. Sovereign to accept Negroes into the order in the South . . . but in case you attempt to force the Negro from the country to make it easy for the K. of L. to continue the inculcation of prejudice and inhumanity, you may run against a greater force than the one you bring to bear upon the Negro.

Three days later the Chicago Colored Women's Club, meeting at the Tourgée Club (named after Judge Albion W. Tourgée), pointed out that Negroes had been residents of this country for two hundred and fifty years, and were "as much American citizens as anybody." "If this country is too small for the Knights of Labor and the Negro," the club members advised, "then let the Knights leave."

Apparently not profiting by the errors of its predecessors, the American Railway Union in 1894 wrote into its constitution a clause limiting membership to "railway employees born of white parents," despite vigorous opposition by President Eugene V. Debs and more than a few delegates. Colored workers promptly formed the Anti-Strikers' Railroad Union. Later that year great numbers of Southern Negroes and newly arrived Polish immigrants were secured to break the Chicago stockyards strike.

In 1885, a year before the strife-torn assembly of the Knights of Labor in Richmond, a convention of colored citizens of Illinois had met in Springfield to consider the special problems of their race as well as the general concerns of humanity. Resolutions were passed favoring free trade and the independence of Ireland. Then, striking closer home, a delegate whom Fate, as in the case of the author of "My Country, 'Tis of Thee," tried to conceal by naming Smith, arose to invite contemplation of the prospects awaiting young Negroes fortunate enough to acquire a college education. Most of them had to be content, he maintained, with jobs as flunkies—often in gambling joints, saloons, houses of prostitution—or as the lowest grades of manual laborers. Smith said:

> Shut our young men out of the factories and throw them into brothels and clubrooms, and you dwarf their manhood and ruin their morals. It is as a plant transplanted, a rose turned into a thorn. You keep a man from rising from the position of a menial or a serf—keep him always in temptation and adverse circumstances. In short, you can't grow an angel in hell and you can't grow a good citizen by keeping him in the worst position in society. The interests of the colored people today are not with any political party but with the great laboring masses of the country. If we would only form an alliance with them, the door of every factory in the land would open as if touched by a magician's wand.

Long after the Civil War, colored persons for the most part were restricted to the field of domestic and personal service—as butler, coachman, maid, cook, housekeeper, valet, or janitor. Negroes occasionally conducted businesses, were employed as skilled artisans, and successfully pursued professions, but the greater number of the race gainfully employed were found in the occupations named above, in agricultural work, and at unskilled labor.

The tasks at which Negroes were employed were a reflection of the limited opportunities afforded members of the race earlier in the South and of the fierce competition they met in the North when they attempted to invade fields other than those to which they were attached by tradition. Few of those below the Mason and Dixon line who had mastered trades—and a surprisingly large number were skilled workmen—migrated until several decades after the Civil War.

Both the eagerness of Negroes to leave the South and their lack of acquaintance with the principles of trade unionism were often exploited by employers bothered by strikes and other dissension. The coal mines offered a good field for this tactic, for miners ordinarily lived in company houses, bought food and clothing from company stores, and were even buried in company coffins when they died. Hence, they were absolutely dependent upon the whims of the mining company, and any trouble with it automatically meant the almost immediate loss of shelter and food. Some miners, it is true, managed to extricate themselves from the company store and to live in other than company houses, but their financial dependence upon the mine was only slightly less. The mining sections of northern and southern Illinois had an early acquaintance with the Southern rural Negro in the role of strikebreaker. In March 1887 more than a hundred Southern Negroes arrived in Peoria to take the place of striking white miners. The Chicago *Evening Journal* observed:

> Outside a few of the more skilled and organized trades, if a body of workmen generate sufficient temerity to ask for less hours or an advance in wages, the Goliath in command had only to utter the magical word "Negroes" to drive them back into the ruts in fear and trembling for their positions.

At Spring Valley, Illinois, the "Goliaths" used a double play, as it were, on the native-born white coal miners. First, they were induced to come to the thriving "boom" town in the late eighties by absentee owners who also sold them property on the installment plan at fancy rates—townsite lots staked out shortly before on pasture land bought from farmers at low rates by the acre. When the native-born miners began to complain about poor conditions and a cut in pay, the owners, snugly remote from the scene, nonchalantly ordered the mines closed down. The miners were left to starve in leisure. When the company opened the mines again, it imported Italian, French, and Belgian immigrants who couldn't speak a word of English, and who thought the wages offered were quite handsome. The suffering of the Spring Valley miners attracted national attention, and the New York *World* sent a correspondent to investigate. He sent back heart-rending dispatches with such captions as "Dying to Escape Slavery—That's What the Coal Miners of Northern Illinois Are Doing," and "In Starvation's Grim Grip."

The correspondent visited the shack of Sylvester McDonnell, and found the family of fourteen—from grandparents to grandchildren—"in rags and tatters" with "pinched faces and hollow cheeks showing that the cupboard had often been empty."

"I fought for the Negroes," said the patriarch, a veteran of the Civil War, "and now I am fighting for myself and the folks. It's the principle of the thing I am starving for. I am an American citizen, and I claim the right to educate my children as Americans should be educated."

"The story of Spring Valley," wrote Henry D. Lloyd, a prominent humanitarian author of the day, "needs but a change of names and a few details to be the story of Braidwood, Illinois, where babies and men and women wither away to be transmuted into the dividends of a millionaire coal miner of Beacon Street, Boston. It needs but a few changes to be the story of Punxsutawney—where starving foreigners have eaten up all the dogs in the country to keep themselves loyally alive to dig coal again when their masters reopen the coal kennels."

The alien miners gradually faded into the texture of the community so that the few native Americans who had managed to remain in Spring Valley (most of them had been boycotted by the mining company) almost forgot that the foreigners had come to town as "scabs." The foreigners learned to speak broken English and hoped to make real Americans of their children. But it was hard to do on the wages paid by the coal company. In 1894 the Italians and the French and the Belgians decided they had more than they could stand. They struck.

The coal barons were ready this time too. Soon the town was filled with black men from the South and their women and children. They found the wages much better than those they had been able to make back home, and the conditions couldn't be any worse. The Italians, French, and Belgians—all beginning to think they were Americans—fumed silently for a while at this invasion. Then they went into action. Before the bewildered black men and their women and children knew what was happening to them, they were fleeing into the hills, hiding behind bushes—trying to hide anywhere from mustached men shouting an unintelligible gibberish and brandishing pick handles, knives, and pistols. The amazed and terrified newcomers from the South could distinguish one word, "Scab!" "Scab!"—over and over again, bitter and accusing. Most of them identified it with the crust that forms over a sore. Nobody knows exactly how many Negroes died before the tumult subsided, but as years went by colored folks, at least, referred to the incident as the "Spring Valley Massacre."

Again the eyes of the nation rolled with irritation or distress toward Spring Valley. Some Negroes—and of course antiunion newspapers and individuals—cried out at the injustice of native-born Americans—the Negroes imported as strikebreakers—being set upon and murdered by foreigners. On the other hand, the Italian consul in Chicago voiced a complaint against the treatment of Italian nationals which had forced them to seek such a drastic recourse in opposition to those strange-looking black men who were taking the bread and butter out of the mouths of their children.

In the fall of 1898 the Chicago-Virden Coal Company at Virden, Illinois, installed three hundred Alabama Negroes, and seventy-five armed guards to protect them, in the place of employees who had walked out in protest against the company's refusal to recognize the terms of an agreement between the Illinois Coal Operators' Association and the union. In the ensuing riot, ten striking miners and six guards were killed and about thirty persons injured.

The United Mine Workers of America, formed in 1890 by the joining of Knights of Labor elements with the Progressive Miners' Union, never tolerated the injection of the racial issue into strikes. They fought the imported Negroes as strikebreakers only, and never as Negroes. Furthermore, they freely admitted Negroes to membership, even in the South. Naturally, there were aberrations and even some locals upon which white chauvinists imposed their will, but they were the exception. Rural Negroes from the South continued to figure as strikebreakers as late as the general strike of 1922, but in the meantime many of their race had become loyal members and officials of the union.

The story of Andrew W. Springs, M.D., is that of a Southern Negro who became a prominent member of an Illinois mining community. He was born in 1869 at Charlotte, North Carolina, of an Indian father and a Negro mother. His mother had been a slave in the Presbyterian College for Girls, and endeared herself so to the students that they secretly taught her how to read and write. Instruction of slaves in these arts was forbidden by law.

At nineteen Andrew went to Durham, where he worked for an affable white woman who listened with interest to the story of how the lad's slave mother had triumphed over the barrier which prevented her from enjoying the fascinating-looking volumes at which she had often gazed curiously as she dusted them in the college library. Andrew confessed that he had an ambition to outdo his mother—he wanted to go to college. The white lady helped him, and in 1898 the young man found himself at Fisk University, the recipient of a scholarship.

He made a name for himself at Fisk—football and track star, head of his class, editor in chief of the Fisk *Herald*. A wearisome interlude teaching at a Negro school in Cairo, Illinois, and he had enough money saved to put himself through the National Medical School in Chicago. Returning to southern Illinois, he set up shop in Dumoir. In the course of time he became company doctor for the Madison Coal Company and also a scoutmaster and an honorary member of the Veterans of Foreign Wars. In 1908 he organized a first-aid class, something unknown in the vicinity before.

On October 27, 1914, however, came Dr. Springs's big opportunity to show what he could do. There had been an explosion and fire at the North Mine at Royalton, and fifty doctors had been summoned from the surrounding territory. When Dr. Springs arrived, he found more than two hundred men lying around in the washhouses, some dead, others overcome by fumes. Unpacking his pulmotor, the doctor set to work. He was the only physician thereabouts to own such an instrument, and the only one who knew how to use it. At the bottom of the smoke-filled shaft were fifty-two more miners. Down went Dr. Springs—the only doctor to descend into the pit. For the day's work he was awarded a Carnegie medal.

Throughout the depression of the thirties Dr. Springs maintained a soup-and-coffee kitchen where anybody could come and get a meal with no questions asked.

He couldn't quit yet, he said, when a stroke of paralysis overcame him in 1939. He struggled painfully and managed to keep going. "Old Man Paralysis slapped me on the right side of my smiling face," he laughed. "I ran and didn't turn my left side to him. Gee! You ought to have seen me! My right eye looked like a glass eye; my lips were warped and twisted till they looked like a question mark." He had to be up and about, though, for a lot of folks in that section wouldn't have anybody but old Doc Springs fooling with them. He hobbled around waiting on his patients till at last he seemed almost as good as new again.

For several years before he died in the early summer of 1944, Doc Springs used to run a mile before breakfast. He was very touchy about his physical condition, and would angrily deny that the mile trip was any more difficult for him than it had been twenty years before. The last few weeks, however, he had to give up and acknowledge that he couldn't make it. Nearly everybody in the neighborhood owed him a debt of gratitude and came to see him lying quiet in his casket—resting for the first time in many years. A lot of them followed him to the grave too. Not many of the old-timers could remember as big a funeral.

In the same year Doc Springs started his first-aid class in 1908, the coal miners were striking in Alabama. White and black struck together, for they were all union brothers—members of the United Mine Workers of America. Evicted from the company shacks, the miners set up a tent colony. The coal company proceeded to exploit the race issue and did it so successfully that a mob put the torch to the tent colony. A "citizens' committee" warned the union officials that a race riot would result unless the miners returned to work at once. Striking by blacks and whites together would not be permitted. All right, said the union officials, we'll send the Negroes away and make it a white man's strike. This offer of appeasement did not mollify the company and the citizens' committee, however, and after a few sanguinary skirmishes the strike was called off. One night, while the strike was still in effect, William Miller, a Negro union member who lived near Brighton, Alabama, awoke from an uneasy sleep and hurried to the window, obeying some alarming and irresistible impulse. Ghostly sheeted figures were stealing from the woods to surround his cabin. One of the figures carried a rope, and within a half-hour William Miller, who had been accused of dynamiting the home of a "scab," was swinging by the rope from a limb of a tree. The "whitecaps" were doing their bit for "law and order."

Also in the same year Doc Springs began to teach a group of people how to help victims of illness and injury, an incident farther North in Illinois proved that the Negro, no matter how long his stay in a place, might suddenly be forced to realize that circumstances could again make him a hunted and despised stranger.

On the night of August 14, 1908, Mrs. Mable Hallam, a white woman of Springfield, Illinois, wife of a streetcar conductor, reported that she had been dragged from her bed and raped by a Negro. George Richardson, a Negro who had been working near by, was charged with the crime and identified by Mrs. Hallam as her assailant. Richardson, born in the city and described as "a man above the ordinary intelligence," who talked "with great sincerity and earnestness," contradicted Mrs. Hallam's story. A mob, clamoring for the blood of Richardson as well as that of a Negro tramp and drug addict jailed shortly before for fatally wounding a white man, besieged the jail. When members of the mob realized that the prisoners had been spirited away, they vented their fury upon the restaurant and automobile of Harry Loper, white, who was believed to have assisted the authorities. The shop of Scott Burton, Negro barber, was demolished and the proprietor dragged by the neck through the streets, mutilated, and burned. The torch was applied to a block of Negro hovels, while more practical rioters seized the opportunity to loot a number of stores.

Shrieking at the head of the mob was Kate Howard, an amazon who had had more than casual acquaintance with the police. On the very night of the riot she was at liberty under $4,000 bond. When the zest for torture and murder seemed to die down a bit, Kate spurred on the rioters with taunts of "coward! coward," fortified by others unprintable. Kate had long been an advocate of direct action to cope with the Negro menace. She had made a trip through the South, and observed with admiration the patterns of segregation there tending to keep the Negro in his place. Why, in Springfield they wouldn't get off the sidewalk for you, and they'd even come and sit down by you in a restaurant! Women like Kate are usually eager to command respect from *somebody*, even if drastic measures are required. The excitement was too much for her to stand, however, and she committed suicide before she could be brought to trial for her part in the outbreak as well as her previous crimes. Her life had ended in a gratifying blaze of glory, anyhow, for during the bloody shambles she had been called the "Joan of Arc" of the riot.

Rioting continued throughout the next day and night. The police, it appeared, were both unable and unwilling to cope with the mob. A brigade of militia arrived, but was not immediately successful in quelling the disorder.

On the second day William Donegan, eighty-four, known as a friend of Abraham Lincoln, a substantial Negro citizen who had lived in Springfield for fifty years and owned half the block upon which his house stood, was jerked from a rocking chair in which he was peacefully dozing in his yard and hanged from a tree across the street from his home. Militiamen intervened and cut the aged man down, but he died the next day. Donegan's only offense seems to have been that for thirty years he had been married to a white woman—a circumstance which previously had not excited animosity. Donegan's daughter later said that the mobsters, appearing to be young hoodlums, had told the old gentleman that he "owned too much property for a nigger." On the night before, Eugene W. Chafin, Prohibition party candidate for President of the United States, had interrupted a stump speech to befriend an intended victim by pretending that he had a revolver in his pocket and allowing the fugitive to escape while he held the mob at bay.

The rioters, as they charged through the streets of the Negro section, cried, "Abraham Lincoln freed you; we'll show you where you belong!" In the feathering-out districts, where white and black residences might intermingle, the mobsters paused often to look at doorposts. Just as on St. Bartholomew's Eve a white cross marked a house to be spared from destruction, so a white handkerchief was nailed on the doorposts of houses where white people lived. The rioters hurried by these houses

When the tumult subsided, it was found that in addition to the two Negroes lynched and the four white men killed during the disorders, seventy-nine persons had been injured and several blocks of Negro homes razed by fire. The city of Springfield, under the State law holding the community responsible for destruction of property resulting from mob violence, was burdened with judgments totaling $39,000.

Hundreds of Negroes fled the city during and immediately after the riot. It was estimated that one hundred and fifty to two hundred had made their way to Chicago within two days. Some of these were given shelter by friends, while others taxed the facilities of hotels and lodging houses catering to Negro guests. Others boarded trains for other cities to make a fresh start. Two hundred refugees arrived in St. Louis, Missouri; twice that number had escaped to Alton and East St. Louis. Southern newspapers took advantage of the opportunity to invite the Negroes to return to the more congenial atmosphere of the South, but few heeded the summons. Senator Vardaman commented smugly: "Such sad experiences as Springfield is undergoing will doubtless cause the people of the North to look with more toleration upon the methods employed by the Southern people."

A grand-jury investigation completely exonerated Richardson when Mrs. Hallam confessed that her assailant had been a white man whose identity she refused to divulge. Ironically enough, the victims of assault, lynching, and arson were further penalized for their enforced participation in the riot.

The city discharged more than fifty employees who had the misfortune to be Negroes. It was acknowledged that their efficiency and fidelity were not questioned—many of them were among the most satisfactory of the municipal job holders, and some of them were veterans in the service. If Negroes continued to hold city posts, particularly on the police force, it was argued, a recurrence of the trouble might be expected at any time.

Though both mob victims were industrious, well-behaved, and respected property owners, apologists for the rioters chose to attribute the disorders to the presence of Negro criminal elements and the immunity granted them by vote-seeking politicians.

The Illinois *State Journal* of Springfield faintly deplored the disgraceful affair, but maintained that "conditions" alone were to blame. "Many citizens," the *State Journal* said, "could find no other remedy than that applied by the mob. It was not the fact of the whites' hatred toward the Negroes but of the Negroes' own misconduct, general inferiority, or unfitness for free institutions that were at fault."

The Chicago *Tribune,* under the caption "Dens of Sin Wiped Out," expressed its conviction that "one good thing" had resulted from the burning of the Negro district, and went on:

> The houses of this black belt were hovels. Whites and blacks lived together. Children ran through the streets of this miserable settlement who knew not their parents. Their hair indicated one race and their fair skin the other. The worst grades of whisky and gin were served in the barrooms. Drugstores thrived on the sale of cocaine and other drugs. Along Cocaine Alley huts of deepest squalor were the hiding places of the drug fiends. Sandwiched in between these dens were white resorts where the lowest forms of depravity existed.

Pursuing the theory that political conditions precipitated the riot, the *Tribune* concluded:

> It was the knowledge of this political power and their long immunity which made the Negro unbearable in Springfield. It was this that drove the mob to destroy the entire district. The reign of the Negro has ended.

As the European powers squared off after the shot at Sarajevo, the demand for Negro labor in the North became acute. In this period occurred an incident well illustrating the Biblical fable of the mote and the beam. Less than two years before East St. Louis, Illinois, was to be visited by a great catastrophe involving a racial clash, the *Journal* of that city discoursed (October 19, 1915) on the hanging of Joe DeBarry, a Negro, at Murphysboro. The ceremony had been made a gala occasion, with more than a thousand witnesses created temporary "deputies." Upon hearing of the circumstances, Governor Dunne wired Sheriff James A. White that the affair was a "scandal and disgrace to the state" and requested that Elston Scott, another Negro scheduled for hanging the following Friday, be dispatched with "decorum, decency, and privacy." On November 2 the *Journal* chided:

Murphysboro seems to gloat over the brutal Negro hanging pulled off a few weeks ago. The movies in that place were showing the uncivilized scene and the exhibitions were crowded. Foreign-missionary activities ought to be somewhat diverted to Murphysboro.

East St. Louis has been called a "satellite" city, most of its prominent businessmen and industrialists preferring to make their home in St. Louis, Missouri, across the Mississippi River. Politicians and police authorities have been charged with winking at prostitution, gambling, and other lawlessness, since these activities prove a profitable source of revenue. "Black Valley," a section of dilapidated shacks in close proximity to the city hall, became one of the most renowned vice districts in the world. The industrialists who had invited Negro laborers to the city were inclined to be indifferent toward their housing, social, moral, and educational problems.

It has been estimated that between 10,000 and 12,000 colored workers from the South flocked to East St. Louis and its neighboring St. Clair County industrial communities from the autumn of 1916 to the spring of 1917. Some of these, labor leaders asserted, were imported as strikebreakers.

On May 25, 1917, the *Journal* commented editorially on the "Negro Influx Problem" and pointed out that "thousands have come into East St. Louis . . . and they are still coming." While East St. Louis was agitated at the invasion, Southern planters were complaining that fields which might supply food and clothing for soldiers and civilians were lying fallow because most of the able-bodied laborers had fled North. The *Journal* concluded:

> But they are here in East St. Louis, and the problem must be met in a humane and patriotic spirit. Settlements and abodes should be provided for them. In order to avoid friction, our officials, civic and business organizations should take hold of the matter, and, in co-operation with colored church pastors and other Negro leaders, work out a plan that will be satisfactory to all, and maintain good relations.

The "humane and patriotic spirit" was destined to be manifested in peculiar ways. Mayor Mollman exerted pressure on railroad agents and exacted a promise that they would no longer encourage or, indeed, permit the importation of Negroes. Representatives of organized labor presented their protests. Nearby Belleville warned "strange Negroes" that they must not stop in that city, and Mayor Duvall assigned patrolmen to the railroad stations with instructions to chase away all "undesirables."

Hundreds of "labor sympathizers," including sixty representatives of the Central Body of Trade and Labor Unionists, met in the East St. Louis city hall auditorium to protest the continued employment of Southern Negroes by industrial plants.

The unionists suggested that the industrial plants be warned that if they persisted in bringing Southern Negroes into the city police and fire protection would be denied them. The Aluminum Ore Company had imported hundreds of Negroes to break a strike by white workers.

The familiar devices employed to harry "undesirables" were used by East St. Louis authorities. "Vagrancy" and "loitering" charges, arrests for "suspicious conduct" might be anticipated by any Negro—and particularly one new in town—regardless of his behavior or financial status. Minor "incidents" between the two races multiplied. One was precipitated by the apprehension of William Engram, a Negro, by Patrolman Thomas Gebhardt, who repaired with his prisoner to Thomas Boston's saloon, his intention being, he said later, to call for additional help to conduct Engram to police headquarters, there to book him for "spitting on the sidewalk." Gebhardt had been followed by several Negroes who were incensed at the plain evidence of discrimination, since spitting on the sidewalk certainly was not uncommon, nor were any others save Negroes jailed for it. Boston, described as "a well-known politician," ordered the crowd around his door to disperse, and when it did not comply as quickly as he wished, he shot and critically wounded George Lee, Negro.

On May 28 a rumor that a white man had been slain by a Negro was circulated widely, and a white mob made the rounds to assault a number of Negroes, beating some of them severely.

These events were climaxed on the night of July 1, when one or two automobiles—witnesses do not agree as to the number—careened wildly through streets inhabited by Negroes, the occupants peppering dwellings with bullets. Surmising that the

Negroes might be organizing for retaliation, policemen drove to the neighborhood—ostensibly for the purpose of preserving order. At any rate, the result was that a group of Negroes fired on the automobile, killing one policeman and fatally wounding another.

Throughout the next two days the city was ruled by a mob which killed, burned, and pillaged at will. Militiamen summoned to quell the disturbance fraternized with the rioters, and even assisted them. White women and children participated in acts of almost incredible cruelty. Colonel Tripp, commanding the five companies of Illinois National Guards sent to the scene, secluded himself in the city hall. When asked why he was not active in command of his men, he is said to have retorted: "The President never goes out of *his* office."

By Independence Day the disorders had abated, after fearful carnage and destruction of property totaling almost $400,000. The exact number of dead will never be known. Estimates range from fifty to several hundred.

Oscar Leonard, superintendent of the Jewish Educational and Charitable Association of St. Louis, wrote in *Survey*:

> . . . I went in the company of a young Russian Jew, a sculptor who had witnessed and bears the marks of more than one anti-Jewish riot in his native land. He told me when he viewed the blocks of burned houses that the Russian "Black Hundreds" could take lessons in pogrom making from the whites of East St. Louis. The Russians, at least, he said, gave the Jews a chance to run while they were trying to murder them. The whites in East St. Louis fired the homes of black folk and either did not allow them to leave the burning houses or shot them the moment they dared attempt to escape the flames.

Leonard interviewed observers who testified that a great number of Negroes were burned alive in their homes and consequently were not counted among the dead. Some expressed their conviction that a hundred or more perished in the flames consuming a deserted theater where they had sought sanctuary from the mob's fury. Leonard went on:

> Thrifty black folk, who were doing their bit [to win the World War] by raising vegetables, were murdered. I saw ruins of their homes, into

which had gone the labor and savings of years. The little thrift gardens had escaped the flames, and the orderly rows where seeds had been planted gave the plots the appearance of miniature graveyards.

More than six thousand refugees fled from the State of Abraham Lincoln across the river to Missouri, a former Slave State. John Schmoll, director of public welfare in St. Louis, complained that the East St. Louis authorities were disposing of their problem by sending their homeless Negroes across to the St. Louis municipal lodging house. All day long trucks chugged up to the lodging house. Some of the refugees had brought household goods. Some of them were sick or wounded. Soon the four-story building was jammed to the roof. The restless crowds milled about in the street, and the trucks began depositing their loads upon the city hall lawn across the way.

A poll conducted among the four thousand temporarily quartered in the lodging house revealed that less than 15 per cent were willing to return to the South, though governmental and private agencies in more than a dozen cities—including Atlanta, New Orleans, Louisville, and Mobile—had invited the wayfarers back home to protection and jobs.

As on other occasions, the absence of the Negro workers at once made itself felt. The East St. Louis manager of the Swift Packing Company reported that three hundred of the seven hundred Negroes normally working in the plant had left their jobs and that it might be necessary to close down. The general manager of the Armour Company added:

> We have lost more than one hundred Negroes, most of them hard-working men who were as glad to get the good wages as we were to pay them. Continued terrorizing of Negro laborers will drive many more of them away. We are working as fast as we can on contracts for the United States Army and Navy, and if a considerable portion of our force is driven out of the city it will interfere with the most important of all war munitions—the food.

The manager of the Morris plant stressed the fact that the one hundred and fifty men who had left his employ were not come-lately "ficaters," but solid citizens. "The 'ficaters' don't mind a little thing like a riot," he said. "But these men with families and homes do not feel like taking chances of being assaulted on their way to and from work."

The East St. Louis Chamber of Commerce met behind closed doors to debate this problem. It was pretty generally agreed that some effort ought to be made to bring the Negroes back. But what about protecting and housing them? That was the rub.

The national agitation about the East St. Louis riots culminated in a Congressional investigation. So revolting were the details of the mob's fiendish cruelties and the indifference and even collaboration of those in authority, that Representative Cooper of Wisconsin, a member of the committee, cried out, "Indians could do no worse!" Representative Baker of California added, "What chance has a poor, innocent Negro in a place like this?"

The Congressional committee was particularly touched by the story of Minneola McGee, a Negro girl who, far from the scene of the rioting, had had her arm shot off near the shoulder, two policemen and three soldiers having used her for a living target.

"I wuz in a outhouse in de garden," she told the committee. (The stenographer who recorded her testimony appears to have been affected by the dialect style of Octavus Roy Cohen.) "I hea'd de shootin' and started fo' de house. When I got putty nigh de house a soljer histed his gun and pinted it right at me and shot my arm off when I hadn't done nothin'. When he shot me I fell on de ground and didn't know nothin'."

The Congressional committee severely criticized the municipal and military authorities for their conduct, but commended Assistant Attorney General Middlekauf, in charge of the subsequent prosecutions, for showing "neither fear nor favor." Eleven Negroes and eight white men were sentenced to the State penitentiary. Two additional white men were given prison terms, fourteen received jail sentences. The night chief of police and three policemen were among twenty-seven men fined when they pleaded guilty to a charge of rioting.

Dr. LeRoy A. Bundy was indicted with fourteen other Negroes for the murder of the policeman slain on the night of July 1. On testimony of white witnesses, who declared that they had seen armed Negroes in the vicinity of his home on the night in question, Dr. Bundy was sentenced to life in prison. In 1920, however, the Illinois Supreme Court reversed the decision.

On May 30, two months before the East St. Louis riot, the Chicago *Tribune* had commented on the growing racial tension and recurring "incidents" in East St. Louis and elsewhere:

> They say down South that "niggers are all right in their place," but where is that place? South? At Memphis, Tennessee, a Negro was recently burned alive. North? At East St. Louis, Illinois, Negroes are mobbed, beaten, and run out of town. We taunt the South with race prejudice when it burns a "bad nigger," but just see how we Northerners detest even "good niggers." The real race prejudice is ours. Our very philanthropists betray it. They say to a black man, "God bless you, good-by," whereas the South says, "—— you, come here!" Or put it this way: The Northerner is a great friend of the Negro, but not of a Negro; the Southerner is a great friend of a Negro, but not of the Negro.

And Rough Rider ex-President "Teddy" Roosevelt took notice of East St. Louis too. Not many years before he had outraged die-hard Southerners by inviting Booker T. Washington to dinner at the White House. Some anonymous and venomous bard composed a bit of doggerel which was repeated for a long time by little children, usually in all innocence:

The Statue of Liberty hung her head;
Columbia dropped in a swoon,
The American eagle drooped and died,
When Teddy dined with the coon.

Perhaps Teddy was thinking of this jingle as well as the valor of the Negro troops who fought under him in Cuba as he said in his Fourth of July speech at Forest Hills, Long Island:

> There has just occurred in a Northern city a most lamentable tragedy. We who live elsewhere will do well not to feel self-righteous about it, for it was produced by causes which might at any time produce just such results in any of the communities in which we individually dwell. There have been race riots with dreadful accompaniments of wholesale murder and arson. The first necessity is that the

government should use its strength to stop and to punish the violators, and once more to install the ordinary instrumentalities of law and order, but this is not enough. The causes, social and industrial, should be fearlessly and thoroughly investigated, so that the primitive remedy may be found, and the investigation should blink no fact, however ugly. I reverently believe in facing truths by officially acting on the knowledge thus gained, so that when order has been restored, we can establish a permanent working system of justice.

Fine words, these! But the Negro was not unaccustomed to hearing fine words.

CHAPTER XI

The Exodus Train

TWO LANKY NEGRO YOUTHS, their overalls powdered with the red dust of a Georgia road, paused at a street corner to listen to their friends and neighbors discussing Kaiser Bill, the Battle of the Marne, the boll weevil, "doodlum," and other matters interesting to a Saturday-afternoon street-corner crowd in a small town of the Georgia farming country.

"Why'n't y'all get outa this whole mess?" one of the youths inquired. "Go North where you can make big money and live like a man besides."

"How you gonna go?" one of the elder sharecroppers inquired mockingly. "Ride shank's mare?"

"Don't have to. Don't even have to ride a freight. A Chicago labor agent's gonna be in town today. Carry all the hands he can get up there free and on the cushions. Stockyards in Chicago's crying for fifty thousand men to take the place of them foreigners they used to hire. Listen to this, what I got out of a Chicago paper for colored folks called the *Defender*."

He fished a creased newspaper clipping from his pocket and began to read:

> *"Some are coming on the passenger,*
> *Some are coming on the freight,*
> *Others will be found walking,*
> *For none will have time to wait."*

A deputy pushed through the crowd and laid his hand on the boy's shoulder.

"Reckon you'd better come with me, son," he said. "The sheriff wants to see you."

"What for? Ain't done nothing but read a little old poem."

"That's just it! Got orders to arrest all you colored boys I catch reading poetry out of that Chicago *Defender*. Been a lot of that stuff read and it's raising hell all over the South. Hands leaving the plow right in the field and running away from their honest debts to traipse North. You'll likely be charged with 'inciting to riot in the city, county, and throughout the State of Georgia.' Yes sir, son, looks like you're bound for the prison farm."

The boll weevil, an insect migrant from Mexico, invaded Texas in 1892. Armed with its sharp proboscis for puncturing tender young cotton bolls, it ranged northward and eastward at a speed reaching one hundred and sixty miles annually, leaving behind it thousands of wilted and devastated cotton fields. In 1915 and 1916 the boll weevil was particularly destructive, while unprecedented storms and floods added to the desolation of Southern agriculture. The credit system enslaved the lord of the porticoed mansion as inexorably as it did the sharecropper in his ramshackle cabin. The sharecropper or field hand, living on a hand-to-mouth basis and depending on the credit which the landlord was no longer able or willing to give, could not afford to wait for better times. He had to do something and do it fast. Inevitably, the paralysis spread to the cities.

Consequently, World War I, which cut off the supply of European immigrant labor, was at first considered an indirect blessing by impoverished planters who could no longer command credit with which to operate. Northern factories needed laborers, and the Southern Negroes needed work.

The Nashville *Banner* expressed the opinion that the migration might serve . . . "to relieve the South of the entire burden and all the brunt of the race problem, and make room for and create greater inducements for white immigration that the South so much needs." The Vicksburg *Herald* concurred, and added: "Then, too, a more equitable distribution of the sons of Ham will teach the Caucasians of the Northern states that wherever there is a

Negro infusion, there will be a race problem—a white man's burden—which they are destined to share."

But Southerners who had professed to see in the Negro a liability rather than an asset to the economy of the region, took alarm as the migration assumed tidal proportions. This movement was more or less leaderless, and spontaneous; there was no "Moses" comparable to "Pap" Singleton directing it. Nevertheless, as in Singleton's time, it looked as though nobody would be left to till the fields and do the hard work. The Birmingham *Age-Herald* pointed out:

> It is not the riffraff of the race, the worthless Negroes, who are leaving in such large numbers. There are, to be sure, many poor Negroes among them who have little more than the clothes on their backs, but others have property and good positions which they are sacrificing in order to get away at the first opportunity. The entire Negro population of the South seems to be deeply affected. The fact that many Negroes who went North without sufficient funds and without clothing to keep them warm have suffered severely and have died in large numbers has not checked the tide leaving the South. It was expected that the Negroes would come back sorry that they ever left, but comparatively few have returned.

The fact that Southern planters and manufacturers sought to hamper the activities of labor agents sent South to recruit workers served only to convince the skeptical that there must be something to the reports of high wages and better living conditions. Clubs of migrants secured special rates from the railroads, or traveled free on passes supplied by agents. The Illinois Central Railroad alone is credited with having transported tens of thousands of colored plantation hands to Illinois, principally to Chicago. Chicago was known to all. It was the big town by the lake from which the mail-order catalogues came, and thus vaguely associated in the minds of hinterland folks with everything desirable but hitherto unattainable.

Securely established Negro citizens were perturbed by the avalanche of their rustic brethren whose manners and personal appearance were not always so prepossessing as they might be. Feet used to a plowed field found it hard to steady themselves on a lurching streetcar, so that migrants stepped on toes and jostled their fellow passengers. A great many of the new arrivals found employment at the stockyards and boarded public conveyances without changing from their malodorous work clothes. Others were still glowering with resentment over their treatment down South, and were inclined to vouchsafe their new freedom a bit too aggressively—a little beyond the limits of common courtesy. Unfortunately, the whites of the New Canaan were not without their prejudices, for the virus of racial hate has never been confined below Mason and Dixon's line. The awkwardness of the migrant—his unfamiliarity with city mores—was given all sorts of unfavorable interpretations. Some behavior traits common to certain individuals of all races often were indicated as manifestations peculiar to or inherent in the Negro character. For example, hostile white Chicagoans frequently complained that Negro factory hands always boarded elevated trains by way of the window. Impartial observers noted that fully as many whites as Negroes used this means of entrance when doors were congested.

The migrants kept coming to Chicago. The Chicago *Defender* received thousands of letters out of the Deep South, as did the Chicago Urban League, the organization to which the paper usually referred prospective migrants inquiring about employment.

The legend of the Great Northern Drive, as the reported mass movement was popularly called, spread rapidly months before the appointed date, May 15, 1917. The Birmingham staff correspondent noted on March 10:

The Great Northern Drive spoken of by the Chicago *Defender* is taking place long before the time set by the paper. They are leaving here by the thousands. The Birmingham *Age-Herald* is trying to make light of so many leaving but they seem to have the *Defender* tonic in their system and are heading North.

A month earlier a Savannah correspondent had said:

The word has been passed along from father to son, from mother to daughter, brother to brother and sister to sister, prepare for the day is coming. This spring a general movement will be started northward by millions of members of the Race from all over the South. It is expected before that time, however, that thousands will have left despite the fact that many educated men of the Race who have hid behind the cloak of schoolteachers and ministers of the gospel, aided by the publicity to their acts given them by the white press, have tried to scare them with the cold-weather gag. Not only this but some of the more trifling kind took advantage of free transportation given by railroads and other industries, went North without desiring to work, and found out that there was no white man in that section of the country who would give him money to tattle on Jim or John, has come back with some excuse. These fellows are "good niggers" and find their names in print the day following their arrival back home.

Letters requesting information about the Great Northern Drive flooded the *Defender* office for months. Anxiety and desperation pervaded most of them. One from New Orleans read:

I reads your paper and I am asking about the drive of May the 15. We want more understanding about it for there is a great many of us that wants to come and the depot agent never gives us any satisfaction when we ask for they don't want us to leave. Please put in your paper Saturday, just what time the train will be here, and the fare so we can be there on time. Many women are wanting to come. They are hard-working women, the white folks tell us we have to have plenty of money to come north, if this is right let us know, also let us know where the train is going to stop.

A New Orleans woman wrote:

Please sir, will you kindly tell me what is meant by the Great Northern Drive to take place May 15, on Tuesday. It is a rumor all over town to be ready for the 15th of May to go in the drive. The paper said the first drive was to be the 10th of February. My husband is in the North already preparing for the family but hearing that the excursion will be $6.00 from here North and having a large family I could profit by it if it is true. Do please write at once and tell me of this excursion to leave the South. Nearly the whole of the South is ready for the drive. Please write at once. We are sick to get out of the South.

The exodus was helped along by such poems as William Crosse's "The Land of Hope," which appeared in the Chicago *Defender*.

I've watched the trains as they disappeared
Behind the clouds of smoke,
Carrying the crowds of working men
To the land of hope,
Working hard on southern soil,
Someone softly spoke;
"Toil and toil and toil and toil,
And yet I'm always broke."

On the farms I've labored hard,
And never missed a day;
With wife and children by my side
We journeyed on our way.
But now the year is passed and gone,
And every penny spent,
And all my little food supplies
Were taken 'way for rent.

Yes, we are going to the north!
I don't care to what state,
Just so I cross the Dixon Line,
From this southern land of hate,
Lynched and burned and shot and hung,
And not a word is said.
No law whatever to protect—
It's just a "nigger" dead.
Go on, dear brother; you'll ne'er regret;
Just trust in God; pray for the best,
And at the end you're sure to find
"Happiness will be thine."

"Farewell—We're Good and Gone," "Bound for the Promised Land," and "Bound to the Land of Hope" were slogans often chalked on the sides of special trains carrying "exodusters." In many instances local authorities tried to divert or halt the emigrants. The *Defender,* after reporting the addition in Memphis of two eighty-foot steel coaches to the Chicago train in order to accommodate "exodusters," printed the text of a telegram just dispatched:

THIS IS TO NOTIFY BRAVE CHIEF OF POLICE PERRY THAT THE CHICAGO DEFENDER HAS MORE THAN 10,000 SUBSCRIBERS IN THE CITY OF MEMPHIS WHO GET THEIR PAPERS DIRECT THROUGH THE UNITED STATES MAIL, AND TO ACCOMPLISH HIS PURPOSE OF PREVENTING RACE MEN AND WOMEN FROM READING THE DEFENDER, WE WOULD SUGGEST THAT HE HAVE HIS ENTIRE POLICE FORCE ARREST EVERY MAIL CARRIER LEAVING THE MEMPHIS POST OFFICE ON THE MORNING OF JUNE 1, 1917.

Even those labor agents who had succeeded in getting their charges aboard an exodus train sometimes encountered the opposition of Southern industrial and agricultural interests as expressed through the law-enforcing agencies. The following letter from Brookhaven, Mississippi, indicates that such expedients were but puny obstacles to the mighty torrent of the Great Northern Drive. The will to quit the South was irresistible.

Following a continual exodus of members of the Race from this section of the country by labor agents, the police, spurred by the continual wail from the lumber mills of their losing all the help, arrested a white man by the name of Kelly on the arrival of a North-bound train. At the time of his arrest Kelly was in charge of two carloads of laborers on their way to Bloomington, Illinois. After the arrest of Kelly the police made the trainmen switch the two cars on a side-track and there the occupants spent the night. An account of the men in the coaches shows there were 125 in all. The word having passed around, some 100 more crowded the station seeking to go North. The police used more brutal force to disperse them. The sawmills, railroads, and other concerns are badly in need of laborers. Every member of the Race that can leave for the North has gone. One section gang left their tools on the spot, not stopping to get their pay. The treatment of the Race in general, coupled with the open way some of the women members of the Race live with white men and with no thought of marriage, the seducing of the daughter, the Jim Crowing and other cases including lynching, has set the members of the Race to a pitch of unrest, and nothing will be left undone until the Southern sections of the country have been cleared of every soul with a bit of black blood in their veins will remain in the South unless the whites put the Negro Race back on their statute book as a man with all the equality accorded to the law and constitution of the United States.

This letter came from Rome, Georgia:

I've just read your ad in the *Defender* on getting employment. So I will now ask you to do the best for me. Now Mr. —— I am not a tramp by any means I am high class churchman and businessman. I am the Daddy of the Transfer Business in this city, and carried it for ten years. Seven years ago I sold out to a white concern. I prefer a job in a Retail Furniture store if I can be placed, I'll now name a few things that I can do. Viz. I can reparing and Finish furniture I am an expert packer and Crater of furniture I pack China cut glass and silver war. I can enamel grain and paint furniture, and repair violins guitar and mandolins, and I am a first class Umbrella-man. I can do anything that can be done to a Umbrella and parasol. I can manage a Transfer business. I know all about shipping H. H. Goods & Furniture, and can make out bills of Lading and Write Tags for the same.

If you can place me in any one of these trades it will be O. K.

The desire for better educational facilities, either for themselves or for their children, actuated the writers of many letters. One from West Palm Beach, Florida, read:

While reading the *Defender* I saw where you needed laborers in Chicago. I have children and I lost my wife a few years ago. I would like to properly educate them. I am a barber by trade, and have been barbering for twenty years. I have saved enough for our fare. If I could make more money in Chicago, I will come there where they can get a good education. I am a church man and don't drink whisky.

A resident of the same city wrote:

I saw your advertisement in the *Defender* for laborers. I am a young man and want to finish school. I want to look out for me a job working mornings or evenings. I would like to get a job in a private family so I could continue taking piano lessons. I can do everything around the house, but drive and can learn that quick. Send me the name of the best high school in Chicago. How is the Wendell Phillips College. I have finished grammar school. I can not come before the middle of June.

This letter came from Alexandria, Louisiana:

I am planning on leaving this place about May 11, for Chicago and wants to know everything about the town. My job for the past eight years was with the Armour Packing Co., of this place. I know all about the office and what goes on in a packing company. I am doing the smoking in this company now. I am thirty-six years old and have a wife and two children. I have been here all my life and would like to go somewhere I could educate my children so they could be of service to themselves when they gets older, and I can't do it here. I will pay you for your trouble if you can get me a job with any of the big packing companies there, if not I will accept any job you can get.

Professional and business men often followed or accompanied their departing clients. Many preachers led their entire flocks North and established their churches anew, usually in vacant storerooms. A *Defender* reporter interviewed Reverend R. H. Harmon, who had arrived with his wife and twenty-eight members of his congregation in a carload of "exodusters" from Harrisburg, Mississippi, and other Southern points. Reverend Harmon said:

I am working at my trade. I have saved enough to bring my wife and four children and some of my congregation. We are here for keeps. They say that we are fools to leave the warm country, and how our people are dying in the East. Well, I for one am glad that they had the privilege of dying a natural death there. That is much better than the rope and torch. I will take my chance with the Northern winter.

Most of the preachers toiled each weekday at some other job, putting aside their work clothes to occupy the pulpit on Sundays or for "prayer meetings" and other occasions, such as protracted "revival" services held nightly.

A great number of less daring preachers nevertheless were perturbed at the course of events. One of these wrote from Newborn, Alabama:

We desire to know if you are in a position to put us in touch with a reliable firm or private family that desires to employ two young women; one is a schoolteacher in the public schools of this country and the other is a high school pupil. The teacher has a mother and sisters to care for and she is forced to seek employment, because wages are so low. The high school pupil is able to work in a private family. Wages are terrible here a grown man is forced to work for 50 cents a day. Sometimes he may earn 75 cents for all kinds of work. Here a man is only able to get a peck of meal and from three to four pounds of bacon a week, and he is treated as a slave. As leaders we are powerless for we dare not to resent such or even show disapproval. Only a few days ago over a 1,000 men and women left here for the North and the West. The white man says that we all can't go but he doesn't raise our pay. As a minister of the Methodist Episcopal Church I am on the verge of starvation simply because of the above conditions. I shall be glad to know if I could be of any real service to you as director of your society. Thanking you in advance for an early reply, and for any suggestions that you may have and be able to do for us.

From Greenville, Mississippi, came this letter:

Please inform me as to whether there is employment for colored insurance agents by company as industrial writers, sick and accident and death in a company that handles colored agents, in Chicago or suburban towns. Please see whether the supt. of a company could use a live reliable agent. I am planning on moving to Illinois. This is confidential. I have been working for 15 years as agent in an insurance company.

There were similar appeals from barbers, automobile mechanics, schoolteachers, and others who had been left stranded by the exodus.

The *Defender* maintained its role as the friend and adviser of the "exodusters" after they had settled in the city. However, the columnist "Wise Old Owl" early in March 1917 saw fit to add a word or two of advice. After discussing desirable objects and outlining the civil rights to be demanded in the North, "Wise Old Owl" concluded:

But it must be remembered that these rights are not to be abused and the rules governing them are the same for white and members of the Race alike. Be clean, ladies and gentlemen; water is cheap and deportment should be at a discount; avoid loud talking, and boisterous laughter on streetcars and in public places; keep away from the buffet flats like you duck a smallpox sign; help starve out the gypsy fortuneteller—they are conducting an illegal practice and there is a gang of them every day in the police courts for thieving; and don't show your ignorance by entrusting your money with anybody without a proper receipt for same, and then only with responsible people. In thinking all this over and while praising the Lord for your deliverance from the bloody zone in the South where the lynch-billies are supreme, remember and deal only with your own race and shop where A MEMBER OF THE RACE IS EMPLOYED. If you do these things you will be doing yourself and your people an inestimable good and at the same time you will be pleasing the WISE OLD OWL as he deserves for the worrying he is doing about your welfare.

The *Defender* did not relax its vigilance. An item published a few weeks later struck a grim note:

The Chicago *Defender* wishes to impress firmly upon the minds of the newcomers to carry an identification card in their pockets all the time. If you are a newcomer and your family are still in the South, carry their name and address and your nearest relative's name on you at all times. In case of accident we may be able to notify them. Twenty deaths and accidents occurred last month and the bodies of these persons are still at the County Morgue, unidentified.

In May the paper found it necessary to repeat some of the advice offered by "Wise Old Owl."

Laboring men who have been placed at shops and factories are urged to appear on the streetcars and in public places in clean decent clothes. They can leave their working clothes where they work, and put on better ones when they leave. In the North a man is usually judged by the clothes he wears, how clean they are, and they have cars and elevated roads to keep themselves clean going to and from work. It is different here in the North. In the South they don't care how they dress; here they make it a practice to look as well in the week as they do on Sunday. We have seen a number of Southern women wearing boudoir caps. They don't seem to know when to wear them. Don't wear them on the street and on the cars. They are to be worn in the house with a kimono. . . . Also wear your kimonos in the house.

The *Defender* warned against "scheming preachers and labor agents getting rich off newcomers," the latter "charging them a dollar a month for the entire year." That fee, the paper said, was "outrageous," and asserted that "half of those sent do not know anything about the work or what they are going for, and consequently there is a breach between labor and the employer, who is dissatisfied with his new laborers and gets a grudge against all members of the Race." The *Defender* also condemned "scheming preachers through this section of the country and the East, who for fifty cents and a dollar find one a job. You go to the place and they want no labor, but your money is gone." Censure was directed at twenty men who had declined "to leave the 'bright lights' of the city and 'State Street' " to accept out-of-town jobs procured for them by the Urban League. Though it stoutly championed the cause of "the hard-working man, the steady fellow with a family, who has come North to be able to associate with the whites on an equal basis," the paper was not inclined to coddle idlers. In one issue it complained:

> With conditions more promising than at any time in the history of the city, a *Defender* reporter found many loafers hanging around the poolrooms near Thirty-first and Thirty-fifth on State Street. When asked if they wanted work, they shook their heads in the negative. The bright lights are attracting them strongly. They care not how they live or where they stay. It is only a question of time before these people, poorly clad, without proper food, will succumb to the white plague. In addition to the foregoing there is another class that depends on gambling for a living, and they imbibe too freely of whisky. The police are gradually cleaning up this sort, and the judges are getting severe. This class we do not want here, and the better element of the city will do all they can to see that those who do not behave themselves will be handled by the proper authorities.

Though the *Defender* urged courtesy and respect for the rights of others, it did not advocate servility. Workingmen were admonished:

> Quit calling the foreman "boss." Leave that word dropped in the Ohio River. Also captain, general, and major. We call people up here Mister This and Mister That. When your pay day comes, take it home. Depend on your work to keep you in a job and not the dollar or two you have been used to slipping the foreman. Cut that out. If you are working for $18 keep it.
>
> Your employer pays the foreman much more than you, and if he has got to graft let him go to the employer. If you can't stay because you don't pay, quit and go somewhere else, or go in person to your employer and complain.

When you get among white workmen, treat them as you want them to treat you—AS A MAN—not as his inferior. Keep your hand off your hat when you pass men in and around the shop or plant. There is no law that requires you to tip your hat to a man because he is white.

The South sought to restrain the "exodusters" first by blandishments and minor concessions, and then, if necessary, by force. The perpetual debt under which most Southern Negroes (particularly those in the rural sections) struggled was a convenient weapon, as were unpaid fines for minor offenses. Moving to the North, perforce, was construed as evasion of such obligations and consequently a criminal offense. Even in the North, the refugees were not always safe, for Dixie employers and planters honing for the services of fleeing bondsmen were quick to take advantage of the extradition laws. The *Defender* reported a typical case:

Southern kidnapers made a bold and successful raid on Chicago citizenship Saturday when in broad daylight a sheriff from Mississippi went to the railroad yards at Eighteenth Street and with the help of Chicago police "captured" a man named James Halley, and in less than two hours had this man handcuffed and on a train bound for Holly Springs, Mississippi, to stand trial for selling a pint of whisky, made a penitentiary offense for the purpose of establishing a new form of slavery in the South and setting forth a complicated condition of affairs in the state which the Race has started to fight in order to protect its own citizens from illegal kidnaping.

Attorney Ferdinand L. Barnett interested himself in these kidnapings, ordinarily effected with the assistance of Chicago police. Another "exoduster" was saved from extradition on the charge of having "insulted a white woman in Memphis" when his wife summoned Barnett in time for the attorney to procure a writ of *habeas corpus*. The Southern officers prudently refrained from pressing their charges in court, and departed without their intended victim. One hard-working migrant was astonished when a detective from Atlanta approached him and informed him that he was wanted back home for "spitting on the sidewalk."

The *Defender* ran this notice:

ATTENTION NEWCOMERS

IF THE POLICE ATTEMPT TO MOLEST YOU AND YOU ARE NOT GUILTY, OR IF YOU GET IN TROUBLE, SEND FOR ONE OF THE FOLLOWING LAWYERS.

F. L. BARNETT—184 W. WASHINGTON STREET
ELLIS AND WESTBROOKE—3000 SOUTH STATE STREET

Enterprising advertisers sometimes profited from the *Defender*'s insistent warnings to gullible "exodusters" who might fall prey to city slickers. The State Theatre offered a motion picture entitled *Beware of Strangers,* exposing "methods of blackmailing and facts about clairvoyants," and "endorsed by the United States Department of Justice." Directed to the "Attention Newcomers from Southland," the advertisement read:

Little did Hinton Clabaugh think when he brought to justice a blackmailing syndicate preying on the unsuspecting public that he was laying the network of a moving picture. An eight-reel play exposing the organizations of crooks and showing how they operate. It is not the proper food for juvenile minds so children must stay at home. The subject is of paramount interest and is worth seeing. Selig made this a worth-while picture and not one of those fly-by-night things. Its moral is "beware of strangers."

No matter how suave, sweet, or smiling Mr. Stranger may be do not entrust in him either yourself or your money. If you do you are liable to get blackmailed or go to jail. This and the reason why are pointed out in this film. The cast includes Fritzi Brunette, Thomas Santschi, Jack Richardson, Bessie Eyeton.

Whatever might befall them, few of the "exodusters" even contemplated a return to the South. Sparrell Scott wrote for the *Defender:*

WHEN I RETURN TO THE SOUTHLAND IT WILL BE

When lions eat grass like oxen
And an angleworm swallows a whale,
And a terrapin knits a woolen sock,
And a hare is outrun by a snail.

When serpents walk like men,
And doodle-bugs leap like frogs,
When grasshoppers feed on hens,
And feathers grow on hogs.

When Tom cats swim in the air,
And elephants roost in the trees,
When insects in summer are rare,
And snuff can't make you sneeze.

When fish live on dry land,
When mules on velocipedes ride,
And foxes lay eggs in the sand
And women in dress take no pride.

When a German drinks no beer,
And girls deck in plumes for a dime,
When billy goats butt from the rear,
And treason is no longer a crime.

When the mockingbird brays like an ass,
And limburger smells like cologne,
When plowshares are made of glass,
And the hearts of true lovers are stone.

When ideas grow on trees,
And wool on cast-iron rams,
I then may return to the South,
But I'll travel then in a box.

Though they had been glad to escape from oppression, nostalgia for the more pleasant associations of the homeland assailed the exiles. Homesick for familiar speech, faces, and scenes, they banded themselves into social and fraternal clubs named for the States and localities from which they had emigrated. There were the Alabama Club, the Mississippi Club, the Vicksburg Club, the Louisiana Club, the Arkansas Club, et cetera.

An establishment on State Street bore the cumbersome but expressive name of the "Florida East Coast Shine Parlor," while the "Carolina Sea Island Candy Store" opened its doors for business on Wabash Avenue.

Store-front churches, too, helped in the readjustment process. These sprang to life in abandoned or condemned buildings formerly housing retail shops such as grocery and dry-goods stores. The established places of worship maintained their formalities of dress and conduct, but no such rules circumscribed the store-front congregation. The preacher usually worked somewhere during the day, and sometimes lived in the rear of the long room furnished with crude benches and a goods-crate altar. Front windows were rudely painted in imitation of the stained-glass windows of more pretentious edifices.

But the most important thing about the store front was that everybody participated. Untrained but powerful voices joined in hymns sung in such an unorthodox manner that they gave rise to a whole new body of gospel music. The preacher might be illiterate, but he spoke a homely, straight-from-the-shoulder language understood by all. The names of the store-front churches were as picturesque as their services—Willing Workers' Spiritualist, Israel of God, Canaan's Pilgrims, Spiritual Love Circle, Blessed St. Martin, Peter's Rock Baptist, Prophetic Spiritual, Purple Rose Mystical Temple, Crossroads to Happiness, Followers of Exodus, Church of Lost Souls.

A churchwoman who had heeded the call of the "Promised Land" sent back this report to her church sisters:

My dear Sisters: I was agreeably surprised to hear from you and to hear from home. I am well and thankful to be in a city with no lynching and no beating. The weather was a great surprise to me. I got here just in time for one of the greatest revivals in the history of my life —over 500 joined the church. We had a holy-ghost shower. You know I like to run wild at the services—it snows here and even the churches are crowded and we had to stand up last night. The people are rushing here by the thousands, and I know that if you come here and rent a big house you can get all the roomers you want. I am not keeping house yet, I am living with my brother. I can get you a nice place to live until you get your own house. The houses are so pretty, we has a nice place. I am very busy I work in the Swift Packing Co., in the sausage department. My daughter and I work at the same place. We get $1.50 a day, and the hours are not so long, before you know it, it is time to go home. I am so thankful the Lord has been so good to me. Work is plenty here, and we don't loaf we are glad to work. Remember me to Mrs. C. and T. and tell all the children I am praying for them. Hurry up and come to Chicago it is wonderful. I hope I see your face before I die.

Pray for me I am heaven bound. Let me know if you are coming soon as I will meet you at the railroad and bring you to my house, and what a good time we will have thanking God and going to church.

And enclosed was this special greeting and request:

DEAR ———: How are you. I am fine the family is well to. I am working and have been since I left. I make $90 a month with ease. Hello to all the people of my home town. I am saving money, and have joined the K of P up here. Send me five gallons of country syrup. Love to all yours in Christ.

CHAPTER XII

Trouble in Canaan

"THEY SHALL NOT PASS!" The French armies under Pétain and Nivelle, fighting to hold Verdun, had been saying it stubbornly for more than two years when a huge banner bearing the same slogan was strung across Grand Boulevard (later to become South Parkway) at Forty-third Street in Chicago.

This banner, however, did not refer to the European enemy against whom the forces of democracy were then pitted, but to black American citizens pressing south out of the overcrowded segregated district. With each new arrival of migrants from the South, the pressure became more and more intolerable.

A Negro who had become rather well known throughout the nation for his repertoire of selections from Shakespeare and his reading of the poems of Paul Laurence Dunbar chose to ignore this warning, and moved five blocks past the boundary—to 4805 Grand Boulevard.

The elocutionist had hardly settled in his new home when an automobile drove past one night. It careened to the curb as it sped by; and a white hand, reaching from the window of the machine, threw a length of gas pipe against the stoop of the newcomer's house. The homemade bomb exploded in orange flame and a puff of black acrid smoke. Fragments of metal pinged against the walls of surrounding buildings. The stoop lay in splintered ruin, while all the windows of the first floor were shattered.

This was the first of four similar hints to Richard B. Harrison that Negroes were not wanted south of Forty-third Street. Harrison was a man of peace, not unlike the benevolent character he portrayed so long and to such great acclaim in *The Green Pastures* a good many years later. But he also had some iron in his gentle make-up, and he refused to be intimidated by the form of persuasion employed by the "protectors" of the neighborhood. Harrison was often out of the city entertaining at Liberty Bond rallies, and he worried about the safety of his family while he was away.

Not all the victims of bombing were as fortunate as Richard B. Harrison. A blast which wrecked the lower floor of a house at 3365 Indiana Avenue some time before had killed a six-year-old Negro girl. In the period from July 1, 1917, to March 1, 1921, there were fifty-eight bombings of residences occupied by Negroes in contested districts, thirty-three of these in the area bounded by Forty-first Street and Sixtieth Street, Cottage Grove Avenue, and State Street.

In the Kenwood and Hyde Park neighborhoods a determined and organized effort was made to keep Negroes from crossing State Street in the area between Thirty-ninth and Fifty-ninth Streets. The Kenwood and Hyde Park Property Owners' Association, justifying itself by the statement that an influx of Negroes automatically caused a depreciation of property values, made no bones about admitting that its purpose was to "keep Hyde Park white." In October 1918 this organization scattered throughout the district a handbill urging property owners to come to a meeting at which some action might be decided upon.

"Shall we sacrifice our property for a third of its value and run like rats from a burning ship, or shall we put up a united front to keep Hyde Park desirable for ourselves?" the handbill inquired.

The zealous white realtors and property owners did not recognize (or professed not to recognize) the fact that Negroes were compelled to move into neighborhoods already depreciated in value—into ancient, vermin-infested, long-outmoded structures which white occupants had rejected as unfit for their occupation. The depreciation in value, therefore, had already occurred.

Within the decade following 1910 the Negro population of Chicago increased from 44,103 to 109,458. As a consequence, the Negro community began bursting its bounds. More than 90 per cent of the migrants settled on the South Side, in areas of established Negro residence, but before long they were forced to seek living room in sections previously inhabited exclusively by whites. It has been estimated that 50,000 Negroes, a majority of them fresh from the South, came to Chicago within an eighteen-month period after the first of January 1916. Chicago figured as a distribution center, too, a large number of the migrants proceeding directly or after stops of various lengths to Detroit and other industrial centers.

Negro parents who had come to Chicago to provide a more wholesome environment for their children had good reason to seek living quarters outside the congested "black belt," aside from lack of space. Most of the buildings were dilapidated and lacked modern conveniences, but this disadvantage was by no means the principal worry of Negro mothers and fathers anxious to give their offspring a better chance than they themselves had had.

In 1911, several years before the Great Migration began, the Vice Commission of Chicago had published a report at the request of Mayor Busse, in which it was pointed out that "licensed" vice had always been relegated to Negro neighborhoods, and ". . . nearly every time a new vice district was created downtown or on the South Side, the colored families were in the district, moving in just ahead of the prostitutes."

"So," the report continued, "whenever prostitutes, cadets, and thugs were located among white people and had to be moved for commercial or other reasons, they were driven to undesirable parts of the city, the so-called colored residential sections."

The Chicago Urban League made the housing and employment problems of Negro migrants its chief concern, and its South Wabash Avenue headquarters became a rock in a weary land to the perplexed outlander. The league fought vigorously (and with some measure of success) to open doors to jobs hitherto closed to Negroes. It took cognizance of grievances arising from discrimination in places of employment and made an effort to adjust them. The National Association for the Advancement of Colored People offered legal assistance to migrants whose civil rights had been abused.

The insistence of realtors and others in referring to Negro penetration of white residential sections as an "invasion" helped to develop a fear which communicated itself to persons who might not have been affected under ordinary circumstances. Business firms and even churches often fled ahead of the "invaders" or shortly after they arrived. In many cases fear was aggravated into hysterical panic.

Pilgrim Baptist Church moved into a synagogue purchased from members retreating before the advancing newcomers. A Hebrew inscription adorned its façade. Other white congregations sold out and moved to new locations. Some of the churches gradually changed their membership from white to colored. First Church, the oldest white Baptist church in the city, transferred its building to Olivet, the rapidly expanding Negro institution originally an offspring of First Church. The pastor, Reverend Perry Stackhouse, has written of the last services on Sunday evening, September 15, 1918:

> For nearly one half a century they had worshiped God in that sanctuary. It was filled with sacred associations. They recalled the happy days . . . when the seating capacity of the great building had been taxed to accommodate the crowds that gathered. . . . They prayed together, listened to a sermon, no doubt shed a few tears, and, having sung a final hymn, that remnant of a great church went out without a church home of their own and without a field for a new ministry.

Four years later, when the church had settled in a building farther south, the pastor observed:

> The decade closed with a spirit of enthusiasm and hopefulness concerning the future. Meanwhile the Negroes are steadily pushing down the alleys southward with their carts of furniture, but Forty-seventh Street running east and west still stands as a breakwater against the economic tide. If it crumbles there will be some new history for the First Church.

Before many years the "economic tide" had flowed far past First Church's new location.

The pastor's lament sheds significant illumination on the racial problem as it sometimes affects even men of good will. The church people were wont to express earnest sentiments about the

Brotherhood of Man, but they could not or would nor accept the Negro as a full-fledged brother. Instead, infected by the "invasion" panic, they moved away from him, and hoped that he would stay where he was and not follow them. But he couldn't stay; there wasn't room. Realtors, practical fellows, expressed their disinclination toward extending the hand of fellowship to the Negro more realistically—and more violently—than did the religionists.

So Chicago did not quite live up to its reputation for equality of opportunity and lack of prejudice. Some white people disputed the right of colored citizens to use beaches, playgrounds, and other public facilities. Restaurants found means for discouraging Negro patrons ranging from bald refusal to inattention, overcharging, and similar subterfuges. Not a few of the Loop office buildings required Negroes to use the freight elevator when they had business transactions.

Minor clashes between Negro and white boys occurred in Washington Park which was gradually being flanked on three sides by Negroes, so that a disgruntled white property owner suggested that it be rechristened "Booker T. Washington Park." These skirmishes often were provoked by gangs of teenage white boys organized into "athletic clubs." The members of these organizations, some of which boasted of political connections, pursued most of their athletic activity—aside from attacking Negroes with brass "knucks," rocks, blackjacks, and sometimes knives and guns—in the poolrooms which served as their headquarters. "Ragen's Colts" was one of the most aggressive of clubs, and the "Colts" frequently made Washington Park a battleground.

On Sunday, July 27, 1919, Eugene Williams, a Negro youth, floated on a raft across an imaginary line dividing the Twenty-ninth Street Lake Michigan beach into "white" and "colored" sections by a sort of unvoiced agreement. Soon afterward a number of Negro men approached white patrolman Daniel Callahan and asked him to arrest George Stauber, white, who, they said, had pelted young Williams with stones until he fell, unconscious, into the water, where he drowned. Negroes later charged that Officer Callahan refused to arrest Stauber. Upon being attacked by the incensed Negroes, Callahan enlisted the support of white men and boys on the beach, and the battle was on. The trouble radiated from the beach to other parts of the South Side.

Throughout the night the occurrence on the beach was the chief topic of conversation in the "Black Belt." Widespread clashes between the two races took place, and as the night wore on the tempo of violence increased. White men and boys stopped streetcars and attacked colored passengers, while Negroes retaliated with similar action. Members of the so-called "athletic clubs" ranged through the Negro district, shooting and beating indiscriminately every Negro or group of Negroes unequal in size. "Ragen's Colts" were in the vanguard, but "The Hamburgers," "Our Flag," "The Sparklers," and several other organizations were also active. The poolroom athletes and other hoodlums did not find the campaign all beer and skittles, for some Negroes resisted fiercely.

Nicholas Kleinmark boarded a streetcar with a number of other white men, intent on beating the Negro passengers, mostly stockyard workers, with clubs. Nicholas Scott, one of the Negroes belabored by Kleinmark and his associates, defended himself with a pocketknife so well that Kleinmark received a fatal wound. A coroner's jury in dismissing a charge of murder brought against Scott commented: "It is the sense of this jury that the conduct of the police at the time of the riot at this point, during the subsequent investigation, and at the preliminary hearing at which Nicholas Scott was bound over to the grand jury without counsel, was a travesty on justice and fair play."

Clarence Metz met a similar fate when he and several companions assaulted three Negro men and three Negro women coming home from the theater. One of the Negroes, a United States Army lieutenant, stabbed Metz with his pocketknife. Of this incident the coroner's jury said: "We find that the group of colored people, en route to their home, were acting in an orderly and inoffensive manner, and were justified in their acts and conduct during said affray."

Not all of the participants in the riot were hoodlums—many were peaceable citizens under ordinary conditions. Others were precipitated into the maelstrom against their wills. This, of course, was particularly true of Negroes, though not a few white people were unwillingly involved in the disorders. And in the excitement the maddening virus of racial hatred infected many who might never have consciously felt it otherwise—or at least not have expressed it in violence.

The first general riot call since the 1886 Haymarket trouble rallied nearly 2,000 policemen, but they failed to restore peace. Often enough, it was charged, they sided with the white rioters. Wild rumors dispensed by newspapers and individuals helped to keep the fires of animosity burning. It was rumored that a Negro had telephoned a dealer in firearms to order $3,000 worth of revolvers, shotguns, rifles, and ammunition, saying he would be after the goods with a truck. Other yarns spoke of the looting of South State Street pawnshops by rioters in search of shotguns and revolvers.

Some of the rumors in the Negro community were strangely like the atrocity stories told of the Germans a short time before. It was said, for example, that Negro women of the stockyard district had had their breasts hacked off after being subjected to sexual violence; other reports had it that Negroes were being soaked in gasoline, set afire, and made to run like living torches until the flames overcame them and consumed their bodies. A white man with a bottle of gasoline in his hand was hauled out from under a Negro residence. He admitted that his intention was to burn down the house and justified himself by saying that he had heard that Negroes were setting fire to the houses of white people in the stockyards district. There were the usual stories of Negro men raping white women. The most persistent rumor was the one that told of the discovery of Negro riot victims' bodies in the fetid waters of Bubbly Creek, a small stream receiving sewage from the stockyards. Some witnesses even swore that they had seen bodies reclaimed from the creek, but there was never any proof accepted by sober-minded investigators as positive. Rumor set the total dead as high as five hundred.

Alderman Joseph McDonough returned from the riot area in a state of alarm, warning that the Negroes possessed enough ammunition for "years of guerrilla warfare." The chief of police detailed sixty detectives armed with rifles to the task of guarding the city hall, explaining that he feared an assault in force by Negroes.

Five days of disorder ensued during which a large force of State militiamen arrived. The death toll of the riot was officially placed at twenty-two Negroes and sixteen whites, with more than five hundred people known to have been injured in varying degrees. The actual number of fatalities probably was much larger.

Shortly before Mayor Thompson admitted the inability of city police to cope with the situation and requested the help of State troops, a delegation of Negro citizens called on the mayor to complain of police indifference toward or complicity with white lawbreakers. Attorney Beauregard F. Moseley, at a meeting of Negro business and professional men in the Idlewild Hotel, expressed his opinion, according to newspaper reports, that Negroes from the South had been responsible for a lot of the trouble, and reminded his hearers that "this is a white man's country." The Chicago *Tribune* quoted him as saying:

> Some of us forget that the white man has given us freedom, the right to vote, to live on terms of equality with them, to be paid well for our work, and to receive other benefits. Now if the white man should decide that the black man has proved he is not fit to have the right to vote, that right might be taken away. We might also find it difficult to receive other favors to which we have been accustomed, and then what would happen to us?

It was noticed that the madness of the riot was felt only faintly where Negroes and whites were accustomed to working together, as in the stockyards. There were instances of white stockyard workers coming to the aid of their Negro fellow workers, and vice versa. The *New Majority,* official organ of the Chicago Federation of Labor, addressed an appeal to white union members:

> Let any white union worker who has ever been on strike where gunmen or machine guns have been brought in and turned on him and his fellows search his memory and recall how he felt. In this critical moment let every union man remember the tactics of the boss in a strike when he tries by shooting and terrorizing striking workers into violence

to protect themselves. . . . Well, that is how the Negroes feel. They are panic-stricken over the prospect of being killed. . . . Right now it is going to be decided whether the colored workers are to continue to come into the labor movement or whether they are going to feel that they have been abandoned by it and lost confidence in it. . . . All the influence of the unions should be exerted in the community to protect colored fellow workers from the unreasoning frenzy of race prejudice. Indications of the past are that organized labor has gone further in eliminating race hatred than any other class. It is up against the acid test now to show whether this is so.

Representatives of forty-seven business and philanthropic organizations, called together by the Chicago Association of Commerce, passed a resolution urging Governor Lowden to appoint a committee "to study the psychological and economical causes underlying conditions resulting in the present race riot and to make some recommendations as will tend to prevent a recurrence of such conditions in the future." The governor responded by creating the Chicago Race Commission, composed of six Negro and six white citizens, which published a voluminous report as a result of its investigation.

Of the Chicago riot and one which had occurred in Washington on July 19, the President, Woodrow Wilson, said in an article in the *Nation:*

The evidence at hand points not only to a failure of the civil authorities to act promptly and so prevent loss of life; it goes to prove that in each case the white race was the aggressor. This makes the matter infinitely worse; it casts a stain upon every one of the majority group in our land. It is the more censurable because our Negro troops are but just back from no little share in carrying our cause and our flag to victory. As they stood by the majority, so must and should the majority stand by them with true Christianity.

The violence and bloodshed of the July 1919 riot did not cause any diminution in the campaign of the Kenwood and Hyde Park Property Owners' Association to keep Negroes confined to the "black ghetto." Indeed, the tone of its official organ, the *Property Owner's Journal,* seemed to indicate approval of drastic steps. In its January 1, 1920, issue the publication said:

As stated before, every colored man who moves into Hyde Park knows that he is damaging his white neighbor's property. Therefore, he is making war on the white man. Consequently, he is not entitled to any consideration and forfeits his right to be employed by the white man. If employers should adopt a rule of refusing to employ Negroes who persist in residing in Hyde Park to the damage of the white man's property, it would show good results.

In another issue the *Journal* was moved to exclaim:

What a reputation for beauty Chicago would secure if visitors touring the city would see crowds of insolent, idle Negroes lounging on the South Side boulevards and adding beauty to the floricultural display in the parks, filling the street with old newspapers and tomato containers, and advertising the Poro-system for removing the marcelled kinks from Negro hair in the windows of the derelict remains of what had once been a clean, respectable residence.

The *Journal* finally overplayed its hand with such intemperate fulminations that even those white people who were opposed to Negroes moving into the "white" neighborhoods protested. It suspended publication, but the embattled Negrophobes did not give up the struggle.

Another and even more effective weapon was discovered then—the restrictive covenant. The restrictive covenant was an agreement between a certain percentage of property owners within a district not to sell or rent their property to Negroes. In spite of their obvious effects of segregation and discrimination, the legality of the restrictive covenants was upheld by lower courts until the United States Supreme Court ruled against them in 1948. Thus the Chicago black ghetto was hedged in by industrial plants to the west, the Loop business district to the north, and the Oakland, Kenwood, and Hyde Park districts to the east, barring access to the lake. In the latter districts were the sedate, wide-lawned, and many-roomed mansions of Chicago's industrial and financial pioneers. Most of the old families fled long before World War II to "better" residential sections, and for many years the ancient houses slumbered out the years undisturbed save by a caretaker who usually lived in the carriage house in the rear, kept the lawn mowed and the trees reasonably well trimmed. Just across Cottage Grove Avenue more than 80,000 Negroes were confined in each square mile of space. The restrictive covenants had placed the old mansions under protective glass—transfixed as museum pieces.

Though the postwar years brought a slackening of the demand for laborers and finally an acute depression, the trend of migration was toward and not away from the North. During the depression years of 1930 to 1935, the number of white farm operators in the Southern States increased by 264,047 (11.3 per cent) while the Negro farmers decreased by 65,940 (7.5 per cent).

Negroes in the South complained that they were being given the little end of relief work and relief food—AAA payments were made to the landlord for keeping the cotton land idle, while the sharecroppers sat around watching their shadows grow thinner. In the North the relief payments were more substantial, and all the white men weren't put on WPA jobs before a Negro was considered.

But even in the North there wasn't complete equality of opportunity by a long shot. A great many Negro workers were still unskilled factory laborers—they were barred by custom or union regulations from most of the desirable industrial jobs. Not only that, but the Negro, as Reverend Harold S. Kingsley put it, had been a "fringe" worker—the last hired and the first fired.

Negroes were justifiably incensed to see only white clerks in stores where they spent all their money. Many of the customers were unemployed themselves; others had relatives and friends unable to find a job. A Negro newspaper, the Chicago *Whip,* founded in 1919, hammered away with the slogan: "Don't spend your money where you can't work." The *Whip* in 1929–30 spearheaded a job campaign resulting in the employment of thousands of Negro men and women in manufacturing plants, stores, and offices. Not only neighborhood merchants but corporations and chain stores capitulated and hired Negroes for the first time. One of the *Whip*'s first targets was the Metropolitan Life Insurance Company, which had many Negro policyholders but no Negro collectors. When the company declined to change its attitude, Negro insurance companies profited by the acquisition of many policyholders who had been affected by the "don't-spend-your-money-where-you-can't-work" propaganda and had quit the Metropolitan.

Such organizations as the Urban League and the NAACP participated in the jobs campaign. Recalcitrant employers often found their places of business surrounded by pickets.

For obvious reasons, advertisers were inclined to shun the *Whip,* and it ended its troubled course in 1932. An even more aggressive exponent of the jobs-for-Negroes idea soon took up the cudgels, however.

H. George Davenport, a roving sign painter, arrived in Chicago sometime during the thirties and began to write acrimonious comment for the Negro press, principally the *World.* Editors often rejected or censored his vitriolic pronouncements, and in 1936 Davenport, an adept craftsman whose business motto, "I Made Signs Before I Could Talk," was somewhat justified, invested his savings in a personal mouthpiece, *Dynamite.* The tabloid-sized journal usually ran four pages, though sometimes it had eight. From 1,000 to 5,000 copies were printed weekly, and distributed free. While readers enjoyed Davenport's tirades against prominent individuals and organizations, they successfully resisted his attempt to make them pay two cents a copy for *Dynamite,* and free distribution was resumed. Eight evils were sentenced to death under a front-page caption: "This Vicious Circle Must Go." Listed were organized vice, racial discrimination, restrictive covenants, unfair business and professional men, false race leaders, unfair labor unions, brutal police, and rent hogs.

Announcing that *Dynamite* would "blast everything that stands in the path of the Negro and his progress," Davenport expressed his determination to "use the the power of the press in the same sense as dynamite is used in getting what we think rightfully belongs to us." The militant sign painter was forced by lack of capital to suspend *Dynamite* for six months in 1937, but managed to re-enter the arena early in 1938. When the Negro Labor Relations League was formed for the purpose of directing the jobs-for-Negroes movement, *Dynamite* endorsed it with characteristic gusto. The league, while it welcomed and acknowledged Davenport's support, was embarrassed by some of his anti-Semitic utterances. Advertisers boycotted the pugnacious tabloid, readers would not pay for the privilege of reading it, and late in 1938 it ceased publication.

As the depression deepened, a paradoxical situation developed on the South Side. Migrants were still arriving in the city, but there were always vacant apartments. Pedestrians often found it necessary to step into the street, detouring around a pile of household goods deposited on the sidewalk. Near it there might be a weeping woman with tearful children clinging to her skirts, a man silent and cold with hate or frantic with anxiety. Landlords wanted their rent, depression or no depression, and when it wasn't forthcoming the process servers came—finally "the law" to move everything outside.

It seemed at first as though there were no place for the homeless ones to turn. They had no money with which to rent another apartment. Sometimes a neighbor or passer-by would stop to offer a word of condolence or hollow encouragement, again a small coin or two would be dropped unostentatiously into a saucer—infrequently a faded dollar.

Later on the restless crowds gathering around the pile of furniture telling of another eviction for nonpayment of rent began to galvanize into a coherent unit with a definite purpose. Landlords and issue-seeking politicians said that the spark was supplied by Communist agitators, more intent upon advancing the theories of far-off Moscow than solving the Negro's problems. The resistance to eviction took shape in shabby little halls above dingy shops where black men and white men, bound together by a common misery, met together. Pennies dearly spared went into crudely mimeographed, passionate leaflets.

Then they started moving the furniture right back into the flats after it had been set out on the sidewalk. As they worked, the members of the Unemployed Councils sang, using the name of some leader in their ranks:

> "——— *is our leader;*
> *We shall not be moved!*
> ——— *is our leader;*
> *We shall not be moved!*

Just like a tree that's planted by the water,
We shall not be moved!"

At times the song was punctuated by the angry, defiant, and upraised clenched fist. There were white men and women among the movers-back, some of them undoubtedly Communists. This, however, seemed to perturb the newspapers and the politicians more than it did the Negroes, who were grateful for vital, immediate help.

Clashes with the police became frequent. On occasion the crowd failed in its attempt to restore the furniture. A climax came in August 1931, when more than two thousand people left a meeting in Washington Park which served the Unemployed Councils as an open-air forum and proceeded to a house on Dearborn Street. The belongings of an unemployed woman had been dragged out on the sidewalk in the usual way. The procession gathered strength as it moved to its goal, singing "We Shall Not Be Moved." By the time a squad car full of policemen from the Wabash Avenue Station arrived, there were five thousand on hand.

The policemen shouldered their way through the throng, arresting several black and white men they judged to be the leaders of the demonstration. But the crowd was in a nasty mood. It started shoving back, laying hands on the cops to restrain them, shouting angrily. When the tussle was over, the policemen having drawn and fired their guns in the midst of the crowd, three Negroes lay dead on the ground. A great many others were nursing wounds.

Presently a rain of leaflets fell on the South Side:

HOLD SOLIDARITY DEMONSTRATIONS AGAINST THE
MASSACRE OF OUR UNEMPLOYED COMRADES!

Visions of another riot comparable to that of 1919 came before the city officials. This time, of course, it wouldn't be a race riot. A Negro and white guard of honor stood by the bodies of the men killed by the police as they lay in state in Odd Fellows Hall; it was estimated that eighteen thousand mourners filed by to gaze briefly at the dead men who had become martyrs. An immediate result of the whole thing was that the Renter's Court temporarily held back eviction orders in process.

In an effort to halt the movement of indigent migrants to Illinois, the Legislature in 1939 passed a law requiring recipients of relief to prove three years' continuous residence in one of the one thousand four hundred and fifty-five governmental units of the State. In the fall of that year it was discovered that about 4 per cent of all relief clients had lived in their local units less than the specified time. Negroes comprised about 20 per cent of these. Cook County, with 35 per cent of all the cases in this category, counted Negroes as 80 per cent of the total.

On August 19, 1940, Mayor Edward J. Kelly of Chicago, testifying at the Chicago hearings of a Congressional committee investigating the interstate migration of destitute citizens, referred to the three-year residence law, and said:

> I think three years is too long. I know of many instances where it has been a real hardship. I can cite one case of a young colored man who came here thinking that he could get work, or get relief. Of course he was not recognized. He became a highwayman. He shot a policeman. The policeman shot him. He got one hundred and ninety-nine years in the penitentiary. It does not seem to me as though there was anything else for that man to do. He was starving. He could not get anything. He finished up with one hundred and ninety-nine years.

Ishmael P. Flory, organizer of the Chicago Council of the National Negro Congress, called the attention of the committee "to the plight of at least 8,000,000 white and colored citizens of the South who suffer under a system of debt slavery which had its counterpart only in the feudal system of the Dark Ages," and continued:

> Here on Chicago's South Side we have thousands of Negroes who have fled from the South to escape the burden of debt slavery. More arrive each month, so that it is estimated that at least 50,000 Negroes here—one sixth of the colored population—have no regular place of abode, begging their meals at back doors and on the streets, sleeping in parks, hallways, or on the floors of already overcrowded apartments.

Refugees from the debt slavery mentioned by Flory were not entirely out of the woods when they crossed Mason and Dixon's line. But those who sought to return them to bondage met with less and less success.

Three modern slave catchers from Oglethorpe County, Georgia, notorious for its peonage system, came to grief in their attempt to return Otis and Dock Woods and Solomon McCannon to Sandy Cross Plantation near Lexington, Georgia. William Toliver Cunningham, owner of the plantation, arrived in Chicago in September 1939, accompanied by his attorney, Hamilton McWhorter, and a deputy sheriff. Enlisting the aid of Cook County Deputy Sheriff Keenan, McWhorter succeeded in having the three Negroes arrested for the theft of two bushels of corn in 1935. The tenants had remained on the plantation a year after the alleged theft, the charge being brought against them only after they had departed for the North. While in Chicago, McWhorter also made an effort to apprehend Clyde Smith, Ella Smith, and Edward Raines, Negro refugees from Oglethorpe County, but failed because he had no warrant.

Though he did manage to have Otis and Dock Woods and Solomon McCannon lodged in jail, McWhorter's plea for extradition to Georgia was denied by Governor Henry Horner. Moreover, through the efforts of Colonel William Henry Huff of the Abolish Peonage Committee and several allied organizations, Cunningham and McWhorter were indicted by a federal grand jury for "conspiracy to retain and hold Negroes in a condition of peonage and slavery." In January 1942 the United States Supreme Court in a unanimous decision voided the Georgia debt law. The Elberton (Georgia) *Star* had complained that the "two worthy citizens" of Georgia would be railroaded in a "Negrophile locality" like Chicago. The "worthy citizens" did at last engineer a change of venue, and a benevolent Georgia court soon exonerated them.

CHAPTER XIII

"Beloved and Scattered Millions"

ON A WINDY DAY late in March 1916 a young Negro from Jamaica, destined some years afterward to captivate hundreds of thousands of his racial brethren with his proud assertion that he was a "full-blooded black man," made an inconspicuous entry into New York's Harlem. He had come to rally the "beloved and scattered millions of the Negro race."

Marcus Mosiah Garvey, born on August 17 in the year of 1887 in the small town of St. Ann's Bay on the northern coast of Jamaica, was not prepossessing at the first (nor even the second) glance. He was short and squat, with a heavy head set close to his shoulders. Garvey's boast about his pure African blood was justified. Marcus and Sarah Garvey, his parents, were indeed of unmixed Negro blood. Marcus the elder was a skillful master mason whose beautiful work in brick and stone was greatly admired. He also was a man of some learning, and often offered free legal advice to his friends and neighbors.

Reading the books in his father's well-selected library, Marcus (at an early age called derisively "Ugly Mug") developed a yearning to see how his people lived in other parts of the world. His formal education must have been skimpy at best, though he later claimed to have attended two colleges. At the age of fourteen, he had been apprenticed to a printer. Working in a Kingston printshop, he organized a union and led an unsuccessful strike. When the strike was broken and his fellow workers were permitted to return to their jobs, Garvey was black-listed. The government printing house, however, ignored the black list and put him on the payroll. Before long he was editing a rebellious periodical called *Garvey's Watchman* and organizing a political club which issued a fortnightly magazine named *Our Own*. To raise money for the club and his publishing venture, Garvey took a job as a timekeeper on a banana plantation in Costa Rica. The wretched conditions suffered by his fellow Jamaicans moved him to protest vainly to the indifferent British consul. Financed by an indulgent maternal uncle, who was also alarmed at his nephew's radical activities, Garvey then traveled to Panama. There he established *La Prensa,* a newspaper which illness and discouragement soon induced him to abandon. He returned to Jamaica.

The year 1912 found Garvey in London. From this vantage point, he hoped to gain a more comprehensive idea of the conditions of Negroes throughout the world. The British colonies, he knew, held many of them. It has been said that he managed to attend law classes at London University. Certainly, he was influenced by Duse Mohammed Ali, an eccentric half-Negro and half-Egyptian scholar who had during the previous year published a volume called *In the Land of the Pharaohs: A Short History of Egypt from the Fall of Ismail to the Assassination of Boutros Pasha*. Duse Mohammed was so well impressed with the fiery and earnest young Jamaican that he put him on the staff of his monthly magazine, *Africa Times and Orient Review*. The inquisitive West Indian found a rich treasure of information in London libraries. He also learned from African and West Indian students and workers with whom he came in contact. Everywhere he saw his people in subjection and poverty. He wrote:

> I read *Up from Slavery* by Booker T. Washington, and then my doom—if I may call it—of being a race leader dawned upon me . . . I asked: "Where is the black man's government? Where is his king and his kingdom? Where is his president, his country, and his ambassador, his army, his navy, his men of big affairs?" I could not find them. I declared: "I will help to make them."

Garvey began corresponding with Washington on problems of common interest to them both, and the sage of Tuskegee, Garvey reported, had urged him to come to the United States.

Returning to Jamaica in 1914, Garvey set about organizing the

Universal Negro Improvement Association, the purpose of which was to "take Africa, organize it, develop it, arm it, and make it the defender of Negroes the world over." Garvey had long been irritated by the caste system of Jamaica, with the light-skinned mulattoes at the top of the heap and the blacks at the bottom. He resolved never to apologize for his color, but to glory in it. As an adolescent boy he had been wounded deeply by a white girl, daughter of a clergyman, who had told him when she reached the years of maidenly discretion that it was socially inadvisable to associate any longer with a "nigger."

Garvey intended in 1915 to accept a rather diffident invitation from Booker T. Washington to come to Tuskegee for a conference. Washington's death changed things, for his replacement, Robert Russa Moton, was distinctly cool toward Garvey and his organization. On that wind-worried day in March, 1916, however, the man from Jamaica arrived in New York City to plant the UNIA banner on United States soil. The general attitude of important Negro leaders toward him was one of hostility. In the forefront of his critics was Dr. W. E. B. Du Bois, brilliant Negro scholar and editor of the NAACP's *Crisis*.

Nevertheless, the UNIA prospered. Garvey was a persuasive speaker, and an able organizer. Four busy and for the most part triumphant years passed before he, as president-general of the UNIA issued his eloquent call to the "Beloved and Scattered Millions of the Negro Race." In January 1918 he had established the *Negro World*, "indispensable weekly, the voice of the awakened Negro, reaching the masses everywhere."

The 1920 convention of the UNIA in Madison Square Garden was attended by 25,000. It had been preceded by a parade through Harlem by the African Legion, nattily attired in blue uniforms with red trouser stripes, and a company of 200 white-clad Black Cross nurses. The assembled delegates, among them an African prince and a number of tribal chiefs, lustily sang the UNIA official anthem, "Ethiopia, Thou Land of Our Fathers." A red, black, and green tricolor was unfurled. This banner, the delegates hoped, would one day fly proudly over a free and united Africa. Marcus Garvey was proclaimed Provisional President of Africa by enthusiastic acclamation.

One of the UNIA's pet projects was the Black Star Steamship Line, incorporated for the dual purpose of returning race leaders and American Negroes to their homeland in Africa and of opening up commercial relations with the African continent. Garvey contended that Negro scholars, scientists, and industrialists should match wits on African soil with white interlopers and thus regain supremacy.

The cry of "Africa for the Africans" was not new, of course. Colonization of Negroes in Africa as a proposed solution for the racial question had been advocated by white men and both slave and free black men for various reasons. As early as 1800 the legislature of Virginia, alarmed at Gabriel Prosser's abortive slave rebellion, had authorized the governor of the State to confer with the President of the United States on the possibility of colonization of malcontents "dangerous to the peace of society." Free men of color were increasing in number, and, in the opinion of the slaveholders, setting a bad example for Negroes still in bondage. Their insubordination and independent attitudes were irksome to those in power and authority, and it was thought that they would be much less dangerous if settled at a safe distance beyond the Atlantic Ocean. From time to time, too, slaveowners were assailed by qualms of conscience or became convinced that the institution of slavery itself was economically unsound, and manumitted their bondsmen. Usually, the owners preferred that those freed be sent as far away as possible.

Thomas Jefferson in 1811 indicated his belief in the desirability of settling American Negroes on the coast of Africa, and in 1814 wrote a letter to Governor Edward Coles of Illinois in which he discussed colonization of Negroes in the West Indies, particularly in the Negro republic of Santo Domingo. Jefferson was convinced that members of the colored race eventually would drive all white people from the Caribbean islands.

British foes of the slave traffic—such as William Wilberforce, Thomas Clarkson, and Granville Sharp—took practical steps toward colonization in Africa, and it was mainly due to their efforts that four hundred Negroes, principally soldiers and sailors who had fought on the British side in the Revolutionary War, and sixty

European females were settled on the Sierra Leone peninsula in 1787. The Europeans have been described as "mostly women of abandoned character," white prostitutes rounded up in the slums of English cities and deported by force—or given a choice between deportation as mates for Negro colonists and prison sentences. Some fugitive slaves who had sought refuge in London were included in the number, and these were joined later by freed slaves from Canada and the West Indies.

Paul Cuffee, a New England Negro sailor who had acquired some wealth and had embraced the Quaker faith, was the first American to supplement theory with action. In 1815 he sent, at his own expense, thirty-five Negro colonists to Africa. Cuffee's feat is believed to have inspired the formation of the American Colonization Society in 1816, with Henry Clay and Francis Scott Key as officers. This organization established settlements which were bound together in the independent Republic of Liberia in 1847. Joseph Jenkins Roberts, an ex-slave, arrived in the colony in 1829, assembled and trained a force of militiamen, and was appointed governor in 1841. Upon the establishment of the republic, Roberts became its first president.

The colonization scheme was opposed by various forces. Not many slaveowners were willing to part with their black chattels, and the colonization enthusiasts dared not compel free Negroes to quit the United States in the face of the abolitionists' rising protest against the expatriation. Most free men of color were as firmly rooted in the national life of America as any other citizens, and they called mass indignation meetings throughout the North to protest against the African venture. A majority of the emigrants, therefore, were manumitted slaves who had no choice in the matter, their masters for one reason or another desiring to be completely rid of them.

The British had freed their West Indian slaves in 1838, and there followed considerable emigration to Haiti, Trinidad, and British Guiana. Despite the general unpopularity and seeming ineffectuality of the American Colonization Society, interest in colonization did not die. In 1853 a conclave of Negro leaders took up the problem of emigration and divided into three factions favoring respectively the Niger Valley in Africa, Central America, and

Haiti. Martin R. Delaney, foremost proponent of the first group, journeyed to Africa and negotiated agreements with eight African kings who promised to accept American Negroes as citizens. The Haiti faction is credited with directing two thousand settlers to that country, but only a third of them established permanent residence.

The Civil War halted all emigration or even consideration of it for a time. Abraham Lincoln had entertained the idea of sending freedmen to Liberia, but little official action in that direction actually was taken. A legend persists among poor whites of the South that Lincoln, had he been permitted to live, would have had all the Negroes out of the country.

The American Colonization Society celebrated the fiftieth anniversary of Liberian independence in 1897, and announced that it had dispatched during that period 147 ships carrying nearly 12,000 African colonists. Freeborn among these numbered about 4,500, while approximately 6,000 had been freed on condition that they go to Liberia. A minority of 345 had freed themselves by self-purchase. The society was not the only one sending colonists to Africa. The Maryland State Colonization Society in 1831 had founded the "Maryland-in-Africa" colony, which maintained its independence until 1858, when it was incorporated into the governmental structure of Liberia as Maryland County. The Maryland State Colonization Society had transported 1,221 colonists, while the United States Government had returned to their native land 6,772 Africans who had been smuggled into America, depositing them in Liberia.

The bark *Azor,* chartered by the Liberia Exodus Association, set sail from Charleston, South Carolina, on April 22, 1878, with 250 passengers bound for the Negro republic. Their destination was Bopara, near Monrovia, the capital city.

Bopara had been founded by a freedman from Charleston, whose reported success story was in the tradition later to be made famous by Horatio Alger. Coming to Liberia penniless, this colonist, it was said, had soon acquired a flourishing plantation bringing him a clear income of three thousand dollars each year. The Liberian Congress had granted the head of each immigrant family aboard the *Azor* a free grant of twenty-five acres of land with the privilege of occupying as much more as he desired at fifty cents per acre.

Negroes had good reason to get out of the South as the Democrats returned to power. Some of the freedmen, who saw ominous portents of a return to slavery just as onerous as that of antebellum days, answered the call of "Pap" Singleton, and headed for Kansas. Others, sick of it all, thought of Africa—feeling some nostalgic urge for that hot, rich land with its copper sun, luscious fruits, and bright green vegetation.

Before long charges of swindling were being brought against some of the emigration societies, and no doubt some of them were justified. The fees were not excessive—could not be, for the prospective emigrants would have found it impossible to raise large amounts. The Emigration Society of Raleigh collected from each of 700 Negro families (averaging six people to the family) the sum of twenty-five dollars. It was expected that further aid would be forthcoming from benevolent societies formed for the purpose of aiding emigrants. Atlanta newspapers complained in January 1891 that 2,000 Negroes from Texas and Mississippi, induced by the United States and Congo National Emigration Steamship Company to head for Savannah and thence to Liberia, were stranded in the city. It was in the midst of a cold snap, and the municipality was forced to feed and shelter the hungry and shivering emigrants. No arrangements had been made in Atlanta for transportation to Savannah or beyond, and many of the prospective colonists loudly cried that they had been swindled. Since each one had paid such a small sum and most of the victims were penniless, it was impossible to interest any lawyer in taking the matter to court.

Bishop H. M. Turner of the African Methodist Episcopal Church, who had been commissioned by President Lincoln as the first Negro chaplain in the United States Army, became convinced that segregation of a large number of Negroes in Africa would be the best immediate step toward solution of his people's problems after reaction and Ku Kluxism had displaced the military administrators and "carpetbaggers."

Bishop Turner came to Chicago in 1893 to observe Colored American Day at the World's Columbian Exposition. Here he made a speech advocating emigration to Liberia, which met with opposition from Frederick Douglass.

The New York *Press* observed on April 14, 1895:

"Africa for the Negro" is being re-echoed in the South. No good can come of this emigration. Nothing is said of the fevers and famine to be met on African shores. Douglass' call to stand up in America and fight was a clearer note than Turner's cry to run away to an unknown land. American Negroes should become Americans.

The Colored Emigration and Commercial Convention, meeting in Chattanooga, Tennessee, in May 1901, passed a resolution requesting Congress to appropriate $500,000,000 for the purpose of colonizing Negroes desiring to quit the United States. Bishop Turner was named as "the leading spirit of the movement." By this time, however, colonizing schemes attracted but faint interest. Negroes dissatisfied with the South usually preferred to try the portion of the United States north of the Mason and Dixon's line rather than a foreign land. The call of Africa became dimmer and dimmer.

Nevertheless, Marcus Garvey was determined to reawaken the cry of "Africa for the Africans" and to hurl it farther and more challengingly than anyone else ever had. Once he got his Black Star Steamship Line going, his task would be simplified. The ships, manned by all-Negro crews, would take to African shores cargoes of repatriated Negroes and machinery with which to build the homeland into a self-sufficient empire. They would return with the exotic natural products of the fabulously rich Dark Continent—ivory, mahogany, rubber, spices, gold and bronze art objects wrought by native craftsmen. But all this took a lot of money for pump-priming.

Garvey would not permit white people to buy stock in his enterprises. And rather than seek capital from wealthy Negroes, of whom there were few, he appealed to the masses for small investments. These responded so enthusiastically that he found a movement on his hands. His glorification of the color black, as evidenced by his demands for a Black House as well as a White House, Black Cross nurses, et cetera, fostered intense nationalistic feeling and racial pride. He revived the "Back-to-Africa" movement on a scale never remotely approached by other evangels of the idea. Garvey himself wrote a poem in which he saluted "The Black Woman" as "Goddess of Africa, Nature's purest emblem!"

and assured her that "Black men worship at thy virginal shrine of purest love, /Because in thine eyes are virtue's steady and holy mark . . ."

The UNIA's lively house organ, the weekly *Negro World,* was eagerly read by Negroes everywhere. It eventually reached a circulation conservatively estimated at from 75,000 to 100,000.

It must not be supposed, however, that Garvey's course was all smooth sailing. Negroes from the South did not get along any too well with West Indians in Harlem. The Southerners were incensed by the islander's air of superiority, his pride in his status as a British citizen, and his propensity for "talking a good fight." The West Indians, on their part, made no bones about expressing their disdain for the crude outlanders. Garvey further increased his handicap by assailing mulattoes and all Negroes with even a small amount of white blood in their veins. He had erroneously supposed that the West Indian caste system, regulated by lightness of skin, with Negroes just a shade darker than white at the apex and in the favored position, was a burning issue in the United States too.

American Negroes in Harlem soon dubbed Garvey's followers "monkey chasers" and began composing satirical ditties about the Back-to-Africa movement such as:

When I get on the other side,
I'll buy myself a mango,
Grab myself a monkey gal
And do the monkey tango.

Of the leader himself the skeptical Harlemites sang:

Garvey, Garvey, is a big man
To take his folks to monkey-land.
If he does, I'm sure I can
Stay right here with Uncle Sam.

Nevertheless, all of Garvey's seeds of discontent did not fall on stony soil. The North had not fulfilled the legend about it that had prevailed throughout the South. Prejudice, segregation, and violence attended the Negro seeker still. Garvey's attractive word paintings of a bright future in the African homeland might prove as delusive as "Pap" Singleton's idealization of Kansas or the Chicago *Defender*'s enticing picture of the big city by Lake Michigan, but it was something to think about anyhow. There *must* be a place *somewhere!*

Garvey's vituperative tongue rallied against him a group of formidable enemies. W. E. B. Du Bois battled with the genteel weapons of reason and logic. He gave the crusading Jamaican credit for sincerity and capacity for leadership, but disputed his economic views and his advocacy of a return to Africa as a solution of the American Negro's problems. Other adversaries—such as A. Philip Randolph and Chandler Owen, editors of the *Messenger,* took issue with the combative UNIA leader on his own ground.

"Mudsill of Jamaican society" and "Supreme Negro Jamaican Jackass" were two of the comparatively mild epithets hurled at Garvey by the *Messenger*. Robert W. Bagnall, writing of him in the March 1923 issue described him as:

> . . . Squat, stocky, fat, and sleek with protruding jaws and heavy jowls; small, bright, piglike eyes, and rather full doglike face. Boastful, egotistic, tyrannical, intolerant . . . gifted at self-advertisement . . . promising ever, but never fulfilling . . . a lover of pomp, tawdry finery, and garish display . . . a sheer opportunist and a demagogic charlatan.

As with many another spellbinder whose effectiveness rests upon the skill of his oral delivery, Garvey's pronouncements always sounded better than they read. His recipe for success was conventionally orthodox, as expressed in this admonition to his followers:

> Ask Rockefeller where he came from, ask Carnegie where he came from, ask Henry Ford where he came from; and they will tell you that they came from the lowly places of life; they started out with the dollar and then made the ten dollars and, after, the millions.
>
> Man, do not beg and remain idle, but borrow a dollar or beg a dollar and start your career today. Buy a handful of newspapers and sell them, buy a few heads of cabbage and start to become a merchant,

buy a few oranges from the dollar and later on you will be buying barrels. Why! take a dollar and invest it in bananas and sell them at a profit. Do not eat up all your capital and your profit on the first day. Let every day be like the day before, and then you will find how quickly you are ascending the ladder of commerce, to be probably one of its captains.

It was not hard for an astute economist and sociologist such as Du Bois to point out serious defects in the various organizations set up as adjuncts to the UNIA, such as the African Communities League, the Black Star Steamship Line, and the Negro Factories Corporation. Du Bois pointed out, accurately enough, that the only concrete achievement of the latter organization was visible in a few grocery stores, a laundry or two, and a printing press. All these enterprises soon failed.

The Black Star Line was equally unsuccessful. The *Yarmouth,* bought for $140,000 and rechristened the *Frederick Douglass,* was impounded for debt after three unprofitable trips to the West Indies. Then it was sold under the auctioneer's hammer for $1,625. The *Antonio Maceo,* formerly an ocean-going yacht, ran up a repair bill of $70,000 or $80,000—far more than its original cost of $60,000. Its ultimate fate is shrouded in mystery. One supposition is that it was either wrecked or seized for debt in Cuba. The *Shadyside* made several excursion trips up the Hudson to the accompaniment of great fanfare, the resulting propaganda being the principal benefits accruing.

The palpable failure of Garvey's grandiose schemes had a deflating effect on the enthusiasm of followers who had been charmed by his silver tongue. In addition, he made some incautious references which could be interpreted as at least a left-handed endorsement of the Ku Klux Klan's argument that the United States should be made "a white man's country." Garvey's point, of course, was that Negroes should pull out for Africa and leave the white men to run the country as they pleased. But this distinction was too fine for most Southern Negroes, who had good reason to resent any sort of approval of the Klan.

One of Garvey's first major defeats was administered in Chicago, a major tower of his strength. The issue of West Indian versus United States Negro was practically nonexistent in Chicago, and there were many migrants from the South who were growing more and more disgruntled with their lot in the promised Paradise of the North. By 1920 UNIA membership in the city was said to total 7,500, while branches flourished in East St. Louis, Springfield, Mounds, Alton, Cairo, and other Illinois communities. William H. Wallace, later a State Senator, gave up a thriving bakery business to head the Chicago movement.

When Robert S. Abbott, publisher and editor of the *Defender*, took up the cudgels against Garvey and his organization, the man from Jamaica was not a little perturbed. Abbott enjoyed power and prestige, and he was easily Garvey's equal in the art of invective and rough-and-tumble debate.

Jeering at Garvey's purchase of the dilapidated *Yarmouth* and advertisement of it as the maiden ship of the Black Star Line, the *Defender* made a sarcastic comparison to a similar ship bought by "Chief Sam" of Kansas, a predecessor of Garvey whose plans for setting up an independent kingdom in Africa had gone awry—some said because of British antagonism toward the venture, others alleging that "Chief Sam" was a fraud who had collected huge sums solely for his own enjoyment. Garvey held to the latter viewpoint, and filed a libel suit against Abbott demanding a million dollars as compensation for damage to his character. Though he won a moral victory and finally was awarded one cent, the cost of litigation severely damaged the UNIA's financial equilibrium.

Before the case was decided Garvey announced his intention of invading Chicago. It was October 1919, less than four months after the race riot that had gone so far toward disillusioning refugees from Dixie with the New Canaan. It seemed a propitious time for Garvey to appear with his Back-to-Africa appeals. Many black Ishmaels were again yearning toward a "better place" somewhere. Garvey rented the Eighth Regiment Armory and from its platform denounced Abbott more vigorously than before. At the close of the meeting he was arrested for selling stock in the Black Star Steamship Line in violation of the Illinois Blue Sky Law, which governed the sale of stock certificates and shares. Garvey later claimed that the arrest had been engineered by Abbott, who, he said, had arranged to have a Negro detective posing as a prospective investor insist upon buying stock from none other than the leader of the UNIA, the purpose being to incriminate him. Released on bail, Garvey departed from the city, never to return. "Abbott has always through rivalry and jealousy been opposed to me," said Garvey later, "and especially through my not being born in America and my criticism of his dangerous newspaper policy of always advising the race to lighten its skin and straighten out its hair which was kinky."

Trouble continued to hound Garvey. In 1922 he was indicted on a charge of using the mails to defraud in connection with the sale of stock in the Black Star Steamship Line. He conducted his own defense, having no confidence in Negro attorneys and scorning to employ a white one. His bombastic and imperious manner in the courtroom alienated both judge and jury. After litigation lasting a year, he was sentenced to five years' imprisonment in the federal penitentiary at Atlanta. Garvey obtained bail, and by appeals delayed the execution of sentence until 1925.

In the meantime, he had formed the Black Cross Navigation Company and bought the S. S. *General Goethals,* which he renamed the *Booker T. Washington* for the great leader at Tuskegee who had expressed interest in his plans. Like its predecessors, the *Booker T. Washington* was dogged by ill luck. Putting in at a Cuban port, it was seized for debt. Nearly twenty years later a World War II Liberty merchant ship was named for the Sage of Tuskegee, and commanded by a Negro captain, Hugh Mulzac. Ironically enough, the name of Robert S. Abbott, Garvey's nemesis, was bestowed upon another. But, Garvey would have retorted, even though these ships might be manned and officered by Negroes, they did not *belong* to them or to the Negro race.

When Garvey was at last consigned to federal prison, he addressed his followers in a customarily flamboyant editorial, "If I Should Die in Atlanta," published in the *Negro World*:

> Look for me in the whirlwind or the song of the storm, look for me all around you, for with God's grace I shall come and bring with me the countless millions of black slaves who have died in America and the West Indies and the millions in Africa to aid you in the fight for liberty, freedom, and life.

Garvey's sentence was commuted by President Coolidge late in 1927, but immigration laws required that he be deported immediately to Jamaica. He was not even permitted to visit UNIA headquarters in New York. Several hundred followers assembled on the docks at New Orleans to pay homage to their champion as he departed from the United States, never to return. Without its dynamic leader the UNIA floundered about uncertainly, rent by schisms and dissensions. Enterprising organizers and local chairmen seized the opportunity to promote various schemes of their own.

Two years before Garvey's indictment there appeared in Chicago a white man named R. D. Jonas, reputed to have been an organizer for the UNIA in East St. Louis. With the assistance of Grover Cleveland Redding, a Negro who claimed to be a native of Abyssinia, Jonas organized the Abyssinian Movement. Since one of its principal aims—according to its literature and speakers—was to facilitate the emigration of American Negroes to Africa (specifically to Ethiopia) not a few of its converts believed the UNIA and the Abyssinian Movement were at least affiliated.

On Sunday, June 20, 1920, Redding, astride a white horse and clad in what was supposed to be the costume of an Abyssinian prince, appeared on East Thirty-fifth Street, leading a parade of his followers. At Prairie Avenue the procession halted while Redding produced a United States flag, poured either liquor or gasoline over it, and set it afire. A Negro policeman rushed up to remonstrate, and was shot down by one of the "Abyssinians." In the ensuing melee a white sailor and a white shopkeeper were killed.

Police seized Redding on the spot, and later rounded up Jonas. Redding and another Negro subsequently were hanged for their part in the affray. Jonas tried to save himself by giving information about the movement. Redding, he said, had not confined his propaganda activities to Chicago, but had visited several other cities, handing out blanks which, when properly filled out, would procure membership in the Star Order of Ethiopia and identify the signer as an "Ethiopian Missionary to Abyssinia." The signer expressed his loyalty to the "mother country," and renounced the name of Negro, given him against his will by a race other than his own. A subtle bait was embodied in the clause expressing the new member's willingness to proceed to Ethiopia to fill any position for which he might be qualified. Most of the positions represented as being open were important and lucrative ones.

During the trial Redding comported himself with a great deal more dignity than did his white confederate. He resolutely and unrepentantly addressed the court in these words:

> My mission is marked in the Bible. Even if they have captured me, some other leaders will rise up and lead the Ethiopian back to Africa. The Bible says, "So shall the King of Assyria lead away the Egyptian prisoners and the Ethiopian captives, young and old . . . to the shame of Egypt." The Ethiopians do not belong here and should be taken back to their own country. Their time was up in 1919. They came in 1619. The time is up. The burning of the flag last Sunday night by me was a symbol that Abyssinians are not wanted in this country. That was the sign the Bible spoke of.

In 1925, as Garvey paced up and down in his newly occupied cell in Atlanta, a small Negro wearing a flaming red fez similar to those worn by Turks appeared in empty lots and on street corners of Chicago's South Side to proclaim a startling new doctrine. He was Noble Drew Ali (born Timothy Drew in North Carolina), Prophet of Islam, and founder of the Moorish-American Science Temple. Little is known of Drew Ali's early history. He is reputed to have been an expressman in New Jersey, where he is said to have founded the first temple as early as 1913. There is also some evidence to indicate that he had established branches of his cult in Pittsburgh and Detroit before he came to Chicago.

Drew's main contention was that the people commonly known in America as Negroes are of Moorish descent and thus Asiatics. He further insisted that they are not black at all, but olive-hued. Act six of his *Divine Constitution and By-Laws* reads:

> With us all members must declare their nationality and their Divine Creed that they may know that they are a part and partial [sic] of this said government and that they are not Negroes, Colored Folks, Black People, or Ethiopians, because these names were given by slaveholders, in 1779 and lasted until 1865, during the time of slavery, but this is a new era of time now, and all men must proclaim their

free national name to be recognized by the government in which they live and the nations of the earth, this is the reason why Allah the Great God of the Universe ordained Noble Drew Ali, the prophet, to redeem the people from their sinful ways. The Moorish Americans are the descendants of the ancient Moabites who inhabited the North Western and South Western shores of Africa.

Prophet Noble Drew Ali did not immediately rally many disciples to his banner, the Moorish star and crescent on a field of red. But he persisted, and at length was able to set up permanent headquarters. Though semiliterate, he possessed an eloquent tongue, a persuasive manner, and a native shrewdness that enabled him to sway the poor and unlettered people who listened to him. Most of them remembered the race riots of 1919; all of them had experienced discrimination and other wrongs. Drew Ali was offering them pride of race and dignity. In 1927 a successful convention encouraged Drew Ali to expand his proselytizing activities to other cities. It is difficult to ascertain just how many temples resulted, but those in Pittsburgh, Detroit, Philadelphia, Kansas City, Charleston (West Virginia), Lansing, and Youngstown are fairly well authenticated.

Drew Ali had written and published his *Koran*, a slim pamphlet consisting of a curious mixture of the Mohammedan holy book of the same name, the Christian Bible, the words of Marcus Garvey, and anecdotes of the life of Jesus—the whole bound together with the prophet's own pronouncements and interpretations. Garvey was eulogized at every meeting as the John the Baptist of the movement. The prophet began to do a profitable business in various nostrums and charms he had concocted—among them Old Moorish Healing Oil, Moorish Purifier Bath Compound, and Moorish Herb Tea for Human Ailments.

More and more "Asiatics" flocked to the star and crescent standard. They flaunted their fezzes on the street and treated the white man with undisguised contempt. Many of them affected formidable-looking beards. Drew Ali announced that each devout Moorish American must carry a card bearing his credentials and his real (or Asiatic) name, signed by the prophet with his seal. Often enough "slave" names were transformed into "real" ones by the simple addition of "El" or "Bey," these being titles signifying Moorish dignity. The membership card and button, when displayed to Europeans, would convince them that the bearer was enlightened and a member of an organization to be feared and respected.

To the prophet this theory of new-found independence had been a more or less purely ethical or theoretical point, and he had not reckoned on its practical effect among his zealous followers. Alarming reports of street brawls, threats, insults, and minor violence centering around Moorish Americans soon were brought to his notice. Members were accosting the white enemy on the streets, showing him their membership cards and buttons, and proclaiming in the name of Drew Ali that they had been emancipated from "European" domination.

Recalling the downfall of the militant Abyssinians and contemplating the current difficulties of the Garvey movement, Drew Ali issued this ukase:

> I hereby order all Moors that they must cease from all radical or agitating speeches while on their jobs, or in their homes, or on the streets. Stop flashing your cards before Europeans as this only causes confusion. We did not come to cause confusion; our work is to uplift the nation.

The increase in dues-paying members (estimates have placed the peak as high as 10,000 in Chicago alone) as well as other rewards of temple leadership attracted a number of converts more eager to cut in on the benefits of temple leadership than to spread the Islamic doctrine among the unsaved. Drew Ali on his part began to be hampered by his lack of formal education as the business affairs of the cult became more complicated. He enlisted the aid of several men who proved to be more cunning than scrupulous.

Drew Ali's leadership was soon contested. In 1929 he became embroiled in a quarrel with Sheik Claude Greene, small-time politician and former butler of the philanthropist Julius Rosenwald. One day Drew arrived at his office to find that Greene had moved all the furniture outside and declared himself the grand sheik. A civil war ensued, each faction enlisting support from temples in other cities. Greene was shot and stabbed to death in his offices at the Unity Club on the night of March 15, 1929.

Drew Ali was arrested as he sat with his wife and a group of followers celebrating, authorities charged, the murder of his rival. The prophet, from prison, issued a message to his flock:

TO THE HEADS OF ALL TEMPLES, ISLAM

I, your prophet, do hereby and now write you a letter as a warning and appeal to your good judgment for the present and the future. Though I am now in custody for you and the cause, it is all right and it is well for all who still believe in me and my father, God. I have redeemed all of you and you shall be saved, all of you, even me. I go to bat Monday, May 20, before the Grand Jury. If you are with me, be there. Hold on and keep faith, and great shall be your reward. Remember my laws and love ye one another. Prefer not a stranger to your brother. Love and truth and my peace I leave you all.

Peace from
Your Prophet
NOBLE DREW ALI

This proved to be Drew Ali's final official proclamation. Released on bond, he died under mysterious circumstances a few weeks later. One theory is that he succumbed to injuries inflicted by the police during his imprisonment; another is that he was set upon by partisans of Greene and beaten so severely that he never recovered.

After Drew Ali's death his attorney attempted unsuccessfully to hold the group together. Each among several of the prophet's disciples announced that he alone was the rightful inheritor of Drew Ali's leadership. Each established a little temple of his own. More than one sought to lend additional weight to his claim by professing to be the reincarnation of the prophet.

Among Negroes caught in a World War II dragnet and subsequently convicted of conspiracy to thwart the Selective Service Law was Mrs. Mittie M. L. Gordon, leader of the Ethiopian-Pacific Movement, an outgrowth of the Peace Movement of Ethiopia.

The Peace Movement of Ethiopia was formed originally to help the Ethiopians in the Italo-Ethiopian war of 1935–36. When the conflict was over, the members, who had in the meantime separated into warring factions, carried on a nationalistic and "Back-to-Africa" campaign. Though all the Chicago organizations directly descended from the UNIA boasted a combined membership of less than 1,000 members, they united in 1939 to sponsor enthusiastically a proposal by Senator Theodore ("The Man") Bilbo of Mississippi that Negroes desiring to go back to Africa should be speeded on their way with federal assistance. Three hundred Chicago lobbyists representing remnants of the Garvey legions assembled a fleet of dilapidated trucks and headed for Washington to lend moral support to "The Man." Most of them never arrived, for the rickety trucks began breaking down before they had left the Chicago city limits behind.

Mrs. Gordon was first summoned before federal authorities on August 25, 1941, to answer to the charge of influencing young Negro men against registering for the draft. She denied this allegation, and asserted that the principal object of her organization was to transport American Negroes to Liberia. She said that approximately 4,000,000 people were affiliated with the movement, since all of them had signed petitions endorsing the Bilbo recommendation. Thomas Jefferson and Abraham Lincoln, she pointed out, had favored similar action. She went on:

> Those men knew the two races couldn't live together. And our race is dying out through amalgamation. There are 8,000,000 mulattoes in the United States now. Whites should remain white and blacks should remain black. Africa is our country and that's where we want to go —to the soil of Liberia.

She then produced a letter from Edwin Barclay, President of Liberia, in which he somewhat cautiously said that the country "would welcome selected emigrants who were fitted for the pioneering life." "The government should use the relief money now being spent on blacks here to transport all self-respecting blacks to Liberia," said Mrs. Gordon, herself on the relief rolls.

As she spoke, many observers had long since decided that the picture of Liberia ("Land of the Free") as a snug harbor for the tempest-tossed arks of the Negro seekers was a slightly illusionary one. And more than a century after the republic's establishment, a railroad superintendent for the Republic Steel Corporation's mining compound in the Bomi Hills near Monrovia was still taking a distinctly pessimistic viewpoint. Luther Henry Lemley wrote in 1963:

> Enforced labor is prevalent now. When a government worker wants some work done, usually at a private farm, he merely tells a clan chief to have sufficient men at the job site the next morning, and the men will be there waiting to work. The men will receive no pay for their labor, except perhaps a cup of rice during the day.

Era Bell Thompson, Negro American journalist and editor for the Johnson publications, felt a nostalgic tug pulling her toward her ancestral motherland in Africa and responded. Though she felt optimistic about the future for the black republic, she found conditions there somewhat less than idyllic in 1954. She recalls her first impressions of the streets of Monrovia, the capital:

> As startling as was the nudity, and as pathetic the obvious poverty, what surprised me most were the Syrian and Lebanese proprietors behind the counters. It was a black man's country, but there was the same lack of business leadership found in Negro neighborhoods in the States. Even the better-class stores on the hill were owned mostly by white immigrants and staffed by white clerks. According to Liberian law, only the descendants of Africans could own property or become citizens (the President could make one a citizen on sight), but somewhere along the line control of their own trade had got out of hand. The question of white monopoly over a black country's business was a sore one, I soon found.

From passive resistance, as manifested by her agitation against registration for the draft, Mrs. Gordon and her followers were said to have shifted to open advocacy of the Japanese cause after Pearl Harbor. At least she was sentenced to a term in a federal penitentiary for her subversive activities. Nevertheless, the Peace Movement of Ethiopia survived the war, and was still functioning on a small scale on South State Street in Chicago in the 1960s. Several other organizations and their leaders preached hatred for the white man and fraternity with the Japanese because they were a colored race. Among these were the Pacific Movement of the Eastern

World and the Iron Defense Legion. Members of the latter organization wore uniforms imitating those of Nazi storm troopers, and were reputed to have drilled with rifles.

Though Mrs. Gordon and the Peace Movement of Ethiopia sought to apply Garvey's remedy for the Negro question—migration to Africa—the "Moors" and also the Islamites (as we shall see in the following chapter) tried to escape by seceding—or attempting to secede—from the white man's society as well as from the ranks of American Negroes and also by establishing their inherent superiority over the white man. The "Moors" insisted that their identification with an ancient culture gave them an immediate advantage over the Johnny-come-lately paleskin, who until quite recently had been living in caves and drinking blood from skulls. The Islamites abhor the "cavy" as an effete, bleached-out mutation of the "original" black man. The "cavies" have further corrupted themselves by mating with beasts, so that they have in fact become beasts themselves. This, it may be remembered, is a *volte-face* from "Professor" Charles Carroll's theory that Negroes are not really human for a similar reason. The "Moors" at one time talked vaguely of "taking over the government of the United States." During World War II, perhaps impelled by prudence, they modified drastically even that nebulous ambition. In the years following the war the membership of the Moorish-American Science Temple dwindled to an infinitesimal fraction of its peak strength. In Chicago and two or three other cities temples sustained mainly by the ghost of Noble Drew Ali existed precariously. Most of the more ardent members had defected to the Lost-Found Nation of Islam. As to the Islamites, they always spoke of a return to Mecca in a symbolical or spiritual sense. Neither of the "Asiatic" cults expressed more than an academic interest in a "Back-to-Africa" movement.

While "Moors," Islamites, and leaders of the Peace Movement of Ethiopia and the Pacific Movement of the Eastern World were eulogizing Marcus Garvey and hailing him as John the Baptist of the campaign to arouse the Negro to proud racial consciousness, the founder of the UNIA was trying to rebuild his shattered organization from exile in Jamaica. Somehow or other he managed to keep his magazine the *Black Man* going. He eventually gave up the struggle in Jamaica and went back to London, perhaps hoping to revive some of the evangelical zeal he found there when he first conceived the grandiose scheme of recapturing the continent of Africa for its rightful heirs. In 1938 he appealed in the *Black Man* for one thousand students to attend his School of African Philosophy. He planned to train a corps of diplomats, interpreters, economists, and other specialists to be ready for service when Africa's hour should strike.

A dwindling band of the faithful stuck with Garvey through thick and thin. On May Day 1938 a parade of the Royal African Legions marched through Harlem. They were the titled dignitaries of UNIA—the dukes and lords and knight commanders of the Distinguished Order of Ethiopia and the knight commanders of the Supreme Order of the Nile. Their uniforms were resplendent, their heads high and proud. But the procession was only two blocks long, a sad comedown from the palmy days. A huge limousine carried in its back seat a life-size portrait of the absent leader. Harlemites assembled along the line of march to cheer the image of the cocky little Jamaican.

At the head of the parade pranced a richly caparisoned horse bearing the majestic figure of a gigantic Negro arrayed in barbaric splendor. Reporters tried to question him, but discovered that the interrogation had to be done through an interpreter. It was explained that the rider was an African prince who neither spoke nor understood English.

"We are showing the world Dr. Garvey isn't forgotten, although he is many miles away," the black prince said gravely.

Marcus Garvey died in London in 1940. He was not an old man—only fifty-three—but unceasing failure since his release from Atlanta had embittered him and worn down his spirit. Perhaps as he lay dying he thought of a derisive jingle he had heard often during his sojourn in Harlem:

When a monkey-chaser dies,
Don't need no undertaker.
Just throw him in the Harlem River—
He'll float back to Jamaica.

But Garvey was never going back to Jamaica. What was more, he would never set foot on the hot, rich soil of Africa he had sworn to wrest from the white interlopers. Curiously enough, he had never found the time or the opportunity to visit the land of his ancestors. Ironically, too, his implacable adversary, William Edward Burghardt Du Bois—the scholar who had ridiculed Garvey's "Back-to-Africa" crusade, some said because it had wrecked his own Pan-African movement—died August 27, 1963, in Accra, Ghana. He had come there at the invitation of President Kwame Nkrumah to supervise the preparation of the *Encyclopedia Africana*. The project materialized a long-cherished dream of Du Bois. Many years before he had written an introductory study for a proposed *Negro Encyclopedia*. Now it was being sponsored by the government of the first Negro republic in the resurgent New Africa. President Nkrumah, on his part, frequently had taken occasion to praise Marcus Garvey as a prime catalyst of that resurgence.

Garvey's connubial voyages were scarcely less tempestuous than his public career. When he went to New York in 1916 he was accompanied by pretty Amy Ashwood, who had been a secretary for the UNIA in Kingston. While Garvey's private secretary at the UNIA in New York, she bravely tackled a demented gunman who had fired two shots at him, one of which grazed his temple. Amy unhesitatingly threw her own body into the line of fire before Garvey himself subdued his assailant. In December 1919 he was married to Amy. When she abandoned the role of secretary for that of housewife, she was replaced by another Amy—Amy Jacques, a good-looking girlhood friend of hers whom she had urged to come up from Jamaica. Soon Amy I was charging that Garvey's attitude toward Amy II was somewhat more ardent than that proper in an employer-employee relationship. The couple separated, and while Amy I was absent in England Garvey obtained a divorce by default. Amy I unsuccessfully challenged the divorce's legality. She then manifested extraordinary candor in revealing intimate details of her life with the head of the UNIA, thus providing the heavily anti-Garvey Negro press with delightfully juicy material about her ex-spouse's eccentricities and misbehaviors.

Time served to modify the rancor of Amy I, however. In 1960

Lerone Bennett, Jr., of *Ebony* interviewed her in London, where she was conducting the Afro-Peoples Centre, an organization pledged to the Garvey slogan of "Africa for Africans." She spoke indulgently of her former mate:

> Like the rest of us, he was made of mortal clay and he carried his full burden of human weakness and limitation. His chief failing was his inability to share responsibility. He was autocratic, vain, and he loved to hog the spotlight. He erred in trying to shine too brightly.

Then she added:

> He must be resting peacefully and joyously in the certainty that history will give the verdict that he neither lived nor labored in vain and that his successes by far outweighed his faults and mistakes. Ghana's Black Star Line is a living compliment to Garvey. Nkrumah hasn't forgotten him.

Amy Jacques Garvey, still a vigorous and eloquent evangel of Garveyism in 1965, maintained that hostile white and Negro newspapers had distorted the intent of Garvey's "Back-to-Africa" slogan in order to ridicule and discredit him. She said that the movement was mainly one of the heart, mind, and soul—it essentially was a spiritual crusade. Its principal goal, she contended, had been won, for it had awakened the slumbering race consciousness of black men everywhere and galvanized it into deeds.

The second Mrs. Garvey was standing proudly by on November 4, 1956, when Mrs. Norman Manley, wife of Jamaica's prime minister, unveiled a bust of Garvey, the work of the Jamaican sculptor Alvin Marriott, in Kingston's George VI Park (once the town's racecourse). On a platform built near by for the ceremony were representatives of local and foreign governments, labor unions, churches, and other organizations. The military band of the Old West Indian Regiment, clad in uniforms as colorful as those once worn by the Royal African Legions as they marched through Harlem to the cheers of black multitudes thronging the sidewalks, had led a preceding parade. William L. Sherrill, heading a delegation of five UNIA pilgrims from the United States, delivered a eulogy in which he said:

> Because Garvey lived, Jamaica is different; because Garvey lived, Negro America is different; because Garvey lived, Africa is different. His work and teachings gave birth to a new Negro, a New Africa. . . . He did more to crystallize National sentiment in so-called backward countries than any single individual in our times. Measured by the standard of change, Garvey rises to the heights of greatness.

Sherrill, who once represented Garvey at the League of Nations, still maintained, as its president, headquarters of the UNIA in Detroit. Three years before the dedication in Kingston, an estimated 2,000 Garveyites had assembled on August 1 at a UNIA rally in Harlem, a date celebrated since 1949 as Marcus Garvey Day (the first UNIA convention had begun on August 1, 1920). A number of speakers noted with satisfaction that the nationalistic fires lighted by Garvey were burning fiercely in several nations of Asia and Africa. "Miss Africa, 1953," winner in a beauty contest sponsored by the convention, was awarded a silver loving cup appropriately inscribed "Marcus Garvey Day,1953."

Was Garvey "a sheer opportunist and a demagogic charlatan," as Robert W. Bagnall had called him? Few among either white and Negro historians or among the "beloved and scattered millions" to whom he addressed his fervent appeal would agree with that ungenerous estimate a quarter century after his death. Whatever he was, he had graven his name deep. Even W. E. B. Du Bois, his unrelenting enemy, had been moved, upon hearing of Garvey's death in 1940, to comment:

> It was a grandiose and bombastic scheme, utterly impracticable as a whole, but it was sincere and had some practical features; and Garvey proved not only an astonishing popular leader, but a master of propaganda. Within a few years, news of his movement, of his promises and plans, reached Europe and Asia, and penetrated every corner of Africa.

CHAPTER XIV

Registered with Allah

The Asiatic black man is the original man, and ruler of the universe, the eight inhabited planets and this planet earth. Islam is the true religion. A religion which can be proved by mathematics in a limit of time. The Muslims have the wisdom. We're not afraid of the devil, this so-called white man. We talk right up to them. They're afraid of you if you've got the Truth. Just tell 'em, "White man, you're a devil. You were grafted from the original black man." He'll say, "Yes, you're right." He'll admit it, 'cause you got the power. Just say, "You're a beast; you've got one-third animal blood." He won't deny it, 'cause it's true. When they were driven from the Holy City of Mecca, they lived in the caves of Europe and mingled with the beasts. Christianity is the religion of the so-called white man. Have you ever noticed that the very things he teaches us that the devil does is the very things *he* is doing? *He* is the devil.

—from a sermon by a minister of Chicago Temple No. 2,
Lost-Found Nation of Islam.

SOMETIME before 1930 a Negro, or at any rate a dark-skinned man, appeared in the "Paradise Valley" Negro neighborhood of Detroit, selling silks and raincoats from door to door. He soon made it clear that he was not to be regarded as an ordinary itinerant peddler. He introduced himself to prospective customers in this manner:

I am W. D. Fard, and I came from the Holy City of Mecca. More about myself I will not tell you yet, for the time has not yet come. I am your brother. You have not yet seen me in my royal robes.

He proclaimed that his mission was to secure "freedom, justice, and equality" for his "uncle" living in the "wilderness of North America, surrounded and robbed completely by the cave man." "The uncle of W. D. Fard" became a symbolical term for all Negroes of North America, while the white man was referred to as a "cave man," a "satan," a "blue-eyed devil" or a "Caucasian devil." Sometimes he would be called familiarly or contemptuously a "cavy" or "common ca."

While Fard maintained that he was racially identical to North American Negroes, he also claimed to have been born in Mecca, the son of a wealthy member of the tribe of Koreish to which the prophet Mohammed belonged. He was reputed to have been educated in England or at the University of California; to have been trained for a diplomatic career in the service of the kingdom of Hejaz. A less respectful report is that he was jailed at least once in California as a narcotics pusher before he arrived in Detroit. Though it had been surmised from his talk that he must have been a follower of Noble Drew Ali at some time or other, Elijah Muhammad, Fard's right-hand disciple who was destined to head the Black Muslim movement in Chicago, denied that the two ever met. Fard has been pictured as light-colored for a Negro, with an Oriental cast of countenance. This description, if accurate, would lend credence to his contention that he was of Arabian descent.

Fard at times in his apocryphal career used various other names. Among these were Walli Farrad, Professor Ford, Farrad Mohammed, and F. Mohammed Ali. After his disappearance in 1933 or 1934, his followers deified him as the God Allah. Fard himself is said to have told Elijah Muhammad, "I am Mahdi; I am God."

While pursuing his trade as a peddler, Fard never lost an opportunity to lecture Negroes into whose homes he was invited. One of his converts said of him:

> He has told us that the silks he carried were the same kind our people used to make in their home country, Arabia, and that he had come from there. So we all asked him to tell us about our own country. If we asked him to eat with us, he would eat whatever we had on the table, but after the meal he would begin to talk like this:

"Now, don't eat this food. It is poison to you. The people in your own country do not eat it. Since they eat the right kind of food they have the best health all the time. If you would live just like the people in your home country, you would never be sick any more."

So we wanted him to tell us more about ourselves and our home country and about how we could be free from rheumatism, aches, and pains.

Fard began to arrange meetings in the homes of those willing to listen to him, and before long had gathered a small but devoted band of followers. His excoriations of the "white devil and his so-called spook civilization" became more and more virulent. He extended his condemnation to the Christian religion, though he frequently quoted from the Bible. In his *Secret Ritual of the Nation of Islam,* Part 2, Section II, Fard declared:

Me and my people have tried this so-called mystery God for bread, clothing, and a home. And we have received nothing but hard times, hunger, naked, and out of doors. Also was beat and killed by the ones that advocated that kind of God.

Most of Fard's converts had arrived recently from the South, and were inclined to agree with his contentions about the outrages perpetrated by the "white devils" who were running everything to the disadvantage of the black man. Challar Sharrieff, who had rejected the "slave" name of Charles Peoples, told of hearing the prophet explain:

The Bible tells you that the sun rises and sets. This is not so. The sun stands still. All your lives you have been thinking that the earth never moved. Stand and look toward the sun and know that it is the earth you are standing on that is moving.

This was indeed a revelation to Sharrieff. He went on:

Up to that day I always went to the Baptist church. After I heard the sermon from the prophet, I was turned around completely. When I went home and heard that dinner was ready, I said: "I don't want to eat dinner. I just want to go back to the meetings." I wouldn't eat any meals, but I goes back that night and I goes to every meeting after that. Just to think that the sun above me never moved at all and that the earth we are on was doing all the moving. That changed everything for me.

The Negroes of Detroit could see all about them justifications for Fard's accusations against the white man and his civilization. As the depression tightened its grip, numbers of them were laid off while white men were retained. In other instances, Negroes of long service were replaced by white newcomers. "Hard times, hunger, naked, and out of doors" assumed an immediate significance for the "original" black men. When they were obliged to apply for public assistance, the more sensitive Negroes keenly felt the humiliation attached. It was not hard to convince them that they were objects of special discrimination. Fard and his rapidly increasing band of disciples made considerable hay in the Negro community. It has been estimated that 8,000 Detroiters joined the cult during its first four years.

After Fard had succeeded in establishing permanent headquarters in the first Temple of Islam, he "registered" all the members, promising to restore their "righteous" or "original" names to replace the "slave" names forcibly fastened on them by the "Caucasian devil." To obtain his "righteous" name, the applicant for membership was required to write Fard a letter asking that he be freed of his "slave" name. While waiting for his "righteous" name the acolyte was designated by his first name and a simple "X." It was pointed out later that the "X" stood for "unknown," as in algebra. It was assumed that Fard knew the "righteous" names by virtue of the spirit of Allah within him, or that they would be made known to him by divine revelation at an appropriate time. There were complications in this system of nomenclature, however. At one time the prophet reportedly bestowed three different surnames on as many brothers, not being aware of their common parentage. When confronted with this discrepancy, he blandly asserted that he had perceived that each of the brothers had a different father.

The rapid growth of the first temple in Detroit was accompanied by the birth of various subsidiary departments. The Fruit of Islam (FOI), a semimilitary defense corps, was trained in the use of boxing, karate, and judo. It was charged, but emphatically denied, that they also drilled with rifles. The Muslim Girls Training Corps Class instructed young women in the domestic arts and taught them the behavior expected of a Muslim wife and mother. Fard's especial pride, though, was the University of Islam, to which the children of Muslim families were sent rather than to the public schools.

At the university (in reality an elementary school with some high school subjects) pupils were taught the "knowledge of our own" as distinct from that of the "spook civilization of the Caucasian devils." Courses were offered in "higher mathematics," astronomy, and what was termed the "general knowledge and ending of the spook civilization." All this specialized knowledge was deemed necessary to combat the "tricknollogy" learned by the "Caucasian devils" in their schools. The "higher mathematics" consisted mainly of a variety of "problems" usually embodying a symbolical meaning obscure or unintelligible to the uninstructed and containing a dizzying number of digits. The symbolism perhaps was designed to counter the "tricknollogy" of the "blue-eyed devil." Several of these problems were read at each meeting of the cult as well as in classes of the University of Islam. This is a characteristic problem:

> A lion, in a cage, walking back and forth sixty feet per minute, seeking a way out of the cage. It took him nearly four centuries to find the door. Now, with modern equipment, he is walking three thousand feet per minute and he has three thousand miles by two thousand miles to go yet. How long will it take him to cover this territory of said three thousand by two thousand miles at the above walking rate? He also has seventeen million keys, which he turns at the rate of sixteen and seventeen one-hundredths per minute. How long will it take him to turn the whole seventeen million? Sixty minutes equals one hour, twenty-four hours equals one day, three hundred and sixty-five days equals one year. The above figures do not include rusty locks.

An obliging cult member shed some light on this problem by identifying the lion as the "original" black man, or Asiatic, held in bondage four centuries within a trap fabricated by the "Caucasian devil." The seventeen million keys represent a like number of

"Asiatics" enslaved in the "wilderness of North America." "Modern equipment," naturally, means the teaching of Islam by which the "original" man is enabled to progress rapidly toward emancipation. "Rusty locks" are recalcitrant "Asiatics" who have not yet accepted Islam.

Here are three more problems:

(1) What is the physical standard of a devil against the original? How many ounces of brains does an original have? What is the exact percentage of tricknollogy used by the devil in the so-called spook civilization? How long has the devil on the planet been using tricknollogy? Tell us how and who invented the devil.

(2) The total atoms equal 10,000,000,000,000,000,000,000,000,000,000,000,000,000,000,000,000,000,000,000,000,000,000,000,000,000. How many atoms are there in North America?

(3) The uncle of W. D. Fard lives in the wilderness of North America, surrounded and completely robbed by the cave man. He is working sixteen hours out of twenty-four hours for very little pay. He has eight in his family to support, besides other little bills to meet each month. On top of that, a cave man came along and sold him an old touring car, which travels downhill at the rate of forty-eight miles an hour. If it is shown by actual test that a force of two hundred fifty pounds is required to maintain this rate at downhill speed, what horsepower must the engine deliver at the wheels? Thirty-three thousand pounds equals one horsepower.

At one time attendance officers of the Detroit Board of Education attempted to break up the University of Islam and to compel its students to attend the public schools, claiming that the university's teaching standards were below an acceptable level even for the elementary grades. This move precipitated violent resistance. Fearful of causing race riots, the courts released almost all of those arrested for physical interference with the school board's orders.

More serious difficulties arose over the question of human sacrifice. It was rumored in Detroit that Fard had stipulated the sacrifice of four "Caucasian devils" as a prerequisite of the pious Muslim's eventual return to the Holy City of Mecca. On November 21, 1932, the people of Detroit became acutely conscious of the cult through its first widely publicized human sacrifice. Robert Karriem, a prominent cultist whose "slave" name had been Robert

Harris, erected an altar in his home and invited his roomer, John J. Smith, to offer himself as a human sacrifice so that he might become "the Savior of the world." Smith agreed, according to Harris, and at nine P.M.—the appointed time—Harris plunged a knife into his heart. The next day the Detroit *News* commented:

> An Asiatic trend among Negro dole recipients of the Elmwood district, noted at the time as a passing whim, today came back with horror to two women welfare workers on learning that the fanatical Robert Harris had intended them for human sacrifice as infidels . . . Harris stated to the police that each of these was a "no-good Christian" and that they would have been sacrificed if he knew where he could find them.

By 1933 the Prophet of Islam had organized the Detroit temple so efficiently that he felt able to recede into the background, appearing with less and less frequency to his followers during his final month in Detroit. This mysterious withdrawal only served to strengthen the belief that he was indeed the "Supreme Ruler of the Universe" (or, as he called himself, the God Allah) temporarily assuming a mundane form in order to fulfill a divine mission. Not all of his followers believed in Fard's divinity, and controversy over this question was one of the several causes of dissension in the movement. Another was the objections of some patriotic Muslims to what they judged to be Fard's disloyal attitude toward the United States government. One of these was Abdul Mohammed, who had been one of Fard's trusted lieutenants. Abdul refused to swear sole allegiance to the Moslem flag when he was ordered to do so, and seceded to form a small group of his own. As a direct consequence of internal disputes, the Chicago branch of the Nation of Islam came into being in late 1933 or early 1934.

Fard himself was last seen in Detroit at about the same time, or shortly before. He then disappeared altogether as far as any authoritative record is concerned. On one occasion Elijah Muhammad, his successor as head of the Lost-Found Nation of Islam but not heir to his divinity, stated that he had been with Fard at the airport when he was deported. The police record of a courtroom riot on March 5, 1935, involving members of the "Allah Temple of Islam" on South State Street, named the cultists' leader as "W. D. Fard, or Fard Mohammed, or Elijah Mohammed." An unsuccessful search was made for him. A newspaper account of the riot said that Noble Drew Ali had been the original prophet of the cult, described as "a secret organization of national proportions." Nothing that was disclosed definitely indicated that Fard was present at the riot, or, indeed, that he ever came to Chicago after leaving Detroit.

Fard's disappearance did not cause a real leadership hiatus. It had been apparent for some time that it had been his intention to place the Nation of Islam under the stewardship of Elijah Muhammad. Muhammad, whose "slave" name had been Elijah (or Robert) Poole, was born in 1897 in Sandersville, Georgia, the son of a Baptist preacher who tried to make a living for his wife and thirteen children as a sharecropper. At sixteen, having managed to struggle through the fourth grade in a ramshackle "colored" school, young Elijah left the parental nest. There followed a number of ill-paid and short-lasting jobs before he was married to Clara Evans. In 1923 the couple moved with their two children to Detroit, a Mecca of freedom and opportunity in the minds of many of Elijah's racial brethren held in bondage in the Egypt land called Dixie. Elijah said later that he has witnessed enough of the white man's cruel brutality in Georgia to last him 26,000 years. Detroit was somewhat less than the utopia he had envisioned. Prejudice and hard times had not been entirely left behind. Then a fortuitous meeting with W. D. Fard, probably when Elijah was working on the Chevrolet assembly line, brought a momentous change in the life and attitude of the transplanted Georgia boy. He always thereafter credited Fard with taking him out of "the gutters in the streets of Detroit" and teaching him the true knowledge of Islam. Elijah soon was an assiduous laborer in the temple vineyard. Fard at first bestowed upon him the "original" surname of Karriem, but later changed this to the more impressive cognomen of Muhammad in recognition of his yeoman service to the cause. When Fard dubbed him "Minister of Islam and Messenger of Allah," he was virtually choosing him as his successor.

After Fard's disappearance, Elijah's faction (those favorable to the deification of Fard), severed all connection with the parent group, assumed the name "Temple People," and set up headquarters in Chicago. The Detroit branch floundered uncertainly for a while without aggressive leadership, then came under the hegemony of Elijah. Both branches soon began to enjoy a moderate amount of prosperity.

In September, 1942, FBI agents collared Elijah Muhammad and several other members of the Chicago temple. Some newspaper accounts gave Elijah's "real" name as Robert Poole. The Muslims were charged with evading the draft and influencing others to do so, and also with maintaining seditious relations with the Japanese government. The latter indictment more or less petered out. The Islamites would be likely to feel at least passive sympathy for any nation of colored people at war with the "blue-eyed Caucasian devils," but the government failed to prove that there was any active link between the Nation of Islam and the nation of Japan. The Muslims' aversion to any sort of registration other than that with Allah had antedated the war with Japan by a good many years.

The temple people had isolated themselves politically, socially, and economically not only from white men but from Negroes who declined to reject Christianity as an evil ally of the "white devil." The economic confusion and upheaval attending the depression they explained by quoting Elijah's assertion that the white man's allotted rule of the world actually had ended in 1914, and that Allah was preparing to wipe out his "spook civilization." It had been existing on borrowed time. As we have seen, the Islamite's refusal to register for the draft indicated no new tendency. Cult members had always been particularly vociferous in their denunciations of President Franklin D. Roosevelt and the New Deal. In their opinion, the WPA and other alphabetical agencies spawned during the depression were subtle efforts on the part of white men to save what was left of their dying civilization by getting "original" black men to sign up and be given a number. They eschewed social security and relief case numbers as manifestations of the aptitude of the "white devil" in the devious art of "tricknollogy." They had no intention of giving the expiring "spook civilization" a revitalizing blood transfusion by embracing it or even collaborating with it. A typewritten piece of temple literature read:

Roosevelt gave you a social security number just to hold you, and now he's getting ready to call in these numbers and give you a stamp . . . He's going to put a stamp on you, the mark of the beast. You signed up with the devil and he gives you the filthy crumbs from his table like the rich man gave the man Lazarus.

Elijah Muhammad spent three years in the federal prison at Milan, Michigan. He does not seem to have languished idly there, but appears to have managed to maintain a connection with and a grip on the Black Muslim organization. (Muslim people for some reason objected to the "Black" attached to their name, even though they regarded black as emblematical of superiority. The term became so common, particularly after the Muslims engaged in public relations activities in the sixties, that they apparently ceased to resent it.)

After his release in 1946, Elijah vigorously resumed his organizational activities.

His imprisonment had the effect of glorifying him as a martyr to the cause of black men. It was easy for him to establish in the minds of many Negroes hitherto impervious to his exhortations that he had been persecuted for their sakes. There were at the time of Elijah's return to active control four temples in operation, those in Milwaukee and Washington, D.C., having been added to No. 1 in Detroit and No. 2 in Chicago. In the 1950s a period of spectacular expansion began. By the end of 1960 there were as many as sixty-nine temples or missions distributed throughout twenty-seven states extending from Massachusetts southward to Florida and westward to California. A comparatively small number of the buildings housing the temples or mosques were owned by the sect. Some of the Muslim groups met in rented quarters or even in the homes of members. Membership, of course, had zoomed accordingly. It has been variously estimated from the less than 7,000 (not even half as many as in 1960–61) cited in 1965 by Aubrey Barnette, a disillusioned dropout from Boston's Temple No. 11, to the undoubtedly overexuberant claim of 200,000 sometimes made by Muslim spokesmen. About 100,000 would seem to be a more credible figure. In addition to the hard-core, tithe-paying members there are many thousands of Negroes who secretly or openly admire the Islamites for their defiance of the white man and for the exemplary personal life to which they are pledged.

In the 1950s the Black Muslims discarded to a great extent their policy of secrecy about their doctrines and activities. Rather, they seemed to court publicity from the white man's media of communication. Elijah Muhammad held forth regularly on a network of radio stations. White reporters were invited to the annual conventions, being admitted to the hall after a thorough but polite frisking by the FOI. The 1956 convention, held in a Protestant church in Chicago, was the first large one to exhibit this new tolerance if not deference toward the opinions of the "blue-eyed white devils." The 1960 convention in the Chicago Coliseum, which was called the "Thirtieth Session," attracted an audience of about 2,000, which included six white men, one white woman, and an Indian. The messenger of Allah arrived an hour late, clad in a conservative blue suit and wearing the black velvet skull cap, adorned with jewels and a crescent, that had become his badge of office for such ceremonial occasions. In the course of his long oration he enlightened his audience, which often interrupted him with cries of approbation, with these rather startling cosmogonical revelations:

> Sixty-nine trillion years ago, what is now earth was called moon. That part which is now moon blasted off from the moon and went 12,000 miles away. What is now earth left its pocket and went 36,000 miles away. When the part that is now moon blasted off, it dropped water on the other part now earth, covering three-fourths of its surface. Hence the ocean . . . Life has been going on for more than 66 trillion years. It has been here for 79 trillion years. Africa was then East Asia. The black man is of the tribe of Shabazz that came from Asia to the jungle of East Africa. There they became tough and hard. We are descendants of the Asiatic black people, according to the word of the Almighty Allah.

Elijah Muhammad also gave an account of a trip he had taken late in the previous year, accompanied by two of his sons, to Mohammedan sections of Asia and Africa, culminating in a pilgrimage to the Holy City of Mecca. He spoke of having been hospitably received everywhere. He found Cairo a "paradise" he was reluctant to leave. Taking exception to the Messenger's glowing account was one Talib Ahmad Dawud, leader of one of the several groups of "orthodox" Moslems in the United States that had branded Muhammad as an impostor and his cult as a fraud. Dawud had erroneously predicted that the Messenger of Allah would not be permitted to set foot on the soil of Saudi Arabia, much less make the traditional pilgrimage to Mecca. Dawud, a West Indian Negro who had been a musician with various jazz bands before being converted to Mohammedanism in 1940, was married to jazz singer Dakota Staton, also a Moslem. In 1950 Dawud took a large role in forming the Moslem Brotherhood, Inc., which set up temples in Philadelphia, Detroit, and Harlem and boasted of a membership of 100,000 "true" Moslems—a figure undoubtedly inflated. Dawud consistently jeered at Elijah Muhammad's assumption of divine authority, calling him "plain Elijah Poole of Sandersville, Georgia." At one time he and his wife tried unsuccessfully to legally enjoin the Lost-Found Nation of Islam from using the name "Muslim." He also inspired a series of anti-Elijah articles in the Chicago *New Crusader*. One of these alleged that W. D. Fard was in fact a white man, and produced a photograph to prove it. Plainly unfounded was the assertion that Fard was a Turkish agent for Hitler, and that Elijah Muhammad had met him in prison while doing his World War II stretch.

Despite the aspersions, it became evident that Elijah Muhammad's 1959 trip had had some impact upon the Moslem establishment in Cairo, Mecca, and elsewhere. The extent of his success in gaining recognition for his cult was difficult to gauge.

With the new candor about its doctrines and activities, the Lost-Found Nation of Islam outlined a rather elaborate mythology which borrowed in some of its latter aspects from the Christian Bible. The antihero or "devil" of this mythology is Yacub, who about 6,800 years ago was a dissident member of the original black tribe of Shabazz in the Holy City of Mecca. Precocious Yacub entered school when he was four; by the time he was eighteen he had graduated from all the existing colleges and universities. He was not overly modest about his capabilities, and his big talk irritated the Mecca authorities so much that they exiled him with 59,999 of his followers to the island of Patmos. Smarting under this rebuff, Yacub plotted revenge. He was a scientist skilled in genetics, and started a long series of breedings and crossbreedings that eventually developed a debased white man named Adam. Adam's descendants, at first walking on all fours and living in caves and trees (also mating with beasts), stayed on Patmos for six hundred years before they escaped to the mainland. They soon caused trouble for the "original" black men, over whom they at length gained mastery by resorting to underhanded dealings and low trickery. Tolerant Allah gave the white cave men six thousand years in which to perpetrate their knaveries and follies. When this time was up in 1914, he granted them an indefinite period of grace in which to reform. Unfortunately, they had not taken advantage of this benevolent reprieve, but recklessly persisted in their devilish ways. Prognostications of imminent doom became a regular feature of Muhammad's sermons in *Muhammad Speaks*, the cult's well-edited newspaper which began as a biweekly in 1960 and became a weekly in February 1965. On the front cover of the February 26, 1965, issue was emblazoned this lugubrious pronouncement by the Messenger: "FALLING, FALLING THE OLD WORLD!" In the accompanying article, beginning also on the front cover, Muhammad continued:

> America's burden in trying to protect herself from the attacking nations of the world is tremendous; one that she will not be able to carry. Therefore she must succumb to the powerful forces that are coming against her. The fall of a nation makes way for another. As the earth continues, all nations and their civilizations are limited upon it, except the original nation, which takes on renewal and changes . . . . Though in appearance America seems steadfast, she is moving toward an ultimate end.

The "so-called Negro," Muhammad went on, is due to inherit the earth—or what's left of it:

> Salvation must come to the so-called Negro. Everyone's eyes should be opened. The time of the ending of this world is now, and not yet to come, as you so foolishly think. The end is predicted and hinted in many places. Daniel (in the Bible) however gives you a better knowledge of it than in any other place. And, the Qur-an's prophecy is exact. Do not expect 10 more years. The fall will be within a few days.

This deference toward the "blue-eyed devil's" Scriptures is characteristic of the Messenger's curious ambivalence—making in one paragraph approving references to both the Holy Qur-an (Koran) and the Bible of the detested Christians.

With expansion both in membership and, presumably, affluence, the Nation of Islam became more practical-minded and economics-oriented. Taking a leaf from Marcus Garvey's book as well as from that of Soviet planners, Elijah Muhammad evolved a grandiose blueprint for a Muslim center in Chicago which was to cost $20,000,000 financed in large part by weekly contributions sent in by the faithful. Solicitation for funds became a regular feature in *Muhammad Speaks,* which also ran a double-page spread picturing Muhammad's conception of the proposed educational center: a bulbous-domed mosque flanked on one side by an elementary school and high school and on the other by a college and university. Atop the mosque's dome was a golden star and crescent of the Islamites. The illustration, in color, had been executed by staff artist Eugene Majied, who, after noting that "an architect's drawing will be presented when suitable grounds are secured," continued:

> The Honorable Elijah Muhammad's idea as shown in the picture conveys to us the true, and noble aims of the man. He wants to see the so-called American Negro lifted up to something which bespeaks that of his own. The school, the Mosque, agriculture, manufacturing, engineering—these foundations will build for us that which we can call our own. Note that he has no crosses, which represent murder and death, but the Crescent, which represents Life. His Sign lives forever. Let ALL so-called Negroes help him, for ALL shall benefit from this great achievement. This is not for Muslims exclusively, but for the whole black nation. The Honorable Elijah Muhammad says: "Let the Negro build his tabernacle in the wilderness."

Majied's exhortation was supplemented by this appeal: "Send your contributions today to: Muhammad's Mosque No. 2 Educational Fund, 5335 Greenwood Avenue, Chicago, Illinois 60615."

(The reference to "suitable grounds" recalled a dispute over a five-acre tract the Black Muslims had bought in the Chatham-Avalon district on Chicago's far South Side for a reported $150,000.

When it was learned that the Muslims intended to build their center on this site, both white and Negro residents of the community protested to such effect that the Chicago Park Commission, which had made the sale to the Muslims in the first place, set aside the tract as a park in 1960. The Muslims sued and won a settlement amounting to $165,000, a sum larger than the original price. To complicate matters, the properties on Greenwood Avenue were scheduled for razing as part of the Hyde Park renewal project.)

In the meantime, various small business enterprises, mostly of the service type, had blossomed under the Nation of Islam aegis in several cities: restaurants, bakeries, dress shops, barbershops, groceries, and cleaning establishments. These were part of an ambitious three-year Economic Plan.

As was the case with Garvey's commercial ventures, there were skeptics who ridiculed and low-rated the Messenger's economic program. One of these was Aubrey Barnette, whose disillusionment had led him to resign as secretary of Muhammad's Temple of Islam No. 11 in Boston. His apostasy, he charged, had earned him a severe beating by a Muslim goon squad in August 1964. Visiting Chicago, Barnette says he discovered that the University of Islam was little more than an unaccredited grammar school. (The university previously had been castigated by Illinois State Senator Arthur R. Gottshalk as hate-breeding and substandard.) The only one of the several Muslim commercial enterprises that could be called a going concern, Barnette maintained, was the dress shop, and its solvency was mainly due to its monopoly on the ankle-length robes worn by Muslim sisters.

It had been the custom of the Messenger himself to preserve a dignified silence in the face of such animadversions, but no such restraint circumscribed his high-ranking functionaries. John Ali, national secretary of Muhammad's Mosques of Islam, paid his respects to dropout Barnette in an article captioned "Folly of the Paid Informer" in the February 26, 1965, issue of *Muhammad Speaks*. (Barnette was branded an "informer" because his exposé of the cult had appeared in the *Saturday Evening Post*.) Ali fervently avowed his loyalty at the conclusion of his article:

No man in America, or anywhere in the world, loves his people more than Messenger Muhammad. No man in America or anywhere in the world has given or continues to give so much of himself for his people as Messenger Elijah Muhammad. The garbage of the Aubrey Barnettes, the Malcolm Littles and other hypocrites, disbelievers and devils shall take its place in disgrace, regret and a lake of fire.

The "Malcolm Little" mentioned was being downgraded from Minister Malcolm X of Muhammad's Temple of Islam No. 7 in Harlem. Until his suspension by Elijah Muhammad late in 1964, he had figured as the most articulate and most intelligent spokesman for the Black Muslims and probably the aging Elijah Muhammad's heir apparent. His eloquence and nimble wit had made him welcome on television and radio shows and as a speaker before college groups. He once said, with pardonable complacency, that the New York *Times* in 1963 rated him as second in popularity on college campuses, only Barry Goldwater being more desirable.

Born Malcolm Little in Omaha, Nebraska, in 1925, Malcolm X was one of eleven children of a Baptist preacher who was also a militant and outspoken Garveyite. The elder Little's outspokenness provoked the Ku Klux Klan into burning down the family's home in Lansing, Michigan. After he accepted the Muslim dictum that all white men are congenital devils, Malcolm became convinced that his father's death beneath the wheels of a streetcar was not an accident as supposed but murder at the hands of white racists. They had first killed him and then laid him on the tracks to cover up their deed.

In his late teens Malcolm Little was a big-time vice lord in Harlem. His reddish hair and complexion caused him to be nicknamed "Big Red," and he blamed them on the ravishment of his grandmother by a "white devil" on the island of Grenada in the West Indies. "I hate every drop of that white rapist's blood that is in me," he said, after confessing that before he saw the true light of Islam he foolishly believed that his light color constituted some kind of status symbol. Malcolm was taking in as much as two thousand dollars a month from narcotics, bootlegging, policy, and prostitution. He wore two-hundred-dollar suits in which he kept a fat thousand-dollar roll for the benefit of less exacting lawmen willing to grant immunity for a price. Such whited sepulchers as rutting social workers and randy clergymen sought him when they craved a liaison with one of the colored whores he had in his stable. The hypocrisy of these pillars of society deepened his contempt for white men and their low-down ways. He also catered to the wishes of Negro men who wanted white women.

A jail cell was already familiar terrain to Malcolm when in 1947 he was committed to the maximum-security prison in Concord, Massachusetts. There he was visited by his brother Reginald, who had joined Muslim Mosque No. 1 in Detroit. Reginald converted his wayward brother, and upon his release Malcolm went to Chicago to see Messenger Elijah Muhammad. Elijah personally indoctrinated the acolyte so well that Malcolm X, formerly sinner Malcolm Little, was named assistant minister of Detroit Temple of Islam No. 1 in the summer of 1953. A month-long training session then ensued in the Messenger's home, a nineteen-room red brick mansion at 4847 Woodlawn Avenue in Chicago. Elijah Muhammad treated Malcolm like a son, and for some time after his graduation from private lessons on Woodlawn Avenue the Messenger gave every evidence that he was proud of his brilliant protégé and had the utmost confidence in him. Sent to Philadelphia in March 1954, Malcolm had organized Temple No. 12 there before the first of June. His next post was as minister of Temple No. 7, then housed in a Harlem store front. Minister Malcolm X became a familiar figure on Harlem street corners, holding large audiences spellbound. In January 1958, with the blessing of the Messenger, he was married to Sister Betty X of the Harlem mosque, the ceremony being performed by a justice of the peace who was "an old hunchbacked white devil." The witnesses were "white devils" too.

More and more did Malcolm X emerge as the voice of Islam. The Messenger, growing old and plagued by failing health, dispatched him as his personal envoy on a tour of Africa and the Middle East in the summer of 1959. He was made editor of the *Messenger Magazine,* one of the several predecessors of *Muhammad Speaks.* "I thank Allah for my Brother Minister Malcolm," Elijah Muhammad told a Milwaukee audience.

For a long time Malcolm's devotion to Elijah made him impervious to such snide remarks as those made in 1957 by Thurgood Marshall, a NAACP leader who later was made a Federal judge and then U. S. Solicitor General. Marshall declared that the Nation of Islam was "run by a bunch of thugs organized from prisons and jails and financed, I am sure, by some Arab group." As early as 1961, however, Malcolm recalled after his suspension, he had felt misgivings and had troubling doubts about the morals and the financial responsibility of his leader. Nasty rumors, at first whispered and then spoken aloud, reached his ears. When in 1963 two ex-secretaries in Los Angeles accused the Messenger of getting them with child, Malcolm wrote to Elijah at his new home in Phoenix, Arizona, telling him he was being talked about. The Messenger had chosen the Arizona location because the climate was kinder to an asthmatic affliction which seemed to grow worse as he grew older. The upshot was that Malcolm was invited to fly to Phoenix for a conference. Elijah greeted him affectionately, and told him that his understanding of prophecy and of spiritual things would enable him to analyze correctly the situation when he explained:

> I'm David. When you read about how David took another man's wife, I'm that David. You read about Noah, who got drunk. That's me. You read about Lot, who went and laid up with his own daughter. I have to fulfill all those things.

Outside observers had thought for some time that self-interest eventually would compel Elijah Muhammad to cut the popular Malcolm X down to size. According to Malcolm, the Messenger's opportunity came as a result of the assassination of President Kennedy on November 22, 1963. Malcolm, along with other ministers, had been ordered by Muhammad to make no comment on the tragic event. But in the question-and-answer period of a meeting at the Manhattan Center in New York Malcolm observed that the President's murder was a case of the "chickens coming home to roost." He afterward insisted that he had meant by this that the murderous spirit vented in the slaying of an innocent black man might be expected to spread like a poison virus through the social and political structure until it destroyed even the white President.

Elijah's reaction was to "suspend" Malcolm for ninety days. After some ineffective efforts to reason with the Messenger, Malcolm formally broke off relations with the Lost-Found Nation of Islam in March 1964, and founded the Muslim Mosque, Inc. in

New York City. Later in the year he journeyed to Egypt and Saudi Arabia, studying Mohammedan doctrine and listening to Islamic scholars. In Mecca he was received by Crown Prince Faisal. For having made the pilgrimage there, he was entitled to the honorary name of El Hajj Malik El-Shabazz. In Ghana and Nigeria he conferred with government officials, intellectuals, and diplomats from other African nations. The most significant experience of his trip, however, he wrote about in a letter dated April 25 and mailed from Mecca to a friend in New York City. In Mecca, he said, there were more than 226,000 devout Moslems gathered for the annual Hajj (pilgrimage). They had come from every part of the world, and were "of all colors and ranks." He continued:

> I have eaten from the same plate, drank from the same glass, slept on the same bed or rug, while praying to the same God . . . with fellow-Muslims whose skin was the whitest of white, whose eyes were the bluest of blue, and whose hair was the blondest of blond.

As an inevitable sequel he rejected in a letter dated September 22 "the 'strait-jacket world' created by my strong belief that Elijah Muhammad was a messenger direct from God" in the narrow-minded confines of which he had lived "for 12 long years." He emphatically disaffiliated himself from ". . . Elijah Muhammad's racist philosophy which he has labeled 'Islam' only to fool and misuse gullible people as he fooled and misused me."

When his plane landed in New York on May 21, 1964, he was surrounded by "probably 50 or 60 reporters and photographers." He informed them of his change of heart about white men, that he didn't now feel that all of them were "blue-eyed devils." Malcolm soon proclaimed the birth of the Organization of Afro-American Unity, and announced his intention of lifting civil rights into the area of human rights. The OAAU would stress political and social action more than did the spiritually oriented Nation of Islam. It would maintain, too, that in places like Mississippi and Alabama where the government is unable or unwilling to defend the Negro, he should defend himself with whatever weapons he might find available. To some this sounded like a declaration of war against the KKK. The agitation for a separate sovereign state for Negroes was to be discarded as impractical in the immediate situation. (The Nation of Islam had already abandoned its demands in that direction, substituting a milder proposal: "As long as we are not allowed to establish a state or territory of our own, we demand not only equal justice under the laws of the United States but equal employment opportunities—NOW!")

In July 1964 Malcolm attended the second meeting of the Organization of African Unity in Cairo, where the heads of thirty-three independent African states had gathered. He said that he intended to add a new dimension to the civil rights struggle in the United States, to attract international attention by having the United States cited at the United Nations for discriminatory practices. In a memorandum submitted to the conference he made this accusation:

> The American government is either unable or unwilling to protect the lives and property of your 22 million American brothers and sisters. We stand defenseless at the mercy of American racists who murder us at will for no reason other than we are black and of African descent. Our problems are your problems. We have lived for over 300 years in that American den of racist wolves in constant fear of losing life and limb.

Malcolm failed in his endeavor to have the United States cited, but he seems to have stimulated some interest in his organization and perhaps made some international ties. Later in the year he wrote from Mecca that he had been named United States representative of the World Muslim League, the supreme religious body of the Muslim world. He had been given the authority, he reported, to open a Muslim Center in New York City. Fifteen authorized teachers would be sent for the center, and fifteen scholarships for study at the Islamic University in Medina would be made available.

The defection of Malcolm X, who for some time had been in the public eye as the foremost spokesman of the Lost-Found Nation of Islam, was a severe blow to the Muslims. Elijah Muhammad, a small and unprepossessing man with a reedy and undramatic voice, appeared to be getting more and more cautious and cagey. His denunciations of the "blue-eyed devils" became less and less vitriolic and his emphasis on a conventional means of emancipation—the three-year Economic Plan—more marked. It was a matter of common knowledge that the more impatient and hotheaded Islamites considered him about ready to fade out.

Nevertheless, those who foresaw an imminent collapse of the movement were not aware of its essentially strong and deep roots in the Negro community. In the despair-haunted slums where vice and crime flourished like a noxious weed the Muslims' exemplary conduct shone like good deeds in a naughty world. The brothers were always neatly and quietly arrayed; the sisters seemed enshrouded in untouchable chastity. If they inspired revulsion or fear, they also commanded respect. Becoming a dedicated Muslim seemed like taking Holy Orders. One had to renounce illicit sexual enjoyment, pork, gambling, liquor, dancing, movies, lying, dishonesty, and every other frailty, folly, or vice to which the human flesh is all too prone. The more enlightened might laugh at the sect's preposterous flights into the realm of science and other branches of knowledge, but these ludicrous aspects were not visible to the unlettered ghetto dweller. He could see only the living exemplars of what appeared to be the good and virtuous life to which all could ideally aspire. Though many of the poor were averse to active participation in any organization that might provoke the attention of the police or even the disapproval of the white man, their sympathies were with the proud and stiff-necked Muslims who had the nerve to look the "Caucasian devil" defiantly in the eye. A not uncommon attitude was: "I wouldn't join them, because I'm too pleasure-loving for that kind of life, but they're for my side and if the chips were down I'd have to be for them, too."

The press—even the Negro press—customarily viewed the activities of the Black Muslims either with jocosity or hostility. Take the question of violence. Though the tough FOI squads are trained to resist violence, they seldom have been the aggressors—and particularly not in brushes with the "Caucasian devil" and his police. Usually their skill in karate and other esoteric forms of combat is expended to settle internecine warfare or to discipline some erring brother who has strayed from the fold. A typical incident was that in Los Angeles on April 27, 1962. In a clash with the police that developed after two young Muslim brothers engaged in fisticuffs with two policemen who suspected them of having stolen men's suits, one Muslim was shot to death and six were wounded while one police officer was slightly wounded. (It was discovered after the carnage was over that one Muslim was merely handing a suit to the other so that he might take it to the dry cleaner's.) Several Muslims from a near-by temple got involved in the fracas. Chased by the policemen, they fled to sanctuary in the temple. In the meantime several squad cars arrived in response to a radioed appeal, and thirty police officers with drawn pistols invaded the temple. A meeting was just breaking up. The cops gunned down seven of the Muslims, dragged them to the sidewalk, and manacled them. Then they proceeded to stomp the handcuffed and wounded Islamites. One of them died. It was disclosed at the trial of nine Muslims indicted before the grand jury for assaulting and resisting the police that the only "weapon" used by the Islamites during the melee was a water jug with which the wounded policeman's elbow was struck. Though a number of witnesses testified to police brutality, no action was taken. The Muslims, expressing contempt for the white man's courts of law, refused to testify. A young policeman told of being surrounded by Muslims who were chanting, "Kill the white devils!" Or at least that's what he *thought* they were chanting. They were chanting in Arabic, which he couldn't understand.

This and other incidents tended to fortify the Muslims' contention that their characteristic role was as recipients of violence rather than instigators of it.

Just what direction would have been taken by Malcolm X and his Organization of Afro-American Unity can only be conjectured in the light of what happened. It was scarcely off the ground when he traveled to Selma, Alabama, where on February 4, 1965, he spoke before several hundred Negro students assembled to demonstrate for civil rights. He warned them that they might be forced to abandon their nonviolent tactics. "The white man," he said, "should thank God that Dr. King has held his people in check, because there are others who don't feel that way—others who are ready to lead a different kind of movement." This statement could be interpreted as indicating that Malcolm was announcing his availability as leader of such a movement.

On the afternoon of February 21, 1965, Malcolm X. Shabazz (as he then usually was called) entered the Audubon ballroom in upper Manhattan where about five hundred Negroes were waiting to hear him. It was a meeting of the Afro-American Unity group, and no whites had been invited.

Walking down the aisle toward the rostrum, Malcolm saluted his followers with the prescribed Muslim greeting: "As-salaam salaam" ("Peace be unto you").

"Wa-alaikum salaam" ("And unto you peace"), they chorused in response.

As Malcolm mounted the speaker's platform, what was later known to be a diversionary scuffle started near the rear of the hall. He had uttered only three words, "brothers and sisters," when he was cut down by a burst of gunfire, apparently directed by three men who had taken advantage of the confusion to run down the center aisle. His body riddled by eleven bullets and two shotgun blasts, Malcolm died before he arrived at Presbyterian Medical Center.

A man accused of being one of the assassins with a shotgun was winged in the leg by one of Malcolm's bodyguards as he tried to flee. He proved to be Thomas Hagan, who had a previous police record as Talmadge Hayer. Hagan (or Hayer) declined to say whether he was a Black Muslim. In Chicago Elijah Muhammad denied any knowledge of him. Another suspect was nabbed, Norman 3X Butler. Identified as a Black Muslim "enforcer," he was out on bail for having shot and wounded a withdrawee from the Temple of Islam.

(The digit before Norman's "X" showed that there were others in his temple with the same first name. Distinct identity was preserved by prefixing a number. The name James is of such common occurrence that one member's name is James 67X. When the movement was smaller, "righteous" surnames—for which the "X" stood until the head of Islam revealed them by divination—were assigned rather frequently. Later on, it was common for a member to use an "X" for years before the "righteous" or "original" name was granted him.)

While Muhammad's organization would seem to be the logical beneficiary of Malcolm's death, there were other candidates. "A

Harlem dope racket with supply lines stretching to Cuba and Red China was responsible," the New York *World-Telegram and Sun* decided. This jibed with the paper's previously stated theory that "left-wing extremists have been peddling dope to finance their revolutionary activities." The Ku Klux Klan was not overlooked as a possible culprit. And what about the New York cops, in whose flesh the pyrotechnic black nationalist had long been a festering thorn? In the September 12, 1964, issue of the *Saturday Evening Post* Malcolm had written: "So, some of the followers of Elijah Muhammad would still consider it a first-rank honor to kill me. Also I know that any day, any night, I could die at the hands of some white devil racists." New York Assemblyman Percy Sutton, Malcolm's attorney, said that Malcolm had told him the day before that he knew he would be killed. He added that the slain leader had intended to read in the meeting the names of those who were intent on doing away with him.

Retaliation by Malcolm's followers was of course expected. Its only immediate manifestation seemed to be the destruction by a fire bomb of Muhammad's Temple of Islam No. 7, over which the murdered man had once presided. When the annual Black Muslim convention was held in the Chicago Coliseum February 26-28, 1965, it was not only accompanied by a heavy police guard but an augmented contingent of the FOI kept constant vigil over every movement of the Messenger of Allah. He repeatedly insisted he was not afraid. "I'm not to be killed," he declared, ". . . and anyone who attempts to harm me will come to a bad end." Though Elijah Muhammad expressed serene confidence in Allah's protection, his police and cult guards were not taking any chances they could avoid. A newspaperman jokingly noted that only the top of Elijah's bejeweled fez was visible among the forest of heads belonging to FOI elite guards. Chicago policemen were not stationed inside the Coliseum, but watched all the entrances and the immediate vicinity.

Fear of reprisal by partisans of Malcolm X was thought to be the main factor in reducing attendance to 3,000 or less, down from a high of about 6,000 the preceding year. Most interest was aroused on the second day when heavyweight champion Cassius Clay (renamed Muhammad Ali after his conversion to Islam) entertained with an exhibition bout. For the most part quiet prevailed. The only violence wreaked by the FOI was upon a young Negro named Willie Eugene Greer, who was severely beaten and thrown bleeding outside into the arms of Chicago policemen. Hospitalized for facial cuts and possible fractures of both legs and several ribs, Greer said he was not a member of the Black Muslims but was interested in their message to the extent that he had attended other meetings in the past. The official Muslim explanation of the incident was that Greer had been recognized as one who had made derogatory remarks about the Messenger of Allah on a former occasion. His ejection came on the third and last day when Elijah made his major address.

At the final session Elijah Muhammad spoke for more than three hours, and, as usual, imparted confidential information not to be had elsewhere. For example, he said that Allah (undoubtedly in his W. D. Fard incarnation) had talked to him many years ago about a trip to Mars during which he (Fard) had found the Martians to be about nine feet tall. Though their life expectancy was 1,200 years, they ranked below the American Negro in brain power. Allah at the same time advised any mortal from trying to make a trip to the moon. Landing would present no insuperable difficulties, but if the earthman drank any of the available water on the lunar surface his eyes would pop out of his head. Of more imminent concern to Elijah's hearers was the disclosure that more than two decades ago a group of businessmen had sunk $210,000,000 in the construction of a superplane that remained aloft a year at a time, traveling so fast that it is invisible. At the end of a year the plane merely drops down a tube into the atmosphere and siphons up enough oxygen to do it another year. Whatever could be the use of such a marvel? Why, Muhammad darkly hinted, the high-flying camarilla might just decide to use it to wipe out the United States government in Washington before the Black Muslims got around to it.

What had been Malcolm X's impact on his people and his times, and how would it be projected into the future—reflected in coming events? Few would venture a precise prediction, but all could agree that Malcolm's martyrdom brought an immediate and, in some respects, spectacular response. His body, lying in state for a week at the Unity Funeral Home, was viewed by at least 30,000. Another 3,000 came to All Faith Temple Church of God in Christ, where his bullet-ridden body, swathed in the white cerements of Muslim ritual, reposed in a bronze casket above which hung two murals picturing Jesus Christ. The funeral obsequies (February 27, 1965) included a fervent panegyric by Ossie Davis, Negro playwright and actor. Malcolm, he said, had been one of Harlem's "brightest hopes—extinguished now and gone from us forever." The defector from the Black Muslims, Davis continued, had stopped being "Negro" years before. The word had become too puny and weak for him. "Malcolm was bigger than that. Malcolm had become an Afro-American and he wanted—so desperately—that we, that all his people, would become Afro-Americans too."

To those who would turn away from him as "not a man but a demon, a monster and a subverter and an enemy of the black people," Davis recommended this answer:

> Did you ever talk to Brother Malcolm? Did you ever touch him or have him smile at you? Did you ever really listen to him? Did he ever do a mean thing? Was he ever himself associated with violence or any public disturbance? For if you did you would know him. And if you knew him, you would know why we must honor him: Malcolm was our manhood, our living black manhood! This was his meaning to his people. And, in honoring him, we honor the best in ourselves.
>
> However much we may have differed with him—or with each other about him and his value as a man, let his going from us serve only to bring us together, now. Consigning these mortal remains to earth, the common mother of all, secure in the knowledge that what we place in the ground is no more now a man—but a seed which, after the winter of discontent—will come forth again to meet us. And we shall know him then for what he was and is—a Prince—our own black shining Prince!—who didn't hesitate to die, because he loved us so.

Ahmed Ossman, introduced as head of the Islamic Center in Switzerland, expressed shock at the reaction of Carl Rowan, Negro director of the United States Information Agency, who had been disturbed by reports that the African and Pakistani press were hailing El Hajj Malik El-Shabazz as a great Negro leader whose assassination would be a great blow to the integration movement. Two days previously Rowan had said in a speech before the American Foreign Services Association in Washington:

> This will come as rather startling news to those Negro leaders who knew Malcolm X and his followers preached not integration but black supremacy and the separation of the Negro . . . All this about an ex-convict, ex-dope peddler who became a racial fanatic. I can only conclude that we Americans know less about what goes on in the minds of other peoples than we thought, or the need to inform is even greater than we in the USIA thought it to be.

Ossman reaffirmed that Malcolm X had renounced his racist views after his pilgrimage to Mecca. And in an interview with Jack Barnes and Barry Sheppard in the March–April 1965 issue of *Young Socialist,* the head of the new Organization of Afro-American Unity did indicate that he had undergone a drastic change of heart. One of his most emphatic pronouncements was this:

> First, I'm not a racist. I'm against every form of racism and segregation, every form of discrimination. I believe in human beings and that all human beings should be respected as such, regardless of their color.

Younger members of the new radical left, particularly those on college campuses, seemed intent on enshrining Malcolm X's scarcely cold corpse in the pantheon of revolutionary deities. A leaflet of the Spartacist (Trotskyite) Committee, distributed in the Bay Area shortly after Malcolm's funeral, began this way:

> Of all the national Negro leaders in this country, the one who was known uniquely for his militancy, intransigence and refusal to be the liberals' front man has been shot down. This new political assassination is another indicator of the rising current of irrationality and individual terrorism which the decay of our society begets. Liberal reaction is predictable, and predictably disgusting. They are, of course, opposed to assassination, and some may even contribute to the fund for the education of Malcolm's children, but their mourning at the death of the head of world imperialism had a considerably greater ring

of sincerity than their regret at the murder of a black militant who wouldn't play their game.

Did the Black Muslims kill Malcolm? The Trotskyites would not give the New York police, who "had good cause to be afraid of Malcolm," a clean bill of health, but they added:

> . . . The Muslim theory cannot be discounted out of hand, because the Muslims are not a political group, and in substituting religion for science and color mysticism for rational analysis, they have a world view which could encompass the efficacy and morality of assassination. A man who has a direct pipeline to God can justify anything.

As for Elijah Muhammad, he lacked the flamboyant flair of Garvey and the eloquence and "charisma" (as more than one had called it) of Malcolm X, but he was a good organization man. His son-in-law, the loyal Raymond Sharrieff, was supreme chief of the FOI. Five of his six sons have held important posts in the administration. Shortly after Malcolm X was expelled from the movement, son Wallace withdrew. He charged his father with mishandling the temple's financial affairs. During the 1965 convention, however, he was reported to have asked and received his father's forgiveness and with it readmission to the ranks. The defection of Akbar Muhammad early in January 1965 was for doctrinal and ethical reasons. A twenty-five-year-old student of Islamic law at Al Azhar University in Cairo, Akbar said he could no longer agree with his father's antiwhite and nationalistic views. Many of the high-ranking temple leaders, he claimed, did not want to go along with Elijah Muhammad's stand but stayed on because of the good salaries they received. Though Akbar's announced opinions coincided closely with those of Malcolm X, he had not joined the Organization of Afro-American Unity when Malcolm was assassinated. The attitude of the Messenger of Allah toward these vipers in his bosom was voiced in his official mouthpiece, *Muhammad Speaks:* "Only those who wish to be led to hell, or to their doom, will follow Malcolm."

Perhaps the most judicious assessment of Malcolm X and the meaning of his life, death, and transfiguration was made in the

April 7, 1965, issue of *The Christian Century*, by C. Eric Lincoln, author of the excellent study *The Black Muslims in America* (1961). Lincoln pointed out that Malcolm was no sooner dead than "his critics turned on him with the fervor of self-righteousness and his defenders sought to elevate him to martyrdom." The "American ideal" and Christian morality should dictate that Malcolm's criminal past not be held against him, Lincoln held, particularly since he had surmounted the mistakes of his youth. On the other hand, he pointed out, the hailers of a "new" Malcolm may have been a trifle premature. "He was a true revolutionary," Dr. Lincoln said, and went on:

> He was indoctrinated to believe that racial strife is the inevitable means of bringing about a reversal in the black man's status, and he passionately believed in and longed for that reversal. True, his conversion to Islam and his desire to be acceptable to orthodoxy may have ameliorated his aggressive tendencies; but the evidence that at the time of his death he was prepared to join the nonviolent crusade is scanty, if indeed it exists at all.
>
> Malcolm X must be taken for what he was. He was a remarkably gifted and charismatic leader whose hatreds and resentments symbolized the dreadful stamp of the black ghetto, but a man whose philosophies of racial determination and whose commitments to violence made him unacceptable as a serious participant in peaceful social change. He had ideological followers—far more than the handful of men and women who belonged to the Organization of Afro-American Unity. His spirit will rise again, phoenix-like—not so much because he is worthy to be remembered as because the perpetuation of the ghetto which spawned him will not let us forget.

On Sunday, August 8, 1965, Elijah Muhammad, clad in the white summer uniform just adopted by the cult, addressed the assembled faithful from the podium of Cobo Arena in Detroit. Scoffing at the Voting Rights Bill signed by President Johnson a few days before, he likened the President's statement that the bill was "a triumph for freedom as huge as any victory that's ever been won on any battlefield" to "saying to a child that his toy airplane is greater than any real airplane which can raise itself from the earth and mount into the air at a terrific speed of 2,000 MPH, while the little toy plane has no motor and no way of conquering space." The Messenger of Allah made it plain that in his opinion the lot of the "so-called Negro" was no better in the North than it was in the South, as he pointed out:

> He is a beggar for freedom, justice and equality here as well as in the South. His head is also beaten by brute police force. He is shot down at will by that same force as in the South. He has to vote for the white man in the South or one of his Uncle Toms who the white man of the South will allow in office.

Only ten days later an occurrence in riot-devastated Los Angeles lent this jeremiad a timely relevance. Mayor Samuel W. Yorty had denounced the Black Muslims as "a very dangerous organization because they openly preach hate" and said they had been distributing pamphlets which inveighed against the "blue-eyed Caucasian devils." It was no wonder, then, that an anonymous tip to the effect that members of Muhammad's Mosque No. 27 were toting a truckload of weapons into the temple brought a quick response. A contingent of one hundred policemen hurried to the scene. They later claimed to have been greeted by a sniper's bullet from the second floor and a shotgun blast from the roof.

Preceded by a mighty fusillade of five hundred to a thousand rounds that shattered the temple's windows and doors, the lawmen stormed into the building. There they found sixty Islamites, but no weapons of any kind. Though both front and back doors had been guarded, it was surmised that the wily disciples of Muhammad had somehow contrived to spirit the incriminating guns away—possibly down an open sewer. Tear gas fired into the sewers brought nobody up. No Black Muslim was killed, as in the 1962 melee, but nine were cut by flying glass. Marched away with shotguns aimed at their heads, nineteen of the Islamites were arraigned on suspicion of assault to commit murder and the others were detained on suspicion of conspiracy.

Once again it had been demonstrated to the children of Allah that verbal violence from a Black Muslim is apt to beget physical violence from the "Caucasian devil." Islamites consistently maintain that the white man will fall a victim to his own folly and the divine wrath of Allah rather than from any aggressive action on the part of the original black man. But this is too abstract a consideration for the gendarmerie, and as a consequence it is the black man who usually is the recipient of violence rather than the dispenser of it.

CHAPTER XV

Calling the Children Home

THE FREE COLORED ELEMENT in the New Orleans population underwent a great change in the fifty years that followed Adah Isaacs Menken's runaway marriage to her young Jewish music teacher. Throughout the rest of the century the group was steadily reduced by the "passing" of those who were indistinguishable from whites into the American melting pot. As often as not, the "escape" was abetted by white friends or relatives, and sometimes it involved no more than moving into another neighborhood in New Orleans. Not infrequently, of course, local complications made it necessary for individuals to leave the city or the state, and the persons of mixed ancestry moved to Los Angeles or Denver or Chicago or Cleveland. Many of them moved into other Southern cities. A few allied themselves with strongly anti-Negro elements.

Small remnants of this relatively proud and cultivated segment of ante-bellum society survive in New Orleans to the present. In 1895, however, it was still an important part of the colored population and still sharply aware of its background of freedom. It had not yet gone all the way toward amalgamating with the children of the slaves. Nevertheless a certain leveling was in process. As the ex-slaves rose through freedom, education, and new opportunities, the group that had produced Basil Croquére and Victor Séjour and Thomy Lafon, the group that had sent its children to Paris for education, the group that had organized and supported a one-hundred-piece symphony orchestra in New Orleans, the group from which the composer and conductor Edmond Dédè had sprung, the group that had published an anthology of better-than-average poetry in 1845—that group had been progressively debased in status as in accomplishment. By the end of the century it was a wistful, backward-looking tribe still hurt and perplexed by what had happened to it.

A part of this caste was the Morton family living at the corner of Frenchman and Robertson. The head of the house was in some way connected with the wine business. A six-year-old son named Ferdinand took guitar lessons from a Spanish teacher. By the time he was eight or nine this boy Ferdy was not only playing what he had been taught but had also begun to show an ear for street music. He picked up such tunes as "Alice Fields," "Isn't It Hard to Love?" and "Make Me a Pallet on the Floor" and played them on his guitar. Presently his interest switched to drums, and a year or two later he began studying the piano.

How long Ferdy's formal training in music continued is not known, but the indications are that he never gave it his undivided attention. For a while he was employed in his uncle's hairdressing shop. Later he learned to make barrels and worked at this end of the wine business. In each capacity he was exposed to a variety of musical forces. The French opera was still a fresh tradition in the circles in which Ferdy's people moved. At the hairdressing establishment, no doubt, mandolin clubs were a subject of everyday conversation. Brass bands were always passing along the streets, often accompanying funeral processions. Blues and ballads and other folk songs could be heard in back alleys. And in still more out-of-the-way places a ragtime rhythm was beginning to rock the pianos. Through all of this Ferdy absorbed musical influences from France, Spain, and Africa, not to mention a few other possible sources. He took in the new along with the old, the refined with the bawdy, the classical with the folk. By the time he was sixteen, a tall, frolicsome, big-footed boy of light chestnut brown, he was an American original: a product of all these rich influences.

It was about this time that Ferdy heard of Mamie Desdume (Desdunes?) and arranged to be introduced to her. Mamie, according to Ferdy's later account, was musically limited, but she sang and played with wonderful effect,

Two-nineteen done took my baby away
Two-nineteen done took my baby away
Two-seventeen bring her back someday.

This piece, of course, was pure folk blues, and it had a tremendous effect on the boy who had not yet given up his conventional piano studies. From the point of view of his middle-class parents, no doubt, it ruined his life. He was completely fascinated by Mamie Desdume's song as music, and he contrived excuses to hang around her place till he had learned it, till he had mastered the rhythmic pattern and caught the subtle twists and nuances. Before long Ferdy was on the ragtime road. He was invited one night to substitute for an absent sporting-house pianist in a place on Rampart Street. He went, leaving his parents under the impression that he was making wine barrels, and every night thereafter he returned to play for food and tips. Eventually his secret was exposed. There was a family quarrel, and Ferdy left home. Inevitably he gravitated to Storyville, New Orleans' notorious red-light district.

Within three years the boy who loved street music and blues was quite a man in the resorts on Basin, Iberville, Bienville, Franklin, and Liberty streets. Generally he worked alone, in response to the demand for soloists in such establishments, but at least one suggestion that he may have played for a while with a local band during this period has been found. Meanwhile, one may assume, he made himself at home with the unrighteous women of his environment, for he became known as "Jelly Roll," a folk expression with strong connotations in this realm. And it was as Jelly Roll Morton that the young ragtime pianist and vocalist took to the road in 1903.

This musical odyssey, the first of many he was to take in the next forty years, has a certain historical importance, but surviving details are sketchy, to say the least. Jelly became a big talker in later life, and he recorded a sort of musical autobiography for Alan Lomax and the Folksong Archives of the Library of Congress, but he failed—despite an excellent memory, especially for tunes—to fill in all the gaps to the complete satisfaction of biographers like Max Jones, editor of the British publication *Jazz Music.*

But the indications are, according to Jones and others, that Jelly's rounds took in Natchez and Vicksburg in this period. He often mentioned musicians from these places. He traveled with Will Benbon's road show for a time, barnstorming through Mississippi, Tennessee, Kentucky, and Illinois. Presently he was back on the Gulf Coast, traveling alone and doing such towns as Bay St. Louis, Pass Christian, Long Beach, Ocean Springs, Gulfport, Biloxi, Pensacola, and Mobile. Along the way he met and matched rhythms with a host of roving musicians and gin-mill artists, among them Baby Grice, Frank Raphael, Frazier Davis, Brocky Johnny, Skinny Head Pete, Old Florida Sam, and Porter King. It was the latter who inspired Jelly Roll's well-known early composition "King Porter Stomp."

Late in 1904, or early the following year, Jelly returned to Storyville. This time he was ready, so to speak, for it was on this second sojourn in the area that he began to impress his musical contemporaries with his style and material and to earn relatively big money for himself. This lasted about four years, with Jelly Roll winning a place among Storyville musicians second only to that of Tony Jackson. Jelly, who has never been accused of false modesty, admired Jackson warmly and never claimed equality with the other pianist, though actually the time came when Jelly outplayed his rival in one of the piano contests so popular among ragtime men of the period. But Jelly Roll's ascendency to the musical throne of Storyville occurred in 1908, the year Tony Jackson left New Orleans. During the next four years Jelly was in and out of the district, but his position was unchallenged. Moreover, he earned money by the hatful—and spent it all.

Jelly Roll Morton became a flamboyant figure in those days. His flashy clothes created a legend, as did his singing and playing. No one thought of him, however, as a creative force in popular music. His personality was much too vivid to permit such considerations. Those who came under the influence of his remarkable improvisations were concerned with what the music did to them, not with what it was. And this seems to be all that Jelly expected.

But Storyville didn't satisfy Jelly, even when he was its king-pin pianist. He made trips to Greenville, Vicksburg, Jackson, and Memphis, playing in the theaters of Fred Barasso, and he spent a season with McCabe's Minstrels and got as far north as St. Louis before leaving the show. Authorities differ on the time of his first Chicago jaunt. Whether or not he hit the town in 1908, as some assert, or 1910 or later can be left to jazz researchers, but there is evidence that he was already on hand when the migrants of the World War I period began to arrive. In 1914 he took a five-piece band into the Elite Café on Thirty-first and State.

While Jelly's combination was playing at the Elite, the original Creole Band with Freddie Keppard on trumpet and Will Johnson, Jelly's brother-in-law, on string bass came to the Grand Theatre on Chicago's South Side. The Creole boys turned the town upside down as their gifted trumpet player treated the folks to an art that had been taking shape in New Orleans for a number of years. Jelly's show was eclipsed; and, to make his embarrassment complete, his trumpet player quit and joined the other band.

The migration had brought jazz to the North. A new note had been sounded in popular music. A new idiom had been suggested. The crowds went to the Grand, not the Elite. But Jelly Roll Morton was not through. He gave himself more seriously to composing and arranging music. He continued to make excursions into the outlying country with his band, and he kept on playing the piano. About four years later he went to California.

In Los Angeles Jelly decided to form another band. But where would he get the players? He would need men who could play the music that had made such an impression on Chicagoans. There was only one place for him to find such talent: New Orleans. He quickly sent home for Buddy Petit, Frank Dusen, and Wade Waley. Dink Johnson, who had been the drummer for the Creole Band, had gone West with Jelly and was available. A combination of this size would be just right for Jelly's style of playing. Could he get the boys from home?

The New Orleans musicians were only too glad to come. Waley got off the train with his clarinet sticking out of his back pocket. Petit brought his cornet in his suitcase. Dusen's trombone protruded from a paper bundle which he carried under his arm. All three of the men wore box-back coats of a style borrowed from the macks of St. Louis but still popular with New Orleans jazz musicians. Jelly met them at the station and rushed them into seclusion till they could be provided with less spectacular raiment. Soon the band was performing successfully in night clubs and dance spots in southern California.

Jelly Roll's experience in putting together this West Coast group followed a pattern which became general in the migration of jazz musicians from the South. If a whole band wasn't needed and sent for, a cornettist might be fetched or a drummer or a bass, as occasion arose. Friends spotted opportunities for friends who were still at home waiting for a break, and those who had been helped often felt a duty to help others. If one member of a combination which had played together in the South found a place in a Northern aggregation, he could generally be counted on to remember the boys he had played with down home and to speak a good word for them where he thought it would do the most good.

The subsequent wanderings of Jelly Roll Morton cannot be followed closely. Jelly was too restless, too casual, and he lived too much in the moment to be bothered with marking the trail he followed. But it is definite that for the rest of his life he was first in one place then in another. He never settled down, and he was never at peace.

In Los Angeles his fortunes flourished. He rode in an impressive automobile, dressed like a mad prince. He was in his glory during the engagements he played at Leak's Lake on the outskirts of Watts. To the large barnlike pavilion on this property he came several times a week after twelve o'clock when the Los Angeles dance halls closed. The small combination with which he played was made up partly of neighborhood musicians, including Ben Albans, Jr., a high school boy. Jelly patiently taught the young cornettist, as well as the other musicians he had found in the community, the style of playing he required. He brought two or three of his regular men with him. The results were most satisfactory. Crowds of Jelly's admirers filled the place regularly. Many of them had known him in New Orleans and Chicago, and he seemed happy to be among them.

A year or two later Jelly was in St. Louis. E. Simms Campbell has recorded his memories of him in those days. Later it was New York and then Washington. Then New York again and back again to California. Toward the end illness reduced his energies, and his playing became more and more introspective. Playing for a young visitor in a cheap cabaret in Washington, after all other guests had gone and the tables had been turned upside down on top of each other, he gave the impression of trying to remember something he had forgotten, some brightness that had once flashed before his eyes and then vanished. His great memory and his equally great power of creative improvisation remained strong, but when he got started, he played only for himself. A vastly different man from the one who had played with such a compelling sense of power and influence to an admiring crowd at Leak's Lake!

What had come over this one-time noisy extrovert? What was it old Jelly had forgotten? What was he trying to recall?

The answer is not simple. It goes back to New Orleans and has to do with an aspect of the whole story of jazz and the men who created it. And it involves considerations often regarded as basic in the criticism of other art forms but frequently neglected entirely by students of jazz music. In short, it has to do with the personal lives of the creative men of jazz music and the social environment in which they developed.

Naturally, inquiry of this sort leads at once to the general problem of the Negro in the South, but in the case of Jelly and his contemporaries in New Orleans it also points to the peculiarities of the situation in Louisiana. Behind such men as George Baquet, Emanuel Perez, Kid Ory, Honoré Dutrey, and Sidney Bechet were the cultural traditions of the Creoles. They were the products of the "intellectual tolerance" which to W. Adolphe Roberts, for example, was the essential difference between the Gallic and the Anglo-Saxon attitude toward dark people. Jelly Roll Morton was of the same group.

Jelly's uptown friends, on the other hand, had a very different background. Buddy Bolden, the John Henry of Negro cornettists in New Orleans, Bunk Johnson and King Oliver and Freddie Keppard, his contemporaries and followers, and Louis Armstrong, the end product of their combined influences, were the offspring of the emancipated slaves. As a group they had nothing behind them but the dark night of bondage. They were, in one sense, an infant race exploring the world with a fresh and innocent outlook. Musical extroverts, they played for the world. They played to exert power.

They played to change people. From Buddy Bolden's ten-mile notes in Johnson Park, "calling his children home," to Armstrong's amazing high C's, their purpose was always the same. Not satisfied with the world in which they were born, they were out to make a new one. And the incredible part about it is that, within certain limits, they succeeded.

Certainly that part of their country's social life that rests on jazz music would not be as it is without this dynasty of cornet players. Bolden was a Franklin Street barber who played for the entertainment of clubs such as the Buzzards and the Mysterious Babies and for public dances in the pecan grove in Gretna. His cornet-playing days went back to the years before the Spanish-American War, but the high point in his career, no doubt, came in Johnson Park when he gladdened the night with a wondrous tone as a means of drawing his uptown crowd away from the music of John Robichaux's Orchestra over in Lincoln Park. "Now it's time to call my chillun home," the great Buddy would say as he put his lips to the mouthpiece and poked his horn through a hole in the fence. He could be heard for miles on a still night. Presently the crowd would start trickling back to where they belonged. Johnson and Oliver and Keppard followed in Bolden's footsteps. They were just like Bolden, the homefolks would say, but they were *not* Bolden—even though Keppard and Oliver played in Chicago in later years and achieved reputations that reached far beyond Franklin Street and Johnson Park. Louis Armstrong, a product of a waifs' home, learned from Bunk Johnson the tricks that Bunk had picked up in his association with Bolden; and in Armstrong, Buddy Bolden finally lived again. Together they gave America its hot trumpet.

But Ferdinand Joseph Morton grew up in a house where the music of the colored Edmond Dédè was still remembered among people who talked about Paris and the Opéra, in circles of folk whose parents knew Victor Séjour before he went to France to become a popular playwright. Jelly Roll began the study of music at the instigation of parents whose hearts were set on comparable achievements by their own children.

Life in New Orleans, from the point of view of these people, had sustained a peculiar damage since the time of their grandparents. In the French tradition no determined effort was made to rob colored people of their beauty. Part of the general sin of the South since Reconstruction has been a studied plan to represent all Negroes as ugly and all aspects of their lives as base. In stories, for example, the most unattractive characters have been offered as typical of the best the group can produce. The most stupid, the most disagreeable, and the most ungainly have been held up before the world. Naturally, such a plan also includes suppression of everything that would tend to neutralize this impression. If a Negro is wise, he must be called "unstable." If a woman of color is lovely, then something filthy must be said or implied against her. No newspaper report can be allowed to state any fact in such a way as to permit readers to assume that either beauty or virtue is possible in any individual of Negro or mixed blood.

But there was a day when New Orleans newspapers described Basil Croquére, the mulatto swordsman and mathematician, as the handsomest man in the city. They described the elegance and taste of his clothes, and no one, so far as is known, complained against or disputed the report. True, old New Orleans passed laws intended to prevent mulatto and quadroon girls from looking more beautiful than whites. In 1788 Governor Miro passed an ordinance which made it an "evidence of misconduct" if a free, unmarried woman of color walked abroad in silk, jewels, or "plumes." The only head covering the ordinance allowed them was the madras handkerchief or *tignon*. But these *femmes de couleur* devised such attractive ways to wear the *tignon* that they set a fashion which lasted beyond the effective period of the law and spread to the cities of the West Indies. The total effect of the law was to flatter the colored women and to increase their reputation for exotic beauty.

Jelly Roll Morton and the other musicians of the colored Creole group started life in surroundings that still retained an occasional hint or suggestion of the old ways. They heard constant complaints from old people trying, rather inarticulately, to convey what had happened. To them, of course, the outlook seemed hopeless. And a symptom of this hopelessness was the tendency for musicians of the group to gravitate to Storyville.

When the ragtime vogue which followed the publication of Scott Joplin's "Maple Leaf Rag" and other related works reached New

Orleans, it found a ready reception. But in no part of the city was it more warmly accepted than in the red-light community. Here a great demand for ragtime pianists and musicians developed. This brought in increasing numbers of colored men. Women of color had already established themselves there in a more primary capacity. But in the positions of both colored men and women in Storyville there reappeared—in a tawdry and soiled reproduction—a deteriorated facsimile of the old pattern of New Orleans life. As musicians, playing a new and infectious music, colored men were able to realize a sort of power. They were able to weave a spell, to take white people out of themselves. As denizens of the houses the women maintained the traditional authority of their station. Through it all a sort of democracy prevailed. Likewise a respect for attractiveness, a cheap perfume, a kind of melody, and an illusion of beauty like a face seen in a dream.

For a short time sixteen-year-old Ferdinand Morton may have imagined that he had found what he had been led to expect of life. But Storyville passed away, and with it went the last figment of the world his grandparents knew. Pushed steadily downward, the children of the free men of color had finally become Negroes—part of the great mass whose main portion consisted of children of slaves. A certain mental reservation had broken down at last. The uptown men and those from the "French" section formed bands together. When they made jazz, they made it together.

Yet that didn't keep old Jelly Roll from dreaming in the sundown years of his career. There was something—something he had forgotten. Perhaps that is why he played for himself, improvising and recalling lost melodies, while young Louis Armstrong set his horn and his will toward making a new world.

CHAPTER XVI

Trail of the Whitetops

OTHER NEGROES FOLLOWED James P. Beckwourth to the Western passes. Among the earliest was George William Bush, born a free man in the State of Pennsylvania. As a youth Bush had offered his services to his country in the War of 1812, and he had fought with Andrew Jackson as a part of the intrepid colored unit which won the praise of that tough commander at the battle of New Orleans. Afterward, as a man of peace, he appears to have accumulated some wealth and to have ventured into the rugged, dangerous Western country to see what it was like. On this first trip, the exact date of which is not now known, Bush must have repeated the experiences of old Jim Beckwourth. But the struggle against hunger and hostile Indians, the breath-taking perils of the journey appear to have awakened in him a desire to settle in this exciting region, and in 1844 Bush and his family joined a party of four white families heading for the Oregon country.

This expedition of prospective settlers, including Michael T. Simmons, James McAllister, David Kindred, and Gabriel Jones and their households as well as the Bushes, and numbering twenty-eight souls in all, traveled by ox teams, and in 1845, after several months at the Dalles in Oregon, arrived at the spot where the city of Olympia, the capital of the State of Washington, now stands. Here again they pitched tents; then all took up homes in the section which later became Thurston County, and a prosperous community began to grow.

Almost immediately, however, George William Bush and his family found themselves struggling against racial prejudice, the same old enemy that had driven them from their home in the East to seek a new life in an unsubdued wilderness. In Oregon they found themselves unable to settle—though their short sojourn at the Dalles was undisturbed—due to a law which prohibited Negroes or mulattoes from entering the Territory. In the Puget Sound country, whence they had come at the suggestion of their white friend Michael T. Simmons, opposition did not show itself till the Bushes sought the right to homestead the land on which they had squatted. Then it was, as it seemed to them, that the influence of the white South entered Eden and spoke through the serpent in the tree. Negroes were denied the right to homestead land. But thanks again to Simmons and the other white friends with whom the colored family had come West, Bush was able to secure title to six hundred and forty acres of land by special act of Congress. This came in response to a petition which besought that body to exclude from the provisions of the anti-Negro act those colored settlers who had been in the section before 1850.

On the plot of land thus acquired Bush spent the rest of his life. It became known as Bush Prairie. The family of George William Bush continued throughout the rest of the century to be leaders in the community. One of the sons became a member of the first State legislature. Another son raised wheat on this land which won the first award at the Centennial Exposition at Philadelphia in 1876. And B. Ezra Meeker in his *Pioneers of the Puget Sound* tells how the farming Bushes divided crops worth thousands of dollars with newcomers who had struggled across the plains and thus helped many of them to establish themselves on the frontier.

Some of the same pioneers may also have been aided at the other end of their journey by a Negro. In the city of Independence, Missouri, the jumping-off place for many of the early expeditions, Hiram Young owned and operated a factory on Liberty Street. His establishment had twenty-five forges with two men working at each forge. Young specialized in building wagons, and his products were said to have been as good in quality as any without iron axles. He also did general blacksmithing. Regrettably, Young used mainly slave labor.

In 1853 Washington became a Territory, parting from Oregon. In 1889 it became a State. Meanwhile, in 1855, another band of homeseekers included a Negro in their number. This man, known as George Washington, had first migrated from Virginia to Illinois, possibly via the Underground Railroad, but he had been disappointed in Illinois when he was required to post a heavy bond in order to remain. So presently he set about to assemble a company of friends interested in the Far West. The journey took months, and being unable to qualify for a homestead under the special act passed by Congress for the benefit of George William Bush, Washington found it necessary to get a white friend to homestead for him, paying the latter twenty-eight hundred dollars for the land thus obtained. Later on the Northern Pacific ran tracks through the farm, giving Washington a townsite; the city which grew on this spot was called Centralia.

Three years after George Washington reached the Territory, one of the most colorful characters of the frontier period appeared in the region of the Sound. He was William Gross, "the biggest man in the Northwest." In his prime Gross weighed four hundred pounds. Born in Washington City in 1834, he joined the Navy at the age of seventeen and served on the sloop of war *Vincent*. He was on the vessel during its search for Sir John Franklin. Three of his years of service were spent in the Indian Ocean and the waters around Japan. Gross was in Japan when Commodore Perry made his treaty. When he had completed his period of service, he was discharged at San Francisco and made his way to the mining district around Montezuma. There he remained till an influx of Southerners resulted in the expelling of all Mexicans, Negroes, and Chinese from the area. Gross headed for Puget Sound.

He found employment as steward on the mail boat *Constitution* operating on the Sound and continued to work in this capacity till the early sixties. Then he took up restaurant work in Seattle. He started the lunch counter in Rube Low's saloon and became widely known throughout the roaring region as "Big Bill the Cook."

A more significant figure, however, came into the region in those days with much less bluster and noise. He was an intellectual, and the restlessness and discontent which drove him West were compounded with self-consciousness, a knowledge of history, and a tendency to worry about the place of Negroes in American democracy. A few years earlier he had graduated from Alcorn College in

Mississippi, then under the direction of Hiram Revels, former United States Senator from that State. Thereafter for several years the wanderings of this small, articulate mulatto had been almost Homeric, but in Seattle he discovered what he was seeking: a chance to make a new life in a community far removed from the things he found intolerable in Mississippi.

His name was Horace Roscoe Cayton, and he was the son of a black man who refused to remain in slavery and a white woman who annihilated the sensibilities of her slaveholding parents by bearing a dark child to the high-spirited runaway. So the furies that drove Cayton out of the South had mustered before he was born. And to make the situation completely unbearable, he was endowed by nature with sharp comprehension and a sense of right and justice.

The migrating Cayton carried a number of vivid impressions out of the South. As a small child he saw Pemberton surrender to Grant at Vicksburg. He saw the former slaveholders of the section leave their plantations and "go somewheres." At the age of ten he saw black men cast their first vote. Five years later he was working in connection with local elections, doing stunts to pep up the campaigns. The following year he saw Negroes driven from political power—the beginning of their disfranchisement.

The unsettled youth pulled himself together in Seattle, went to work for a printer, and eventually learned the trade. He married the daughter of Hiram Revels, one of the two colored men ever to sit in the United States Senate, and began to plan a normal life for himself and his family. Almost his first enterprise was a weekly newspaper for the Negroes of the community. He called his paper the *Republican,* and on January 4, 1896, when it was nearing the end of its second year of publication, he began his New Year's message with these words:

> On behalf of the Negroes of the state, the *Republican* extends greetings to all, whatever their color or their nationality; be they rich or poor, Jew or Gentile, Greek or Chinaman, or whether they be native or foreign.

He concluded the two-column message as follows:

> . . . We live in the present and in the future, and not the past; let bygones be bygones, and today let all men, irrespective of race, color, creed, or nationality, meet on one common ground, smoke the pipe of everlasting peace, and bow without murmur or complaint to the inevitable. Let there be one flag and one country for all manner of man that swears allegiance thereto. Let America be for Americans, without either color or race distinction cutting any figure in the contest. Let the race be for all, and the prize to the winner, irrespective. Let us join in the brotherhood of man, and form a nucleus, both defensive and offensive, around which we will gather the elements of American humanity, now repelling each other, and thus move grandly on to a goal, and with our combined forces defy the world should it threaten our liberties or endanger our institutions.

In the same issue he printed an article by Miss Susie Sumner Revels (after Senator Charles Sumner who introduced her father to the Senate), soon to become his wife, in which she described the Dahomey village and the Negro building at the Atlanta Exposition and commented on the celebrated speech made by Booker T. Washington, a speech which, she felt, could not have been given had there been no Negro building. The article praised the exposition for presenting the Negro in an honest light. Much political news of local interest was also included in the same issue of the *Republican*. The impression is unmistakable that Cayton's strong feelings about the "brotherhood of man" and "one flag and one country for all" were already influencing the publication away from the original idea of a weekly newspaper for the Negroes around the Sound toward the more general concept of a political sheet for the whole community.

The complete change in the policy of Cayton's newspaper came as an aftermath of a turbulent Republican State convention in Spokane. Cayton had been named as one of two Negro delegates to this convention out of deference to the twenty-five hundred Negro voters which represented about one in one hundred of the total constituency. Instead of doing as he was told by the county caucus, however, Cayton joined seven white delegates in a rebellion and walked out on the "gang." Cayton became spokesman for the bolters and delivered a fiery challenge to the regulars. The result was wild applause from his faction, hisses and derision from the others. A fist fight, with the stormy little brown man at its very center, brought down the curtain on the session, and Cayton was publicly assured by the old guard that he had attended his last Republican convention.

The newspaper of which he was editor and publisher became the organ of his faction. By means of it, Cayton drew around himself a number of active white workers and captured the ward delegation for the next county convention. He became the chairman of the group. But the fight had only begun. Years later he recalled:

> . . . on the day of the caucus, which elected the delegates to the county convention, a colonel of the great Civil War was stationed at the polls to curse me during the entire voting period and shame white voters for bowing down to a nigger leader. Be it remembered there was not another Negro voter in the entire ward. My followers pleaded with me to have my adversary arrested, but I pleaded with them to leave him alone, knowing full well it was a well-laid plan to bring about the defeat of my faction. I won, and from then on I was always taken into consideration. My paper became state wide in circulation and many took it without knowing my racial identity. If perchance I was introduced at some public function the other fellow was usually greatly surprised.

Cayton's strength as a ward politician continued to increase, but there is evidence of an increasing tendency on his part to withdraw from the spotlight and work behind the scenes. Of course he did not admit to employing any such tactics. "If a Negro feels that he can hold his own among white campaigners and wants to play the game, though without a Negro constituency," he once said, "he should 'back his ears and pitch in.' If he gets knocked down, never admit it was on account of his color and never sulk in his tent." But he also confessed to "knowing full well I would not be the recipient of any of the fat jobs in the state." What he did reap, though much less than he might have expected had not the "nigger objection" remained so handy for his opponents, was nevertheless rather exceptional under the circumstances.

Scores of candidates put their publicity campaigns in Cayton's hands. On one occasion, he recalled, "a gubernatorial candidate employed a well-known local leader as his man and then the publicity man came to me and engaged me to do the work at my own price providing I kept it a secret." The campaign came off as pleasantly as a marriage ball, despite the fact that Cayton's part in it was suspected and mentioned as soon as copy began to reach the newspapers. Later he was put to work on the campaign of a United States Senator seeking re-election. In the heat of the campaign someone asked the Senator, "What are you going to do for Cayton when this fight is over? He has done masterly work and is deserving of the best you have to give." The Senator's answer was blunt, cruel, and realistic. "Nothing," he said. "If I give him what he merits, the opposition will use it against us in the next fight. If I give him an insignificant place, the opposition will belittle me." If Cayton appeared to take this bitter dose with a strange equanimity, it was because he had set his eye on "the governorship of the Philippine Islands in case my senatorial candidate and President Taft won." Unfortunately, both candidates lost.

Cayton's weekly again became a Negro newspaper during the migrations of the World War I period. Reports of riots against colored industrial workers brought into Northern cities from the rural South, accounts of the bombing of the homes of the newcomers, rumors of the mistreatment of black soldiers of the United States Army, and other evidences of the spread of leprous racial hatred convinced him that the infection had to be resisted by direct methods. There was no escape for the man of feeling and understanding, not even in faraway Seattle.

Back again to the point at which he started, Cayton ended his career as a zealous race man, working in a cause which was just then beginning to gather its forces throughout the country. He had lived long enough to discover that the Emancipation he had witnessed as a child was a half measure. It lifted the slave only to the status of an alien in the United States—despite the Fourteenth and Fifteenth Amendments. That wasn't enough. Full citizenship was the basic right of the native-born man, no matter what his color or previous condition. Cayton had also lived long enough to assure himself that his wife and children would entertain no vain and wistful hope of solving their problems by withdrawing from the main body of Negroes in the United States. The back-trailing began a few years after his death.

In succeeding years Cayton's oldest son, Horace, Jr., followed the sea for a while, completed college at the University of Washington, and—a decade later—became the director of the Parkway Community House in the heart of Chicago's largest Negro neighborhood. Revels, the second son, launched a career in labor by organizing the cooks and stewards on the coastal steamer *H. F. Alexander*. He rose through the Maritime Union on the San Francisco waterfront, and within a few years he had become a State vice-president of the CIO in California. The daughters and the wife of the elder Cayton followed Horace, Jr., back to Chicago. There the mother died, and somewhat later Madge, the oldest daughter. The memory of the first Cayton's adventure into the Northwest had begun to grow dim.

Meanwhile, another procession of hopeful Negroes moved into California. When Captain John C. Frémont's expeditions surveyed that territory in the years following 1843, the parties generally included Negroes. Bancroft names Jacob Dodson among the twenty-five persons selected by Frémont for the journey which ended in the discovery of Klamath Lake. Dodson was also with Frémont on the famous ride from Los Angeles to Monterey. James Duff, who later settled in Mariposa County, where he lived to be ninety-three years old, was said to have gone West with Frémont. One of his surviving neighbors retained a picture of the old man as late as 1919—a picture which revealed the pioneer, who apparently made no secret of his colored blood, as a man not easily distinguishable as a Negro. Both of these Negroes as well as John Grider, Joe McAfee, Charles G. Gaines, Billy Gaston, and an individual known only as Ben, the personal servant of one of the officers, were probably present at the Bear Flag Party, where the bear insignia of California was created. The *Western Outlook* of San Francisco, October 7, 1914, describing an admission day parade in the city of Vallejo, called attention to newspaper reports that "John Grider, the only survivor of the Bear Flag Party, rode in solitary state in an automobile, a vehicle his wildest imagination never pictured in the strenuous days of California's fight for membership into the Union." Newspapers had neglected, the *Outlook* pointed out, to mention that Grider was a Negro, but word got about later, and interviews with him brought out the testimony that these other colored men, too, had been present at the Bear Flag Party.

A more arresting character than any of these, however, was Biddy Mason, a slave woman who came to San Bernardino in 1851. The party which brought her West from Mississippi consisted of three hundred wagons, mostly drawn by ox teams, and Biddy's task was to follow behind driving the cattle and livestock across the plains. At the same time she had to care for her three young daughters, Ellen, Ann, and Harriett. Her owner settled in San Bernardino with his family and slaves, remained there three years, and then decided to move to Texas. But he failed to take into consideration the State laws and the antislavery sentiment in the community. Passing through Los Angeles County, the party encamped in a canyon near Santa Monica; it was here that Sheriff Frank Dewitt, having been notified of this attempt to remove slaves from the free State of California, overhauled the master and issued a writ preventing the move. Biddy Mason and her family secured their freedom, and the mother took her children to Los Angeles, where she found employment as a confinement nurse with a Dr. Griffin.

According to Biddy's daughter, there were only eight white families living in the town at that time. There were, however, other Negroes, and one of them was Robert Owens, livery-stable keeper. At this house Biddy and her brood were received with warm hospitality. And it was not long before Biddy herself was in a position to befriend newcomers. Almost immediately she began to acquire property. In later years the values of her holdings in Los Angeles increased fabulously, and Biddy was regarded as a woman of considerable wealth. Her benevolence became a legend. Inmates of jails and hospitals and destitute families knew her as Grandma Mason. She secured and held church property for her people. And during the destructive flood of the early eighties Biddy left an open account with a small grocery store on Fourth and Spring Streets to be used by any family made homeless by the rains.

At least one of the daughters of Biddy Mason was sent to Stockton to attend the school for colored children conducted by J. B. Sanderson, himself a mulatto migrant, on Elk Street between Market and W. This was the thing to do in the years following 1856, for Sanderson's reputation as a tutor was excellent, and educational opportunities for young Negroes were limited. This same daughter married Charles Owens, son of the livery-stable keeper, and sent her own children to the public schools of Oakland for elementary education and then to Sanderson for "a business education." In Stockton they boarded in the home of the teacher. Back in Los Angeles, after the completion of their work with Sanderson, they were permitted to attend evening classes at one of the business schools. And in the early years of the present century the descendants of the slave woman Biddy Mason and Robert Owens still owned valuable property in the business section of Los Angeles.

The great migrations which reached their height at the time of World War I brought in so many Negroes from the South and East, with so much fresh vitality, they turned the page on the early settlers and opened a new chapter on Negro migration to the West Coast. Los Angeles as a whole was filling up with new people, and its Negro communities expanded proportionately. When the depression reduced the tide temporarily, the colored population of Los Angeles was already among the larger ones in major cities of the United States. And the adjustment of this group to the community as a whole was perhaps better than that of any group of equal size in any other American city. This despite the predominance of Southern whites in the general population. Perhaps the Japanese and the Mexicans are to be thanked. They drew off much of the racial hostility which otherwise might have been concentrated on the Negroes. And when Japanese-American citizens were removed from cities of the Coast to inland relocation camps following Pearl Harbor, their places were quickly filled by another wave of Negro migrants.

Typical of these, in some ways, was Edwin Louis Petty, born in Memphis in 1912, the son of the pastor of the Gilfield Baptist Church of that city. Petty headed West in 1932, not waiting for the depression to lift, and landed a three-dollar-a-week job with a Japanese produce broker in the city market at Ninth and San Pedro streets. Three years later he was made a salesman in the firm. Later he went into the wholesale produce business for himself, and in 1942—following the evacuation of the Japanese—he became a State licensed broker, buying from farmers and selling to local stores, markets, et cetera. In 1944 he opened his own commission house, with a setup comparing favorably with any in the city market.

Los Angeles in legend became "Paradise West" to Negroes still languishing in the Egyptland of the South, and not without some justification. For one thing, there was more space in which a man could breathe. The city covered a wide area, so that even in a Negro section one might have a small front yard with a few flowers and a palm tree or maybe even a little vegetable garden in the rear. It was possible in some places to keep a few chickens. And jobs, within certain restricted categories, were not too scarce.

The story of the renowned architect, Paul Revere Williams, provides an example of the achievements of some Negro Angelenos with talent and persistence. His parents, Chester and Lila Williams, came to Los Angeles from Memphis in the 1890s. Paul was born there in 1894. His father died when he was two, and two years later the death of his mother made him an orphan. He was raised by relatives who did their best for him and managed to send him to school.

As a child he was not very much aware of prejudice, but when he grew older and applied for a part-time job to help pay his school expenses he was shocked to realize that he had been rejected because of his dark skin. He later spoke of this experience:

> I passed through successive stages of bewilderment, inarticulate resentment, and, finally, reconciliation to the status of my race. I found in my condition an incentive to personal accomplishment, an inspiring challenge.

He was imbued with a fierce determination to "show himself" rather than to "show them." His obsessive aim was to ". . . vindicate every ability I had . . . to prove that I, *as an individual,* deserved a place in the world."

Even before he enrolled at Polytechnic High School, Paul had decided he would be an architect. There a not unkindly instructor, when the boy confided in him, asked if he had ever heard of a Negro architect. Paul had to admit that he hadn't, but kept the goal before him as he worked his way through the University of California. While attending the Beaux Arts Institute of Design, he won the Beaux Arts Medal.

His schooling over, Williams began an insistent telephoning of architectural firms. Did they need an architect—a Negro architect? The answer was monotonously no, until, near the end of the fat volume, he found a firm willing to take a chance. Beginning as a junior draftsman, he soon forged to the top as head man. He was admitted to the Los Angeles Society of Architects. Now is the time to go it for myself, he thought, and opened his own office.

His business flourished like the green bay tree, and on some occasions he had as many as thirty-three draftsmen—some of them white—working for him. He designed all kinds of buildings, but won international fame as a favorite architect of the Hollywood movie set. Among his clients were Will Hays, Grace Moore, Bill "Bojangles" Robinson, Corinne Griffith, Zasu Pitts, and Frank Sinatra. In the course of time he was admitted to the growing-less-exclusive club of Negro millionaires.

It did not require the success story of Negroes like Paul R. Williams to convince his racial brethren that California was the land of dreams, the legendary Fortunate Isles where there is always a golden sun and the winds blow warmly and softly. Los Angeles, one often hears, has the prettiest Bar-B-Q carhop girls in the world. Most of them came West fired by the sleazy cinema-nurtured phantasmagoria that has a firm place in the American mythology: every girl has a good chance of becoming a movie star. The ambitions of the Negro migrants usually were less grandiose: they'd settle for a little of the freedom and wide-open spaces for which the West was noted, for a job that paid enough to live on in modest comfort, for a home with a tree in front of it and a little grass and a few flowers.

World War I brought a great many job seekers to the Negro district nearly ten miles south of downtown Los Angeles called Watts. Settled residents were inclined to be hospitable and often took in relatives and friends fleeing from bondage and hard times in Mississippi, Alabama, Georgia and other areas of the Darkest South. There was room in the neat, one-story frame and stucco houses.

But World War II and the years following it brought a deluge. Servicemen who had grown fond of the benign climate and the not-too-bad racial atmosphere either stayed or returned, bringing wives and families. The aircraft industry and other wartime activities had attracted many who chose to remain. And throughout the South and other sections of the country the urge to try fabulous Los Angeles persisted.

Overcrowding and the annoying social behavior of some of the greenhorns with cottonseed in their hair and red Georgia clay between their toes eventually caused a flight by the more solid mainstays of the community, who yearned to disaffiliate from their uncouth racial brethren. An ambition to get out of Watts as fast as possible became general among the old-timers. Renters swarmed into the vacated homes, often crowding eight or ten in one or two rooms. The neat cottages became shacks. Slums encroached on the periphery of the original settlement. Absentee landlords collected as much rent as they could without expending anything for upkeep. By the 1960s, Watts was derisively labeled "a ghetto with palm trees."

A report called *Migration and the Southern California Economy,* issued in 1964 by the Southern Research Council of Occidental College, stated that "Southern California is a land of opportunity for the educated, the skilled, and the successful." Unfortunately, few if any of those who came hopefully to Watts possessed these essential qualifications. The report went on:

> Another major problem brought about by migration to Southern California is that there are too many potential unemployable workers among the migrants. Unemployable migrants are typically young (teenagers) and/or unskilled. A disproportionate share of these are non-white. These groups gravitate toward the older sections of Los Angeles, accentuating the crowded conditions there and creating new slums, crime, delinquency and requiring increased police coverage.

By 1965 Watts had a population density of 27.3 per acre, compared with a Los Angeles County average of 7.4. Two thirds of its residents had not completed high school, and the school dropout rate was more than twice the city average. Restless, bitter, disillusioned boys aimlessly roamed the streets. Boredom, frustration, and despair hung in the air like a heavy pall. Justifying their surveillance by the existence of a very high crime rate in Watts, the police were always watching and often apprehending and frisking Wattsians. Most of those supervised were from the South, where the typical lawman is a contemptuous oppressor and natural enemy. "Every time I stop to look at something I feel a white cop's eyes boring into my back," one black citizen complained, "and I see them everywhere I go."

Civil Rights workers would refer to the 205 police officers in Watts, only five of them Negroes, as an "occupying power." An image of "Whitey"—any white man—as the principal architect of the district's misfortunes grew larger and larger. A constant target of Negro organizations was Los Angeles Police Chief William H. Parker, who frequently lectured on the subject: "Man Is by Nature a Predatory Animal Who Must Be Restrained." Negroes contended that he displayed more zeal in restraining them than he did in handling white lawbreakers, and that he sanctioned police brutality toward dark-skinned Angelenos.

James Tolbert, a Negro attorney who once lived in Watts and served five years as a probation officer, offered this comment:

> The key word in Watts is hopelessness. The trouble is that the hero there is the bad guy, not the good guy. The feeling too often is that "I had rather be a delinquent than be nothing."

Against such a background the long-predicted happening took place just as the hot day of August 11, 1965, was drawing to a close. Shortly after seven P.M. Lee Minikus and Bob Lewis, state highway patrolmen, stopped an automobile at the intersection of Avalon and One Hundred Sixteenth Streets. They ordered the driver, a twenty-one-year-old Negro named Marquette Frye, to step out, and when he did they accused him of drunken driving. The ensuing events have been described in a dozen different ways by as many eyewitnesses. One story is that Frye's pregnant mother heard the ruckus and emerged from her nearby home to reprimand Marquette for being drunk. Another is that she was pleading with Marquette to submit peaceably to the officers. At any rate, there followed an argument participated in by Frye, his mother, his older brother (who was with him in the car) on one side and the policemen on the other. The officers claimed that Frye struggled and had to be restrained. Negro spectators did not see it that way. They maintained that the cops had beaten Frye before throwing him in the police car, and to make matters worse, had stomped his pregnant mother. The upshot was that all three Fryes were driven off to jail.

As always is the case, a curious crowd had gathered. One of the policemen is reported to have held the onlookers at bay, saying something like: "Get back, you niggers! Clear out of here, you niggers!" Squad cars with flashing lights and screaming sirens began to arrive in dozens, and soon there were seventy-five policemen with menacing guns. Only one of these was a Negro, and he is credited with making some ineffectual efforts to restore calm and order. One thing is certain: all hell broke loose. Angry, shouting Negroes began throwing rocks or anything else handy, smashing windows, and manufacturing Molotov cocktails out of Coke bottles filled with gasoline. These they hurled into buildings, usually those housing white-owned businesses. Often, before the establishment was put to the torch, desirable merchandise was hauled away. There was no such thing as a leader, unless you could call the one who first kicked in a window a leader. Once the breach was made, others quickly followed. Television sets, furniture, and even refrigerators were hauled away in coaster wagons and shopping carts. Foodstuff was not neglected, and liquor was high on the loot priority list. "That man been robbin' me for years, now I'm gettin' some of it back" was a frequent excuse.

Negro shopkeepers hastily posted such signs as "Blood Brother," "Colored-Owned Business," or simply "Blood." The rioters sometimes spared these places, though not always. In the course of the six-day disorders, 1,000 fires were reported by the Fire Department, 300 being of major proportions. Entire blocks were reduced to smoking ruins resembling those of bombed-out cities in World War II. A conservative estimate of the property damage placed it at over $40,000,000.

During the first day of rioting more than 1,500 people, mostly young Negroes, were ranging the streets, throwing rocks and other missiles into store windows and stoning the cars of passing motorists who appeared to be white. On several occasions light-skinned Negroes were accorded the same treatment.

By Friday, the mob was in complete control. More than a thousand city policemen, deputy sheriffs, and State highway patrolmen were helpless. "Burn, baby, burn," the theme song of a popular Negro disk jockey called "the mighty Montague," took on a ghastly literalness. "Get Whitey! Get Whitey!" was another often-shouted slogan as white pedestrians and motorists were set upon and beaten, none fatally. After unaccountable hesitation, Mayor Samuel W. Yorty asked Lieutenant Governor Glenn Anderson (in charge while Governor Edmund G. Brown was vacationing in Europe) to send in the National Guard. There was further delay as Anderson also displayed some indecisiveness, but on Saturday the guardsmen moved into the battle zone. Eventually there were 12,500 of them. They sealed off the area, imposing a quarantine appropriate for the black death or the bubonic plague. Severe restrictions were placed upon Negroes going in and out of Watts, even doctors being submitted to a search. It was easy enough to get out, but hard to get back in. Food shortages became grave. Negroes who had taken no part in the rioting were embittered. Many had huddled in their living rooms, watching on television the hell-raising going on only a block or so away.

Included in the loot from raided stores had been a number of rifles and revolvers. A certain amount of sporadic sniping took place, usually from rooftops. Police cars searching for a sniper threw a floodlight on a Negro housewife sitting on her front lawn. Blinded by the glare and enraged at the intrusion, she shouted:

> I ain't out in the street, dammit! Dammit, don't bother me in my house! Y'all ain't right! That's the trouble! Y'all ain't right!

Another woman was compelled to get out of her house and stay in her front yard while guardsmen searched for a sniper they thought had fired from the roof. It didn't seem right to her, either, and she lamented:

> You shot into a house full of babies. I love my black babies as much as you love your white ones, and all I see around me is white faces with guns.

When all the hysterical talk about Negroes with guns simmered down, it was learned that of the thirty-four known dead in the riot, only three were white. And only one of the white casualties could have been shot by a Negro. Law-enforcement officers consistently referred to the rioters as "terrorists," but it was disclosed that the lawmen themselves knew a little about terrorism. The rioters were terrorists, all right, but their terrorism rarely had lethal consequences. It was aimed at Whitey's property more than at his life. One elderly Negro gentleman, who remembered Watts before the deluge of migrants came, shook his head sadly and said:

> These youngsters goin' around, hopped up tree-top tall on goof balls and shisky, playin' the scare-Whitey game! They scare him all right, but they scare the livin' daylights out of me, too. And they scare theirselves plenty, you bet your boots.

Observers began to wonder about Chief Parker's riot control program, of which he had often boasted. The conventional methods of riot control—tear and nausea gas, fire hose, etc.—were never put into use. The wide streets of Watts lent themselves to such tactics. Instead, the police—and later the guardsmen—relied largely upon clubs and firearms. Flashing red lights on police cars and ambulances and screaming sirens added to the pandemonium, whereas in other cities it has been considered wise practice to eliminate such provocations of excitement. Nicholas Von Hoffman of the Chicago *Daily News*, one reporter who observed things for himself and did not rely upon police say-so or canned press releases, had a number of questions to ask.

He pointed out that the 664 Los Angeles city policemen sent into action chalked up two thirds of the slain, while the 12,500 National Guardsmen in the same area could be credited with only about four casualties. Very often the familiar question, "Who's in charge here?" seemed to be unanswerable. Von Hoffman quoted a white reporter as remarking: "On Thursday night, clearly no one was in command. I saw police going up and down beating people with their sticks and smashing car windows."

When uneasy calm descended upon Watts, everybody seemed to be affected with a case of psychic hangover. Most Negroes, young and old, walked about silently, either sullen or sad. There was no more communication between them and the white power structure than there had been before the holocaust. As for the men on top, mutual recriminations and accusations began to fly about as thickly as the brickbats had. Everybody wanted to get in the act, as Jimmy Durante complains. Governor Brown, flying hastily home from Greece, could see no employment opportunity or voting privilege significance in the situation. He went on:

The riot took place in a scene of broken families and broken hearts, of lonely children and aimless adults, of frustration and poverty . . . It is a tragedy that must not become a prophecy for this or any other great city in America.

With this in mind, he appointed an eight-man commission, headed by John A. McCone (formerly director of the Central Intelligence Agency), to investigate the riots, with subpoena powers "to make sure that all of us have access to the whole truth." The function of the investigatory commission, he said in a television speech, would be ". . . to probe deeply for the immediate and underlying causes of the Los Angeles riots and to recommend means to prevent their recurrence." Later on, he was to say in San Francisco that statements by Chief Parker had "hurt the whole cause of race relations in Los Angeles." One of these, undoubtedly, was Parker's exultant crowing that "We're on top now and they're on the bottom," referring to the rioters.

As for Parker, he could see no blemish or flaw in his conduct or that of his men. There had been too much handling of Negroes with "kid gloves" in the recent past, he concluded. Replying to accusations that police brutality not only had helped to precipitate the riot but had contributed to its prolongation, he made it plain that he was not going to suffer "in silence under such criticism" as did "the average police chief in America." Then he made a revelation:

We have learned that a large proportion of the rioters in custody have criminal records. The feeling of the rioters has been to gloss over Negro crime and blame mistreatment by police.

Mayor Yorty concurred, and cited a favorite bête noire (albeit it was red-hued!). He dismissed the charges of police brutality by identifying them as ". . . part of a big lie technique shouted all over the world by Communists, dupes, and demagogues, irrespective of race."

Evangelist Billy Graham, surveying still smoldering Watts from the vantage point of a helicopter, envisioned "a dress rehearsal for revolution" instigated by "sinister forces trying to set race against race and class against class with the ruthless objective of overthrowing the government." This led the *Christian Century* in its September 1, 1965, issue to inquire editorially:

> What sinister forces, Mr. Graham? Are you implying with the John Birch Society that the Negro's rebellion is communist-inspired, communist-directed? Or do you mean by "sinister forces" the centuries-old rapaciousness of the white man, the white Christian's cold indifference to the plight of his Negro brother, the inactivity of genteel churches, the bitter despair which the Negro sucks from his legacy of abuse? Don't you know that it was your ancestors and ours who set race against race, class against class? If you believe that the nation is being ruined by sinister forces, name them.

Municipal Court Judge Loren Miller, a Negro attorney noted for his civil rights activities and for his incisive articles in the *Nation* and elsewhere, thought that the overwhelming vote for Proposition 14 in the November 1964 election had something to do with the hedged-in, wanting-to-bust-out feeling that had stirred discontent among the Wattsians, who felt that they were being enclosed within four walls. Proposition 14 had the effect of nullifying all fair housing legislation that had given Negroes a measure of at least legal protection. "The people distrust the police, and the police distrust the people," Judge Miller added. "They move in a constant atmosphere of hate."

Saul D. Alinsky, a community organizer whose work in the Chicago "Back of the Yards" neighborhood brought him international attention, offered—from his home in Carmel—two "conditions of reconstruction." The first was to give Police Chief Parker his walking papers. The second was to retire "that un-Christian, prehistoric muttonhead" James Francis Cardinal McIntyre, archbishop of the Los Angeles diocese. Alinsky elaborated: "I would recommend Parker to be security chief in Disneyland. And Cardinal McIntyre would be apostolic delegate to Taiwan, with the hope that we would then follow John Foster Dulles' suggestion and unleash him on the Chinese mainland."

Mayor Yorty had no power to implement the second recommendation, and he vigorously spurned the first. Dr. Martin Luther King, after a ninety-minute conference with Governor Brown, reported that the governor, too, defended Parker's conduct, but acknowledged that "his zeal for law enforcement could be misinterpreted as prejudice." Dr. King had said in Miami before he came to Los Angeles:

I strongly deplore the violence. It is absolutely wrong, socially detestable and self-defeating. On the other hand, I equally deplore the continuation of ghetto life that millions of Negroes have to live in. They are in hopeless despair, and they feel they have no stake in society.

Alinsky's indictment of Cardinal McIntyre was not the only one. Civil rights leaders and liberal-minded Roman Catholic laymen and clergymen had previously assailed him for his censure and punishment of priests and nuns who had taken part in civil rights activities or had even spoken favorably of them. In 1964 Father William DuBay addressed an open letter to Pope Paul VI requesting that Cardinal McIntyre be dethroned. Late in the same year, Father John Coffield asked for and received a three-year leave of absence from his pastorate at Ascension Church so that he might go to Chicago to work in a Negro parish and to study psychology at the University of Chicago. He said frankly that the Cardinal's strictures on the race question had influenced his decision to leave Los Angeles.

Harlem Congressman Adam Clayton Powell, Jr., never at a loss for words, had some strong ones:

In Los Angeles, the incinerating fuel for last week's explosion had been smoldering for years—police brutality. The arrogance of Police Chief Parker in refusing to heed the pleas of responsible Negro leadership steadily worsened the situation. More recently, the refusal of the Mayor to evolve a comprehensive anti-poverty program to siphon off many of that community's unemployed further was regarded as a kick in the stomach by many Negroes.

Ex-President Eisenhower, in characteristically muddled syntax, used these words to reprove the rioters:

This kind of senseless violence—I don't care what the condition of these people who started it—they have made the conditions far worse. They have burned their homes and stores. They have cost an immeasurable amount of money that could have been spent in their favor.

Senator Robert F. Kennedy (D.–N.Y.) was moved to retort when he heard of Ike's homily:

It is pointless to tell Negroes living in Northern slums to obey the law. To these Negroes, the law is their enemy . . . By and large, white politicians in the North are completely out of touch with the ferment and hatred that exists among slum Negroes. They have traditionally done business with a small coterie of Negro leaders who, until 1962, could be depended upon to deliver the Negro vote as a bloc in return for a few political jobs and specified sums of money.

And what of the "terrorists" themselves? A few were still bellicose, but more were chastened and repentant. "It seemed like fun at first," one boy confessed, "throwing rocks at Whitey's big new cars. We didn't aim to hurt anybody, just mess up the cars. At least, not at first. Then it seemed like the stuff we took was just there for us. If we didn't take it, somebody else would. But then it got not to be so much fun at all but just trouble." Other contrite rioters recalled that some of the "Whitey" merchants hadn't been "devils" after all, but had occasionally done a kindness for them. But if the window is already broken, and the stuff you really need or want is just lying there for the taking, you got to be strong not to jump in and get your share.

The McCone commission issued a 101-page report in December 1965. It named unemployment as the most distressing problem in Watts, and deplored the "sickness in the center of our city." There were recommendations for job training programs, a more wholesome home life for children, and a "strengthened" police commission. Very few personal references were made, though Acting Governor Anderson was mildly chided for not calling in national guard troops soon enough. This dire warning was sounded:

So serious and so explosive is the situation that, unless it is checked, the August riots may seem by comparison to be only a curtain raiser to what could blow up one day in the future.

CHAPTER XVII

Karamu

THIS IS THE STORY of a good deed shining in a naughty world. When Russell W. Jelliffe was growing up in Mansfield, Ohio, one of the members of the First Congregational Church, which his family attended, was Mrs. Annie Bradford, a Negro woman who occupied a pew directly in front of theirs. To him there was nothing remarkable about Mrs. Bradford's presence there. That much he took for granted. His people had been on the side of freedom for generations. But when the old colored woman died, it was learned that she had provided in her will for the establishment of a library in the church. The books were made available to members of the church, and Russell, to whom books were already beginning to be an important part of life, did not neglect the opportunity to read them.

In those days there was no public library of any sort in the community, but it remained for a Negro member of the church to feel this cultural lack strong enough to do something about it. However, the grateful members soon repaid her thoughtfulness and generosity by hanging a portrait of the late donor near the shelves of books. And the whole experience became one of the sweetest and strongest of the boy's childhood memories. He grew to manhood praising this church member, without reference to her color, because she had been concerned about the intellectual life of her Christian brothers and sisters and had had the good sense to decide upon books as her contribution toward the improvement of that life.

But another childhood experience left an equally vivid impression on young Jelliffe's mind. He and Boyd Hick, a Negro boy, who happened to be his playmate, presented themselves together for admission to membership in the local Y.M.C.A. When the colored youngster put down his twenty-five-cent fee, the money was refused. When Russell, standing beside his friend, offered his own quarter, it was promptly accepted. The two boys were embarrassed, hurt, confused. No one attempted to explain this incomprehensible act to them.

Both experiences have borne fruit in the adult lives of Russell and Rowena Jelliffe, founders of Cleveland's beloved Karamu House. When these two classmates, who had met as freshmen, became seniors at Oberlin College in 1914, they made up their minds that racial prejudice is "the weakest link in the democratic chain." The next year both of them went to Chicago on scholarships, worked in the slums, at Hull House and other settlements, took masters' degrees, got married, and began casting about for the kind of work into which they could put their hearts.

Rowena Woodham Jelliffe had roots in the Midwest too. Her folks were old Illinois people whose pioneering aim had been to help build a unified nation. Neither they nor she had thought very much about Negroes one way or another. But a relative of Ernest Hemingway advised the girl's mother to send Rowena to Oberlin, a college to which that branch of the Hemingway family was sentimentally attached. And at Oberlin, where she majored in sociology and psychology, Rowena met Negroes and learned something of their problems.

Without a very definite plan the young couple returned to Cleveland in 1915, at the invitation of the Second Presbyterian Church, and began settlement-house work in a slum neighborhood which was by no means predominantly Negro. They moved into an old frame house that had once been a funeral parlor, made it their home as well as the headquarters of their work, and began a five-year period of experimental study of human personality and the storms and stresses by which it is assailed in a harsh environment. But while they worked and learned, the migration engulfed them.

Thousands of Negroes poured into "the Roaring Third," the community in which the Jelliffes' welfare center was located during those first years. Nearly all of the newcomers were fresh from the

South, migrants brought in to work in defense plants and other industrial establishments. And almost immediately the results of bad housing, overcrowding, and inadequate health and recreational facilities began to be noticed: disease and delinquency. With equal swiftness the city as a whole began to mistake effect for cause. The Jelliffes were faced with a problem of analysis and comprehension as well as the responsibility to act in the situation they themselves had elected.

The result was Karamu House and the philosophy which it has come to represent. As the name, a Swahili word, suggests, Karamu thought of itself both as the "center of the community" and a "place of enjoyment." Its "recreational" activities, begun as a side line, became its basic technique. Art, as one observer pointed out, began to wag the welfare. But this was not art with a capital *A*. The Jelliffes observed early in their experience that a certain facility for artistic expression was not at all uncommon among the poor, the lonely, the hurt youngsters who ventured into their center. Indeed, they soon discovered that some of these teenage Negroes, socially repressed and apparently backward, possessed unusual talents. This fact put them on the alert, and they began to note early symptoms of the artistic impulse—careless snatches of song on the playground, pretty flourishes of movement thrown into the games, jigs, struts, and hippety-hops, spontaneous impersonations, casual bits of inspired make-believe, shy attempts to help beautify Karamu's buildings and grounds. This was their lead. They would offer young Negroes an opportunity to liberate themselves, so to speak, through artistic expression. Careers in the arts, fortunately, could be pursued by colored Americans with less opposition than was to be met in most other fields.

Neither of the Jelliffes had special training in any of the arts. They simply worked with the youngsters who came to them and learned as they went along. Their first project in this new area was a children's theater started by Mrs. Jelliffe. The little troupe did so well that older youths and adults began asking for a grown-up company, and soon one was organized. This unit was a lot of fun for the participants from the beginning, but essentially it was just another Little Theater company. Little, if anything, had been added to the stereotype. Then the great Charles Gilpin came to Cleveland to play the title role in Eugene O'Neill's *Emperor Jones*. He attended a performance by the Karamu Players and gave them the suggestion that transformed their group from a carbon copy of every other Little Theater company in the nation to a creative force which has exerted a real influence.

"Look here, you're all wrong," Gilpin said to the group sitting along the apron of the crude stage. "Why don't you take yourselves seriously and really do something? Make this a real Negro theater. You could do it. Look at the material all around you. Learn to see the drama in your own lives, and someday the world will come to see you. If there aren't any plays, get somebody to write them." To show that he was sincere in his criticism, he added, "Here's fifty dollars toward your cause."

This was a blunt and shocking speech, purposely so perhaps, and it came from a disconsolate actor who had suffered his own ups and downs and was even then being criticized for his part in the play which was at last bringing him deserved recognition in the American theater. And the amateurs to whom it was directed were by no means unanimous in approval of the idea. In fact, a serious discussion began after Gilpin left the hall. But after all was said, the actor's suggestion prevailed, and the group decided to make a fresh start along lines which Gilpin had indicated. Their immediate step was to change their name to the Gilpin Players.

Launched on a program of Negro plays, the Karamu group soon discovered that it was *not* following the line of least resistance. Some white people, of course, wanted then—as now—to see the Negro only in ridiculous situations, whether on the stage, screen, or in story. They did not want to be reminded of the essential humanity of colored people, for this throws a burden on the mind and the conscience. Some Negroes resented transcriptions of their lives for very different reasons. They hated to be reminded of their serfdom and their ghetto existence. They especially hated to have these transcriptions exhibited to the world at large, for they feared the world would think Negroes are plantation serfs by choice or that Negroes consent to or approve of the indignities of segregation. The Gilpin Players had to justify their course in the face of such attitudes. It seemed to them that the right kind of plays—assuming such treatments could be found—would answer everything. The search for scripts became their first enterprise.

The members of the theater group attempted to write plays themselves. Nothing much came of this particular zeal, but their letters to more experienced writers throughout the country did not go unanswered. Their first play was Ridgely Torrence's *Granny Maumee*. Other plays on Negro themes followed. In time the group produced everything written in this field by Torrence and Paul Green and Willis Richardson and Langston Hughes, not to mention works by many less well-known writers.

Meanwhile, they converted an old German saloon into a theater, rebuilding it themselves out of contributed materials, and decorated it with Karamu art work, using an African motif. The research and the creative activity which this involved did worlds of good. It stimulated the art program of Karamu as well as the theater. And it reached a climax when the Gilpin Players raised fifteen hundred dollars, mainly through admissions, toward a fund to purchase specimens of primitive African art to be brought to Karamu House. The African Art Collection has since been given to the Cleveland Museum of Art and to the Cleveland Historical Society. With another three thousand dollars of the company's earnings the Gilpin Players established a scholarship fund at the Cleveland School of Art for Karamu's most promising students. But the important fact was that the Gilpin Players were able to squeeze this kind of money out of their operating budget at all. Charles Gilpin's fifty dollars was the only subsidy they ever received. Thereafter, thanks to his common-sense suggestion, they not only covered all their production expenses but did right by the authors whose plays they used.

When war brought to a temporary halt the activities of the Gilpin Players, the group had already produced one hundred and forty plays, more and more of them having been written especially for a first performance at Karamu. It had given training and experience to more than four hundred actors and stagecrafters. Some of this group had gone on to the professional stage. Many others had found places in colleges and schools and social agencies as teachers and promoters of drama. John Marriott, a Gilpin Players graduate, toured with Tallulah Bankhead in *The Little Foxes*. Frances Williams, another, was in *You Can't Take It with You*. At the same time Edward Tyler, a twenty-year-old baritone, was showing great promise. The Karamu Dancers gave special performances at the 1939 World's Fair in New York, where they were photographed in action by Gjon Mili's speed camera for *Life* magazine. And Langston Hughes who, as a student at Central High, had come to Karamu to enjoy its facilities while teaching lettering to other youngsters, saw *Mulatto*, one of his plays—first written for the Gilpins—run ten months on Broadway before going on extensive tours. Perhaps these are some of the reasons why the *Theatre Arts Magazine* called the Gilpin Players "the greatest single democratizing force" in their community.

The other art enterprises of Karamu were equally sound, if sometimes less spectacular. Fred Carlo, Elmer Brown, and Zell Ingram were among those who came to the center in short pants. Carlo became the first Negro to make the International Print Show; and Brown, a fugitive from a Mississippi chain gang, became the second. Ingram progressed from puppets to oils and sculpture.

On Karamu's twenty-fifth anniversary the city of Cleveland presented to Russell and Rowena Jelliffe the Charles Eisenman Award, the city's highest civic prize. Dorothy Maynor and Paul Green helped to pay homage to the founders of Karamu over a national broadcast. Said playwright Green: "The Jelliffes are the kind of dreamers who have made America great." And the six hundred Cleveland citizens who came to honor the Jelliffes expressed their approval.

But there were still some Americans who asked, Why an arts program in a settlement house? To them Rowena Jelliffe has replied:

We came upon the Arts Program through a searching for a way by which the Negro could come to feel that his energies headed straight into the main stream of American living. He needed to escape the sense of separateness which is so wasteful to energy and initiative. So much of his living has gone on in the little eddies at the side of the stream. We were looking for a way of challenging and using his best, not his eighth, ninth, or tenth best, but his very best. And it had to be something real enough and challenging enough to make him feel that by use of it he became a participating part of his community.

The field of the arts was the place where prejudice was less of a handicap for the Negro in making his contribution.

The Negro had obvious creative talents, and in the twenties America was just becoming aware of the fact that she hadn't a culture of her own and she decided that she would build one. Obviously, the Negro had much to offer in this structure.

And, too, it was a means of telling his story to America. It is not art for art's sake. It is art as it touches the lives of common people, and becomes a means of telling their sufferings, their joys, their yearnings, their aspirations. We see it as a means of enabling the Negro to tell his story, the truths about his own life. Indeed, we have come, through use of this program, to suspect that art forms may be the only way in which we really tell truths.

His contributions are recognized in this field. He has a sense of bringing something in hand and putting it before his community and saying, "This is mine, I bring this."

And that has become a keynote with us. We come to our community, not with our hand out asking for something, but with a gift in hand.

The Arts Program enables us to be a part of the growing American culture.

Efforts to build and endow a new and greatly expanded Karamu House began when a fire ravaged the original theater in 1939. A nation-wide campaign for a new four-unit plant at East Eighty-ninth Street and Quincy Avenue was undertaken. World War II halted these plans for a time, but a nursery, built in 1945 as a war-emergency child-care center, provided for after hours, youth activities, and in 1947 a temporary arena theater. In 1949 the new Karamu Theater was opened in a building which also provided facilities for other departments. Ten years later long-deferred plans for a Community Service and Music Building reached fulfillment.

When Russell and Rowena Jelliffe retired in 1963, Karamu was operating in a plant that had cost a million and a half dollars. It was debt free and had an endowment of $1,200,000. The annual operating budget was $250,000. Its board consisted of thirty-nine persons, a fair number of whom had themselves been products of Karamu's programs. Memberships, about equally divided between the sexes and likewise between children and adults, with a 70-30 ratio of Negroes to whites, had exceeded 4,000. A full-time staff of thirty-four, assisted by eighteen qualified part-time employees, conducted the operation.

On this sad but heart-warming occasion Mrs. Jelliffe reminisced:

One speaks softly of a thing one loves, and so would I speak of Karamu. We have evolved through the years many programs as a means of reaching our goals. We believe they are good ones. We shall be seeking always to make them better. But I think that, more important to us than our programs, we have evolved a way of life we have found there. We have found a communication between us that bridges differences in background, differences in heritage, differences in social condition, differences in race and religion, to unite us in a concept of man and his function. We have found trust in each other and understanding—and love among us. And this, I think, is Karamu.

We spoke a moment ago of a dream which we, all of us together, have evolved. It has frequently been said of us that Karamu is a dream come true, that the Jelliffes have seen a dream come true. And this is said in all kindness and with a certain tinge of wonder. But I think it must be said that this is not so. Our dream for Karamu, our common dream for Karamu, is not yet come true. Parts of it came to be; fulfillment is there in some degree. But the dream outreaches our achievements; they may outreach our life span. The Karamu dream is fulfilled when every man has the full free right to live out his full potential, undeterred by any other man or group of men.

This night marks the end of our directorship at Karamu, but it marks, too, the beginning of another man's taking into his hands the shuttle for the spinning on the Karamu dream. They are able hands, willing and eager and strong hands, hands you will trust and love.

As we thank you with very full hearts for what you have given to us through a lot of years, we thank you even more for what you will give in future to Olcutt Sanders, our successor.

And Langston Hughes, whose long association with Karamu would make a story in itself, read a poem of tribute he had written for the occasion:

And so the seed
Becomes a flower
And in its hour

Reproduces dreams
And flowers.

And so the root
Becomes a trunk
And then a tree
And seeds of trees
And springtime sap
And summer shade
And autumn leaves
And shape of poems
And dreams—
And more than tree.

CHAPTER XVIII

Moon of the Migrant Tides

IT WAS NOT LONG after Antoine de la Mothe Cadillac settled in 1701 a band of one hundred French soldiers and civilians beside the straits of the Detroit River that Negroes began arriving in the settlement. They were slaves captured by marauding bands of pro-French Indians from the Southern plantations of Englishmen. When the English took over in 1763, they brought additional slaves—a 1773 census listed ninety-six. The Ordinance of 1787 prohibited slavery in the Northwest Territory, which had become a part of the United States in 1783, but American authority near Detroit was largely nominal until the conclusion of the War of 1812.

After 1830 the trickle of Negro fugitives to Detroit became a sizable stream. Levi Coffin came to the city in 1840 to organize what later became one of the principal stations of the Underground Railroad to freedom in Canada, just across the river. Abolitionist sentiment ran so strong that slave catchers pursuing runaways often found themselves in a hornets' nest of resistance stirred up by both blacks and whites.

On one occasion, in 1833, a group of irate Negroes and whites besieged the jail in which Thornton Blackburn and his wife were confined. Blackburn had been in Detroit since 1830, had a steady job, and was known as a sober and industrious citizen. Somehow or other his Kentucky master got wind of the refugee's whereabouts and sent an emissary to negotiate his return to bondage. The first move of the committee to thwart Blackburn's captor was a ruse engineered by a woman who entered the jail to visit with Mrs. Blackburn. Once inside the cell, she quickly changed clothes with the imprisoned woman, who walked forth unmolested to be ferried in a rowboat across to Canada—the customary transportation for "passengers" of the Underground Railroad who arrived at the Detroit terminal.

The sheriff, determined to succeed at least partially in his undertaking, set forth from the jail with Blackburn, intending to send him on his way back to Kentucky. He was no sooner outside the protecting walls than a furious mob representing both races fell upon him, fractured his skull, knocked most of his teeth down his throat, and triumphantly assisted his charge across the river, where he rejoined his wife. Alarmed by this "first Negro insurrection," as the affray later was called, the authorities jailed every Negro man and woman to be found abroad. Some of these whose participation in the riot could be definitely established were compelled to work in the streets, attached to a ball and chain, as an example to rebellious souls who might be inclined to flout law and order.

On another occasion, in 1850, three companies of volunteer militia were required to quell an incipient uprising when abolitionists intervened forcibly to prevent a slave catcher from carrying off a runaway under the provisions of the Fugitive Slave Law. The militant Detroit Anti-Slavery Society, formed in 1837, galvanized such popular demonstrations reflecting the temper of the community. And on March 12, 1859, a group of earnest men and women met at the home of William Webb on Congress Street to hear Old John Brown of Kansas tell about his plan to strike off the chains of the slaves of Virginia, and eventually those of every black man, woman, and child of the South. Frederick Douglass took part in the meeting, as did such other prominent Negro workers in the cause of freedom as John Richards and George DeBaptiste.

The love of freedom, then, was in the air of Detroit. One unsightly blot on the record was a disturbance coincident with the widespread draft riots of 1863, when disgruntled conscripts and other disaffected elements throughout the nation turned on the Negroes as convenient scapegoats, burning their houses, beating and even murdering them. William Faulkner, a Detroit Negro, had been accused of a sexual offense against a little girl, and a white mob intent on a lynching bee attempted to wrest him away from the sheriff's custody. One of their number was shot down by the officer, and the enraged mobsters vented their fury on all the Negro citizens of Detroit. Many Negroes withdrew across the river to Canada, leaving their homes and possessions behind them in smoking ruin. It was quite a few years before most of them ventured back. Faulkner, sentenced to life imprisonment, was found to be innocent after he had served seven years. The repentant whites of Detroit offered an apology and raised a fund to set the wronged man up in business. It may be presumed that the incident taught them a lesson in racial tolerance and the advisability of keeping a cool head.

Negroes were in Detroit to stay, and more were to come. Down in Fredericksburg, Virginia, Mrs. Maria Louise Richards, a widow with a large brood on her hands, heard about the opportunities, cultural and otherwise, open to colored folk in the city beside the straits. Life was getting to be very hard for free persons of color in Virginia as the "irrepressible conflict" between the pro- and anti-slavery cohorts heated up.

In 1820 Maria Louise Moore, a girl who had a thirst for learning and had managed to acquire some of it, married dashing Adolphe Richards, a native of the island of Guadeloupe, who had been sent to Virginia for his health. She was the daughter of an Edinburgh Scotsman and a free woman of color from Toronto. Some of the free Negroes in Fredericksburg—such as the DeBaptistes, the Cooks, the Pelhams, and the Lees—had attained a measure of wealth and social position. The gradual abrogation of the privileges they had enjoyed alarmed and distressed these more favored ones. Soon their status—in so far as civil rights were concerned—would be little better than that of the slaves.

One of the severest blows to Adolphe and Maria Louise Richards was the prohibiting of schools for Negroes. They set about raising a family in earnest, and eventually had fourteen children. One of the Richards boys attended a school run by an Englishwoman named Beecham, others gathered with their sisters and other colored children at the roomy DeBaptiste home where a white teacher conducted classes.

Later on the wily pedagogues resorted to a dodge to circumvent the letter of the law which specified punishment for anyone imparting knowledge to Negroes "sitting or standing." Pupils reclined at full length on couches or benches while reciting or studying. The law was indulgent toward manual training and the "useful" arts, so one schoolroom was equipped with wood splinters and other materials from which to manufacture matches. When investigators called, the pupils appeared to be busy at a task far removed from the higher realms of education.

Maria Louise Richards saw her brood scattering. One boy lit out for Washington, and the others were restive. To make matters worse, a law passed in 1838 decreed that free persons of color who left the state to attend school would not be permitted to return.

All this and the death of her husband led Mrs. Richards to a fateful decision. She'd go to Detroit, where there were a lot of folks who believed a colored man had a right to a respected role in the community. In 1851 she arrived in the city, and before long most of her friends—the Cooks, the Williamses, the DeBaptistes, the Lees, and the Pelhams—followed her. The group thus formed came to be known as the Richards Colony. Many of its members distinguished themselves.

Will Marion Cook, as most everybody knows, made the grade as a musician and composer. Richard DeBaptiste left his impress throughout the Northwest as a Baptist minister, a crusader for civil liberties, and a newspaper editor. Robert A. Pelham invented a tallying device greatly facilitating the tabulating of census figures, and held several municipal, state, and national appointive positions.

And there was Elijah McCoy, the inventor, whose parents had passed through Detroit in 1837, fleeing from slavery in Kentucky via the Underground Railroad to Canada. Elijah's father sent him to Edinburgh, Scotland, to make a mechanical engineer out of him. His schooling over, he returned to Canada, and then decided to try Detroit. Working as a fireman on the Michigan Central Railroad, he invented a lubrication cup in 1872. Other successful inventions followed, until he had patented seventy-eight devices. Of these, forty-eight were improvements on methods of lubrication, his work in this field winning him recognition throughout the world.

Fannie Moore Richards, after teaching in a private Negro school for several years, entered the public school system in 1868 and remained until 1915, when she was retired on a pension. White business and professional men, city officials and other dignitaries were wont to stop the old lady on the street and present their compliments, assuming that she would remember a former pupil as easily as he remembered her. She had seen so many in her time, and her memory began to be a little tricky toward the last. She would always pretend to recognize the important personage she had last seen as a shaggy and unruly urchin, however. Sometimes, by hedging for time while her erstwhile pupil reminisced, she would manage to drag forth from the dimming recesses of her mind his name and other identifying details.

In 1900 there were 4,111 Negroes living in Detroit. The year before Robert E. Olds had started turning out his Oldsmobile on a small scale. The next year saw the birth of the Cadillac motorcar—named after the city's founder. In 1903 came the Packard and the Ford. These new enterprises didn't mean much to the Negro for quite a while. There were a great many European immigrants employed in the city's industrial plants, but it was still generally considered that a Negro had little or no aptitude for mechanical pursuits. As late as 1910 the 105,159 automobile workers of Detroit included only 569 Negroes.

Though they usually found themselves in heavy and distasteful jobs in the foundry and other places where muscle was more important than intelligence, the Negroes were assigned to a greater variety of jobs in Henry Ford's plant than in any similar establishment. Ford admired the work of Booker T. Washington at Tuskegee, for the automobile pioneer was also an advocate of industrial training. Negro boys from Tuskegee were enrolled in the Ford trade school.

Ford's five-dollar-a-day minimum wage, established in 1914, was a potent lure to the Southern Negro, particularly those who had been compelled to live under the debt-ridden sharecropping system and who seldom saw any actual cash from one year's end to the other.

When the European war set the Negro tides surging out of the South, Detroit was the destination of many migrants. The legend of the city as a citadel of freedom still endured, and there were the fabulous golden rewards of the automobile factories to think about. It seemed as though all America would soon be on wheels. Everybody wanted an automobile, and it took a lot of men to make them. Negroes returning to the South to visit their families or settle their affairs carried the incredible news that black men were taking fares and piloting streetcars in the Michigan city.

As in Chicago, the greenhorns proved to be a trial to the solid citizens—both colored and white. Some of the Detroit Negroes of long residence were ashamed to identify themselves with the newcomers, who gawked open-mouthed at the astounding sights, fell over their own plow shoes in their awkwardness, and were struck with helplessness and consternation when set down abruptly in the city's bustle. Their outlandish garb was enough to betray their rustic origin. They huddled indecisively among their shabby belongings, cluttering up railroad-station waiting rooms, blocking sidewalks.

The Detroit Urban League induced the commissioner of police to assign a colored plain-clothes man as a good shepherd to the new arrivals. Mingling among them, he urged them not to block traffic, told them how to detect and forestall sharpers, advised them to be well-mannered and pleasant but not servile to white people, how to go about looking for a job and a place to stay. When detailed advice was essential or the problem too complicated, he'd simply hand the harried and confused one a card bearing the address of the Urban League, where expert and sympathetic help was on constant tap.

White Southern hillbillies, of course, were just as dazzled by the high wages of Detroit as were the Negroes. The farmlands of the Middle West and even sections as far away as the Pacific Coast and New England contributed their quota, too, but it was the white Southerners—the largest single group—who affected the lives of the Negroes most. Soon the attitudes of the Lily Whites began to provoke racial tension—provoke little clashes on streetcars, in shops, in public parks and playgrounds, and in the factories.

Labor leaders, however, began to regard the Negroes in a new light, and in its August 1918 issue the Detroit *Labor News* told its readers that the American labor movement could no longer disregard the Negro as "a big factor in our industrial life." The paper went on:

> Time and again the selfish masters of industry have used him to batter your organizations to pieces, and instead of trying to win him over, you have savagely fought him, because they used him as a strikebreaker. But the Negro must be made to see the value of organization to himself, and he must be incorporated into and made a part of the great labor movement. . . . Let us work to shift him from his present unhappy position, where he is despised by the big-business element, notwithstanding his utility as a strikebreaker, and hated by unionists for his loyalty to the open-shop element. Unionism must welcome the Negro to its ranks.

Almost twenty years were to pass, however, before this goal was partially realized. In the meantime, the rambunctious white Southerners multiplied in numbers and in noisy aggressiveness. The Ku Klux Klan became a force in local politics and more than once in the twenties came close to electing a mayor. City councilmen were known to be Klansmen.

The "invasion" of Negroes into areas where white people dominated gave the troublemakers an impetus. The principal Negro section, east of Woodward Avenue, was named Paradise Valley by the Negroes themselves—perhaps in acknowledgment of the comparative improvement of their lot, perhaps in irony. Actually, it was just another Mudtown. Thrifty immigrants had built their frame houses here, but as their prosperity increased they moved on to more desirable locations farther away from the smoke and fumes and dust of the industrial plants. A good many of them retained ownership, and did not hesitate to exact exorbitant rent from the incoming Negroes who had little or no choice in the matter. The enterprising property owners also saw no need to keep the premises in repair. Often enough the absentee owner, enjoying his elbow room in a more spacious neighborhood, helped to pay for his improved position by erecting one or more additional buildings on his Paradise Valley lot, shutting off the light from inside rooms and increasing the general disadvantages of overcrowding. Thus, as elsewhere, arose the legend that Negroes destroyed property values by "running down" the buildings they occupied.

The klieg lights of publicity were turned on Detroit and the dilemma of its colored citizens by the Henry Sweet case in the fall of 1925. The youth, a student at Wilberforce University, lived with his brother, Dr. Ossian Sweet, who ventured to break out of the "iron ring" of the black ghetto and bought a home on Griswold Street in a "white" neighborhood.

The Waterworks Park Improvement Association had been formed in the vicinity to repel any Negroes (or "undesirable elements," as the association euphemistically termed them) who might try to move in. One evening, following a meeting in a nearby schoolhouse at which a fraternal delegate from another "improvement association" delivered a speech inciting to violence, a mob composed of members of the audience, gradually augmented by others attracted by the crowd and the excitement, converged on the home of the newcomer and began throwing stones at it. Some stones crashed through the windows.

"Niggers! Niggers!" the "improvers" howled. "Get the niggers! Get the damned niggers!"

The shouting voices and the thundering stones were punctuated by gunshots; the Sweets were convinced they were being fired upon. Henry Sweet grabbed a rifle and took a shot at the mass outside. Leon Breiner, one of the attackers, fell dead at about that moment.

Then—and not until then—policemen who had been diverting the unusually heavy traffic caused by the blocking of the street in the riot zone, and who later maintained that they had been unaware of anything out of the ordinary, intervened to arrest Henry Sweet and the other occupants of the house.

The National Association for the Advancement of Colored People made the defense of Henry Sweet, charged with willful murder, a *cause célèbre*. Dr. W. E. B. Du Bois later voiced his belief that the case ranked in importance with that of Sacco and Vanzetti. Clarence Darrow was persuaded to plead for the defense.

Darrow was in top form. Derisively snapping his suspenders, he jeered at Prosecutor Moll's touching description of the innocent, "neighborly" crowd that had assembled near the Sweet home.

"Neighbors!" Darrow hooted. "Bringing the Sweets greetings and good cheer! . . . Neighbors in the sense an undertaker is when he comes to carry out a corpse—but it was the wrong corpse. . . . Henry Sweet never knew such a man lived as Breiner. Somebody shot into the crowd and Breiner got it. I'll tell you what he was—he was a conspirator in as foul a conspiracy as ever was hatched—to drive from their home a little group of black people and to stab the Constitution under which they lived. If Breiner was innocent, then every man there was innocent. *There were no innocent people there!* They had gathered as the Roman populace gathered at the Colosseum to see the slaves fed to the lions.

"I want to be fair," Darrow said to the jury, referring to the remarkable collusion between witnesses to hide the racial motivation of the affair. "Are the people of this neighborhood worse than other people? I don't think they are. What do you know about prejudice? These people honestly believe that they are better than the blacks. I don't. They honestly believe colored people are an inferior race. They are obsessed with fanaticism. And when people are obsessed with fanaticism they become cruel. But, gentlemen, they oughtn't to ask you to be cruel for them. It's a pretty dirty job to turn over to a jury."

The all-white jury agreed, and reported to Judge Frank Murphy, later to become a justice of the Supreme Court of the United States, a verdict of not guilty.

The Sweet experience was not an isolated instance. Violence against Negroes moving into new neighborhoods had been prevalent for some time. A short while before the Sweet incident, a Dr. Turner had bought a house almost twenty miles away from the scene of the widely publicized riot. A reception committee was waiting for Dr. Turner. His windows were smashed by stones, his Lincoln car wrecked, his furniture pitched into the street. Then the roof was literally torn off his house. With a pistol held against his head, he was obliged to sign an agreement to give up his property. When V. A. Bristol, a colored undertaker, moved into a new location, he was greeted by a surly, muttering gang of "neighbors." When the men appeared to be hesitant about getting rough with Bristol, a hysterical woman is said to have mounted a goods crate and shrieked: "You yellowbellies! Do you call yourselves men? If you ain't men enough to chase these dirty niggers out, us women will have to do the job for you." Thus rebuked, the men proceeded to "do the job."

The Southern Negroes who found their way to Detroit were always pursued by the nemesis of the intolerant white Southerner. Bible-thumping Holy Roller preachers followed the procession, and were a powerful force in keeping the fires of intolerance and fanaticism burning fiercely. More than one church service was interrupted as white-robed and masked Klansmen marched ceremoniously to the altar to deposit a cash offering, while the grateful preacher voiced his admiration of Klan principles. The doctrine of White Supremacy was the "higher law" of the transplanted white Southerners.

With the onset of the depression in 1930, many Negroes were thrown out of work as factories curtailed their production. During 1931 there were 22,000 Negro families on the relief rolls; the next year there were 48,000. Social workers and others exerted pressure on indigent Negroes to return to the South, where—it was pointed out—they would require less clothing and food was easier to get. There were more coming in than going out, however, for hard times had struck the South too. You could get more relief in the North if you could contrive to get on the relief list. And few of those settled in the North would have consented to go South even at higher wages as long as Jim Crow ruled in Dixie.

The provisions in the National Recovery Act affecting organization of labor unions encouraged a spirited unionization campaign in the automobile factories. There had been several small unions—such as the Automotive Industrial Workers' Association and the Associated Automobile Workers—but the vast bulk of the workers had remained unorganized. The American Federation of Labor had made sporadic and ineffectual attempts. Under the Blue Eagle, however, the workers—including Negroes—thronged into the United Automobile Workers, CIO, and secured union contracts with Chrysler in 1936, General Motors in 1937.

Ford, of course, was the whale—and also the hardest nut to crack. The Ford Company, the story goes, had long had an arrangement with certain Negro preachers in Detroit whereby the ministers of the gospel would recommend applicants for employment while extolling the labor policies of the corporation. In this manner the management, it was said, hoped to secure Negroes who would be less susceptible to union and "radical" propaganda than others. The exact details of the arrangement have been vague, but the tie was a real and demonstrable one.

The hour of decision for the Negro worker at Ford's struck on April 2, 1941, when the UAW-CIO called a strike. There were about 14,000 Negroes among the 85,000 workers, and a minority group of these elected to stay in the plant. Loyalty to Ford for his ice-breaking role in giving employment to Negroes was believed to have had a great influence. But the UAW had foxy and battle-scarred Walter Hardin and other colored organizers to reason with stay-ins. Walter White of the NAACP, while acknowledging that Negroes had reason to feel grateful to Ford, warned them not to rely on "the personal kindness of any individual" but upon the strength which organization would assure them. White went on to say:

> The attempt to use Negroes as a club over the heads of those who wish to organize themselves in unions, however, is a dangerous move in times like these. It may make for an increase in racial tensions which would hurt the defense program. I regret that a few colored workers, in their desperation for jobs, have lent themselves to staying in the River Rouge plant. They are not helping themselves, the cause of labor, nor labor relations generally.

The UAW strikers returned to work after ten days, when a National Labor Relations Board election was agreed upon. This concession, of course, was a tremendous victory for the UAW.

The conservative Negro preachers, most of whom belonged to the Interdenominational Ministers' Alliance, urged their racial brethren in the Ford plant to stay out of the UAW. If they *must* join a union, let it be the A.F. of L., which had entered the campaign as a diversionary force long after the CIO had done the spadework. The A.F. of L., however, was believed to be tacitly favored by the Ford Company as a lesser evil. But in the election the CIO union garnered 70 per cent of the votes cast.

Not a few Negro preachers commended and helped the CIO. Prominent among these was Reverend Horace A. White, pastor of the Plymouth Congregational Church. And the United Automobile

Workers, by its steadfast opposition to racial discrimination, gradually won the confidence and loyalty of Negroes who had good reason to be suspicious of high-sounding phrases about equality emanating from union leaders. It seemed as though the leaders of the UAW really meant it, for they demonstrated their sincerity with action. It was a monumental job, for the union had hastily enrolled in its ranks Polish Catholics, the foreign-born, rampant Protestants, and Negrophobes from the pellagra-ridden Southern back country, Northern and Southern Negroes, and many others with conglomerate prejudices and intolerant ideas.

From the noxious soil of race prejudice in Detroit sprang the Black Legion, closely allied to the Ku Klux Klan in ideology if not in fact. Antagonistic to Catholics, Jews, Negroes, and "radicals," this terroristic secret society was dedicated to the protection of American institutions and American womanhood from such imminent perils. It distinguished itself by a number of beatings, ceremonial floggings, and other violence directed against those whose race, religion, or social ideas it deplored. In 1936 the murder of Charles Poole, a Catholic WPA worker, brought the Black Legion under police scrutiny, and sixteen of its lesser leaders eventually were sentenced to prison terms. A Detroit legend still current is that the "big bugs" were not molested—that they were *too* "big."

The Black Legionnaires were not to be discouraged by a few indictments and convictions. Most of them were left unscathed, and joined organizations such as the National Workers' League, the Black Guards, the Roseville Riflemen's Association, the Bullet Club, and the Modern Patriots. They carried on their hate-spreading activities with new vigor.

When the preparedness program and, later, World War II made Detroit a center of war production, the hate merchants were of great assistance to the Axis cause. Inside the factories they succeeded in fomenting several "hate strikes" in protest against the promotion of Negroes or their introduction on jobs where they had not previously been placed. One such walkout at the Packard Plant in August 1943 was inspired by the promotion of three Negroes to skilled jobs for which they had demonstrated their ability. More than 20,000 workers were kept idle for a week. The UAW, which joined with the company and with government agencies to bring the unauthorized strike to a quick conclusion, presented the FBI with information indicating that the Ku Klux Klan (or one of its many alter egos) had engineered the stoppage. The caretaker of a "social club" said to be motivated by the Klan ideology was overheard on the telephone exulting over the "good work" which had resulted in the expulsion of that "black alligator bait" out of Packard and making it a "white man's plant" again. Similar strikes in Detroit during the first six months of 1943 cost the war effort six million man-hours. The Fair Employment Practices Commission and Executive Order 8802, forbidding racial discrimination in employment, helped in some measure, but it often had the same effect upon those with violent racial antipathies that a red rag has on a bull.

The Negro housing situation, which had been acute before, became desperate as thousands of colored job seekers made their way to the city's war plants, humming at capacity through three shifts a day. There had been 40,838 Negro residents in 1920, 120,066 in 1930. The figure reached 149,119 in 1940. After the entry of the United States in the war, the rate of increase was unprecedented. In 1944 Negroes living in Detroit and in nearby industrial suburbs were estimated to total nearly 250,000. Needless to say, Paradise Valley and the other small areas of Negro residence had not expanded to the degree necessary to accommodate these newcomers. Such housing developments as the 941-unit Brewster home project, finished in 1937, were steps in the right direction, but pitifully inadequate to the desperate need.

The Sojourner Truth housing project dramatized the situation just as the Sweet episode had in 1925. It was generally supposed—and even announced—that the FHA development would be occupied by Negroes. Polish-dominated Hamtramck lies between the site of the housing project and Paradise Valley. Though there were Negro residences in the vicinity, an organization calling itself the Seven-Mile Fenelon Improvement Association began to agitate against any more of the race settling there. Strangely enough, a few Negro homeowners also objected, having the idea that a government housing project close by would lower the value of their property. The "improvement" association and the rabid National Workers' League, which promptly involved itself, were animated by other concerns, however. They did not object to the project itself—only to the Negroes. The housing authority apparently yielded to reactionary pressure, and announced that only white tenants would occupy the homes and that they would bear another name than that of Sojourner Truth, the dark angel of mercy of Civil War days. The NAACP and various labor, church, and civic groups then raised such a hurricane of protest that the original name was restored, and it was announced that two hundred units would be opened for occupancy by Negroes.

On February 28, 1942, trucks laden with the household goods of the new tenants were met by a raggle-taggle army of twelve hundred pickets well armed with bricks, clubs, knives, and guns. A pitched battle began. Few Negroes or liberals were surprised to learn a little later that the police had arrested more than one hundred Negroes but only half a dozen whites, charging them with disturbing the peace or carrying concealed weapons. But the latter charge could not be correctly applied to the white rioters, for they had not bothered to conceal their weapons.

The bluff of the Seven-Mile Fenelon Improvement Association and the National Workers' League worked until April 9, when a small army of Detroit and State police as well as "home-guard" militiamen escorted sixteen Negro families into the project. Heavily armed guards patrolled the region for several weeks, but the mobsters had no stomach for such opposition. Shortly afterward a federal grand jury indicted three officers and members of the Seven-Mile Fenelon Improvement Association and the National Workers' League for conspiracy but, in accordance with established procedure, the case dragged on until it was eventually dismissed and forgotten.

June 20, 1943, was a hot and sultry day in Detroit, and in the evening large crowds of both Negroes and whites gathered in Belle Isle Park on an island of the same name in the Detroit River. The perspiring citizens of the "Arsenal of Democracy" milled about restlessly, mopping brows and searching throughout the island for a breath of fresh air. About midnight, most witnesses agreed, the igniting spark of one of the most disastrous race riots in American history flared. There are a dozen versions of its genesis, but the one generally accepted is that a white man and a Negro man came into proximity on a bridge and that shoving, a verbal exchange, and a fist fight attracted members of both races who "took sides."

Rumor, as always, fanned the conflagration. A white (or Negro, according to the race of the teller) baby had been hurled into the river and drowned by a member of the other race. Negro men had torn the bathing suits from white girl bathers, raped and murdered them. These and many other inflammable reports agitated the Negroes of Paradise Valley as well as many of the white citizens. Leo Tipton, a Negro who was subsequently arrested for inciting to riot, hurried from Belle Isle to a Hastings Street night club in Paradise Valley. Breathlessly addressing the five hundred or so patrons, he begged them "to take care of a bunch of whites who killed a colored woman and her baby at Belle Isle Park."

While white hoodlums ranged through the area near Woodward Avenue, overturning and burning the automobiles of Negroes and beating Negro pedestrians, Negro bands began a systematic looting of stores owned by white people in Paradise Valley, assaulting any white person who might be encountered. The riot continued through the night. White gangs assembled in Cadillac Square, the hub of Detroit's principal thoroughfares, and dragged Negro passengers from streetcars and busses to maul them, often to their amazement—they were unaware that a riot was in progress. White war workers leaving their shifts were set upon by vengeful Negroes. One of these was John Holyak, fifty-nine, whose son had been captured at Bataan. Holyak died a few days later from the kicking and slugging. Sam Mitchell, a Negro veteran of World War I, trying to escape a mob that had chased him from a streetcar, was shot three times. He claimed that two policemen to whom he appealed for help held both his arms while white rioters, one after another, came up and slugged him at will. This was a common complaint about the police officers, and it was pointed out that there were many white Southerners and ex-members of the Ku Klux Klan and the Black Legion on the force. At any rate, a frequent charge by Negroes was that the police were either unable or unwilling to take drastic steps with white rioters, while ruthlessly shooting down Negroes in Paradise Valley whom they accused of looting.

Of the thirty-four persons reported killed during the disorders, twenty-five were Negroes. Seventeen of these were slain by the police for "looting." More than one observer charged that the officers of the law were extraordinarily loose on the trigger finger when dealing with Negroes and that "looting" too often served as an excuse for the venting of an obvious prejudice.

Late Monday evening Mayor Jeffries acknowledged the inability of his force to restore order. President Roosevelt declared that a state of emergency existed, and by morning 6,000 federal troops had rolled into the area of conflict. Patrolling the streets in jeeps and trucks, they soon squelched all outward signs of disorder. The shooting of a Negro on Tuesday evening by a State trooper in the St. Antoine Y.M.C.A., was recounted in conflicting versions: The trooper maintained that the victim had cried "Heil Hitler!" and reached for his pocket; colored eyewitnesses said that the trooper with two city policemen had invaded the Y.M.C.A., in pursuit of the wounded Negro, addressed the occupants as "black bastards, apes, and sons of bitches." Then, according to the Negro version, they lined up all the men present against the wall and clubbed and beat them.

The residents of Paradise Valley had confidence in the federal troops, but they did not know what would happen to them if they ventured outside the patrolled areas. A good many of the war plants were situated in outlying sections. Absenteeism among Negroes in the war plants ran as high as 90 per cent on the first two days of the riot, and it was some time before full efficiency was restored.

Immediately, of course, the air was full of discussions of the riot, plans to forestall future ones, meetings of committees and organizations. Gerald L. K. Smith, one of the loudest and most tireless fomenters of racial discord in the city, unblushingly came forward with his "solution" for race riots in the July 1943 issue of his magazine, the *Cross and Flag*.

First of all he denied that Southerners had participated in the riot to any extent—the white rioters were "first- and second-generation Europeans." "I am bold to say," Smith announced, "that Eleanor Roosevelt and Henry Wallace and their clan of stargazers have done more to agitate the whites and overencourage the Negroes . . . than any other single group outside the Communists." He illustrated the wisdom of segregation of Negroes and whites by pointing out: "When a husband and wife part in a hotel lobby to go to their respective washrooms, they practice segregation, not because the equipment in one place is superior to the other and not because the question of equality is involved. But the experience of the race has taught us that segregation of the sexes is necessary under certain circumstances."

Negroes, Smith went on, ". . . are brought into our great cities, out of an environment of discipline and restraint from the Deep South into an environment where there is no restraint and where they are actually encouraged by politicians and Communists to make dates with white girls and to flirt with white girls." Communist leaders, Smith quoted a "fine, clean-cut" Negro as saying, tell Negroes at their meetings that "they should be able to proposition white girls, go out with white girls, marry white girls, and flirt with white girls."

Then Smith listed seven "types of interracial mixture" which most white people, he claimed, would find intolerable. These were:

1. Intermarriage of blacks and whites.
2. Mixture of blacks and whites in hotels.
3. Mixture of blacks and whites in restaurants.
4. Intimate relationships between blacks and whites in the school system.
5. Wholesale mixture of blacks and whites in residential sections.
6. Promiscuous mixture of blacks and whites in streetcars and on trains, especially where black men are permitted to sit down and crowd in close to white women and vice versa.
7. Promiscuous mixture of blacks and whites in factories, especially where black men are mixed with white women closely in daily work.

Differing somewhat from the recommendations of Gerald L. K. Smith were those offered by R. J. Thomas, president of the United Automobile Workers. His eight-point program suggested a grand-jury investigation of riot causes, improvement of recreation facilities, more and better housing for Negroes, squelching of racial intolerance and discrimination in the factories, an inquiry into the failure of the police to quell the mobs with drastic action, reimbursement of innocent victims of the riot, and the appointment by the mayor of a biracial committee of ten to make further recommendations.

The Greater Detroit Interracial Fellowship, meeting at the Redeemer Presbyterian Church, enthusiastically seconded all of Thomas' proposals but the last one. The members balked at the creation of a fact-finding body by the mayor. They remembered all too well that such a body had been formed to investigate the Sweet case. Its well-reasoned report had been impotently gathering dust these many years, though sometimes it might be exhumed briefly for the benefit of a seeker after a Ph.D. degree who was writing a thesis on race relations. And another (perhaps the deciding) consideration was that such a committee would be appointed by the mayor, and that it might well result in a whitewashing of the police. Some portents of such a development had already been seen in the municipal statements about "Bloody Monday."

In the course of time, a committee appointed by the governor issued an eighty-five-hundred-word report which tended to prove that Negroes were mainly responsible for the riot. It recalled previous minor clashes that supposedly were caused by aggressiveness or hostility displayed by Negroes toward whites. Law-enforcement agencies were praised for "adequately and properly" dealing with law violators. Occasion was taken to point out that Detroit Negroes, though comprising less than 10 per cent of the population, perpetrated more than 71 per cent of the major crimes. Negro leaders and Negro newspapers were charged with inflaming colored citizens and turning their sympathies toward Hitler by advocating a militant stand for equal rights. These deductions might have been anticipated, since most of the "evidence" to support the contentions about Negro culpability had been supplied by Police Commissioner John H. Witherspoon, who was also a member of the governor's committee. Even the conservative Detroit *Free Press* was moved to denounce the report as a "whitewash."

Though an increasing number of job-seeking Negro migrants from the South began turning their attention to other areas (such as the Pacific Coast region) during and after World War II, Detroit still proved to be an attractive destination. Its Negro population increased by more than 100 per cent during the 1940–50 decade, rising to 300,000. The increase in total population during this time had been only 14 per cent. The Negro population in 1960 was 480,000 and still increasing, this figure representing nearly 29 per cent of the total. Paradise Valley's population jumped from 87,000 in 1940 to 140,000 in 1950. Only 46 per cent of the city's Negroes were living in the black ghetto in 1950, whereas in 1940 it had accommodated 58 per cent.

The desperate necessity for finding new areas of residence brought on a number of incidents similar to that involving Dr. Sweet and his "invasion" of a "white" neighborhood in 1925. The suburbs remained lily-white for the most part. The white racists of Dearborn were fond of boasting that no Negro had better let the sun go down on him in that community. Early in 1964 a federal grand jury indicted Orville Hubbard, mayor of the suburb, for failing his public duty during a racial demonstration that had taken place on Labor Day, 1963. Public Safety Director George W. Lewis and Police Chief Garrison Clayton had previously been indicted on similar charges. Hubbard, Lewis, and Clayton were accused of failing to act when a mob gathered outside the home of Guiseppe Stanzione and pelted it with rocks, overripe eggs, and garbage after a false rumor spread that he had either rented an upstairs flat to a colored tenant or sold his home to a Negro family. All indictments were dismissed, however, in June 1965.

As in Chicago and other cities, the "block-busting" realtors reaped a rich harvest by exploiting the fears of white property owners. These enterprising merchants either contrived to place a Negro family in a previously all-white neighborhood or took advantage of a Negro family's arrival. This was the signal for a high-pressure campaign inducing the white property owners to sell out at a sacrifice figure before it was too late—before Negro infiltration "ruined" the neighborhood. Once the whites had been scared out, the realtors sold their vacated homes to Negroes at greatly increased prices.

This situation prompted the Fitzgerald Community Council to take action against the "block-busters" early in 1965. The council was composed of a group of white citizens who were "very happy with our integrated neighborhood" and wanted to keep it integrated. Cecil Erbaugh, president of the council, complained that sixteen real-estate brokers in the community were pestering white families by mail, telephone, and personal solicitation to sell out.

"If whites are pressured into leaving," Erbaugh said, "we lose the integration we are happy to have and the real-estate companies win a vast market based entirely on racial prejudice."

The twentieth anniversary of "Bloody Sunday" was observed in an extraordinary demonstration of Negro strength and solidarity. Sponsored by a Negro group called the Detroit Council for Human Rights, a "Walk for Freedom" procession swept down Woodward Avenue, gathering momentum as it neared the Civic Center, where Martin Luther King hailed the marchers for dramatizing the effectiveness of nonviolence. Policemen, traditional harassers of dark-skinned citizens, were courteous and respectful. After all, you don't start an argument with 125,000 determined folks marching toward the same goal: Freedom.

His audience in the Civic Center's convention arena shouted thunderous approval when Reverend King told of a dream in which he had envisioned whites and Negroes as brothers in heart and practice, "walking together hand in hand, free at last . . ."

CHAPTER XIX

With Brotherly Love

THE NEGROES of Philadelphia got used to stormy weather at a very early date. The activities of the Quakers in the cause of abolition and their connection with the Underground Railroad encouraged black fugitives from the South to seek a haven in the "City of Brotherly Love." Sympathetic Quakers and abolitionists frequently arranged to give the refugees industrial training or found jobs for them in shops or in domestic service. The pinch of unemployment was not unknown to white artisans of the day, and some of them regarded the interlopers with extreme hostility which at times manifested itself in acts of violence. Despite the good intentions of white benefactors, they were unable to find work for all the Negro migrants as the flood grew in volume.

The Quakers previously had freed their slaves, and not a few of the emancipated ones had acquired considerable wealth. This circumstance gave rise to a demand that free Negroes be taxed to pay for the upkeep of paupers of their own race. It was proposed in the Pennsylvania Legislature in 1815 that further immigration of Negroes be prohibited.

It was not unusual for white people of both sexes to offer a physical demonstration of resentment when meeting Negroes on the street. A free woman of color was stoned to death by three white women in 1819. Six years later a gang of frolicsome white boys dashed into a Negro church, threw a quantity of pepper on a hot stove, and successfully retreated from the stifling fumes they had created. In the ensuing panic, several Negroes were killed.

Free Negroes who sought to celebrate the Fourth of July in historic Independence Square were chased away each year.

The battle of the abolitionists and their proslavery antagonists raged apace in Philadelphia, and when a slavery partisan was bested in a verbal or physical encounter, his thoughts often turned vengefully toward the racial group he considered the primary cause of his discomfiture. In 1834 and 1838 there were sanguinary race riots. In the course of the latter, the Colored Orphan Asylum was bombarded with paving stones and other missiles and a Negro church was burned to the ground. The Negroes ventured a parade in 1842 to celebrate the emancipation of West Indian slaves, and not only were set upon and manhandled by wrathful whites but were castigated afterward by a grand jury for provoking a riot! Seven years later members of a forerunner of the Ku Klux Klan, self-named the Killers of Moyamensing, took their rifles after the colored folk with such deadly effect that the militia had to be called out to subdue them.

In spite of these adversities, the Philadelphia Negroes had accumulated $400,000 worth of taxable property in 1847, and there were five hundred or more colored mechanics working at their various trades—no thanks, we may be sure, to most of their white fellow workers.

In *Dusk to Dawn* Dr. W. E. B. Du Bois says that he, as an assistant instructor in social science at the University of Pennsylvania, was commissioned at the turn of the century to write his *The Negro in Philadelphia* because the city authorities ". . . at that time had a theory . . . that this great, rich, and famous municipality was going to the dogs because of the crime and venality of its Negro citizens, who lived largely centered in the slum at the lower end of the seventh ward." The completed study, he goes on, actually ". . . revealed the Negro group as a symptom, not a cause; as a striving, palpitating group and not an inert, sick body of crime. . . ."

When the outbreak of World War I brought Southern Negroes to Philadelphia, Emmett J. Scott notes, the city ". . . had for years been pointed to as having a respectable, thrifty, and prosperous colored population, enjoying the good will and the co-operation of the best white people in the community. These Northern

Negroes felt that the coming of their brethren in the rough did them a decided injury in giving rise to a racial problem in a Northern community where it had not figured before."

That's the way a lot of the settled-down ones felt in Chicago, Detroit, and other places too. "Once they get the Georgia clay off their shoes and the cottonseed out of their hair," complained a migrant to Philadelphia who had been given the cold shoulder by a solid citizen to whom he had presented a letter from a mutual friend who had stayed South, "they forget they was once strangers themselves."

Jessie R. Fauset, Negro writer and daughter of a Philadelphia minister, asked "an unlettered Southern emigrant" of her race, whom she interviewed in that city as wartime migration began to provoke friction and "incidents" throughout the North, if he would be willing to go back South.

"Miss," he replied earnestly, "if I had the money I would go back South and dig up my father's and mother's bones and bring them up to this country. I am forty-five years old, and these six weeks I have spent here are the first weeks in my life of peace and comfort. And if I can't get along here I mean to keep on goin', but no matter what happens, I'll never go back."

In Robert L. Sutherland's *Color, Class, and Personality* Selma Hale of Greene County, Alabama, also expressed the sentiments of many migrants who came to Philadelphia and other Northern cities during the World War II boom:

> I'd like to have a house that don't leak, a house with no leaks in it anywhere. I wants a comfortable house, a house you won't freeze in in winter. I'd like to have nice things in the house, nice furniture so you could be comfortable. I'd like for it to have smooth floors, not big loose planks.
>
> By being well cared for, I mean to have enough to eat. To have something to eat every day. Lots of days we don't have nothing to eat. It must be nice to have enough to eat every day. . . . I'd like to have some clothes, too, like other girls.

A place to live in—a "job of work" whereby one can earn a little something to buy a bite to eat. One would think these needs were modest enough. Yet they proved to be vexing problems for the new Negro citizens of Philadelphia.

During World War II Philadelphia and its surrounding fringe of industrial communities emerged as one of the busiest war-work areas in the nation. The scarcity of white labor, together with the efforts of the FEPC, can be credited for a tremendous increase in the number of Negroes hired and the variety of places in which they found employment for the first time. The Philadelphia office of the War Manpower Commission issued a report to the effect that 68,436 Negro men and women were employed in the Philadelphia-Camden labor market during March 1944. In the six-month period from July to December 1943, the figure was only 17,602. Principal employers were listed as the Pullman Company, the Pennsylvania and the Baltimore and Ohio railroads, the Philadelphia Transportation Company, the Philadelphia Electric Company, and the New York Shipbuilding Corporation.

At the same time, however, the tree of liberty was yielding strange fruit in Philadelphia. Naomi Nakano, a Japanese-American girl who had spent all the nineteen years of her life in the city, found that the University of Pennsylvania had a new rule barring all persons of Japanese descent from the graduate school. The fact that she had been a brilliant student of the university for some time and that she was a member of Phi Beta Kappa, vice-chairman of the Middle Atlantic Student Christian Association, and president of both the senior class and the Student Government Association made no difference.

Then the Pyramid Club, composed of three hundred and fifty Negro professional and businessmen, decided to reject the membership application of Father William Jefferies, an Episcopalian clergyman well known for his militant advocacy of racial justice. The Pyramid Club's refusal on the ground that the club was "purely social" provoked many protests from both Negroes and whites who recalled that Father Jefferies, because of his labors for the NAACP and other Negro and liberal organizations, had been practically ostracized by many of his racial brethren.

On the other hand, Judge Curtis Bok of the Common Pleas Court dismissed a suit brought by the former owner of a home bought in a "white" neighborhood by Dr. Henry L. Gowens, a Negro physician. It appeared that the "not-too-willing plaintiff," as Judge Bok described him, had responded to pressure by upholders of white supremacy. In rejecting the petition Judge Bok referred to Dr. Gowens as ". . . a perfectly respectable person who has lived in the neighborhood for years, is a doctor in good standing, and by no stretch of the imagination could be held to be . . . a common nuisance."

Meanwhile, the city of Philadelphia gave formal recognition to the fact that a young colored woman who had once scrubbed steps there had become one of its most distinguished citizens when it gave Marian Anderson the Edward W. Bok award in 1941.

Late in 1943 there were several squabbles, accompanied by minor violence, over the occupancy of war housing projects. On streetcars and busses and in places of amusement there were numerous "incidents" arising from racial tension. A fight between colored and white boys in a public swimming pool had to be broken up by the police. In an effort to prevent a recurrence of such clashes, it was decided that Negro boys and white boys should attend school in separate shifts.

While these skirmishes were taking place, the FEPC ordered the Philadelphia Transportation Company to give up its discriminatory practice against the employment of Negroes as motormen and conductors. The company passed the buck to the Philadelphia Rapid Transit Employees' Union (condemned both by the A.F. of L. Amalgamated and the CIO Transport Workers' Union as a "company" union), saying that its contract with that organization forbade a change in "customary" employment policies. The PRTEU, opposing the upgrading of Negroes, stalled for time—demanded a public hearing. In the meantime, a group representing several interracial and Negro organizations had staged a "March on PTC" with more than a thousand pickets in line.

In March 1944 a collective-bargaining election ordered by the Pennsylvania Labor Relations Board resulted in a vote of 2,936 for the TWU, which had carried on a campaign based on the CIO's avowed policy of "no discrimination." The PRTEU, advocating "white supremacy" and "keeping the niggers off" came in second, with 1,294. The A.F. of L. union garnered 1,109 votes. Officially it had maintained a neutral attitude in the dispute, though CIO leaders charged that it had surreptitiously raised the anti-Negro issue as an argument against the TWU.

A logical sequel of the election was the assigning of eight Negro porters as trainees for the job of motorman. Then the defenders of "white supremacy" whipped up such a furor that they succeeded in getting six thousand of the PTC employees to walk out in an unauthorized strike. It was generally believed that only a small percentage of the strikers had their hearts in the action, but the loudmouthed and aggressive minority had depended upon the deep-seated reluctance of an American worker to fail to respond to a strike call, no matter who issues it.

The CIO immediately ascribed the "wildcat" walkout to "collusive action between company officials and the instigators of the strike," and broadcast an announcement in newspaper advertisements and on handbills:

THE CIO STANDS FIRM.

Vicious anti-American forces are at work in Philadelphia. They have been successful in hurting war production, and now they are trying to create racial trouble.

Some politicians are trying to make capital out of this situation. They think by laying the blame for this trouble on the CIO they can stop the forward-moving progress the CIO has made on the political as well as the economic front.

DON'T BE FOOLED!

You know what the national CIO policy has been—JUSTICE AND EQUALITY FOR THE NEGRO!

THE CIO IN PHILADELPHIA HAD NOT COMPROMISED, CHANGED, OR ALTERED ONE SINGLE THING IN THAT NATIONAL POLICY!

Racial clashes were of minor consequence. Several persons were beaten during the first day, most of them whites attacked by Negroes angered by the "hate" strike. Negro boys tripped a coal truck on the sidewalk, pounced upon the anthracite lumps, and began pelting white passers-by with them. The boys fled at the approach of the police. A brick was hurled through a jewelry-store window. One white man was dragged from his automobile and pommeled so badly that he had to be hospitalized. There were the usual rumors of Negroes arming themselves with knives and guns, helped along by the strike leaders. Friction increased during the night, and eleven persons in all were sent to hospitals as a consequence. Saloons and poolrooms were closed. The city government appeared to be unable to do anything about the situation.

President Roosevelt acted swiftly and decisively on August 3 to end the tie-up which was affecting the transportation of a million and a half war workers. The Army moved in and took control, arrested four leaders of the walkout—James McMenamin, William Dixey, Frank Carney, and Frank Thompson. McMenamin, bellwether of the anti-Negro clique, had appeared at Army headquarters with a white woman operator, who, he said, had been slashed with a knife wielded by a Negro fellow worker. A little investigation by newspapermen exposed this move as a provocative hoax. As justification for his opposition to the Negroes, McMenamin maintained that all of them were carriers of bedbugs, and, since both Negro and white employees would be compelled to share wooden benches with crevices affording hiding places for the insects, an inevitable result would be that everybody soon would be crawling with bedbugs.

The walkout ended when McMenamin, just before submitting to arrest, addressed a radio request to the strikers to return to work. The Negroes took their places as motormen without further trouble, and early in October one of them was elected as one of four vice-presidents of TWU Local 234, along with three whites—one a Protestant, one a Catholic, and one a Jew. One Negro newspaper observed:

> What brought this change of attitude? Are not these electors the same strikers? Yes, they are the same men. This new display of democracy on their part reaffirms the fact that the whole strike was a phony. It seems clear that the Negro trainees were used as a scapegoat by the transit company in an attempt to accomplish two purposes. The first was to discredit the FEPC and the second to break the United Transit Workers' CIO.

At the outset of the strike a forty-year-old Negro man, a tasseled red fez askew on his head, strode angrily into the Independence Hall chamber containing the Liberty Bell and hurled a bronze paperweight against its cracked side.

"Liberty! Liberty!" he shouted derisively. "That's a lot of bunk!"

Newspapers at first gave his name as Charles A. White Bey, which, with the red fez, would indicate that he was a "Moslem" from the Philadelphia Moorish-American Science Temple. Later reports dropped the "bey" from his name, probably as a result of his own prudent afterthought. He explained that the spectacle of the "hate" strike against members of his race had induced "an uncontrollable emotional outbreak." He had relatives in the armed forces, he said. Judge Allessandroni freed him after a lecture on patriotism.

By 1965 friends of freedom in Philadelphia as well as elsewhere were pondering a symbol of another sort in the City of Brotherly Love. Girard College, extremely well-endowed, had been encircled by the Negro ghetto, though the terms of founder Stephen Girard's will still barred Negroes from attendance. The NAACP put pickets around what it called Girard's "Berlin Wall," and began to explore legal remedies. Tulane University in New Orleans had broken a similar color bar as early as 1962, as had Rice Institute in Houston, Texas, somewhat later, but Girard was proving an even harder nut to crack.

CHAPTER XX

Freedom's Frontier

"WHERE YOU BOUND?" a Negro tenant farmer in Mississippi asked a neighbor who was waiting with two bulging imitation-leather suitcases beside a back-country road. "Goin' North to Chicago-Deetroit?"

"Naw! Too many already gone there and ain't making it so good. I want to strike out to some place where colored folks ain't already crowded up like sardine fish. I'm taking that Liberty Special for Frisco; California, here I come!"

"When you aim to be back?"

"Never, if I can help it. You reckon that bus driver'll see me if I flag him? Getting most dark. Maybe I'd better build me a little fire. I sure don't aim to let another sun rise on me in this place."

Tremendous activity in the aircraft and shipbuilding industries all along the Pacific Coast lured thousands of Negroes out that way. Chicago, Philadelphia, Detroit, New York—all of them had their drawbacks, such as segregation, race riots, and overcrowding. Now out in the West, where the free-and-easy frontier spirit was said to prevail still, a colored man might be recognized for whatever merit he possessed without anybody sneering at him or taking exception to the shade of his skin. He might have some room to throw out his chest and breathe deeply—even let out a whoop or two.

An overwhelming majority of the Negroes who moved into San Francisco during World War II were fresh from Arkansas, Louisiana, Oklahoma, or Texas. They found a settled colored population of less than five thousand, which their coming swelled to something like fifty thousand in 1944. Here, as elsewhere, the staid citizens of African blood were only a little less perturbed than white San Franciscans at the onslaught of the untamed and boisterous newcomers from darkest Dixie. However, the greenhorns were on the average more advanced than those who made their way to Chicago and Detroit during World War I. Most of them had eighth-grade schooling, while a fifth had finished high school. Eight per cent had acquired college or professional training. Few older people ventured so far afield. The average couples were in their early or middle twenties and had one child.

There was no Negro ghetto comparable in extent to Chicago's South Side or Detroit's Paradise Valley waiting for the dark migrants, but there was a comparatively small one available. The first place in which the new Negroes found shelter was "Little Tokyo" along Sutter Street, completely evacuated by its former occupants. All the Japanese Americans had been picked up by the government and scattered farther away from the sea. Property owners among them had been compelled to sell their property for whatever they could get (as little as a day's notice had been given), and enterprising realtors took advantage of the situation to buy low from the departing Japanese and to sell high to the arriving Negroes.

"Little Tokyo" wasn't anything to brag about, and the other ghetto—San Francisco's famed Chinatown—was about as bad insofar as dilapidation of buildings and overcrowding were concerned. Under threat of Negroes overflowing the quondam "Little Tokyo," "improvement" and "neighborhood" societies sprang into being for the purpose of effecting restrictive covenants. Such covenants directed against the Chinese had not been uncommon in the past. The arguments and activities of the sponsors of San Francisco's restrictive covenants were so similar to those of Chicago and Detroit, already discussed, it would be sheer repetition to elaborate on them. The Property Owners' Protective Association, a veteran of the battle to keep the Celestials squeezed within the boundaries of Chinatown, took cognizance of the changed situation and enlarged its scope to include (or, more accurately, to exclude) Negroes as well.

Public housing projects soon began to offer a soupçon of relief, but the process was painfully slow. When Westside Courts, a low-rent development, was proposed, the "improvement" associations followed their customary bent and emitted anguished howls of protest, envisioning the "ruination" of the neighborhood. A dispute not unlike that which had wrecked the Sojourner Truth project in Detroit then got under way. Which would it be: colored or white? Finally, most of the units were rented to Negroes, but in accordance with the government policy of "no segregation" a "token" representation of five or so white families was included. Segregation never was officially sanctioned in government housing, but it was practiced in certain areas where local managers yielded to pressure by segregationists.

Seven miles outside San Francisco, and near Sausalito, the government built an aggregation of fifteen hundred redwood housing units to accommodate both white and colored workers of the adjacent Oakland Shipbuilding Company. The population of five thousand included one thousand Negroes. There was also a sizable delegation of white Southerners, and some of these snorted and cavorted when they found themselves assigned to the same duplex house with a Negro family or within a few feet of one. After a period of blustering and threats, during which the project manager firmly reiterated the no-segregation policy of Marin City, the objectors usually cooled down. It wasn't easy to find equally desirable apartments at such a low rent. Milla S. Logan in *Common Ground* quoted a Texan who was asked how he liked living next door to Negroes. This was his answer:

> I don't like it at all. But we get along all right. If anybody had told me a year ago I was going to live this way, I wouldn't have believed it. My Negro neighbors are all right. We don't have much to do with them, of course. We say "howdy" to each other and my kids go to school with theirs. We don't have any trouble. There's no trouble between Negroes and whites in Marin City—but it just isn't right to live this way.

In the course of time, Negroes and whites began to mingle in social affairs with little or no friction. If the whites felt any animosity, they ordinarily managed to conceal it with at least a measure of grace and its gradual evaporation became almost visible.

The CIO was a powerful influence toward racial tolerance and co-operation. In August 1943 the Northern Conference on Racial and National Unity, sponsored by the Minorities Committee of the California CIO Council, met in San Francisco. The delegates, some of whom represented A.F. of L. locals, numbered two hundred. They recommended a program including:

1. Abolition of discrimination against minorities in renting units in war housing projects.
2. Educational courses for policemen designed to prepare them for intelligent handling of specific racial problems.
3. Assignment of members of minority groups as police officers.

A.F. of L. unions, in particular the boilermakers', were much less liberal than the CIO, insisting upon segregating the Negroes in Jim Crow locals or—as the only alternative—excluding them altogether. With the merger of the CIO and the A.F. of L. in 1955, the position of Negro unionists was improved.

Migration did not slacken in the postwar period. In 1962 it was estimated that San Francisco had 74,000 Negro residents. The 1960 census counted 1,000,000 Negroes in California. The State was receiving more Negro migrants than any other in the union. San Francisco, a city with a reputation for full acceptance of minorities, developed some racial tension under the strain. Nevertheless, disorders and riots of major proportions did not occur. Housing was understandably a major concern.

A significant experiment was initiated in 1964 with the completion of the racially integrated St. Francis Square garden apartments, sponsored by the International Longshoreman's and Warehouseman's Union. In dedicating the project, Louis Goldblatt, secretary-treasurer of the union, stressed the need for middle-income housing to prevent the larger cities from being inhabited by the very rich and the very poor.

Among the 299 owners of apartment units, 50 per cent were so-called Caucasians, 25 per cent were Negroes, and 25 per cent Orientals. Revels Cayton, a Negro labor leader, was named manager. In the five months before sale of apartments began, he had spoken before church, labor, and civil rights groups to deliver this pointed message: "If you believe in an integrated community, here's your chance to live in it, and benefit yourself at the same time."

The St. Francis Square apartments rose in the midst of an area on which a ramshackle Negro slum had been razed. Slums were still pressing close upon it, and those who lived in them could hardly afford the comparatively modest investment necessary to secure a garden apartment, even if one had been available. The dispossessed had to find another slum, and with the redevelopment program in full swing not many were left. Middle-income folks needed a place, all right, but the very poor, as the Scriptures say, are always with us. And they, too, need a place to lay their heads.

Washington and Oregon accommodated a much smaller percentage of Negro migrants. There were 26,901 Negroes in Seattle in 1960, which amounted to 4.83 per cent of the total population. There were less than 1,000 Negroes in the suburbs, and most of Seattle's colored citizens were living in an area in the central part of the city which was slated for redevelopment razing. Harmony Homes, Inc., and the Fair Housing Listing Service, both organized in 1962, began a campaign against "block-busting" by realtors who schemed to depopulate whole neighborhoods of whites by convincing them that the presence of even one Negro family could topple real-estate prices. Once in possession of the property sacrificed by the fleeing whites, the realtors were able to command a high price from home-hungry Negroes. Harmony Homes began by building homes in middle-class neighborhoods and selling them for a reasonable price to Negroes. The Fair Housing Listing Service cooperated to combat the tactics of "block-busters" by endeavoring to keep neighborhoods truly integrated. An effort was made to preserve some sort of racial quota in selling new homes, so that there were some white buyers and some Negro. Drastic changes in the racial composition of neighborhoods were avoided as much as possible. Propaganda was carried on to instill good feeling among whites and Negroes establishing homes in neighborhoods where none of their race had lived previously.

Most of the westering Negro Argonauts got as far as the Pacific region in their quests for social and economic equality. Very few paused en route. The 1960 census counted 6,514,294 whites but only 123,242 Negroes in the eight Mountain States: Montana,

Idaho, Wyoming, Colorado, New Mexico, Arizona, Utah, and Nevada. Utah had 873,828 white citizens and only 4,148 Negroes. Yet Negro leaders maintained that that State's race problem was potentially the worst in the United States. More than 60 per cent of the whites were members of the Church of Jesus Christ of Latter-day Saints (Mormon). Though Negroes were admitted as members, they were barred from the priesthood even though Japanese and other Orientals were not. Negroes believed that discrimination against them in employment, housing, and public accommodations might be motivated by references in Mormon religious writings to the Negro as a descendant of Cain. Thus he might be regarded as the inheritor of the curse put upon Cain for slaying Abel.

Not many white Southerners are Mormons, but multitudes of them have embraced the doctrine of a curse attached to a black skin. There are those who insist, however, that a goodly number of both groups are beginning to re-examine this shared belief.

CHAPTER XXI

Chicago: Queen of the Inland Sea

With ever-growing brotherhood your children come to live
In peace that only toil and understanding give
Where Kinzie and Du Sable, pioneers of different race,
Used the same log cabin for their dwelling place.
Chicago! Chicago! Queen of the Inland Sea;
Today thy past and future meet to honor thee.

—*Ballad of Chicago,* composed and sung by Win Stracke.

CHICAGO, like most Northern cities, did not need a new wave of Negro migration to complicate the housing problem for dark-skinned situation-seekers during World War II. In the depths of the 1930s' depression many obsolete and dilapidated buildings had been torn down to avoid paying taxes on them. Naturally, a great many of these were in the Negro districts. So, while there had been an increase in population, housing facilities had not expanded at a corresponding pace—had decreased, if anything. Then came difficulties in getting building material, and other impediments hampered the construction of new residential structures.

Negro migration to Chicago during World War II was less sensational than the torrent that had swept up from the South more than three decades before. But the South Side ghetto was already overcrowded when the new migration began. Pushing eastward toward Lake Michigan between Thirty-fifth and Thirty-ninth streets, the colored families established "beachheads" across Cottage Grove Avenue, the boundary guarded so zealously by the Oakland-Kenwood Property Owners' Association.

The organization carried on the provocative tradition of its predecessors in the period following World War I. In a little "throwaway" advertising sheet the association boasted of a new kind of restrictive covenant cooked up to order for the protection of the "leafy avenues of Oakland-Kenwood" against "undesirable residents and conditions which break down a neighborhood." The improved restrictive agreement, it was said, had "withstood all the technicalities which have been presented in the courts" and also had "the advantage of being much more quickly and economically enforced."

There followed not-so-very-oblique incitements to violence in appeals to white residents of the district to "serve as a block worker and warn your neighbor as to what is liable to happen if quick action is not taken" as well as "to report to the association any condition that is harmful to the neighborhood." This admonition was added:

> The undertaking must be completed quickly and thoroughly. There's no time to lose. Unless we all act together—at once—lifetime investments will shrink, home surroundings will become unbearable, and much that you have worked and saved for these many years will disappear.

As a happier solution than the "invasion" of Oakland-Kenwood, the association offered a privately financed housing development to contain fifty-six dwelling units. Construction had just begun on this enterprise, which was to be named for George Washington Carver.

It was estimated in 1944 that 70,000 Negroes had been added to Chicago's population since 1940, when there were 277,000. Density of population in some areas was set as high as 90,000 per square mile. Overcrowded Negro schools were operating in half-day shifts. Thus children of colored war workers when both parents were employed, as was frequently the case, had idle afternoons to while away in the streets or elsewhere. Many of them, it goes without saying, preferred not to spend the time in the small, dark rooms they called home. An appalling increase in juvenile delinquency became an inescapable corollary.

Though Chicago had no big-time rabble rousers and racial hate mongers comparable to Gerald L. K. Smith of Detroit, manifestations of racial intolerance were not lacking. Nor were they directed against Negroes alone. Vandals desecrated Jewish cemeteries, overturning headstones and branding them with swastikas. Synagogues were stoned. There were ghouls who scanned the newspaper obituary notices for Jewish-sounding names, then mailed to the bereaved family this taunt: "Another Jew gone to hell." Jewish boys were assaulted by gangs of young toughs. Tom Y. Chan, a prominent Chinese-American merchant who had been tireless in patriotic activities and had helped to sell more than $4,000,000 worth of war bonds, was denied burial beside his white wife, who had been interred twenty-four years before in Rosehill Cemetery. The cemetery, it was explained, was "for Caucasians only."

The Mayor's Commission on Race Relations, one of the first and most active of many set up in cities throughout the country, was the nucleus for a conference attended by seventy-one leading Negro and white Americans. It met in Chicago in March 1944, at the joint invitation of Marshall Field, publisher of the Chicago *Sun,* Dr. Charles S. Johnson of Fisk University, and Edwin R. Embree of the Julius Rosenwald Fund. Two months later the American Council on Race Relations, a national clearinghouse for information of this kind, was formed as a result of the March conference. The new organization adopted a five-point program:

1. Advancement of knowledge concerning race and racial relations both by the collection and analysis of records of interracial relationships and by original research.
2. Cooperation with public and private agencies and individuals working in the interracial field by supplying needed information, by advice concerning procedures, and by temporary loan of personnel.
3. Assistance of local communities in organizing to meet their interracial problems where the existing program seems inadequate.
4. Assistance in developing materials and programs for use in the public schools and other educational institutions.
5. Increasing knowledge about racial groups by popular education through the radio, press, movies, and other means of mass communication.

Shocked into action by the Black Pearl Harbor of June 1943, in Detroit, civic, religious, and labor leaders assisted in the forming of interracial commissions to deal with the problems of racial tension. Within a year after the Detroit riot, 224 of these commissions had been established.

Unlike the ex post facto committees which routinely make investigations of race riots after they have happened, the Chicago Mayor's Committee on Race Relations, with Edwin R. Embree as chairman and Robert C. Weaver as executive director, set itself energetically to the task of *preventing* these disorders by hammering away at the causes and trying to have them removed. As might have been expected, opposition to this forthright policy soon developed.

In July 1944 the Federation of Neighborhood Associations, comprising seventy "improvement" associations, published a report in which it condemned as "undemocratic, partial, and not representative" a previous statement of Chairman Embree attacking restrictive covenants. He had said:

> At present Negroes are confined to restricted areas with bad houses and exorbitant rent. They are confined to their districts by an atmosphere of prejudice and specifically by conspiracies known as restrictive covenants . . . Once you start that, there's no limit. There already are restrictions against Jews, Catholics, and Negroes. There'll be restrictions against Baptists next.

In reply, the Federation made this remarkable statement:

> Race restrictive covenants do not segregate Negroes. They segregate whites. These covenants do not connote prejudice. They have been signed by persons in industrial and professional life whose activities provide employment for thousands of Negroes.

The restrictive covenant issue receded into the background in 1948 when the United States Supreme Court ruled in the case of Shelley versus Kramer that, while individuals who enter into an agreement not to sell their property to Negroes or other minority groups are not actually violating Constitutional provisions per se, such an agreement is unenforceable in the courts because it contradicts the equal protection clause of the Fourteenth Amendment. This ruling, of course, compelled the resourceful realtors to find other methods of "protecting" white property owners.

Embattled race supremacists had their own ideas about how to control the situation. Direct and violent action was frequent, and they often proceeded to take the law into their own hands when a Negro managed to buy or rent property in a "white" section. Welcoming committees, usually including otherwise demure housewives and frolicsome children, assembled to jeer at the new neighbors. Protests rarely were confined to verbal exhibitions. Bricks hurled through windows, Molotov cocktails (bottles filled with gasoline to make fire bombs) reminiscent of World War II days, and other "persuaders" were put into use.

Frank London Brown, a young Negro novelist in Chicago, vividly described in his first and only novel *Trumbull Park* (1959) his harrowing ordeal and that of his fellow Negroes who moved into the Trumbull Park Homes housing project at One Hundred Seventh and Bensley Streets in 1953. Brown was only thirty-four when his promising writing career was cut short by leukemia. Brown's family was the tenth to occupy a home in that formerly all-white project. Howling mobs of infuriated whites hurling stones and garbage, flinging aerial bombs, and screaming obscenities ranged through the area, virtually unchecked. The new tenants charged that police protection was lackadaisical, to say the least. As late as July 1957, when policemen still on guard in Trumbull Park were assigned to emergency duty elsewhere, Negro residents were waylaid and beaten and a Negro home was ransacked and wrecked by white mobs.

At about this time, a mildly inebriated white citizen was overheard in a stubbornly lily-white bar around which Negroes were steadily encroaching. He was regaling the appreciative and assenting bartender with what both seemed to regard as a hilarious anecdote. A "pushy" Negro had presumed to buy a house on a hitherto unsullied street and was in the act of installing his household effects when partisans of the "improvement" association with jurisdiction over that street rallied quickly. Soon both the house and the furniture deposited on the lawn were blazing merrily. Policemen assigned to watch the property were nowhere to be seen. The victim did manage to call the fire department, or some sympathetic spectator did it for him. When the dawdling smoke-eaters finally made the scene, as the barfly admiringly expressed it, little was left of the house and nothing remained of the furniture. The firemen then seemed to have considerable difficulty in hooking up their hose so that by the time they were ready for action it was just too late to do any good.

Though this particular incident may have owed something to the wishful-thinking, booze-fired brain of the Nordic-proud narrator wallowing in a last-ditch fantasy, it sounded credible in the climate of hostility in which it was related. And real-life occurrences of essentially the same character had not been lacking.

In 1950 the Negro population of Chicago amounted to 13.6 per cent of the total. By 1963 it was estimated to have increased to 25.8 per cent. About 28 per cent of the elementary and 34 per cent of the high school pupils in the public schools were Negro children. Still barred from many jobs and still victims in some industries of the "last hired and first fired" policy, Negroes represented 42 per cent of the unemployed. As a consequence, it was disclosed early in 1964 that Negroes comprised 84 per cent of the people on relief rolls. About 87 per cent of these had lived in Cook County more than five years. More than half, however, had been born in the South or Southeast and had acquired whatever education they had before coming to Chicago.

Looking at the relief and job situation in February 1965, Cook County Public Aid Director Raymond Hilliard said: "If we never have another migrant, the Negro population here will still increase 25,000 a year. And the real problem is jobs, not people." Stressing the need for an open occupancy law in Illinois, Hilliard added: "There are thousands of jobs going begging in the suburbs, but the Negroes can't go there."

Most of the suburbs had managed to remain lily-white, but there were fewer neighborhood reception committees armed with bricks, bottles, garbage missiles, and Molotov cocktails than in "changing" urban areas. Behind this apparent restraint, however, was an ironclad compact between suburban realtors and home owners not to rent or sell or even show to Negroes any house or apartment in which they might express interest.

There was the Deerfield episode. Morris Milgram, president of Progress Development Corporation, announced in November 1959 that his company intended to duplicate in Brookfield, a suburb of Chicago, an experiment which Modern Community Developers, parent organization of Progress Development Corporation, had carried out successfully in Princeton, New Jersey. There a group of interracial housing units had been erected. "I don't want to build homes that my friends can't live in," Milgram explained, "and some of my friends are Negroes." He negotiated for a Deerfield tract of land upon which he planned to place fifty-one homes, about a dozen of which would be sold to Negroes.

The Princeton venture had been preceded by a public relations campaign sparked by clergymen and Christian laymen from local churches who carried the gospel of brotherhood so forcefully to the white community that little or no opposition resulted. Not so, alas, in Deerfield, where no such educational campaign had been undertaken.

When wind of Milgram's intentions got around, aroused white supremacists assumed battle positions. Milgram's dream died aborning because they contrived to have his prospective site set aside as a park. This blatant maneuver provoked protests from Deerfield clergymen and fair-minded citizens, and national obloquy was brought down upon the village. Nevertheless, racism prevailed in the end.

Early in March 1965 a report compiled by Home Opportunities Made Equal (HOME) with the co-operation of the Chicago Urban League and the Presbytery of Chicago revealed that seventy-four Negro families were living in traditionally all-white neighborhoods in twenty-six different Chicago suburbs. Of these, forty-six had moved in during 1964 and five had arrived during the first two months of 1965. Edwin C. Berry, executive director of the Chicago Urban League, found encouragement in the addition of even one Negro family in a number of suburbs during 1964, but referred to something he regarded as an imperative in the campaign to bring about "substantial changes in the present rigid pattern of residential segregation." He said:

Passage of a statewide open occupancy law at this session of the state legislature is an absolute must if we are to consolidate the gains made in 1964 . . . Only by invoking the moral and legal sanctions of such a law can the well-meaning white owner feel free to sell his home to a buyer of any race without disloyalty to his neighbors.

William H. Moyer, a young Quaker, came from Philadelphia in 1964 to become executive director of HOME. Looking over the situation, he observed:

The suburbs are just as much a closed society as the South. Chicago's system of separation of the races differs from Mississippi's only in degree. In Mississippi, the Ku Klux Klan burns churches. Last year, in Chicago, three houses were burned to the ground because they were purchased by Negro citizens.

Within a short time Moyer had organized two hundred suburban volunteers in twenty-five Fair Housing Committees distributed in various suburbs in Chicago. With the notoriously lily-white suburbs to the north and west of Chicago as his principal targets, he sent his volunteers out to canvass owner-for-sale homes. They found a few willing to sell to Negroes, while a larger number had no moral or ethical scruples against such a sale but were restrained by fear of ostracism or even more drastic forms of reprisal by white neighbors. Then HOME would act as a go-between to bring unprejudiced white home owners with houses for sale into contact with Negroes eager to buy them. Moyer pointed out:

Our long-range program is to work ourselves out of a job. We hope to achieve a single housing standard to Negro and white alike somewhat like the single voter registration we hope to have in the South.

It long had been a popular legend among white racists in Chicago that hordes of penniless Negroes arrive daily from the South and immediately contrive to get on the relief rolls, living thereafter on the fat of the land at the expense of hard-working taxpayers and avoiding work as the devil shuns holy water. Negro women, on their part, were said to busy themselves with bearing as many illegitimate children as they could, each by a different father, in as short a time as possible in order to qualify for Aid for Dependent Children Assistance. Confuting this myth, the 1960 Greenleigh Report on Aid for Dependent Children in Cook County asserted:

ADC mothers held out without help for an average of one year and three months (after death, divorce or desertion) . . . They worked at odd jobs until they could no longer care for their children and keep their jobs, or until illness forced them to quit, or until relatives who had helped them also went under with debts . . .

Negro families maintained themselves for a significantly longer period than white families before they became dependent.

A Gargantuan slum clearance and "urban removal" program went into high gear in Chicago in the 1950s and was still going strong in the 1960s. About 65,000 dilapidated buildings were scheduled to fall before the wrecker's swinging ball. A great many of these were located in the Negro ghettos in various parts of the city, the largest, of course, being on the South Side. The public housing projects that displaced the slums could not accommodate all the dispossessed, and in most cases the rent was too high for poor folks with a large family. Cynics began to equate "urban removal" with "Negro removal." Some of the low-rent public housing projects quickly became segregated Negro slums. Such was the case with the Robert R. Taylor Homes, stretching from Thirty-ninth Street to Fifty-fourth Place along State Street. About half of the 28,000 tenants in this world's largest public housing project, opened in 1962, were on relief in April 1965. As usual, upkeep and maintenance were neglected and repairs rarely made. Housing, schools, and jobs continued to preoccupy the attention of black Chicagoans. Organizations pledged to fight for a preservation of racial balance became increasingly effective in the 1960s. The Woodlawn Organization was one of these. In the South Shore community there was the South Shore Commission. In May 1965 Martin Rosene, its president, proposed a code of ethics for real-estate practice. He pointed out:

An integrated community will not just happen in this generation. It must be worked for diligently and honorably. We believe that real estate agents can work toward this end by developing and following a code such as the one we suggest.

Here are some of the provisions of the proposed code:

Advertising should mention neither race nor the word integration. There should be no mass distribution of letters or leaflets urging residents to sell or move.

Harassment by telephone, or pressure to sell in any form, is unacceptable. Each available apartment should be shown to any qualified prospective tenant.

Today there are growing numbers of people receptive to the concept of integrated living. Many of the new residents South Shore is attracting from the universities do not share out-dated prejudices. The concept of "turning" a building is obsolete; the new idea is to rent to desirable tenants, regardless of race, creed, or color. Real estate dealers must become educated in this new philosophy or communities cannot achieve racial stability. Continuing service to all tenants must be stressed.

On Sunday June 13, 1965, the South Shore Open House committee conducted its second annual walking tour through both white and Negro apartments and houses. More than a thousand sightseers from other parts of Chicago were shown impressive evidence that the South Shore community control plan was working. The tour led through colonial, Old English, and swanky luxury apartments renting for upward of fifty thousand dollars a year as well as more modest but well-kept ones where the owners had not let the introduction of a few Negro tenants be the signal for abandonment and deterioration, as had so often been the case in other sections of Chicago. Gracious old homes and aggressively modern residences were exhibited in proximity to less pretentious places where whites and blacks were striving to co-operate with the South Shore Commission's determination to make the community an assimilated, harmonious neighborhood. Not a few of the hosts were more pragmatical than evangelical, emphasizing the practical rather than the idealistic. One woman confessed:

Well, we're not going to bat 100 per cent for integration. But we're trying like mad to assimilate. Some owners panicked when the first

Negroes moved in, but those of us who remained here organized and are really trying to get people—black and white—to keep this place livable.

The Chicago City Council had passed on September 11, 1963, an ordinance forbidding racial discrimination in the sale or rental of real estate. On that day four thousand white pickets opposing the ordinance paraded around City Hall. Their attitude was officially shared by the Chicago Real Estate Board.

Earlier, in July, four Negro families had moved into a white neighborhood in the South Side Englewood district. For days a white mob, at times numbering a thousand, milled about in the surrounding streets. On one occasion they hurled bricks and bottles at an apartment building housing one of the Negro families. It took the strenuous efforts of two hundred policemen to restore a semblance of order after 149 rioters had been arrested. Roman Catholic priests and Protestant clergymen who mingled with the rioters to plead for an end to the violence were credited with some success in their pacific efforts.

As 1963 wore on the question of *de facto* segregation in the schools came into more and more prominence. In August 1953 Benjamin Coppage Willis had been appointed superintendent of Chicago schools. An energetic and in some respects capable administrator, he began a program for building badly needed new schools. A number of streamlined yellow brick buildings arose. Soon, however, there were protests that the new schools had been placed in such a way that they helped to perpetuate racial segregation, leaving Negro pupils in outmoded and crowded buildings. To relieve overcrowding in the Negro ghettos trailer classrooms were put into use. Civil rights leaders charged that these "Willis wagons," as they soon sardonically labeled them, often were set down close to schools with only white students in half-empty classrooms.

Complaints became so numerous and outspoken that in May 1963 the school board finally authorized a report on the school situation. Opposition by Superintendent Willis, it was said, had delayed the authorization eighteen months or more. The report finally was issued in November 1964 as a five-hundred-page survey of the school situation, generally called the Havighurst report for Dr. Walter J. Havighurst, the University of Chicago professor who supervised its preparation. Among its recommendations was the establishment of a set of fifteen to twenty elementary schools from grade five to eight, called "integrated schools." These would be located strategically about the city, as near as possible to areas of Negro residence. They would be open to children living anywhere in the city, white or Negro, but an effort would be made to enroll children of average or superior reading ability, not more than a year below their normal grade level. The Board of Education would be required to guarantee that 60 per cent of the children in these schools would be white or Oriental, in order to preserve a racial balance. The report also called for the setting aside of three large Chicago areas containing about 30 per cent of the city's population as integration and community development areas. There the schools would help local community organizations in an energetic program for stabilizing the white population and maintaining a truly integrated community.

Differences of opinion with respect to this report and its recommendations provided a kind of prologue for a controversy which came to be spoken of as the "battle of Ben Willis."

Early in August 1963 picketing by Negroes at a construction site of twenty-five of the mobile classrooms led to a tussle with the police and culminated in a number of arrests, including that of comedian Dick Gregory. Gregory remained in jail several days rather than sign a recognizance bond. Willis, accused by Negroes and white liberals of fostering *de facto* segregation, resigned his $48,000-a-year job on October 3. (He had been criticized, too, for holding down a $32,000 "moonlighting" job as supervisor of a Massachusetts school survey.) An immediate reason given for Willis' resignation was pique over some enforcements of the Armstrong Law requiring school boards to readjust district boundary lines where they tended to promote racial segregation.

The school board abandoned the "Willis wagons" and prepared to move the children involved into other schools. A few Negro students who had displayed more than ordinary scholastic ability were transferred from segregated neighborhood high schools to schools with honor courses. Some of these schools were picketed by white parents who feared that the transfer plan would overcrowd classes. Willis, allegedly yielding to pressure from these parents, then deleted a number of receiving schools from the plan. The school board promptly reinstated a few of them. Parents of four Negro students then successfully sued to have the original plan restored. Willis reacted by offering his resignation, effective December 31, stating that the school board had encroached upon his administrative responsibilities. He also asked to be released from active duty by October 30.

The rejoicing of Willis' enemies proved to be premature. The school board, by a vote of eight to two, refused to accept the resignation, and Willis consented to stay on. A group of Negro parents sued Willis and the board, charging that their children were receiving education inferior to that provided for white children. Though the suit was dropped upon the promise of an outside survey on school integration, it did spark a study supervised by Dr. Philip M. Hauser, chairman of the sociology department of the University of Chicago. Dr. Hauser's report, issued in March 1964, made a number of recommendations as to measures for combating segregation in the schools. Dr. Hauser later charged, at hearings conducted in July 1965 by the House of Representatives Education and Labor Committee in Washington, that Willis had done nothing to put the measures in force. He claimed that 90 per cent of Chicago's pupils, white and Negro, were enrolled in segregated schools and that the schools in Negro neighborhoods were "unequal and inferior." Dr. Hauser described Willis as "the symbol of segregation" and added: "Willis is performing the same thing for the civil rights movement in Chicago as Governor Wallace has in the South. Some day they may erect a monument to him."

Willis complained to Congressman Adam Clayton Powell, chairman of the committee, that the flight of whites to the suburbs and the moving in of illiterate Negroes from the South had complicated the problem of integration in the schools. Segregated neighborhoods, he pointed out, were sure to breed segregated schools. When Willis produced figures indicating a rapid increase in Negro registrations in Chicago schools with a corresponding decline in white registrations, Powell, feigning folk dialect, observed: "It looks like us colored folks gonna be runnin' the big cities."

Willis' statement that funds for educational development in Chicago were inadequate was apropos. Congressman Powell's *ad hoc* committee was empowered to investigate complaints of school segregation and discrimination. Federal funds could be denied cities found guilty of such practices.

The Havighurst report, which came eight months after Dr. Hauser's, was in substantial agreement with the latter's unflattering analysis of the Chicago school situation. The Hauser and Havighurst reports were destined to serve as the *vade mecum* of the anti-Willisites.

On October 22, 1963, civil rights groups organized a boycott in observance of which 225,000 children skipped school for one day. This represented nearly half the total enrollment. About six thousand anti-Willis demonstrators picketed City Hall and the Board of Education offices. ACT, a militant civil rights organization led by Lawrence Landry, took a prominent part in the boycott. The activities of CCCO later were to overshadow those of ACT, which had an earlier start. A boycott on February 25, 1964—backed by local chapters of CORE, the Student Nonviolent Coordinating Committee, Dick Gregory, and Mahalia Jackson—resulted in 172,350 absences.

Dick Gregory, whose zeal in the civil rights cause cost him many profitable bookings in night clubs, and Al Raby, convenor of the Coordinating Council of Community Organizations, became relentless evangels of the slogan: "Willis must go!" Raby resigned his teaching job to devote full time to the crusade. Gregory, frequently arrested for various activities (once for kneeling in prayer before the Board of Education building), began to lead an almost daily march from Buckingham Fountain in Grant Park to the City Hall. Sometimes the demonstrators resorted to the extreme tactic of lying in the street at the busy corner of State and Madison streets. Their vehemence increased when it was announced that Superintendent Willis would be reappointed at the expiration of his term on August 31, 1965, to serve until he reached the legal retirement age of sixty-five in December, 1966. It had been generally assumed that Willis would either resign or be fired.

A four-page circular entitled "Why We March" became a familiar object on Chicago streets during the spring and summer of

1965. Issued by the Coordinating Council of Community Organizations, it reminded Mayor Daley that he could halt the demonstrations if he would:

Publicly endorse an immediate change in the school superintendency.

Change your advisory commission to include representatives of the civil rights movement.

Publicly endorse a program of quality, integrated education—beginning with your support of the Hauser and Havighurst recommendations.

The circular also exhorted: "OUR VOICES HAVE NOT BEEN HEEDED! WILLIS HAS BEEN REAPPOINTED! THIS IS WHY WE MARCH! LET BEN WILLIS GO!"

The prestige of Raby and Gregory as leaders was greatly enhanced by a huge rally led by Dr. Martin Luther King, Jr., on July 26. The procession was joined by thousands as it moved toward City Hall, so that, according to some estimates, Dr. King addressed a multitude of 50,000 when he spoke in front of the building. Mayor Daley at the time was attending a convention of mayors in Detroit. He said he would have been glad to confer with Dr. King. Shortly after this, he was asked if he thought there was anything to the rumor that civil rights marches and demonstrations were inspired and financed by Communists. Daley conceded they might well be—that some of the Communists who came to Chicago for the express purpose of annoying the Congressional investigators at the sessions of the House Un-American Activities Committee could have lingered on to join and dominate the civil rights movement. Comedian Dick Gregory scoffed: "The dollars we get are cleaner than the dollars Daley gets. If Daley had to prove where his money came from and he was in a fair court he'd never get out of jail."

Raby and Gregory then ventured a bold new move. They began a nightly walkathon from their established starting point at Buckingham Fountain to the mayor's home at 3526 South Lowe Street in the Bridgeport neighborhood, a five-mile hike. The constant threnody of the marchers was "Willis Must Go!" This was chanted and the semiofficial hymn of the civil rights movement, "We Shall Overcome," was sung. Some of the marchers carried signs with a direct appeal: "Daley, Fire Willis." On the first night the demonstrators were met by a mob of about two thousand "neighbors" prepared to unfurl the Stars and Bars and fight to the death in its defense. The marchers numbered a hundred or less. As they trudged along the sidewalk two by two, silent because they were determined not to provoke the Daley partisans, householders turned on their lawn sprinklers to drench them. Others hurled eggs, vegetables, and various small missiles. The more passive ones carried signs proclaiming: "We Love Our Mayor" and "Great Mayor —Great City." A group of grade-schoolers clustered on a corner, harmonizing on a song of which these words were distinguishable:

Oh, I wish I was an Alabama trooper,
Then I could shoot a nigger legally.

The police acted by arresting sixty-four of the demonstrators. When asked by reporters how come the rioters were not also involved, Police Superintendent Orlando W. Wilson replied that it was police procedure to remove the *cause* of an incipient riot. He added:

> If the police have a feeling that matters are building up to a riot, they must take action. The police are concerned with one thing—that is the maintenance of peace, law and order. We don't want riots.

When TV commentator Len O'Connor expressed wonder at this Alice-in-Wonderland reasoning, he received a number of letters and phone calls inviting him to go and live in the Taylor Homes Negro ghetto, to Moscow, or to an even hotter clime.

Mayor Daley complained that his privacy had been invaded by the demonstrators, but the Chicago newspapers were sterner. CCCO, they insisted, had gone much too far. The *Sun-Times* warned that such behavior would surely alienate friendly white people needed in the civil rights movement, and inquired: "What good purpose is served by deliberately antagonizing Mayor Daley's neighbors?" The *Daily News* chided Raby, but offered him space in which to present his side of the story. "And when you and your people laid siege to Mayor Daley's home in Bridgeport, you were 'punishing' the mayor's family and neighbors and the people of Bridgeport," the newspaper scolded, "Again, to what end?" Among other reasons he gave for the "punishment," Raby pointed out:

> Bridgeport is involved in what amounts to a major conspiracy that prevents the Negro from achieving first-class citizenship and human dignity. A web is woven by real estate interests, city officials, the school board, employers, some unions and citizen organizations that entraps the Negro in his ghetto. A city-wide pattern is dramatically illustrated here.
>
> The Bridgeport Homes, operated by Charles Swibel's Chicago Housing Authority, are lily white, which violates Title VI of the 1964 Civil Rights Act. The Negro community in the 11th Ward, whose committeeman is Richard J. Daley, is rigidly hemmed in. There are streets demarcating the ghetto past which no Negro dares tread at night.

Raby also referred to an incident which had occurred during the previous October. John Walsh, a young North Side high school teacher, had taken Mayor Daley's pronouncements about civil rights and equality seriously. Wishing to arrange a practical demonstration of their genuineness, Walsh bought a house at 3309 South Lowe, very close to Daley's, and rented an apartment in it to a Negro student. After a mob had surrounded the house, tried to set it afire, and chunked a rock through the front window, the Negro student surmised that he wasn't wanted in the neighborhood and moved out. Mike Royko, columnist for the *Daily News*, visited the site of the noble but ill-fated experiment, and found some "neighbors" celebrating their victory. A worried-looking elderly man "with an accent that suggested he might have once fled tyranny and poverty for America's democracy and plenty," came along to ask what was going on. He was assured that "they're gone and they ain't coming back." "Dat's goot," the old man said with satisfaction. "Ve don't vant outsiders."

According to Royko, Walsh was surprised when he learned from a reporter that two white tenants had been moved in during his absence. They had leases, too—something the Negro had not been given by the real-estate agent. Walsh considered himself betrayed, for the agent had promised to keep Negroes in the house.

Royko learned from "a reliable political source" that Mayor Daley's Eleventh Ward Regular Democratic Organization had negotiated the "switcheroo" calculated to preserve the lily-white complexion of the neighborhood. This was denied by one of Daley's trusty lieutenants. Royko then admitted:

> I didn't ask Mayor Daley about the departure of the Negro and the move-in of two guys from the neighborhood. Why bother? When he was asked about the Monday night street fighting he borrowed a favorite phrase of Southern politicians and said the rowdies were "outsiders."

There were segregationists, however, who would consider Daley a tool of Moscow. Circulating during the summer of 1965 in a South Side neighborhood menaced by a Negro "invasion" was this poesie entitled "The New Democratic 23rd Psalm":

Lyndon is my shepherd, I shall not want.
He maketh me to lie down in front of theaters.
He leadeth me into white universities.
He restoreth my welfare check.
He leadeth me down the path of sit-ins for the communist's sake.
Yea, though I walk through the heart of Dixie,
I will fear no policeman, for Lyndon is with me.
He prepareth a table for me in the presence of white folks.
He anointeth my head with anti-kink hair straightener.
My Cadillac's gas tank runneth over.
The Supreme Court will follow me all the days of my life,
And I shall dwell in the Federal housing project forever.

Police Superintendent Wilson, who had been a professor of criminology at the University of California, wrought many desirable changes in Chicago's police department, long notorious for its inefficiency and corruption. On the whole, his handling of the racial situation was enlightened. He had been accommodating with the demonstrators, and, after the first arrest of the victims rather than the victimizers, displayed good sense in the Bridgeport situation.

Walter D. Glanze had responded in the *Daily News* "Letters to the Editor" column on the newspaper's sermonizing about the Bridgeport marchers with these words:

Editorialists deplore "noisy, nighttime demonstrations" in the mayor's neighborhood. No matter how we interpret events, it should be noted that the marches are silent. The demonstrators refrain from whispering, even lifting their feet to avoid noise, and do not reply to hecklers. They do not block the sidewalk, as they are marching in twos. In fact, no one in Bridgeport need even notice their presence. Again, no matter what we think of demonstrations, it is a disservice to the public not to acknowledge that these marches are quiet at night and disciplined and peaceful at all times.

Raby himself saw some positive benefits from the marches:

Bridgeport may not like us any better, but the crowds are coming under control and a process of race relations and civil liberties education has begun. It was suggested by the group of clergymen, who refused to be used to control demonstrators as in the past but instead plead for the tolerance and education of the aroused Bridgeport community.

On March 16, 1965, the Chicago Urban League distributed a "Westside Fact Sheet" that sounded an ominous warning about events to come. It defined the Westside as "roughly the area bounded by Lake Street on the north, Cermak Road on the south, Cicero Boulevard on the west, and State Street on the east," and continued:

The Westside has been an established residential area since 1930. Only two per cent of its dwellings have been built since 1940. The area was originally settled by Irish and Germans, later, as these groups started to move north and west, it was, in turn, settled by Jews and Italians. Although Negroes have been living on the Westside as far back as the 1930's, it was not until the postwar period that they began to move to the Westside in large numbers. Within the next decade, if current patterns of race relations continue, it is expected these four areas will be almost entirely populated by Negroes.

The Urban League's carefully prepared fact sheet concluded with this summary:

> The Negro community on the Westside faces the traditional Negro problems of unemployment, under-employment, low income, price discrimination, poor housing, and inferior educational facilities. In most instances, on the Westside, the occurrence of these problems is more acute.
>
> The discrimination and economic deprivations are destructive to individual and family stability. On the Westside, three out of four teenagers drop out of school; one out of four births are illegitimate; the juvenile delinquency rate doubles that of all Chicago; and, there are higher rates of infantile mortality, public dependency, and tuberculosis.

The foregoing facts succinctly set the scene for a 1965 "incident" that occurred Thursday evening, July 12. The ensuing disorders well illustrated the soundness of the "powder-keg" theory about racial tension simmering in such areas as the Westside, building up animosities and frustrations until the pressure is so great that the lid is bound to blow off in a violent explosion. A small incident is often enough to trigger such an explosion.

On the hot evening in question, Dessie Mae Williams was standing on a corner near the firehouse at 4000 West Wilcox Street in the Westside neighborhood of West Garfield Park. A serious, hard-working girl of twenty-three, with only a grade school education, she held a low-paying job as packer in a fishery. She had arrived from Clarksdale, Mississippi, nearly six years before, and had been sending money back home to see the younger Williams children through high school. She couldn't send much, but had hoped to get a better job so as to be able to bring her nine-year-old sister North to live with her.

Just then a fire truck sped out of the firehouse, responding to what proved to be a false alarm. The tillerman who was supposed to steer its rear end had been left behind. It was said later that he was taking a shower when the alarm sounded and couldn't dress in time to take his post. Out of control, the truck smashed into a stop sign near which Dessie Mae was standing. It fell on her and killed her.

Sixty pickets representing the militant ACT organization had picketed the station the month before because it was not integrated. Soon after news of Dessie Mae's death got about, a jeering mob of two hundred or more Negroes surrounded the firehouse. Bricks and bottles began to fly, and piles of debris were set afire. As the riot area expanded, windows were broken and some fire bombs hurled, but there was little looting. The disorders reached a high point the following night. Shouting gangs of Negro teenagers, both boys and girls, pelted policemen and white civilians with assorted missiles. They smashed the windshields of white motorists who ventured into the district, and accosted "Whitey" pedestrians. Sometimes the whites were let off with a warning to get out of the neighborhood and stay out; at other times they were cuffed or beaten. More than seventy-five people, including a number of policemen, were injured in one way or another, none seriously. Frequently it became obvious that some teenagers were animated by liquor.

An all-Negro crew, commanded by a white captain, was hastily installed in the station at 4000 West Wilcox as a placative gesture that came a little late. It was apparent, as the riots continued into a third day, that Superintendent Wilson's course of training for handling racial disturbance had some merit. The five hundred policemen eventually called to the scene exercised considerable restraint. A detachment of one hundred Negro detectives in plain clothes mingled with the rioters and tried to reason with them. A flying squad of clergymen undertook a similar mission. The contingent of 2,500 National Guardsmen put on a stand-by basis by Governor Otto Kerner was never called into action. Of the 169 persons arrested for participation in the rioting, a large percentage were juveniles. A great many were school dropouts.

Who was to blame? Edwin C. Berry of the Chicago Urban League echoed the convictions of many Negroes and whites when he said, "I'm to blame. Everybody's to blame." He spoke at a meeting of fifty-two white and Negro leaders summoned by Mayor Daley to discuss the West Garfield Park problem. "Discrimination against the Negro has become a way of life, not an exception," Berry added. Reverend Carl Fuqua, executive secretary of the Chicago Branch of the NAACP, felt that some benefits might be salvaged from the tragic events in that they had helped to develop concern on the part of white people who had previously looked upon the "Negro problem" as something remote from their own lives. Al Raby expressed dissatisfaction with the meeting, contending that it devoted too much time to the riots per se and not enough to larger problems of the Westside that had brought about the situation underlying them. Most of the rioters, he said, were teenagers and young adults whom an inferior school system, bad housing, idleness, and various frustrations had transformed into hoodlums. John Ascher, deputy chief of the patrol division, said about 50 per cent of the blame could be laid at the door of ACT. He acknowledged, however, that ACT leaders deserved some credit for their role in pacifying residents of the neighborhood. Lawrence Landry, ACT leader, vigorously denied that his organization had tried to fan the flames of discontent by distributing provocative leaflets and exhorting the mob to further depredations.

As West Garfield Park subsided to at least surface placidity, Dessie Mae's mother came to Chicago from Clarksdale to claim her daughter's body. Her first thought was to plead that all violence cease. Hearing that some of the Westside residents planned to establish a Dessie Mae Williams Community Center to serve young folks who didn't have much of any place to go except street corners, she said: "This is a wonderful thing for the children, and I know that her two little sisters will be happy to learn that Dessie Mae is going to be remembered this way."

One of the sponsors of the proposed community center was Sherman Kennedy, an eighteen-year-old boy who admitted having lost his head and who vowed never to let it happen again. But he felt impelled to offer some explanation, if not justification, of his behavior:

> We're sorry about the bricks and bottles, but when you get pushed, you shove back. Man, you don't like to stand on a corner and be told to get off it when you got nowhere else to go. And we want somewhere else to go.

Epilogue

THE DEPRESSION produced its own lore. Not infrequently this included anecdotes reflecting cordial race relations among vagrants, bums, and others who live below the level of polite respect. The one about the white kids and the Negro runaways in a hobo jungle is remembered for its tag line.

They were all headed for Detroit, and they were getting along fine, it seems, raiding nearby orchards co-operatively, venturing even farther away from their base to obtain by illicit means ingredients for a pot of mulligan stew, when a stock character known as a railroad bull suddenly thrashed his way through the horseweeds that screened the jungle from the railroad tracks. He was wearing a ten-gallon dimpled hat, a red shirt, and a tooled-leather holster from which he had drawn the pistol.

"Hold it," he barked. "Don't you move an inch, nara one of you, or I'll drill you till your hide won't hold corn shucks."

He lined the Negro boys on one side of the jungle, the white ones on the other. Then he commenced searching the Negroes. When he found a pocketknife on one of them, he waved it triumphantly.

"Don't you know it's a penitentiary act to carry a weapon like that?" he demanded.

"That? That ain't nothing but a little old penknife that wouldn't cut hot butter," the black kid muttered.

The railroad bull ignored him. Turning to the white boys, he asked without rancor, "What you boys aiming to do?"

"We want to go to Detroit to get a job of work."

"Well, I better not catch you on no Red Ball manifest."

"Can we ride a local out, just so's we don't get on the Red Ball?"

"I ain't saying for you to ride *nothing*. I'm just telling you I'd better not catch you on no Red Ball manifest."

The bull left the white kids but marched the Negro boys away with him. The white ones sat around indecisively. They wanted to get away as fast as possible, and this was the only place to snag a freight. But by now they had lost their appetite for the mulligan they had planned to share.

Before they could get away, however, the three black boys came tumbling through the weeds, rolled on the ground and began pulling off their shoes. With their fingers they burst huge blisters on the soles of their feet, and hot water gushed.

"What's the matter?" one of the white kids ventured.

"That peckerwood bastard made us get up in a carload of hot cinders just emptied out of a firebox. He held that pistol on us while we shoveled out them cinders with our feet frying like bacon. We beat it when he went to take a leak."

"Look out! Here he comes," one of his confederates interrupted. "Don't tell him you seen us here." They dived into the weeds again, and presently the bull returned, pistol still in hand.

"Where's the niggers?" he demanded.

"We ain't seen them since they went with you," a white boy lied.

"Soon as I turned my back they took out. Shows how far you can trust a damned coon—about as far as you can throw a bull by the tail. Thought I seen them heading this way. Say, you wasn't traveling with them by any chance, was you?"

"Naw. We come from the West and they come up from the South. Just *happened* to meet here."

"Well, don't be caught 'sociating with them. Don't forget you're white no matter how low down you get. Just remember you *can't* get as low as a nigger, even if he's wearing diamonds as big as Easter eggs. If I was to catch my chap 'sociating with a nigger, 'y God, I'd take this gun and blow out his brains."

He turned to go, then paused benevolently. "You can ride the local out, boys. I won't bother you if you ride *that*. Only don't let me catch you trying to nail ahold of no Red Ball manifest. If you see them niggers, you come over to the switchman's shanty in the yards and let me know. Promise me one thing, boys. Promise me you won't *never* travel with or 'sociate with no damned niggers."

Suddenly a thundering and puffing filled the air. A Red Ball manifest was pulling majestically out of the train yards, shaking the earth as it moved. A trainman ran ahead to throw a switch to turn the freight onto the northbound line. *This one wasn't going toward Detroit.*

Three limping black boys broke from the cover of horseweeds a short distance from the jungle and made for the train.

"Hey!" shouted a white kid. "You can't ride a Red Ball manifest! They won't allow it."

"They won't allow *us* to do *nothing* if they can stop it," one of the dashing black kids scoffed, speeding up and grabbing hold. "Besides, it ain't going to Detroit! It's going the wrong way."

By this time the Red Ball was moving at a good clip. When the Negro boys caught the grab irons and tried to land a foot on the sill steps, the momentum made their bodies fly out horizontally like flags. After a brief, desperate struggle they wriggled themselves around and secured a foothold.

Chest heaving, voice half choked, one of them yelled, "We don't give a damn *where* it goes, just so it goes away from *here*. Any place but *here!*"

Against the background of revitalized civil rights efforts in the years since 1954 such anecdotes began to sound dated. Nevertheless, those who were quick to call this movement a revolution and to suggest that it represented a dramatic breakthrough in the Negro's struggle for full freedom in the United States were inclined to forget that nonviolent resistance as a means of opposing segregation had been tried repeatedly by Frederick Douglass more than a decade before the Civil War. He employed sit-in tactics in "white" waiting rooms and sections of trains by remaining in his seat until removed bodily by authorities. Teachers from Tuskegee Institute in Alabama, traveling out of Montgomery in the 1880s, were the original Freedom Riders, and they were supported by Booker T. Washington in a letter to the *Montgomery Advertiser*. The National Association for the Advancement of Colored People picketed on the streets and used other public demonstrations before the First World War. A. Philip Randolph's March on Washington movement preceded the events in Montgomery, Alabama, by a decade.

The crusade that started to roll in 1954 got its power not from any new philosophy or any break in the established lines of protest. It moved ahead because other factors had come into play, and efforts which formerly had produced only limited results now began to show spectacular returns. The enemy had grown weaker.

The bus boycott in Montgomery and the throbbing leadership of Martin Luther King, Jr., removed scales from the eyes of an indifferent and unconcerned, if not blind, nation. Suddenly the world became aware of energies and hopes that neither slavery nor slavery's aftermath had succeeded in crushing in American Negroes. But the revolutionary changes had *already* begun and might have been seen by anyone willing to observe. In 1944 the all-white primary was outlawed in the South, thanks to heroic efforts by the NAACP, and within a decade it activated nearly a million black voters in the states of the old Confederacy. Desegregation of the armed forces in the period between 1950 and 1952 was another mighty blow, perhaps a mortal one, to the old order, and the NAACP promptly readjusted its strategy. In 1951 it decided to abandon the legal fight for equalization of separate education and to press for the end of segregation itself. The Supreme Court's historic decision of 1954 followed as a next logical step, and segregation was deprived of legal respectability. What this released in the hearts and minds of Negroes themselves began to express itself in Montgomery in December of 1955.

It was not long before reverberations from the shattering changes down home began to reach the scattered millions in bitter Canaan. How many of them have since had second thoughts about their decisions to migrate out of the region may never be known, but it is worth recalling that Frederick Douglass, the wisest of the Negro leaders of the nineteenth century, had tried his best to persuade their parents and grandparents not to leave. He had been a runaway from slavery himself, and he had reasoned that the slave had a moral right to escape if he could and in the last analysis to attack his enslaver if that were necessary or possible. But after emancipation, Douglass rejected migration as a short-sighted and unsatisfactory solution to the freedman's citizenship problems. The Negro has the same right as any other American to be free in the place where he was born.

But to Douglass' dismay and the dismay of other Negro spokesmen after him, the disinherited masses decided to explore for themselves and see what the end would be. Perhaps it was not so much the hardships and deprivations of the South that they found intolerable as the myths it perpetrated: rustic preachers shouting that Negroes had no souls, no standing with God, so that it was no sin to lie to them, steal from them, or even take their lives; prominent men of John C. Calhoun's era maintaining that Negroes could not be educated, that their skulls hardened prematurely, making intellectual growth impossible.

What the migrants did not anticipate was that the North had its myths too, where they were concerned. One was the myth that Negroes had no history. Look at any schoolbook, any encyclopedia (in those years), where could you find anything worth mentioning about Negroes? Another was the myth of statistics. Count the illiterates, count the delinquents, count the fatherless, look at the matriarchal families. What could you expect? So without claiming that God had rejected Negroes or that they were born without capacity, the North constructed the rationale it needed for maintaining its ghettos, its more subtle and sometimes more deadly discrimination.

If the reception the Negro migrant received in the cities of the North and the West often seemed like a cruel jest, the vision and leadership he has been able to draw from the now changing South is equally ironic. It may not start a reverse migration, but it has at least given the soul brothers in Watts and Chicago and Harlem a new vocabulary.

A Selected List of References and Sources

ABRAMS, CHARLES, *Forbidden Neighbors: A Study of Prejudice in Housing,* New York, 1955.

ADAMS, RUSSELL L., *Great Negroes of the Past and Present,* Chicago, 1963.

AHMAN, MATTHEW, editor, *Race: Challenge to Religion,* Chicago, 1963.

APTHEKER, HERBERT, editor, *A Documentary History of the Negro in the United States,* New York, 1951.

ARNOLD, EDWARD F., "Some Personal Reminiscences of Paul Laurence Dunbar," *Journal of Negro History,* October 1932.

BAILER, L. H., "The Negro Automobile Worker," *Journal of Political Economy,* October 1943.

BAKER, RAY STANNARD, "The Negro Goes North," *World's Work,* July 1917.

BARNARD, HARRY, *Eagle Forgotten: The Life of John Peter Altgeld,* Indianapolis and New York, 1938.

BARNETTE, AUBREY, with EDWARD LINN, "The Black Muslims Are a Fraud," *Saturday Evening Post,* February 27, 1965.

BASS, CHARLOTTA A., *Forty Years,* Los Angeles, 1960.

BEASLEY, DELILAH LEONTIUM, *The Negro Trail Blazers of California,* Los Angeles, 1919.

BECKWOURTH, JAMES P., *Life and Adventures of James P. Beckwourth,* T. D. Bonner, editor, New York, 1856.

BELL, CHARLES R., JR., "A Southern Approach to the Color Issue," *Christian Century,* August 9, 1944.

BENNETT, LERONE, JR., *Before the Mayflower,* Chicago, 1964.

——, "The Ghost of Marcus Garvey," *Ebony,* March 1960.

——, *The Negro Mood,* Chicago, 1965.

——, *What Manner of Man?* Chicago, 1965.

BENYON, ERDMANN D., "The Voodoo Cult Among Negro Migrants in Detroit," *American Journal of Sociology,* July 1937, May 1938.

BERGER, MORROE, "The Black Muslims," *Horizon,* Winter 1964.

BERRY, EDWIN C., "Jobs, Poverty and Race," *Negro Digest,* September 1964.

BLOCH, SARA, "Youth Crusades for a Better Democracy," *Common Ground,* Autumn 1944.

BONE, ROBERT, *The Negro Novel in America,* New Haven, 1958.

BONTEMPS, ARNA, *100 Years of Negro Freedom,* New York, 1961.

BOOKER, SIMEON, *Black Man's America,* New York, 1964.

BOWEN, LOUISE DE KOVEN, "The Colored People of Chicago," *Survey,* November 1, 1913.

BOYD, MALCOLM, "A Voice Through the Wall," *Renewal,* April 1965.

BOYKIN, ULYSSES W., *A Hand Book on the Detroit Negro,* Detroit, 1943.

BRADEN, ANNE, *The Wall Between,* New York, 1958.

BRAWLEY, BENJAMIN, *Paul Laurence Dunbar, Poet of His People,* Chapel Hill, 1936.

——, *Your Negro Neighbor,* New York, 1918.

BRINK, WILLIAM, and LOUIS HARRIS, *The Negro Revolution in America,* New York, 1964.

BRODERICK, FRANCIS L., *W. E. B. Du Bois,* Stanford, Calif., 1959.

BROWN, EARL, and GEORGE R. LEIGHTON, *The Negro and the War,* New York, 1942.

——, *Why Race Riots?* New York, 1944.

BURCH, PETER, *One Gallant Rush: Robert Gould Shaw and His Brave Black Regiment,* New York, 1965.

BUTCHER, MARGARET JUST, *The Negro in American Culture,* New York, 1956.

CAMPBELL, E. SIMMS, "Blues Are the Negroes' Lament," *Esquire,* December 1939.

——, "Jam in the Nineties," *Esquire,* December 1938.

CAREW, ROY, AND DON E. FOWLER, "Scott Joplin, Overlooked

Genius," *Record Changer,* September, October, November 1944.

CARLSON, JOHN ROY, *Under Cover,* New York, 1943.

CARROLL, CHARLES, *The Negro a Beast, or, In the Image of God,* St. Louis, 1900.

CAYTON, HORACE R., *Long Old Road,* New York, 1965.

——, "The Psychological Approach to Race Relations," *Reed College Bulletin,* November 1946.

CAYTON, HORACE R., and GEORGE S. MITCHELL, *Black Workers and the New Unions,* Chapel Hill, 1939.

——, "Negro Housing in Chicago," *Social Action,* April 15, 1940.

CHICAGO COMMISSION ON RACE RELATIONS, *The Negro in Chicago: A Study of Race Relations and a Race Riot,* Chicago, 1922.

CHICAGO CONFERENCE ON CIVIC UNITY, *Human Relations in Chicago, 1949,* Chicago, 1949.

CIO COMMITTEE TO ABOLISH RACIAL DISCRIMINATION, *Working and Fighting Together,* Washington, D. C., n.d.

COFFEY, RAYMOND R., "Negroes, Yes, But How Many?" Chicago *Daily News,* February 20, 1965.

COGLEY, JOHN, "Segregation: the Tender Trap," *Commonweal,* June 14, 1963.

COMMITTEE OF THE NATIONAL DE SAIBLE MEMORIAL SOCIETY, *Some Historical Facts About Jean Baptiste Point de Saible,* Chicago, 1933.

CONANT, JAMES B., *Slums and Suburbs,* New York, 1961.

CONFERENCE ON EDUCATION AND RACE RELATIONS, *America's Tenth Man,* Atlanta, 1942.

CONGRESS OF INDUSTRIAL ORGANIZATIONS, *The CIO and the Negro Worker,* Washington, D. C., n.d.

CONRAD, EARL, *Harriet Tubman,* Washington, D. C., 1943.

COPE, MYRON, "Muslim Champ," *Saturday Evening Post,* November 14, 1964.

COX, OLIVER CROMWELL, *Caste, Class & Race,* Garden City, 1948.

CRONON, EDMUND DAVID, *Black Moses; The Story of Marcus Garvey and the Universal Negro Improvement Association,* Madison, Wisc., 1955.

Current Biography, New York.

DABNEY, WENDELL P., *Cincinnati's Colored Citizens, Historical, Sociological, and Biographical,* Cincinnati, 1926.

DALE, HARRISON CLIFFORD, editor, *Ashley-Smith Explorations and the Discovery of a Central Route to the Pacific, 1822–1829; with the original journals,* Cleveland, 1918.

DELANEY, MARTIN R., *The Condition, Elevation, Emigration, and Destiny of the Colored People of the United States, Politically Considered,* Philadelphia, 1852.

DEMUTH, JERRY, "Race in the Land of Lincoln," *Commonweal,* April 5, 1963.

DE VOTO, BERNARD, introduction to the Americana Deserta edition of *Life and Adventures of James P. Beckwourth,* New York, 1931.

Dictionary of American Biography, 1936.

DONALD, HENDERSON H., "The Negro Migration of 1916–18," *Journal of Negro History,* October 1921.

DOUGLASS, FREDERICK, *Life and Times of Frederick Douglass,* Centenary Memorial Subscribers' Edition, New York, 1941.

DRAKE, ST. CLAIR, *Churches and Voluntary Associations in the Chicago Negro Community* (mimeographed WPA report), Chicago, 1940.

DRAKE, ST. CLAIR, and HORACE R. CAYTON, *Black Metropolis,* New York, 1945.

DU BOIS, W. E. B., "Back to Africa," *Century,* February 1923.

——, *Dusk of Dawn,* New York, 1940.

——, "Marcus Garvey," *Crisis,* December 20, 1920.

——, *The Philadelphia Negro,* Philadelphia, 1899.

——, *The World and Africa,* New York, 1947.

DUNN, ROBERT W., *Labor and Automobiles,* New York, 1929.

DURHAM, PHILIP, and EVERETT L. JONES, *The Negro Cowboys,* New York, 1965.

EISMANN, BERNARD N., "Black Muslim Leadership: Fanatics or Opportunists?" *FOCUS/Midwest,* March-April 1963.

ESSIEN-UDOM, E. U., *Black Nationalism,* Chicago, 1962.

EULAU, HEINZ H. F., "False Prophets in the Bible Belt," *New Republic,* February 7, 1944.

EWEN, DAVID, *Men of Popular Music,* Chicago, 1944.

FALK, BERNARD, *The Naked Lady,* London, 1934.

FARMER, SILAS, *The History of Detroit and Michigan,* 2 vols., Detroit, 1899.

FAUSET, ARTHUR HUFF, *Black Gods of the Metropolis,* Philadelphia, 1944.

FELDMAN, EUGENE P. R., *Figures in Negro History,* Chicago, 1964.

FISHER, MILES MARK, *Negro Slave Songs in the United States,* Ithaca, N. Y., 1953.

FLEMING, WALTER L., " 'Pap' Singleton, the Moses of the Colored Exodus," *American Journal of Sociology,* July 1909.

FLYNN, BETTY, "The Battle of Ben Willis," *Renewal,* March 1965.

FRANKLIN, JOHN HOPE, *From Slavery to Freedom,* New York, 1956.

FRAZIER, E. FRANKLIN, *Black Bourgeoisie,* Glencoe, Ill., 1957.

——, *The Negro Family in the United States,* Chicago, 1939.

——, *The Negro in the United States,* New York, 1951.

FRITCHEY, CLAYTON, "Karamu," *Junior Red Cross Journal,* December, 1941.

GARDNER, JIGGS, "The Murder of Malcolm X," *Monthly Review,* April 1965.

GARVEY, A. JACQUES, *Garvey and Garveyism,* Kingston, Jamaica, 1963.

——, *Philosophies and Opinions of Marcus Garvey,* New York, 1923.

GARVEY, MARCUS, *Aims and Objectives of a Movement for a Solution of the Negro Problem Outlined,* New York, 1924.

GLUCK, ELSIE, *John Mitchell, Miner,* New York, 1929.

GORMAN, HERBERT, *The Incredible Marquis, Alexandre Dumas,* New York, 1929.

GRANGER, LESTER B., "On the Job," *Negro Digest,* June 1944.

HAFEN, LEROY R., "The Last Years of James P. Beckwourth," *Colorado Magazine,* August 1928.

HALDEMAN-JULIUS, MARCET, *Clarence Darrow's Two Great Trials,* Girard, Kans., 1927.

HALEY, J. EVETTS, *A Texan Looks at Lyndon,* Canyon, Texas, 1964.

HANDLIN, OSCAR, *Fire-Bell in the Night: The Crisis in Civil Rights,* Boston, 1964.

HANDY, W. C., *Father of the Blues,* New York, 1941.

HARTGROVE, W. B., "The Story of Maria Louise Moore and Fannie M. Richards," *Journal of Negro History,* January 1916.

HAVIGHURST, ROBERT J., "A Positive Approach," *Renewal,* March 1965.

HAYNES, GEORGE E., *The Negro Newcomers in Detroit,* New York, 1918.

HERNTON, CALVIN C., *Sex and Racism in America,* Garden City, 1965.

HILL, T. A., "Why Southern Negroes Don't Go South," *Survey,* November 29, 1929.

HORWELL, H. W., "A Negro Exodus," *Contemporary Review,* September 1918.

HOWARD, GEORGE ELLIOTT, "The Social Cost of Southern Race Prejudice," *American Journal of Sociology,* March 1917.

HULSIZER, KENNETH, "Jelly Roll Morton in Washington," *Jazz Music* (London), February-March 1944.

HUMPHREY, HUBERT H., editor, *Integration vs. Segregation,* New York, 1964.

HYAMS, JOE, "Negroes Find California Is No Promised Land," Chicago *Sun-Times,* October 25, 1962.

ISAACS, HAROLD R., *The New World of Negro Americans,* New York, 1963.

JOHNSON, CHARLES S., "How Much Is the Migration a Flight from Persecution?" *Opportunity,* September 1923.

——, *Patterns of Negro Segregation,* New York, 1943.

——, *Shadow of the Plantation,* Chicago, 1934.

JOHNSON, JAMES WELDON, *Black Manhattan,* New York, 1930.

JOHNSON, SISTER CHRISTINE, *Muhammad's Children: a First Grade Reader,* Nation of Islam, Chicago, 1963.

JOHNSON, WILBUR, "Landlord's Black Market," *Progress Guide,* October 1944.

JONES, JOHN, *The Black Laws of Illinois and a Few Reasons Why They Should Be Repealed,* Chicago, 1864.

JONES, MAX, "Ferdinand Joseph Morton—A Biography," *Jazz Music* (London), February-March 1944.

KAHN, TOM, *Unfinished Revolution,* New York, 1960.

KENDALL, JOHN S., "The World's Delight: The Story of Adah Isaacs Menken," *Louisiana Historical Quarterly,* Vol. 21, January-October 1938.

KENNEDY, LOUISE VENABLE, *The Negro Peasant Turns Cityward,* New York, 1930.

KESTER, HOWARD, *Revolt Among the Sharecroppers,* New York, 1936.

KISER, CLYDE V., *Sea Island to City,* New York, 1932.

KLEIMAN, CAROL, "Breaking the Housing Barrier," *Renewal,* April-May 1964.

——, "Mission in Suburbia," *Renewal,* April 1965.

LAWSON, WARNER, "Music and Negroes," *Progressive,* December 1962.

LEAVELL, R. H., et al., *Negro Migration in 1916–17,* U. S. Department of Labor Publications, Washington, D. C., 1919.

LEE, ALFRED MCCLUNG, and NORMAN DAYMOND HUMPHREY, *Race Riot,* New York, 1943.

LEMLEY, LUTHER HENRY, *Liberia: The Inside Story,* New York, 1963.

LEONARD, OSCAR, "The East St. Louis Pogrom," *Survey,* July 14, 1917.

LEVENSON, FRANCIS, and MARGARET FISHER, "The Struggle for Open Housing," *Progressive,* December 1962.

LEWIS, EDWARD E., "The Southern Negro and the American Labor Supply," *Political Science Quarterly,* June 1933.

LEWIS, PAUL, *Queen of the Plaza: A Biography of Adah Isaacs Menken,* New York, 1964.

LINCOLN, C. ERIC, *The Black Muslims in America,* Boston, 1961.

——, "The Meaning of Malcolm X," *Christian Century,* April 7, 1965.

——, *My Face Is Black,* Boston, 1964.

LLOYD, HENRY D., *A Strike of Millionaires Against Miners, or, The Story of Spring Valley,* Chicago, 1890.

LOBER, VIVIAN J., "The Mosque: Adaptations of a Muslim Congregation in Chicago," unpublished M.A. thesis, University of Chicago, Chicago, 1958.

LOGAN, MILLA Z., "Racial Discrimination Not Allowed," *Common Ground,* Summer 1944.

LOGAN, RAYFORD, editor, *What the Negro Wants,* Chapel Hill, 1944.

LOMAX, LOUIS E., *When the Word Is Given,* Cleveland and New York, 1963.

LONG, RICHARD A., "Those Magnolia Myths," *Nation*, July 7, 1956.

LOVETT, ROBERT MORSS, "Emperor Jones of Finance," *New Republic,* July 11, 1923.

MACMAHON, DOUGLAS, "The Real Philadelphia Story," *New Masses,* August 29, 1944.

MCWILLIAMS, CAREY, *Brothers Under the Skin,* Boston, 1943.

——, *Ill Fares the Land,* Boston, 1942.

MAILER, NORMAN, *The White Negro,* San Francisco, 1957.

MALCOLM X, "I'm Talking to You, White Man," *Saturday Evening Post*, September 12, 1964.

MAUND, ALFRED, "New Day Dawning: The Negro and Medicine," *Nation,* May 9, 1953.

Mayor's Conference on Race Relations, *City Planning in Race Relations,* Chicago, 1944.

MEEHAN, THOMAS A., "Jean Baptiste Point du Saible—the First Chicagoan," *Mid-America: an Historical Review,* Vol. 19, No. 2.

MEEKER, B. EZRA, *Reminiscences of the Pioneers of the Puget Sound,* Seattle, 1905.

MOTON, ROBERT RUSSA, *What the Negro Thinks,* New York, 1929.

MUSE, BENJAMIN, *Ten Years of Prelude: The Story of Integration Since the Supreme Court's 1954 Decision,* New York, 1964.

NORRIS, HOKE, editor, *We Dissent,* New York, 1962.

NORTHUP, HERBERT R., *Organized Labor and the Negro,* New York, 1944.

NORTHWOOD, L. K., and ERNEST A. T. BARTH, *Urban Desegregation: Negro Pioneers and Their White Neighbors,* Seattle, 1965.

OLIVER, REVILO P., "The Black Muslims," *American Opinion,* January 1963.

OTTLEY, ROI, *The Lonely Warrior: The Life and Times of Robert S. Abbott,* Chicago, 1955.

PARKS, GORDON, "What Their Cry Means to Me: A Negro's Own Evaluation of the Black Muslims," *Life,* May 30, 1963.

PAULI, HERTHA, *Her Name Was Sojourner Truth,* New York, 1962.

PICKENS, WILLIAM, "Africa for the Africans," *Nation,* December 28, 1921.

PLIMPTON, GEORGE, "Miami Notebook: Cassius Clay and Malcolm X," *Harper's,* June 1964.

PORTER, JAMES A., *Modern Negro Art,* New York, 1943.

PORTER, KENNETH W., "Negroes and Indians on the Texas Frontier," *Journal of Negro History,* July-October 1956.

——, "Relations Between Negroes and Indians Within the Present Limits of the United States," *Journal of Negro History,* July 1932, July 1933.

POWDERLY, TERENCE V., *Thirty Years of Labor, 1859–1889,* Columbus, Ohio, 1889.

POWDERMAKER, HORTENSE, *"After Freedom,"* New York, 1939.

PRICE, WILLIAM A., "Malcolm's Death Spotlights Gap Between Negro and White," *National Guardian,* March 6, 1965.

QUAIFE, MILO MILTON, *Checagou: From Indian Wigwam to Modern City,* Chicago, 1933.

——, *Chicago and the Old Northwest, 1673–1835,* Chicago, 1913.

RACE RELATIONS PROGRAM OF THE AMERICAN MISSIONARY ASSOCIATION AND THE JULIUS ROSENWALD FUND, *The Negro War Worker in San Francisco,* San Francisco, 1944.

RAMSEY, FREDERICK, JR., and CHARLES EDWARD SMITH, *Jazzmen,* New York, 1939.

RANDOLPH, A. PHILIP, "The Unfinished Revolution," *Progressive,* December 1962.

REDDICK, L. D., "Du Sable and His Day," unpublished manuscript.

REDDING, J. SAUNDERS, *The Lonesome Road,* Garden City, 1958.

——, *They Came in Chains,* Philadelphia, 1950.

REID, IRA DE A., *The Negro Immigrant,* New York, 1939.

REX, ARTHUR, "Man or Ape," *Protestant,* May 1944.

ROBERTS, W. ADOLPHE, *The French in the West Indies,* Indianapolis, 1942.

ROSEN, HARRY M., and DAVID H., *But Not Next Door,* New York, 1962.

ROSS, M. H., "Labor and the South," *Nation,* July 7, 1956.

ROWAN, CARL, *Go South to Sorrow,* New York, 1957.

ROWLAND, WILMINA, "How It Is in Mississippi," *Christian Century,* March 17, 1965.

RUDWICK, ELLIOTT M., *Race Riot at East St. Louis, July 2, 1917,* Carbondale, Ill., 1964.

SANCTON, THOMAS, "The Race Riots," *New Republic,* July 5, 1943.

SAVAGE, W. SHERMAN, "The Negro in the History of the Pacific Northwest," *Journal of Negro History,* July 1928.

——, "The Negro in the Westward Movement," *Journal of Negro History,* October 1940.

SAXON, LYLE, *Fabulous New Orleans,* New York, 1928.

SCOTT, EMMETT J., compiler, "Letters of Negro Migrants of 1916–1918," *Journal of Negro History,* July 1919.

——, compiler, "Additional Letters of Negro Migrants of 1916–1918," *Journal of Negro History,* October 1919.

——, *Negro Migration During the War,* New York, 1920.

SCROGGS, W. O., "Interstate Migration," *Journal of Political Economy,* December 1917.

SHOGAN, ROBERT, and TOM CRAIG, *The Detroit Race Riot,* Philadelphia and New York, 1964.

SILBERMAN, CHARLES E., *Crisis in Black and White,* New York, 1964.

SIMMONS, WILLIAM J., *Men of Mark: Eminent, Progressive and Rising,* Cleveland, 1887.

SINCLAIR, HAROLD, *The Port of New Orleans,* New York, 1942.

SKLAR, BERNARD, "Crossing the No Man's Land Between Black and White," *Free,* Spring 1964.

SMITH, CHARLES EDWARD, with FREDERIC RAMSEY, JR., CHARLES PAYNE RUSSELL, and WILLIAM RUSSELL, *The Jazz Record Book,* New York, 1942.

SOUTHERN CALIFORNIA RESEARCH COUNCIL, *Migration and the Southern California Economy,* Los Angeles, 1964.

SOUTHSIDE COMMUNITY COMMITTEE, *Bright Shadows in Bronzetown,* Chicago, 1949.

SPERO, STERLING D., and ABRAM L. HARRIS, *The Black Worker,* New York, 1931.

STILL, WILLIAM, *Underground Railroad Records,* revised edition with introduction by James P. Boyd, "William Still: His Life and Works to This Time," Philadelphia, 1886.

STRAUS, NATHAN, *The Seven Myths of Housing,* New York, 1944.

SUTHERLAND, ROBERT L., *Color, Class, and Personality,* Washington, D. C., 1942.

SYRKIN, MARIE, "Jim Crow in the Classroom," *Common Ground,* Summer 1944.

TAEUBER, KARL E. and ALMA F., "The Changing Character of Negro Migration," *American Journal of Sociology,* January 1965.

THOMPSON, ERA BELL, *Africa, Land of My Fathers,* Garden City, 1954.

THORPE, EARLE D., *The Mind of the Negro: An Intellectual History of Afro-Americans,* Baton Rouge, La., 1961.

TINKER, EDWARD LAROCQUE, "Les Cenelles," *Colophon,* September 1930.

TOZIER, ROY and ALMA, "The Battle of the Bible Belt," *New Republic,* March 10, 1941.

TROTTER, JAMES MONROE, *Music and Some Highly Musical People,* New York, 1878.

TURNER, E. R., *The Negro in Pennsylvania,* Washington, D. C., 1911.

VERNON, ROBERT, *The Black Ghetto,* New York, 1964.

VILLARD, OSWALD GARRISON, *John Brown, 1800–1859, a Biography Fifty Years After,* Boston, 1910.

WADE, RICHARD C., *Slavery in the Cities,* New York, 1964.

WALLING, WILLIAM ENGLISH, "Race War in the North," *Independent,* September 3, 1908.

WALROND, ERIC, "Imperator Africanus," *Independent,* January 3, 1923.

WARE, NORMAN J., *The Labor Movement in the United States, 1860–1895,* New York, 1929.

WASHINGTON, F. B., "Welcoming Southern Negroes; East St. Louis and Detroit a Contrast," *Survey,* July 14, 1917.

WECHSLER, JAMES A., "The Cult of Malcolm X," *Progressive,* June 1964.

WECKLER, J. E., and THEO E. HALL, *The Police and Minority Groups,* Chicago, 1944.

WESLEY, CHARLES H., *Negro Labor in the United States,* New York, 1927.

WESTIN, ALAN F., editor, *Freedom Now!* New York, 1964.

WHITE, ELINOR, editor, *Excerpts of the Late Marcus Garvey,* Robbins, Ill., n.d.

WHITE, WALTER, and THURGOOD MARSHALL, *What Caused the Detroit Riot?* New York, 1944.

WILLE, LOIS, "From Malthus to Maremont," *Renewal,* February 1964.

WILLIAMS, PAUL R., "If I Were Young Today," *Ebony,* August 1963.

WILLKIE, WENDELL L., "The Case for Minorities," *Saturday Evening Post,* June 27, 1942.

WILSON, WOODROW, "An Appeal to America Not Yet Written," *Nation,* August 9, 1919.

WISH, HARVEY, editor, *The Negro Since Emancipation*, New York, 1964.

WOOD, EDITH ELMER, *Slums and Blighted Areas in the United States,* Federal Emergency Administration of Public Works, Housing Division Bulletin No. 1, Washington, D. C., 1935.

WOODSON, CARTER GOODWIN, *A Century of Negro Migration,* Washington, D. C., 1918.

——, "Negroes of Cincinnati Prior to the Civil War," *Journal of Negro History,* Vol. 1, 1916.

WOODWARD, E. VANN, "The South in Perspective," *Progressive,* December 1962.

——, *The Strange Career of Jim Crow,* New York, 1955.

WRITERS' PROGRAM OF THE WPA, *Illinois: A Descriptive and Historical Guide,* Chicago, 1939.

——, *Louisiana: A Guide to the State*, New York, 1941.

——, *Missouri: A Guide to the "Show Me" State,* New York, 1941.

ZINN, HOWARD, *SNCC: The New Abolitionists*, Boston, 1964.

Index

Abbott, Robert Sengstacke, 92, 103-07, 202, 203
Abolish Peonage Committee, 190
Abolition, 38, 44, 46, 47, 307
Abyssinian Movement, 204
ACT, 334, 341, 342
Adams, Henry, 54, 56, 62
Adler, Bernie, 120
Adventures, by Jim Beckwourth, 30
Africa, return to, *see* Colonization
"Africa for the Africans," 194, 198
Africa Times and Orient Review, 192
African art, 282
African Communities League, 201
African Methodist Episcopal Church, 81, 197
Afro-American League, 100
Afro-Peoples Centre, 214
Age (New York), 98
Age-Herald (Birmingham), 160, 161
Albans, Ben, Jr., 252
Alcorn College, 260
Ali, John, 230
Alinsky, Saul D., 275
All-white primary, 346
Aluminum Ore Company, 152
American Anti-Slavery Society, 72
American Book and Bible House, 108
American Colonization Society, 195, 196
American Council on Race Relations, 323
American Federation of Labor (AFL), 296, 311, 318
American Railway Union, 140
Anderson, Alfred, 104
Anderson, Glenn, 272, 277
Anderson, Marian, 311
Anthony, Susan B., 101
Anti-Caste Society of Great Britain, 99
Anti-Catholicism, 298
Anti-lynching leagues, 101
Anti-Semitism, 186, 298, 323
Anti-slavery publications, 36, 72-73
Anti-slavery societies, 38, 72, 75, 288
Anti-Strikers' Railroad Union, 140
Archer, Frank, 85
Armour, P. D., 64
Armour Company, 154
Armstrong, Louis, 253, 254, 256
Armstrong, Samuel C., 103
Art, 81-82, 282, 283
Ashley, William Henry, 23-25
Ashley-Smith Explorations, 30
Ashwood, Amy, 213
Associated Automobile Workers, 296
Atlantic Exposition, 261
Automotive Industrial Workers' Association, 296
Avendorph, Julius N., 104

"Back-to-Africa" movement, 198, 199, 211
"Baggage Coach Ahead," by Gussie L. Davis, 85
Bagnall, Robert W., 200, 215
Ball, Thomas C., 81
Ballad of Chicago, by Win Stracke, 321
Baltimore and Ohio Railroad, 310
Bankhead, Tallulah, 283
Banks, N. P., 77
Banner (Nashville), 159

Baquet, George, 253
Barasso, Fred, 251
Barclay, Edwin, 209
Barclay, James Paul, 129
Barnes, Jack, 242
Barnett, Ferdinand L., 98, 99, 101, 170, 171; for his wife, *see* Wells, Ida B.
Barnette, Aubrey, 225, 230
Bear Flag Party, 264
Bechet, Sidney, 253
Beckwourth, James P. (Jim), 21-31, 257; *Adventures,* 30
Bell, Philip, 36
Belle Isle Park, Detroit, 300
Benbow, Will, 250
Benecia Boy, *see* Heenan, John C.
Bennett, Lerone, Jr., 214
Berry, Edwin C., 341
Beware of Strangers (movie), 171
Bilbo, Theodore, 209
Birney, James Gillespie, 72-73
Black Cross Navigation Company, 203
Black Cross nurses, 193
Black Guards, 298
Black Laws, 48
Black Laws of Illinois and a Few Reasons Why They Should Be Repealed, by John Jones, 48
Black Legion, 298, 301
Black Man, 212
"Black Moses," *see* Singleton, Benjamin
Black Muslims, 216, 217-46
Black Muslims in America, The, by C. Eric Lincoln, 244
Black Pearl Harbor, 324
Black Star Steamship Line, 194, 198, 201, 202, 203, 214
Blackburn, Thornton, 287-88
Blackfoot Indians, 26
Bliss, Philemon, 80
"Block busting," 305, 319
"Bloody Monday," 304
"Bloody Sunday," 306
Blues, 114, 249
Bok, Curtis, 310
Bolden, Buddy, 253, 254
Boll weevil, 159
Bombings, 175-76
Bonner, T. D., 23, 29
Booker T. Washington (ship), 203
Boyd, Henry, 83
Bradford, Mrs. Annie, 278
Brawley, Benjamin, 97
Breiner, Leon, 294
Bristol, V. A., 295
British Guiana, 195
Broad Ax, 105
Brooks, Shelton, 120
Brown, Edmund G., 272, 274, 276
Brown, Elmer, 283
Brown, Frank London, 325
Brown, John, 2, 41, 43, 51, 288
Brown, John, Jr., 65
Brown, William Welles, 42
Bruce, Blanche K., 133
Brymn, Tim, 120
Bucktown, Cincinnati, 84-85
Bullet Club, 298
Bundy, LeRoy A., 155
Burleigh, Harry T., 93
Burton, Scott, 147
Bush, George William, 257-58
Butler, Benjamin F., 77
Butler, Norman 3X, 238

Cadillac, Antoine de la Mothe, 287
Calhoun, John C., 347
Campbell, E. Simms, 252
Campbell, S. Bronson, 118
Carew, Roy, 114
Carlo, Fred, 283
Carney, Frank, 313
"Carpetbaggers," 54
Carroll, Charles, 108, 211
Carter, H. C., 77
Carver, George Washington, 322
Casner, George, 21
"Cavy," 211, 217
Cayton, Horace Roscoe, 260-63
Cayton, Horace, Jr., 264
Cayton, Madge, 264
Cayton, Revels, 264, 318
Central Body of Trade and Labor Unionists, 152
Century of Progress, 88
Chafin, Eugene W., 148
Chan, Tom Y., 323
Charles Eisenman Award, 283
Charles P. Taft Museum, 82
Chauvin, Louis, 120
Checagou, by Milo M. Quaife, 12
Chesnutt, Charles W., 133
Cheyenne Indians, 27
Chicago, 1, 3-4, 12, 13, 15, 20, 64, 119-20, 135, 140, 160-74, 175-90, 202, 205, 217, 224, 229-30, 232, 239, 321-42
Chicago Association of Commerce, 183
Chicago City Council, 331

Chicago Colored Women's Club, 140
Chicago Federation of Labor, 135, 136, 137, 182
Chicago Historical Society, 20
Chicago Housing Authority, 337
Chicago Mayor's Commission on Race Relations, 323, 324
Chicago Race Commission, 183
Chicago Real Estate Board, 331
Chicago Urban League, 161, 169, 177, 186, 327, 339, 340, 341
Chicago-Virden Coal Company, 144
Chicago World's Fair (Columbian Exposition), 3, 88-110
"Chief Sam," 202
Childs, A. L., 76
Chittenden, Hiram M., 30
Christian Century, 275
Chrysler Corporation, 296
Cincinnati, 73-77, 81, 84, 93
CIO, 109, 311, 312, 313, 318
Civil Rights law, 68
Civil rights workers, 270, 306, 334-36, 345-46
Clamorgan, Jacques, 19
Clark, Peter H., 81
Clarkson, Thomas, 194
Clay, Cassius, 239
Clay, Henry, 195
Clayton, Garrison, 305
Clere, Richard, 44
Cleveland, Grover, 69
Cleveland, Ohio, 279-86
Cleveland Historical Society, 282
Cleveland Museum of Art, 282
Cleveland School of Art, 282
Coal mining, 141-47
Coffield, John, 276
Coffin, Levi, 287
Colburn, W. F., 76
Cole, Edward, 72
Coles, Edward, 194
Colonization, 54-71, 72; abroad, 49, 50, 67, 70, 194-96
Color, Class and Personality, by Robert L. Sutherland, 310
Colored America, 36
Colored American Day (Chicago World's Fair), 89, 92, 103, 197
Colored Emigration and Commercial Convention, 198
Colored Men's Protective Association, 89, 92
Colored National Labor Union, 137
Colored Orphan Asylum, 308
Columbian Exposition (Chicago World's Fair), 88-110
Commercial Gazette (Cincinnati), 84
Common Ground, by Milla S. Logan, 317
Comstock, Elizabeth L., 65
Congress of Racial Equality (CORE), 334
Conklin, Seth, 40
Conrad, Earl, 41, 107
Conroy, Jack, 107
Conservator, 99, 101
Conway, Thomas W., 61
Cook, John, 93
Cook, Will Marion, 86, 92, 93, 119, 290
Cook County Women's Clubs, 99
Coordinating Council of Community Organizations (CCCO), 334, 335, 336
Cotton, 159, 185
Crampton, Charlotte, 127
Creole Band, 251
Creoles, 123-24, 253, 255
Crisis, 193
Croquére, Basil, 247, 255
Cross and Flag, 302
Crosse, William, 162
Crow Indians, 27
Cuffee, Paul, 195
Cunningham, William Tolliver, 190
Currie, Andrew, 55

Dabney, Wendell Philips, 85, 92, 93
Daily News (Chicago), 336, 337, 339
Dalcour, P., 130
Dale, Harrison Clifford, 30
Daley, Richard J., 335, 336, 337, 338, 341
Dandonneau, *see* Du Sable, Jean Baptiste Point
Darrow, Clarence, 294-95
Davenport, H. George, 186
Davis, Gussie L., 85-86
Davis, Ossie, 241-42
Dawud, Talib Ahmad, 227
Dean, Harry, 103
De Baptiste, George, 46, 288
De Baptiste, Richard, 46, 99, 290
De Barry, Joe, 150
Debs, Eugene V., 140
Dédè, Edmond, 247, 254
Deere, John, 64
Defender (Chicago), 102, 104, 106-07, 109, 158, 161, 162, 163, 166, 167, 168, 169, 170, 171, 185, 202

Delaney, Martin R., 196
Democratic party newspapers, attitude toward Negroes, 89
Democrats, 47
de Peyster, Arent, 13
Depression, 185, 296
Desegregation, in armed forces, 346
Desdume, Mamie, 248
Detroit, 13, 15, 216-24, 287-306
Detroit Anti-Slavery Society, 288
Detroit Council for Human Rights, 306
Detroit Urban League, 292
De Voto, Bernard, 30
Diggs, Charles D., 109
Dixie, William, 313
Dixon, Mill, 120
Dodson, Jacob, 264
Donegan, William, 148
Douglass, Frederick, 41, 43, 46, 49, 51, 60-61, 67, 80, 92, 93, 94, 97, 137, 197, 288, 345, 346
Douglass, Joseph, 93
Douglass, Lewis H., 137
Dred Scott decision, 48
Drew, Timothy, 205-08, 217, 223
Du Bois, W. E. B., 41, 102, 107, 193, 200, 201, 213, 215, 294, 308
DuBay, William, 276
Duff, James, 264
Dumas, Alexandre, *père,* 125, 126, 129-31
Dunbar, Joshua, 93
Dunbar, Paul Laurence, 86, 92, 93-97, 175
Duncanson, Robert S., 81-82
Dunham, Richard C., 110
Durham, Philip, 7
Du Sable, Jean Baptiste Point, 12-20
Du Sable, Jean Baptiste Point, Jr., 17
Duse Mohammed Ali, 192
Dusen, Frank, 251
Dusk to Dawn, by W. E. B. Du Bois, 308
Dutrey, Honoré, 253
Dyer, C. V., 46
Dynamite, 186

East St. Louis, Ill., 150-57
Ebony, 214
Edward W. Bok award, 311
Eisenhower, Dwight D., 277
El Hajj Malek El-Shabazz, *see* Malcolm X
Elijah Muhammad, 217, 222, 223-34, 238, 239, 240, 243, 244
Embree, Edwin R., 323, 324
Emigration, *see* Migration
Emigration Aid Society, 61, 63, 64, 65
Emigration societies, 195-97
Emigration Society of Raleigh, 197
Emperor Jones, 120, 281
Encyclopedia Africana, 213
Engram, William, 152
Erbaugh, Cecil, 305
"Ere Sleep Comes Down to Soothe the Weary Eyes," by Paul Laurence Dunbar, 96
Ethiopia, 67, 204, 208-11
"Ethiopia, Thou Land of Our Fathers," 193
Ethiopian-Pacific Movement, 208
Evening Journal (Chicago), 56, 68, 89, 91, 106, 142
"Exode," by W. H. Stillwell, 53
Exodus (Exodusters, Exodust train), 2, 54, 71, 158-74

Fair Employment Practices Commission (FEPC), 299, 310, 311, 313
Fair Housing Committees, 328
Fair Housing Listing Service, 319
Fard, W. D., 216-23, 240
Faulkner, William, 288-89
Fauset, Jessie R., 310
Federal Civil Rights Act, 50
Federation of Colored Women's Clubs, 99
Federation of Neighborhood Associations, 324
Ferrell, Frank J., 138-39
"Ficaters," 154
Field, Marshall, 323
Fisk University, 98, 145, 328
Fitzgerald Community Council, 305
Flight, by Walter White, 131
Flory, Ishmael P., 189
Fool's Errand, A, by Albion Tourgée, 89
Ford, Henry, 291
Ford Motor Company, 297
Fortune, T. Thomas, 98, 100
"Forty acres and a mule," 57
Fowler, Don E., 114
"Frankie and Johnny," 121
Fraternity, 99
Frederick Douglass (ship), 201
Free Democrats, 47
Free Press (Detroit), 304

Free Speech, 98
Freedman's Aid Society Schools, 81, 98
Freedom marches, 306, 334-35, 345
Freedom Riders, 345
Freeman, H. Lawrence, 120
Freer, L. C. Paine, 46
Frémont, John C., 264
Frey, Donald S., 110
Fruit of Islam (FOI), 219, 226, 236, 239, 240
Frye, Marquette, 270
Fugitive Slave Law, 3, 288
Fuqua, Carl, 341
Fur trapping, 23
Furlough Track, Los Angeles, 5-11

Gaines, Charles G., 264
Gaines, John I., 81
Gans, Baby Joe, *see* Slaughter, Babe
Garfield, James A., 81
Garrison, William Lloyd, 40
Garvey, Marcus Mosiah, 191-94, 198-204, 206, 211-15
Garvey's Watchman, 192
Gaston, Billy, 264
General Motors, 296
Georgia, 190
Gilmore, Hiram, 76
Gilmore High School, 76-77, 80-81
Gilpin, Charles, 120, 281, 282
Gilpin Players, 281, 282, 283
Girard College, 314
Glanze, Walter D., 339
Goldblatt, Louis, 318
Golden, Harry, 107
Goldwater, Barry, 109, 110, 231
Gordon, Mrs. Mittie L., 208
Gordon, Robert, 83
Gottshalk, Arthur S., 230
Gowers, Henry L., 310
Graham, Billy, 275
Granny Maumee, by Ridgely Torrence, 282
Grant, Ulysses S., 50
Great Northern Drive, 161-74
Greater Detroit Interracial Fellowship, 304
Greeley, Horace, 40
Green, Paul, 282, 283
Green Pastures, The, 176
Greene, Claude, 207
Greener, Richard T., 61
Greer, Willie Eugene, 240
Gregory, Dick, 332, 334, 335
Grider, John, 264
Gross, William, 259
Guardian (Boston), 99
Guest of Honor, A, by Scott Joplin, 118

Hagan, Thomas (Talmadge Hayer), 238
Haiti, 195, 196
Hale, Selma, 310
Haley, J. Evett, 109
Hallam, Mrs. Mable, 147
Halley, James, 170
Hamilton, Alexander, 48
Hammond, O. G., 43
Hampton Institute, 103
Handy, William Christopher, 111-12, 113, 121
Hanson, O. G., 46
Hardin, Walter, 297
Harmon, R. H., 166
Harmony Homes, Inc., 319
Harris, Robert, *see* Karriem, Robert
Harrison, Richard B., 94, 175
"Hate" books, 109
Hauser, Philip M., 333, 334
Havighurst, Walter J., 332, 334
Hawkins, August F., 110
Hayakawa, S. I., 107
Hayer, Talmadge, *see* Hagan, Thomas
Hearn, Lafcadio, 84
Heenan, John C., 128; for his wife, *see* Menken, Adah Isaacs
Hemingway, Ernest, 279
Herald (Vicksburg), 159
Hick, Boyd, 279
Hill City, Kans., 68
Hilliard, Raymond, 326
Holy Rollers, 296
Holyak, John, 301
Home Opportunities Made Equal (HOME), 327-28
Homestead laws, 63, 258, 259
Horner, Henry, 190
Housing projects, 102, 299, 311, 317, 318, 319, 322, 325, 327, 329, 336
Howard, Hugh, 15
Howard, Kate, 147
Howard, O. O., 80
Howard University, 81
Howells, William Dean, 96, 97
Hubbard, Orville, 305
Huff, William Henry, 190
Hughes, Langston, 80, 107, 282, 283, 285
Human sacrifice, 222

Ida B. Wells Housing Project, 102
Illinois, 46-49, 58, 135-157, 189
Illinois Centennial Building, 20
Illinois Central Railroad, 160
Illinois Coal Operators' Association, 144
Immigrant (foreign) labor, 70, 139, 142
Immigration, *see* Migration
In the Land of the Pharaohs, by Duse Mohammed Ali, 192
Indiana, 58, 68, 73
Infelicia, by Adah Isaacs Menken, 125, 129
Ingersoll, Robert, 64, 96, 97
Ingram, Zell, 283
Insurance companies, 185
Interdenominational Ministers' Alliance, 297
International Longshoreman's and Warehouseman's Union, 318
International Print Show, 283
Inter-Ocean (Chicago), 60, 64, 66, 91, 101, 139
Iola (pseudonym), *see* Wells, Ida B.
Iron Chest Company, 74
Iron Defense Legion, 211
Islamite (Islamic) Movement, 205-08, 211, 216, 246

Jackson, Gordon, 84
Jackson, Mahalia, 334
Jackson, Tony, 120, 250
Jacques, Amy, 213, 214
Jamaica (West Indies), 191, 192
Jazz, 114, 116, 120, 251, 253, 256
Jazz Music, 249
Jefferies, William, 310
Jefferson, Thomas, 194
Jelliffe, Russell W. and Rowena, 278-86
Jewish Educational and Charitable Association of St. Louis, 153
"John Brown's Body," 58, 69
Johnson, Andrew, 49
Johnson, Bunk, 253, 254
Johnson, Cecilia, 132
Johnson, Charles S., 323
Johnson, Dink, 251
Johnson, James Weldon, 86
Johnson, Prince, 61
Johnson, R. M., 22, 26
Johnson, Will, 251
Jonas, R. D., 204
Jones, Everett L., 7
Jones, Gabriel, 257
Jones, "Golden Rule," 95
Jones, John, 43-52
Jones, Max, 249
Joplin, Scott, 114-19, 120, 255
Jordan, Joe, 119
Journal of Negro History, 74

Kansas, 58-71
Kansas Freedman's Relief Association, 63, 65
Karamu House, 278-86
Karriem, Robert (Robert Harris), 221
Kelly, Edward J., 189
Kendall, John S., 126
Kennedy, John F., 233
Kennedy, Robert F., 277
Kennedy, Sherman, 342
Kentucky Anti-Slavery Society, 72
Kentucky Colonization Society, 72
Kenwood and Hyde Park Property Owners' Association, 176, 183
Keppard, Freddie, 120, 251, 253, 254
Kerner, Otto, 341
Kerr, Orpheus C. (pseudonym), *see* Newell, Robert
Key, Francis Scott, 195
Kidnaping, 170
Killers of Moyamensing, 308
Kindred, David, 257
King, Martin Luther, Jr., 237, 276, 306, 335, 346
King, Porter, 250
"King Porter Stomp," 250
Kingsley, Harold S., 185
Knights of Labor, 137-40, 144
Koran, by Noble Drew Ali, 206
Ku Klux Klan, 57, 201, 234, 293, 296, 298, 299, 301, 308

Labor agents, 160, 164, 168
Labor and labor unions, 135-57, 182, 185, 292, 296-97, 310-13
Labor News, 292
Ladies' Anti-Slavery Society, 75
Lafon, Thomy, 247
"Land of Hope, The," by William Crosse, 162
"Land That Gives Birth to Freedom, The," 59
Landry, Lawrence, 334, 342
Langston, Charles, 80
Langston, John Mercer, 80
Langston, Tony, 104
Language in Action, by S. I. Hayakawa, 107

Latrobe Steel and Coupler Company, 136
Latter Day Saints (Mormons), 320
Lauzetta Quartette, 112
Leak's Lake, Los Angeles, 252
Lee, Mrs. Henrietta P., 104
Lee, William H., 132
Lemley, Luther Henry, 210
Leonard, Oscar, 153
Lewis, Bob, 270
Lewis, George, 305
Liberator, 81
Liberia, 67, 195-96, 209-10
Liberia Exodus Association, 196
Life, 283
Lincoln, Abraham, 43, 47, 196
Lincoln, C. Eric, 244
Little, Malcolm, *see* Malcolm X
Little, Reginald, 232
Little Foxes, The, 283
"Little Tokyo," 4, 316
Living War, 98
Logan, Milla S., 317
Lomax, Alan, 249
Longworth, Nicholas, 82
Loper, Harry, 147
Los Angeles, 5, 236-37, 245, 252, 256-57, 268-77
Lost-Found Nation of Islam, 211, 216, 222, 227, 229, 232, 235
L'Ouverture, Toussaint, 90
Lowe, James, 10
Lyles, Aubrey, 120
Lynching, 98-101, 107, 146

"Macks," 113
Madison Coal Company, 145
Majied, Eugene, 229
Malcolm X (Malcolm Little), 230-44
Manley, Mrs. Norman, 214
"Maple Leaf Rag," 116-17, 255
Marin City, Calif., 317
Marriott, Alvin, 214
Marriott, John, 282
Marshall, John R., 103
Marshall, Thurgood, 237
"Maryland-in-Africa," 196
Maryland State Colonization Society, 196
Mason, Biddy, 265
Maynor, Dorothy, 283
Mayor's Commission on Race Relations (Chicago), 323, 324
Mazeppa, 124, 128, 129
McAfee, Joe, 264
McAllister, James, 257
McCabe's Minstrels, 251
McCannon, Solomon, 190
McCone, John A., 274, 277
McCoy, Elijah, 290
McGee, Minneola, 155
McIntyre, James Francis, 275-76
McKinley, J. Frank, 132
McMenamin, James, 313
McWhorter, Hamilton, 190
Meeker, Ezra B., 258
Memphis, Tenn., exodusters, 163
Menken, Adah Isaacs, 122-31, 247
Metropolitan Life Insurance Company, 185
Messenger, the, *see* Elijah Muhammad
Messenger, 200
Messenger Magazine, 232
Migration, 2-11, 23, 54-71, 131-34, 158-74, 177, 189, 291-92, 308, 315, 318, 319, 321, 346
Migration and the Southern California Economy, 269
Milgram, Morris, 327
Mili, Gjon, 283
Miller, Flournoy, 120
Miller, Loren, 275
Miller, William (lecturer), 37
Miller, William (miner), 146
Minikus, Lee, 270
Mississippi, 170
Mitchell, Charles, 92
Mitchell, Sam, 301
Mixed-blood groups, 123
Modern Community Developers, 327
Modern Patriots, 298
Mohammedanism, 227
Montgomery, Ala., bus boycott, 346
Moore, Joseph, 76
Moorish-American Science Temple, 205, 211, 314
Moorish Movement, 205-08, 211
Mormons, 320
Morris, Edward H., 103
Morton, Ferdinand Joseph ("Jelly Roll"), 120, 248-56
Moseley, Beauregard F., 182
"Moses of the colored exodus," *see* Singleton, Benjamin
Moslem Brotherhood, Inc., 227
Moslems, 227
Moton, Robert Russa, 193
Motts, Robert, 119
Moyer, William H., 328
Mudtown, 5-11

Muhammad Speaks, 227, 229, 230, 243
Mulatto, play by Langston Hughes, 283
Mulattoes, 76, 123, 255, 258
Mulzac, Hugh, 203
Murphy, Frank, 295
Murphysboro, Ill., 150
Music and musicians, 85-86, 111-21, 248-56
Music and Some Highly Musical People, by James Monroe Trotter, 80
Muslim Girls Training Corps Class, 220
Muslim Mosque, Inc., 233
Muslims, Black, *see* Black Muslims
Myers, Isaac, 137

Nakano, Naomi, 310
National Association for the Advancement of Colored People (NAACP), 133, 177, 186, 193, 294, 297, 300, 310, 314, 341, 345, 346
National Colored Convention (Nashville), 62
National Era, 137
National Labor Convention of Colored Men, 137
National Labor Relations Board, 297
National Labor Union, 137
National Recovery Act (NRA), 296
National Workers' League, 299, 300
Neel, S. M., 101
Negro a Beast, The, or *In the Image of God,* by Charles Carroll, 108-09
Negro Cowboys, The, by Philip Durham and Everett L. Jones, 7
Negro Factories Corporation, 201
Negro Labor Relations League, 196
Negro in Philadelphia, The, by W. E. B. Du Bois, 309
Negro World, 193, 199
New Crusader, 227
New Majority, 182
New National Era, 137
New Orleans, 122-23, 127, 131, 247, 251, 253, 255
New Orleans Colored Convention, 62
Newell, Robert, 128
Newspapers, Negro, 89, 97, 104, 185-86
Newspapers, white, attitude toward Negroes, 89, 97
New York, 238
New York Shipbuilding Corporation, 310
Nicodemus (colony), 66, 67
Nkrumah, Kwame, 213, 214
Noble Drew Ali (Timothy Drew), *see* Drew, Timothy
North, Sterling, 103
Northern Conference on Racial and National Unity, 318
Northwest Territory, 287

Oak and Ivy, by Paul Laurence Dunbar, 94
Oakland-Kenwood Property Owners' Association, 321
Oakland Shipbuilding Company, 317
Oberlin College, 86, 93, 279
Octoroons, 123
"Ode to Ethiopia," by Paul Laurence Dunbar, 95
Ohio, 73
Olds, Robert E., 291
Oliver, King, 253-54
O'Neill, Eugene, 120, 281
Oregon, 257, 319
Organization of Afro-American Unity, 234, 235, 237, 238, 244
Ory, Kid, 253
Ossman, Ahmed, 241, 242
Our Own, 192
Owen, Chandler, 200
Owens, Charles and Robert, 266
Owens, Jesse, 4

Packard Company, 298
Paradise Valley, Detroit, 293, 299-301, 305
Parker, William H., 270, 273, 274, 275, 276
Parkman, Francis, 23, 30
Parkway Community House, 264
Passing, as whites, 131-34
Peace Movement of Ethiopia, 208
Pearson, P. M., 97
Pedro Gorino, The, by Harry Dean, 103
Pekin Theater, Chicago, 119-20
Pelham, Robert A., 290
Pelletier, Jean Baptiste, 16, 17
Penn, I. Garland, 89, 98
Pennsylvania Anti-Slavery Society, 38, 41
Pennsylvania Labor Relations Board, 311

Pennsylvania Railroad, 310
Peonage, 190
Peoples, Charles, *see* Sharrieff, Challar
Perez, Emanuel, 120, 253
Perkins, James H., 75
Perkins, Joseph H., 81
Perry, Oliver, 120
Petit, Buddy, 251
Petty, Edwin Louis, 266
Philadelphia, 37, 307-14
Philadelphia Electric Company, 310
Philadelphia Rapid Transit Employees' Union, 311
Philadelphia Transportation Company, 310, 311-13
Philanthropist, 73, 75
Phillips, Wendell, 90
Pinchback, Pinckney Benton Stewart, 67, 77-80
Pinchback, William, 77
Pinkerton, Allan, 43
Pioneers of the Puget Sound, by Ezra B. Meeker, 258
Political Equality League, 102
Poole, Charles, 298
Poole, Elijah (or Robert), *see* Elijah Muhammad
Port of New Orleans, The, by Harold Sinclair, 122
Post-Dispatch (St. Louis), 59
Powderly, Terence V., 138-39
Powell, Adam Clayton, Jr., 133, 276, 333
Presbytery of Chicago, 327
Press, Negro, 89, 97, 104, 185-86
Press, white, attitude toward Negroes, 89, 97
Princeton, N.J., housing, 327
Progress Development Corporation, 327
Progressive Miners' Union, 144
Property Owners' Journal, 183-84
Property Owners' Protective Association, 316
Prophet of Islam, 205, 222
Prosser, Gabriel, 194
Protestant Ministers' Alliance, 101
Pueblo del Rio, 9
Pullman Company, 310
Pyramid Club, 310

Quadroon Ball, New Orleans, 123
Quadroons, 123, 255
Quaife, Milo M., 12
Quakers, 35, 307

Raby, Al, 334, 335, 336, 337, 339, 342
Race relations conferences, 318, 324
Race riots, 37, 153, 179-90, 268-77, 293, 308, 311, 312, 340-42
Ragtime, 114, 116-18, 120, 248, 255
Raines, Edward, 190
Randolph, A. Philip, 200, 345
Ray, Charles B., 36
Reade, Charles, 125
Reconstruction Acts, 79
Red Book, 99
Red Eagle, 6
Redding, Grover Cleveland, 204-05
Relief, 326, 329
Rent evictions, 187-88
Renter's Court, 189
"Report on the Condition of the Colored People in Ohio, 1840," 74
Republic Steel Corporation, 210
Republican, 260, 261
Republican party, 47
Republican party newspapers, attitude toward Negroes, 89
Restrictive covenant, 184, 322, 324
Revels, Hiram, 260
Revels, Susie Sumner, 261
Rice Institute, 314
Richards, Adolphe and Maria Louise, 289-90
Richards, Fannie Moore, 290
Richards, John, 288
Richardson, George, 147
Richardson, Mary, 44
Richardson, Willis, 282
Robert R. Taylor housing project, 329, 336
Roberts, Joseph Jenkins, 195
Roberts, W. Adolphe, 253
Robichaux, John, 254
Robinson, Bill, 120
Robinson, Jackie, 107
Rocky Mountain Fur Company, 23-25
Roosevelt, Mrs. Eleanor, 109, 302
Roosevelt, Franklin Delano, 224, 302, 313
Roosevelt, Theodore, 156-57
Rosene, Martin, 329
Roseville Riflemen's Association, 298
Rowan, Carl, 241-42
Royal African Legion, 193, 212, 214
Royko, Mike, 337, 338
Rust, Horatio N., 65

St. Francis Square, San Francisco, 318

St. Louis, Mo., 112-14, 120-21
"St. Louis Blues," 111, 121
San Francisco, 315-19
Sanderson, J. B., 265-66
Saturday Evening Post, 230, 239
Saunders, Otis, 118
School of African Philosophy, 211
Schools, 75-77, 331
Scott, Dred, decision, 48
Scott, Elston, 150
Scott, Emmet J., 308
Scott, James A., 104
Scott, Nicholas, 180
Scott, Sparrell, 171
Seattle, 319
Secret Ritual of the Nation of Islam, by W. D. Fard, 218
Segregation, 175-90, 258
Séjour, Victor, 130, 247, 254
Selective Service Law, evasion charges, 208
Sengstacke, John H., 107
Seven-Mile Fenelon Improvement Association, 299, 300
Share croppers, 158, 185
Sharp, Granville, 194
Sharrieff, Challar (Charles Peoples), 218
Sharrieff, Raymond, 243
Sheppard, Barry, 242
Sherrill, William, 214-15
Shuffle Along, 120
Sierra Leone peninsula, 195
Sikeston, Mo., 107
Simmons, Michael T., 257
Sinclair, Harold, 122
Sinclair, Patrick, 14
Singleton, Benjamin ("Pap"), 2, 53-71, 160, 197
Slaughter, Babe, 9, 10
Slave labor (Chinese), 139
Slave rebellion, 194
Slavery, 1-3, 32, 72, 190
Slum clearance, 329
Smith, Chris, 117
Smith, Clyde and Ella, 190
Smith, Gerald L. K., 302-03
Smith, John J., 222
Society for the Recognition of the Brotherhood of Man, 99
Sojourner Truth, 65, 300
Sojourner Truth Housing Project, 299, 300
South Shore Commission, 329-30
Southern Research Council of Occidental College, 269
Sovereign, James R., 139
Spartacist (Trotskyite) Committee, 242, 243
Spring Valley, Ill., massacre, 142-44
Springfield, Ill., riots, 147-50
Springs, Andrew W., 144-47
Stackhouse, Perry, 178
State Journal (Springfield, Ill.), 149
Staton, Dakota, 227
Still, Cidney, 33-34
Still (Steel), Levin, 32-37
Still, Peter, 34, 39
Still, William, 34-42
Stillwell, W. H., 53
Stowe, Harriet Beecher, 64
Strikes, 297-98, 312-13
Strikebreakers, 135-57
Strode, Woody, 10
Sublette, William L., 25
Suffrage, 49, 346
Sumner, Charles, 40
Sun (Chicago), 323
"Sunflower Slow Drag," 116-17
Sun-Times (Chicago), 336
Sutherland, Robert L., 310
Sutton, Percy, 239
Sweet, Henry, 294-95, 304
Sweet, Ossian, 294
Swibel, Charles, 337
Swift Packing Company, 154
Swinburne, Algernon Charles, 122, 125-26
Swing music, 114

Taylor, Julius, 105
Temple of Islam, 219, 222
Tenant farmers, 57
Tennessee Real Estate and Homestead Association, 57
Texan Looks at Lyndon, A, by J. Evett Haley, 109
Texas Medley Quartet, 115
Theater, 119-20, 124-25, 281-86
Theater Arts Magazine, 283
Thierry, Camille, 130
Thomas, R. J., 303-04
Thompson, Era Bell, 210
Thompson, Frank, 313
Thompson, Gabriel, 36
Times (Chicago), 90
Times (London), 64
Times (New York), 231
Tipton, Leo, 301
Tobey, H. A., 95
Tolbert, James, 270
Tolliver, Philip, 81
Torrence, Ridgely, 282
Tourgée, Albion W., 89, 140

Tourgée Club, 140
Transport Workers Union, 311, 312, 313
Treemonisha, by Scott Joplin, 118
Tribune (Chicago), 48, 49, 104, 150, 182
Tribune (New York), 100
"Tricknollogy," 220
Trinidad, 195
Trotskyite (Spartacist) Committee, 242, 243
Trotter, James Monroe, 80, 99
Trumbull Park, Chicago, 325
Trumbull Park, by Frank London Brown, 325
Truth, Sojourner, 65, 300
Tubman, Harriet, 40-42
Tulane University, 314
Turner, H. M., 67, 197-98
Turpin, Charles and Tom, 120
Tuskegee Institute, 192-93, 291, 345
Tyler, Edward, 283

Uncle Tom's Cabin, 64, 100
Underground Railroad, 3, 34, 38, 44, 46, 56, 57, 287
Underground Railroad Records, by William Still, 40
Unemployed Councils, 187-88
Union, 86, 93
Unions, *see* Labor and labor unions
United Automobile Workers, 296, 297, 298, 303
United Citizens' Committee for Freedom of Residence, 110
"United Links," 69
United Mine Workers of America, 144, 146
United States and Congo National Emigration Steamship Company, 197
United Transatlantic Society, 70
Universal Negro Improvement Association (UNIA), 193-94, 199-204, 212, 214-15
University of Chicago, 332, 333
University of Islam, 220, 230
University of Pennsylvania, 308, 310
Up from Slavery, by Booker T. Washington, 192
Utah, 320

Verlaine, Paul, 130
Vicksburg Convention, 62
Virden, Ill., strike, 144
Virginia State College, 81
Von Hoffman, Nicholas, 273
Voorhees, Daniel W., 54
Voting, 49, 346

Waley, Wade, 251
Walkathon, 335
Walker, A'Lelia, 84
Walker, Madame C. J., 84
Walker, Mae, 84
Wallace, Henry, 302
Wallace, William H., 202
Walsh, John, 337
War Manpower Commission, 310
Warner, Mrs. John, 132
"Warrior's Prayer, The," by Paul Laurence Dunbar, 96
Washington, Booker T., 156, 192-93, 291, 345
Washington, George, 259
Washington (state), 258, 259, 319
Waterworks Park Improvement Association, 294
Watts, Los Angeles, 9, 268-77
"We Shall Not Be Moved," 187-88
"We Shall Overcome," 335
Weaver, Robert C., 324
Wells, Ida B., 92, 97-103
Wenrich, Percy, 117
Western Luminary, 72
Western Newspaper Union, 104
Western Outlook, 264
"When I Return to the Southland It Will Be," by Sparrell Scott, 171
Whetsol, Arthur, 10
Whip, 185-86
White, Arthur W., 67
White, Charles A., 313
White, Horace A., 297
White, James A., 150
White, Walter, 107, 131, 133, 297
White primaries, 346
"White supremacy," 54, 109, 292, 296, 307, 312
"Whitecaps," 147
"Whitey," 270
Whitlock, Brand, 95, 97
"Why We March," 334
Wilberforce, William, 194
Wilcox, Ella Wheeler, 96, 97
Wilkins, Roy, 133
Wilkins, Thomas, 35
Williams, A. Wilberforce, 104
Williams, Daniel Hale, 133
Williams, Dessie Mae, 340-42
Williams, Eugene, 179
Williams, Frances, 283
Williams, Paul Revere, 10, 267-68
Willis, Benjamin Coppage, 331, 336

Wilson, Orlando W., 336, 339, 341
Wilson, Woodrow, 183
"Wise Old Owl," 167, 168
Witherspoon, John H., 304
Woman's Columbia Auxiliary Association, 89
Woman's Loyal Union, 99
Woodlawn Organization, 329
Woods, Otis and Dock, 190
Woodson, Carter G., 74
World Muslim League, 235
WPA, 185

Y.M.C.A., 279
Yorty, Samuel W., 272, 274, 276
Young, Hiram, 258
Young Socialist, 242

AMERICAN CENTURY SERIES

When ordering, please use the Standard Book Number consisting of the publisher's prefix, 8090–, plus the five digits following each title. (Note that the numbers given in this list are for paperback editions only. Many of the books are also available in cloth.)

The Hoosier School-Master by Edward Eggleston (0001–6)
The Magnificent Ambersons by Booth Tarkington (0002–4)
The Harbor by Ernest Poole (0003–2)
The Flush Times of Alabama and Mississippi by Joseph Baldwin (0005–9)
The Higher Learning in America by Thorstein Veblen (0007–5)
The Shame of the Cities by Lincoln Steffens (0008–3)
Company K by William March (0009–1)
The Influence of Seapower upon History by Alfred T. Mahan (0010–5)
A Daughter of the Middle Border by Hamlin Garland (0011–3)
How the Other Half Lives by Jacob Riis (0012–1)
His Fifty Years of Exile (*Israel Potter*) by Herman Melville (0013–X)
Barren Ground by Ellen Glasgow (0014–8)
Hospital Sketches by Louisa May Alcott (0015–6)
A Traveler from Altruria by William Dean Howells (0016–4)
The Devil's Dictionary by Ambrose Bierce (0017–2)
Moon-Calf by Floyd Dell (0018–2)
The Big Rock Candy Mountain by Wallace Stegner (0019–9)
The Octopus by Frank Norris (0020–2)
Life on the Mississippi by Mark Twain (0021–0)
Troubadour by Alfred Kreymborg (0022–9)
The Iron Heel by Jack London (0023–7)
Georgia Scenes by A. B. Longstreet (0024–5)
The Grandissimes by George W. Cable (0025–3)
The Autocrat of the Breakfast Table by Oliver Wendell Holmes (0026–1)
The Jeffersonian Tradition in American Democracy by Charles Wiltse (0028–8)
The Narrative of Arthur Gordon Pym by Edgar Allan Poe (0029–6)
A Connecticut Yankee in King Arthur's Court by Mark Twain (0030–X)
Theodore Roosevelt and the Progressive Movement by George E. Mowry (0031–8)
The Autobiography of an Ex-Coloured Man by James Weldon Johnson (0032–6)
Jack London: Short Stories (0033–4)
Jefferson by Albert Jay Nock (0034–2)
America Goes to War by Bruce Catton (0035–0)
Hemingway and His Critics ed. by Carlos Baker (0036–9)
Writers in Crisis by Maxwell Geismar (0038–5)
The Best of Simple by Langston Hughes (0039–3)
American Social Thought ed. by Ray Ginger (0040–7)
William Dean Howells ed. by Rudolf and Clara Marburg Kirk (0041–5)
Walt Whitman ed. by Floyd Stovall (0042–3)
Thomas Paine ed. by Harry Hayden Clark (0043–1)
American Moderns by Maxwell Geismar (0044–X)
The Last of the Provincials by Maxwell Geismar (0045–8)
Edgar Allan Poe ed. by Hardin Craig and Margaret Alterton (0046–6)
Jonathan Edwards ed. by C. H. Faust and T. H. Johnson (0047–4)
Benjamin Franklin ed. by F. Mott and C. E. Jorgenson (0048–2)
Indian Tales by Jaime de Angulo (0049–0)
A Time of Harvest ed. by Robert E. Spiller (0050–4)
The Limits of Language ed. by Walker Gibson (0051–2)
Sherwood Anderson: Short Stories ed. by Maxwell Geismar (0052–0)
The World of Lincoln Steffens ed. by Ella Winter and Herbert Shapiro (0053–9)
Mark Twain on the Damned Human Race ed. by Janet Smith (0054–7)
The Happy Critic and Other Essays by Mark Van Doren (0055–5)
Man Against Myth by Barrows Dunham (0056–3)
Something in Common and Other Stories by Langston Hughes (0057–1)
Writers in Transition: Seven Americans by H. Wayne Morgan (0058–1)
The Lincoln Nobody Knows by Richard N. Current (0059–8)
The Disinherited by Jack Conroy (0060–1)
Eisenhower As President ed. by Dean Albertson (0061–X)
Rebels and Ancestors by Maxwell Geismar (0062–8)
Mount Allegro by Jerre Mangione (0063–6)
Thoreau: People, Principles, and Politics ed. by Milton Meltzer (0064–4)
The Big Sea by Langston Hughes (0065–2)
The Golden Age of Homespun by Jared van Wagenen, Jr. (0066–0)
The Senate Establishment by Joseph S. Clark and Other Senators (0067–9)

I Wonder As I Wander by Langston Hughes (0068–7)
Science in Nineteenth-Century America ed. by Nathan Reingold (0069–5)
The Course of the South to Secession by Ulrich Bonnell Phillips (0070–9)
American Negro Poetry ed. by Arna Bontemps (0071–7)
Horace Greeley by Glyndon G. Van Deusen (0072–5)
David Walker's Appeal ed. by Charles M. Wiltse (0073–3)
The Sentimental Years by E. Douglas Branch (0074–1)
Henry James and the Jacobites by Maxwell Geismar (0075–X)
The Reins of Power by Bernard Schwartz (0076–8)
American Writers in Rebellion by H. Wayne Morgan (0077–6)
Policy and Power by Ruhl Bartlett (0078–4)
Wendell Phillips on Civil Rights and Freedom ed. by Louis Filler (0079–2)
American Negro Short Stories ed. by John Henrik Clarke (0080–6)
The Radical Novel in the United States: 1900–1954 by Walter B. Rideout (0081–4)
A History of Agriculture in the State of New York by Ulysses Prentiss Hedrick (0082–2)
Criticism and Fiction by William Dean Howells and *The Responsibilities of the Novelist* by Frank Norris (0083–0)
John F. Kennedy and the New Frontier ed. by Aïda DiPace Donald (0084–9)
Anyplace But Here by Arna Bontemps and Jack Conroy (0085–7)
Mark Van Doren: 100 Poems (0086–5)
Simple's Uncle Sam by Langston Hughes (0087–3)
Stranger at the Gates by Tracy Sugarman (0088–1)
Waiting for Nothing by Tom Kromer (0089–X)
31 New American Poets ed. by Ron Schreiber (0090–3)
Documents of Upheaval ed. by Truman Nelson (0092–X)
Black Pow-Wow by Ted Joans (0093–8)
Half a Man by M. W. Ovington (0094–6)
Collected and New Poems: 1924–1963 by Mark Van Doren (0095–4)
From Plantation to Ghetto (Revised) by August Meier and Elliott Rudwick (0096–2)
Tambourines to Glory by Langston Hughes (0097–0)
Afrodisia by Ted Joans (0098–9)
Natural Process ed. by Ted Wilentz and Tom Weatherly (0097–7)
The Free World Colossus (Revised) by David Horowitz (0107–1)

The Making of America

Fabric of Freedom: 1763–1800 by Esmond Wright (0101–2)
The New Nation: 1800–1845 by Charles M. Wiltse (0102–0)
The Stakes of Power: 1845–1877 by Roy F. Nichols (0103–9)
The Search for Order: 1877–1920 by Robert H. Wiebe (0104–7)
The Urban Nation: 1920–1960 by George E. Mowry (0105–5)

American Profiles

Thomas Jefferson: A Profile ed. by Merrill D. Peterson (0200–0)
Franklin D. Roosevelt: A Profile ed. by William E. Leuchtenburg (0201–9)
Alexander Hamilton: A Profile ed. by Jacob E. Cooke (0202–7)
Mark Twain: A Profile ed. by Justin Kaplan (0203–5)
Theodore Roosevelt: A Profile ed. by Morton Keller (0204–3)
Woodrow Wilson: A Profile ed. by Arthur S. Link (0205–1)
John C. Calhoun: A Profile ed. by John L. Thomas (0206–X)
Ralph Waldo Emerson: A Profile ed. by Carl Bode (0207–8)
William Jennings Bryan: A Profile ed. by Paul W. Glad (0208–6)
Martin Luther King, Jr.: A Profile ed. by C. Eric Lincoln (0209–4)
George Washington: A Profile ed. by James Morton Smith (0210–8)
Jonathan Edwards: A Profile ed. by David Levin (0212–4)
Benjamin Franklin: A Profile ed. by Esmond Wright (0214–0)